The Forms

of the Affects

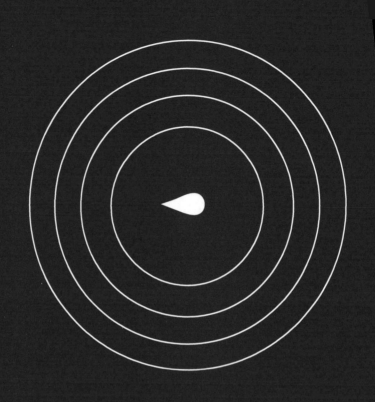

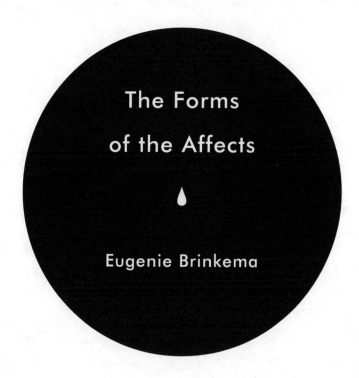

The Forms
of the Affects

Eugenie Brinkema

DUKE UNIVERSITY PRESS • DURHAM AND LONDON • 2014

PRINTED IN THE UNITED STATES OF AMERICA
ON ACID-FREE PAPER ∞
DESIGNED BY AMY RUTH BUCHANAN
TYPESET IN MINION PRO BY COPPERLINE BOOK
SERVICES, INC.

LIBRARY OF CONGRESS CATALOGING-IN-PUBLICATION DATA
BRINKEMA, EUGENIE, 1980–
THE FORMS OF THE AFFECTS / EUGENIE BRINKEMA.
P. CM.
INCLUDES BIBLIOGRAPHICAL REFERENCES AND INDEX.
ISBN 978-0-8223-5644-8 (CLOTH : ALK. PAPER)
ISBN 978-0-8223-5656-1 (PBK. : ALK. PAPER)
1. FILM CRITICISM. 2. FORMALISM (LITERARY ANALYSIS).
3. AFFECT (PSYCHOLOGY). 4. CRITICAL THEORY. I. TITLE.
PN1995.B75 2014
791.4301'5—DC23
2013037965

DUKE UNIVERSITY PRESS GRATEFULLY ACKNOWLEDGES
THE SUPPORT OF THE MASSACHUSETTS INSTITUTE OF
TECHNOLOGY, LITERATURE SECTION, WHICH PROVIDED
FUNDS TOWARD THE PUBLICATION OF THIS BOOK.

TO MY MOTHER, TO MY FATHER

I shall consider human actions and desires

in exactly the same manner,

as though I were concerned with lines, planes, and solids.

—BARUCH SPINOZA

It is the force, at once simple and unexpected,

which consists in saying *cinema and* . . . :

and thus accepting all the consequences.

—RAYMOND BELLOUR

Contents

Ten Points to Begin

Is there any remaining doubt that we are now fully within the Episteme of the Affect? Must one even begin an argument anymore by refuting Fredric Jameson's infamous description of the "waning of affect" in postmodernity? One need not linger in the humanities but might consider newly resurgent neuroscientific work on the emotions; one need not even concern oneself only with scholarship but note the untamed mobility of affects such as terror and disgust, anxiety and hope, in political and popular debates of the early twenty-first century. Indeed, the importance of affectivity has been so well documented in the disciplines of psychiatry, psychoanalysis, literary theory, critical theory, feminist and race studies, philosophy, and studies in representation, including film and new media, that several scholars have started asking broad questions about why it is that so many have turned to affect in the first place. Thus, the newest turn in the theoretical humanities would seem to be a meta-turn that turns toward the turning toward affect itself.[1]

While an intellectual history of the turn to affect would take this book too far afield, I am comfortable joining those who speculate that the contemporary critical investment in affectivity across the humanities has to do with a post-structuralist response to perceived omissions in structuralism—or, indeed, may be part of a post-poststructuralist or anti-poststructuralist response to perceived omissions in poststructuralism. The turn to affect, thus, is part of a larger reawakening of interest in problematics of embodiment and materiality in the wake of twentieth-century Western theory that, for many, was all semiotics and no sense, all structure and no stuff.[2] Given that work on shame, guilt, compassion, and love has been crucial to the "turn to ethics"; scholarship on shock, agitation, and surprise has been key to the "turn to modernity"; cultural studies has been taken over almost entirely by work on identity and emotion (queer rage, gay shame, feminist melancholia); and considerations of sensation, materiality, and distributed agency have been integral to the recent interest in the non-human (animal care, vital matter, the animated environment), we might be better off suggesting that the "turn to affect" in the humanities is and has always been plural, a set of many turnings that are problematically lumped together in a false unity that imagines that one singular intellectual arc could describe them all.

From this set of rotations, what has become visible, what is it that humanistic scholarship has newly encountered? Has this revolution revolutionized readings in the fields in which it is most vigorously represented: literary, film, and media studies? Insofar as affect has been positioned as what resists systematicity and structure, has it in fact been able to recover notions of contingency, possibility, and play? Has the turning toward affect in the theoretical humanities engendered a more complex understanding of texts? Have accounts of affects produced more nuanced, delightful interpretations of forms in texts—and have they recovered the dimension of being *surprised* by representation?

"Affect," as turned to, is said to: disrupt, interrupt, reinsert, demand, provoke, insist on, remind of, agitate for: the body, sensation, movement, flesh and skin and nerves, the visceral, stressing pains, feral frenzies, always rubbing against: what undoes, what unsettles, that thing I cannot name, what remains resistant, far away (haunting, and ever so beautiful); indefinable, it is said to be what cannot be written, what thaws the critical cold, messing all systems and subjects up. Thus, turning to affect has allowed the humanities to *constantly possibly* introject any seemingly absent or forgotten dimension of inquiry, to insist that play, the unexpected, and the unthought can always be brought back into the field. In this way, the affective turn in general is resonant with broader strains in what has been dubbed "metamodernism" as a "structure of feeling" that oscillates between modernist stabilities and postmodern relativisms.[3] One of the symptoms of appeals to affect in the negative theoretical sense—as signaling principally a rejection: *not* semiosis, *not* meaning, *not* structure, *not* apparatus,

but the felt visceral, immediate, sensed, embodied, excessive—is that "affect" in the turn to affect has been deployed almost exclusively in the singular, as the capacity for movement or disturbance in general. (When Lone Bertelsen and Andrew Murphie succinctly declare "affect is not form," it is because they align affects with "*transitions* between states" and the very essence of what is dynamic and unstable, against an impoverished notion of form as inert, passive, inactive.[4]) Deleuzians, with their emphasis on affect as a pure state of potentiality, tend to be particularly guilty of the sin of generality. This terminological lump risks the vagueness of purely negative definitional endeavors and largely cedes specificity—generic, emotional, historical—to cognitivists in literary and media studies, who have taken Aristotelian taxonomizing to heart in their ever-narrowing treatment of, say, startle in horror films, or empathetic weeping in melodramas. There is a formula for work on affect, and it turns on a set of shared terms: speed, violence, agitation, pressures, forces, intensities. In other words, and against much of the spirit of Deleuze's philosophy, which celebrated the minor, the changeable, and the multiple, Deleuzian theories of affect offer all repetition with no difference. When affect is taken as a synonym for violence or force (or intensity or sensation), one can only speak of its most abstract agitations instead of any particular textual workings. Thus, the turn to affect has tended to make the same argument time and again—each a version of, "We urgently have to attend to X!" where X stands for a member of the set {excess, affect, sensation, embodiment, intensity, resistance, whatever}. Each wild agitation for an attention to affection ultimately calls to mind Hermann Lotze's insistence, put to use by Heidegger in his *Habilitationsschrift* in relation to the methodology of modern philosophy, "Das beständige Wetzen der Messer aber ist langweilig, wenn man nichts zu schneiden vorhat" (The constant sharpening of knives is boring if one never gets around to cutting).[5] Lotze does not imply that continual edge-refining is an unproductive or wasteful use of one's time; he does not write *nutzlos* (useless) or *sinnlos* (pointless) but *langweilig* (boring), a bad state in place of merely bad function. To endlessly hone if one does not (perhaps ever) intend to incise is to block the affective possibility of pleasurable anticipation of action itself. The effect of repeatedly intoning a polemic for force is the deforcing and deflating of that very concept. The result is that the defenders of affect are left with only the mild rhetorical force of summary and paraphrase, intoned synonyms, and thematic generalizations. Repetition without difference can have the stultifying effect of invoking, in the end, only the affective modality of tedium.

Critical positions that align affect with what generally and amorphously resists (structure, form, textuality, signification, legibility) hold on to the notion of a transcendental signified, hold fast to the fantasy of something that predates the linguistic turn and that evades the slow, hard tussle of reading texts closely. What I claim in this book is not only that this desire is retrograde and reintroduces an untheorized notion of affect (specifically, one that is fundamentally *incapable* of dealing with textual particularities and formal matters), but that the return to affect on the part of critics from wildly divergent disciplinary backgrounds is, in most cases, a naïve move that leaves intact the very ideological, aesthetic, and theoretical problems it claimed to confront. Thus, even some of the most radical theory coming out of the humanities today begins with the premise that affects and feelings are the forgotten underside of the linguistic turn. Indeed, in some cases the affection for affect has itself been subsumed by a more powerful yearning for a standing before or outside of that very moment in theory that demanded the deep attention required for interminable difficult reading.

The thing is: *Affect is not the place where something immediate and automatic and resistant takes place outside of language. The turning to affect in the humanities does not obliterate the problem of form and representation. Affect is not where reading is no longer needed.*

This drive for some magical mysterious intensity X that escapes signification, while durable and even understandable, is a mode of thinking that only defers the more pressing matter: how is critique to keep grappling with affect and affectivity in texts if, indeed, one cannot read for affects to discover anything new about them? Divorcing affect from reading for form only puts off the moment at which the turning toward affect might be as notable for its critical revelations as for the novelty of its mere turning toward. This book is, among other things, an attempt to defer that problem no longer.

7

If affect is conceived of as synonymous with force, or as intensities, or as the capacity for stage changes or movement as such, then it opens up very few theoretical avenues—Why turn to affect at all? In the end, ethics, politics, aesthetics—indeed, lives—must be enacted in the definite particular. There is no reason to assume that affects are identical aesthetically, politically, ethically, experientially, and formally; but only reading specific affects as having and being bound up with specific forms gives us the vocabulary for articulating those many differences. Otherwise, "affect"—that thing so celebrated for its resistance to systematicity—becomes not only what does not resist, but in fact what confirms every time the same model of vague shuddering intensity. Why ask cinema *and* affect if the answer is to be the same every time and every time in the same way?[6]

8

The one way out for affect is via a way into its specificities. That approach will be called—unsurprisingly, for historically it was always the way to unlock potentialities—close reading. There is a perversity to this: if affect theory is what is utterly fashionable, it is answered here with the corrective of the utterly unfashionable, with what is, let us say, an *unzeitgemässe* call for the sustained interpretations of texts. This book's insistence on the formal dimension of affect allows not only for specificity but for the wild and many fecundities of specificity: difference, change, the particular, the contingent (*and*) the essential, the definite, the distinct, all dense details, and—again, to return to the spirit of Deleuze—the minor, inconsequential, secret, atomic. Treating affect in such a way deforms any coherence to "affect" in the singular, general, universal and transforms it into something not given in advance, not apprehendable except through the thickets of formalist analysis.

9

A consequence of decoupling textuality and theory—which I will argue comes from the tradition of arguing *for* affect by arguing *against* reading for form—is a suffocating dearth of material with which a theorist can press on affect in a text and an almost nonexistent ability to let affect press back against theory. The loss works both ways, for not only do critics fail to find in the details the workings of violence or intensity, but such a reading strategy closes down the paths by which textual specificity might speak back to, challenge, undermine— or perhaps radically revise—the very theory at stake in any argument. How much more arresting is an analysis that allows the particularities of any individual text to disrupt those terms known in advance, to challenge the forms of the affects one is claiming those very texts provoke? What lines of thought might be set loose by interrogating the relationship between a cinematic grid of color and the most visceral of the negative affects, disgust? How might the straits of anxiety be a matter of a broken horizontal line? What, in other words, would happen to the study of both affectivity and form if we were to reintroduce close reading to the study of sensation, not as felt by moved bodies, but as wildly composed in specific cinematic, literary, and critical texts? In this book, the specific structures of any affective form will be closely read *for*—and are not assumed to be an immediate or diffuse unmediated sensation. The turn to affect has corresponded with a disciplinary turn away from detail, from specificity and the local, from the very groundings for the persuasions germane to defending any theoretical movement. Treating affect as a problematic of structure, form, and aesthetics is an attempt to reintroduce particularity to any consideration of affects. It is also an attempt to seize the passions of affect studies for textual interpretation and close reading.

I do not merely mean that we need a return to reading for form in the midst of the ongoing turning toward affect;—I am claiming that we require a return to form precisely because of the turn to affect, to keep its wonderments in revolution, to keep going.

ONE

A Tear

That Does Not

Drop,

but Folds

♦

Consider the shower scene in *Psycho*. It has all come and gone: the black-hole vacuum of the first scream; the striating diagonals of the shower spray; the cool white grid of the cold white tile against which Marion's hand, stretched out and spread, like a claw, grasps, scratches, in bent digitate branches that sink out of the bottom of the frame followed by sodden orthostatic threads of hair, erect at the back of the head as if from terror. And after that, so much water. It rushes, famously mixing with the darkened blood, filling the empty drain with torrents of a sad admixture. The liquid rush moves in a fast counterclockwise, delimiting the contours of the hungry aperture.

But then, at once, the tempo changes, and in place of the frenetic aural shrieks, rapid-fire cuts, and burning stream of wasted water, a slow, almost languid image appears superimposed underneath the churning metal void. It comes into relief first by its opposing orbit, a viscid twisting turn to the right. As the spin weakly makes its journey of sixty degrees, the extremely proximate image of one magnified eye emerges out of the muddy dissolve, its vertical oval centered in a frame in which the edges are the skin's negative space: a flat expanse of shadowy crepe on the left, and two well-etched lines cutting into the forehead on the right. At the very moment the eye stills in its rotation, revealed at the bottom center of the frame, at the darkened corner of the tender inner duct, is one small, fat tear. As the camera pulls out from eye to face, more tears are revealed, first one under the eye, then more, on the bridge and side of the nose, on the upper lip, and all this at the same time as a droplet falls from a matted twist of hair to the bathroom floor. The effect is to retroactively place under suspicion the truth of that tear, that tear that may just be a drop, that tear that does not fall but sits thickly next to the eye without revealing its source or its embodied secret: whether it was secreted at all.

This tear that may not be a tear is an enigma, but historically it has not been treated as such. William Rothman's meticulously detailed close analysis of *Psycho*, for example, considers it an unambiguous emanation of the newly lifeless body. "When the camera spirals out clockwise as though unscrewing itself," he writes, "it is disclosed that the eye standing in for our gaze is, within the world of the film, Marion's, and that it is dead. It emerges stillborn from the drain. The camera keeps spiraling out until we have a full view of Marion's face. Death has frozen it in inexpressiveness, although there is a tear welled in the corner of her eye."[1] Although Rothman too quickly attributes tearness to this drop, he is nevertheless to be commended for noticing the clear bead at all; fifty years of criticism on *Psycho* has so roundly investigated vision, voyeurism, the gaze, the look, dead eyes, sockets, and stares that what it is to be an eye has been conflated entirely with structures of looking, seeing, and being seen.[2] This is a case in which criticism has forgotten all it is that eyes can do—or fail to do, for it is an open question whether the lubricatory productions of the eye are involved here at all. The little pendeloque commands a close examination of its ambiguity and its visual form, the way its shape constitutes one of many curving lines that bifurcate the face with the barely opened mouth, the pronounced nostril, the eyeball on its side, the high dark arch of the eyebrow . . .

Marion's tear that is not immediately legible *as* a tear poses the question of its being—asks: How is it with this tear that is not a tear? Small spherules demand to be read.

CRYING IS STRUCTURED LIKE A LANGUAGE

In the long history of the philosophy of emotion, the tear has been the supreme metonym for the expressivity of interior states at least as far back as Aristotle's *Poetics*. It is fitting that the shortest verse in English translations of the New Testament is the Greek *Edakrysen ho Iesous:* at the death of Lazarus, "Jesus wept" (John 11:35), *and no more needed to be said.* (Bas Jan Ader's film

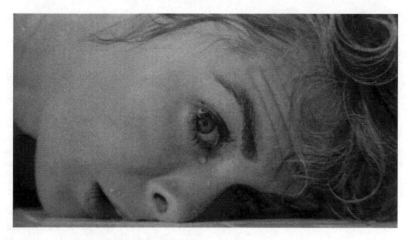

FIG. 1.1. *Psycho* (Alfred Hitchcock, 1960)

I'm Too Sad to Tell You [1971] is likewise three minutes of a wrenching close-up of the man, at just a slight pitch, heaving in the difficulties of the arriving waters; these tears stand in for the entirety of impossible transmission and communion, what is foreclosed in the title. They do all that work.) That is not to say that views of what a tear is or what its attendant leaking forms are—weeping, howling, wailing, crying—have not changed historically or undergone dramatic shifts in meaning, particularly with the Darwinian and Freudian revolutions in the conception of the human. The tear has been a liquid volley in countless debates over whether emotion is an active production or a passive subjection; the relationship between interior states, judgments or beliefs, and exterior expressions; the possibility of the bodily legibility of the amorphous mind or soul; the causality and ordering of physical sensations with mental impressions; either the human's unique difference from the animal kingdom or material sameness to beasts; and the activity of bad faith and falsity (for Sartre) or the interpretable sign of the hysteric's truth (for Freud). That little lachrymal drop has been deployed to work through some of the most significant debates in philosophy about the relation between the body and mind, the interior and exterior, the will and that which overrides will.[3] Because of these theoretical negotiations, the trajectory of the tear in philosophical thought moves from clarity to cloud, from transparency to suspicion, from the sense that we know what a tear is to the sense that a tear is always anything but itself—even that the tear is a lie. In the nineteenth and twentieth centuries, every tear becomes opaque. In turn, from a sense that tears express or convey something—crucial, private, essential—about the interiority of a weeping subject, by modernity the tear is regarded principally as an exteriority and as something that must be interpreted or read. This book will ultimately argue against claims for the immediacy or obviousness or corporeality of affects—specifically, grief, disgust, anxiety, and joy—and will do so by formulating a new approach to affectivity that regards its exteriority in textual form as something that commands a reading. In order to map the scope of the departure of this approach from traditional views of emotion, consider a brief chronicle of the tear.

A summary of the well-trodden differences between Plato and Aristotle on the value of mimesis points to their differing treatments of tears. As with the other arts of imitation, Plato is suspicious of the sopping productions, forbidding in Book III of *The Republic* the charges of the state "whom we expect to prove good men, being men, to play the parts of women." Specifically prohibited is imitating a woman "involved in misfortune and possessed by grief and lamentation—still less a woman that is sick, in love, or in labor."[4] Mourning, birth, sickness and love—all are potential sites for the occasioning of tears, and each is linked to the larger threat of imitation in relation to truth and the education of the young. Aristotle, in his famous definition of tragedy, not only defends the form against Plato's concerns about emotionality but invokes them specifically in its defense: the imitation of "an action that is serious and also, as having magnitude, complete in itself" is to focus on "incidents arousing pity and fear, wherewith to accomplish its catharsis of such emotions."[5] This catharsis (from *kathairein* [to purify or purge]) is linked to both thematic and formal structures: "tragic fear and pity may be aroused by the Spectacle; but they may also be aroused by the very structure and incidents of the play."[6] Pity, so crucial to the definition of catharsis in *Poetics,* is only briefly linked with tears in *Rhetoric,* but it is a telling aside. In the taxonomy of men to be pitied, Aristotle includes acquaintances only if they are not close enough to be kin, for "with the latter their attitude is as for their future selves; hence indeed Amasius did not weep when his son was taken off to be executed, as they say, but did when his friend was begging him—for the latter was pitiable, the former terrible."[7] That is, the "painful and destructive things" that are the objects of pity apply to acquaintances when one is only proximate to suffering, but those very things are terrible when they happen to the self, the future self, or an avatar of the self. Terror, in this account of Aristotle's, is linked to a stifling of tears ("men no longer pity when what is terrifying is near them"); thus, the "fear and pity" of *Poetics* is at more of a remove than the immediacy of a terror that one imagines is around the bend for the thinker.[8] To be able to weep, whether Amasius at his friend's begging or the audience at a tragedy, is a sign of some available distance, a non-coincidence with the feeling of the nearness of terror. All crying, then—even the cathartic kind—is crying at a remove.

These are not the only accounts of tears in early Greek philosophy: Homer's epics are rife with weeping figures, and the Sophist Gorgias wrote in praise of Speech that "there come upon its hearers fearful shuddering (*phrikê peri-phobos*) and tearful pity (*eleos polydakrys*) and grievous longing (*pothos philo-penthês*)."[9] But however brief, this sketch of some of the earliest appearances of the philosophical tear already displays some of the traits that will continue to haunt that drop's future: shameful spilled admission of interior weakness, or instructive and pedagogically valuable purgation; performance of vulnerability, or studied stratagem of the persuading speaker; emotional production of a previously made judgment of distance from the self, or cathartic release that is beneficial to, if not formative of, the self. Crucially, as well, especially in Gorgias and Aristotle, tears are not a static or regulated state, but can be produced, elicited, made to increase, even copiously and strategically, through aesthetic works. These uses to which a tear may be put appear throughout the records of philosophy as stakes in discussions of aesthetics, ethics, cognition, judgment, embodiment, and knowledge—hence, the urgency and difficulty of Roland Barthes's question in *A Lover's Discourse:* "Who will write the history of tears?"[10]

It would be an error to assume transhistorically that tears have been linked only to the negative affects. Already with the Christian medieval tradition of *gratia lacrimarum*—the consoling "grace of tears" or "gift of tears" that accompanies the purest prayer—there is a history of tears that places them apart from matters of suffering, pity, lamentation, and loss.[11] Along with Darwin's fascinating accounts of the tears of laughter or the tears of the mad, one can, as early as David Hume's "Of Tragedy" (1757), find assertions of the intriguing *pleasures* of tearing. The essay is one of many in which Hume is interested in exploring conflicting emotions and mixtures of sentiments. The inquiry opens, as do so many contemporary accounts of the horror film, with the articulation of a seeming paradox: "it seems an unaccountable pleasure which the spectators of a well-written tragedy receive from sorrow, terror, anxiety, and other passions, that are in themselves disagreeable and uneasy. The more they are touched and affected, the more are they delighted with the spectacle." On the matter of tears and their pleasures or pains, the audiences of tragedies are "pleased in proportion as they are afflicted, and never are so happy as when they employ tears, sobs, and cries to give vent to their sorrow, and relieve their heart, swollen with the tenderest sympathy and compassion."[12]

Hume's account is similar to Aristotle's psychological theory of catharsis but is not identical to it, as it places a greater emphasis on tragedy's affective, as opposed to pedagogical, effects. Crucially—and this marks Hume's general work on the passions—pleasure and pain are inextricable and muddled. Hume solves the dilemma whereby an object produces different, even opposing, passions by arguing that a subordinate passion can be converted into a dominant one.[13] In fact, not only is a distinction between pleasure and pain impossible to articulate or hold, but it is the ambivalent murkiness of the difference between sentiments that provides the meta-sentiment of pleasure: the mixture of passions "composes an agreeable sorrow, and tears that delight us."[14] If tears can be converted into that which delights—and one is never so happy as when weeping and sobbing—then it becomes impossible to place the gesture of crying purely on the side of the negative emotions. This shift points to a historical undoing of the clear emotional legibility of the tear that will only amplify over the next two centuries—that is, if it is a mixture of sentiments that composes a pleasurable sorrow, a delightful sobbing, then the tear is not purely an immediate (or unmediated) sign testifying to interior pity or pain but a structural part of a composite sentiment that is not reducible to its physical manifestation.

Around the same time as Hume's essay, Adam Smith was composing the lectures that constituted *The Theory of Moral Sentiments,* his exploration of sympathy as a moral principle. Smith's focus was not on an individual's private feelings but on how the imagination of an "impartial spectator" forms a conception of the emotional experience of the other. He indicts previous philosophers for focusing too much on the tendency and nature of affections instead of considering them in relation to their cause and the context of their excitation. In an interesting anticipation of Levinas's work on the incomprehensibility of the other, Smith poses the problematic of sentiment as part of the larger dilemma of existing in a world with different beings who, ultimately, are opaque to us. We lack the immediate experience of the feelings of others, and sense impressions convey only a representation that must be translated into an understanding. Smith's solution is that through the faculty of judgment and imagination we can represent to the self what the self's sensations would be "if we were" in a situation similar to that of the other.[15] We perceive the situation, conceive how we would feel in such a case, and form an idea or understanding of how the other must be affected. All this is done not from the perspective of our idiosyncratic historical selves but as "impartial spectators" observing and judging the facts of any situation.

Because of the intervention of judgment about the exciting situation, sympathy for Smith does not require a one-to-one correspondence between the experience another is undergoing and our own impressions. We not only feel *with* the other (*sympathy*); we can feel *for* the other in the absence of their (appropriate) feeling (something more akin to *propathy*). In fact, even if the other is incapable of a particular sentiment despite the occasion's warranting it, we can nevertheless imagine ourselves into the appropriate affect and out of emotional isolation. Smith's three case studies of such a situation are encounters with the mad, with the suffering infant, and with the dead, each of which he links to "the calamities to which the condition of mortality exposes mankind."[16] The "poor wretch" deprived of reason is "by far the most dreadful," but despite the fact that he is insensible to his own distressing state, we, the well, do have an uncomfortable if not anguished response to the mad one, and that "cannot be the reflection of any sentiment of the sufferer."[17] Rather, the response of the spectator is due to the horrible thought: What, then, if it were I? Likewise, the mother of the howling infant "joins, to its real helplessness, her own consciousness of that helplessness, and her own terrors for the unknown consequences of its disorder" and thus forms a sense of the infant's distress.[18] In place of the foundational Western trope of the infant joined to the mother at the breast—the nurturing *Madonna del Latte*—Smith offers instead a howling infant joined in helplessness to the mother's consciousness of that sensation, a conjunction based in horror rather than in love.

As for the dead, we sympathize even with them, sympathize through a negative meditation on the losses of finitude. In the philosophical equivalent to Carl Theodor Dreyer's point-of-view shot from inside a coffin in *Vampyr* (1932), Smith's thinker voices the corpse, ruminating, "It is miserable, we think, to be deprived of the light of the sun; to be shut out from life and conversation; to be laid in the cold grave, a prey to corruption and the reptiles of the earth; to be no more thought of in this world, but to be obliterated, in a little time, from the affections, and almost from the memory, of their dearest friends and relations."[19] This call for memorializing the dead as an answer to the imagined suffering at realizing one will be "no more thought of in this world" does not mean that this is an abstract process of judgment only. For Smith's wonderfully hedged account of our sympathy with the dead is that it arises "from our putting ourselves in their situation, and from our lodging, if I may be allowed to say so, our own living souls in their inanimated bodies, and thence conceiving what would be our emotions in this case."[20] The hesitant plea for permission in this account is for a necrophilic blending of living soul or imagination with lifeless body. Throughout *The Theory of Moral Sentiments*, Smith will continue to use this highly physical, even erotic, language to describe the operations of sympathy. (And Mary Shelley's Victor Frankenstein will make a monstrous experiment of just this kind of embodied sympathy in 1818, only sixty years after Smith's treatise.)

Smith's intersubjective account of emotion demands attention to the root *sym-* of sympathy (together or with *pathos* [suffering or feeling]) and does so in a way that explicitly invokes imaginary embodiment, even entry and bodily boundary dissolution. At his theory's most dramatic moment, even the distinction between self and other is obliterated, producing a sympathetic spectator by devastating the difference between that spectator and some other: "by the imagination we place ourselves in his situation, we conceive ourselves enduring all the same torments, *we enter as it were into his body,* and become in some measure the same person with him, and thence form some idea of his sensations, and even feel something which, though weaker in degree, is not altogether unlike them."[21] Feeling is not only communicable or translatable in this account, it is also the means by which a subject can become in some way the same person as another. At stake in Smith's theory of sentiments, then, is a theory of the self as a potentially expanded and composite feeling being. In a lovely metaphor that both aestheticizes and rhythmicizes the experience of being-with, Smith writes, "The man whose sympathy keeps time to my grief, cannot but admit the reasonableness of my sorrow."[22] Although Smith is analytically clear that the imagination forms an impression of the sensations of the other, it is also the case that his language everywhere suggests that sympathy involves the material commingling of affects, keeping time to each other in a slow, locked embrace.

Smith, like Hume, lets the tear waver tremulously at the boundary between pleasure and pain, grief and satisfaction. When the unfortunate speak of their sorrows to another, they are relieved to no longer endure agony in solitude; however, "by relating their misfortunes, they in some measure renew their grief." Tonguing their grief to another awakens the memory of the cause of the calamity: "their tears accordingly flow faster than before, and they are apt to abandon themselves to all the weakness of sorrow. They take pleasure, however, in all this, and it is evident are sensibly relieved by it."[23] The profusion of fast-flowing tears here is both symptom of grief and sign of its alleviation.

Again, as with Hume's paradox by which spectators experience amplified pleasure the more they are made to weep, Smith's treatment of the tear figures it as a highly ambivalent site, linked to grief's presence, amplification, diminishment, and obliteration all at once.

Smith's theory of the transmissibility and translatability of affect (and the moral necessity of both) is a striking departure from the Western tradition that privileges tears as outward signs of an internal, incommunicable experience. In his account of the intersubjectivity of emotional communication, Smith rejects any solipsistic take that treats emotion as something that cannot be shared or that forms barriers between subjects. Furthermore, in suggesting that the judgment of an impartial spectator will produce an understanding of the affections in each case, regardless of what the other is actually feeling, Smith comes very close to suggesting that exciting situations have essential formal analogues in the appropriate affection to each cause. The tradition that this opposes—which emphasizes shaming, catharsis, revelation, and private, even unique, interior experience—cuts across multiple theological and philosophical texts, perhaps the most famous of which is Augustine's account in *Confessions:* "I probed the hidden depths of my soul and wrung its pitiful secrets from it, and when I mustered them all before the eyes of my heart, a great storm broke within me, bringing with it a great deluge of tears. I stood up and left Alypius so that I might weep and cry to my heart's content, for it occurred to me that tears were best shed in solitude."[24] This pitiful privacy of tears stands in marked contrast to Smith's theory of entering the other's body and experiencing emotion in his place. Nevertheless, what Smith's intersubjective tradition and Augustine's antisocial tradition (to frame that difference in a crude shorthand) have in common is a belief that tears express something. Although the two perspectives imagine differently how that expression is read, how legible or illegible it may be to a witness, how private or shared it must be morally, they nevertheless assume that something temporally and causally predates the productive wetness. In this take, tears come *after.*

There is, however, an opposing camp, less well represented in the history of sentiment but still significant, for whom tears are not linked to the release or expression of emotion, or to the purgation of sorrow, or to a legibility of the heart. This other history of the tear locates it far from the soul in the physicality of sensations that precede interior state changes of sadness, sorrow, or pity. Foremost among the thinkers in this other tradition is William James. His argument of 1884 that emotions are physiological states radically revised the causality of emotion, turning the temporal trajectory of sensation to expression on its head. In "What Is an Emotion?" that titular question is answered with a turn to the visceral, the physical, the observable, and the exterior. Indeed, James limits his inquiry to the emotions that lend themselves to that focus, considering only "those that have a distinct bodily expression."[25] This narrowed focus represents a methodological, analytic, and disciplinary shift: James represents the young nineteenth-century discipline of psychology, and with that new field came a very different take on the affections.

James's cause-upending theory of emotion focuses on bodily disruption; his target was previous theories that suggested that one first perceived a fact (Lion!), which then excited an emotion (Fear!), which finally led to a bodily affection (Fight!—or, perhaps, flight). His famous thesis reverses course, stating that

> the bodily changes follow directly the PERCEPTION of the exciting fact, and that our feeling of the same changes as they occur IS the emotion. Common sense says, we lose our fortune, are sorry and weep; we meet a bear, are frightened and run; we are insulted by a rival, are angry and strike. The hypothesis here to be defended says that this order of sequence is incorrect, that the one mental state is not immediately induced by the other, that the bodily manifestations must first be interposed between, and that the more rational statement is that we feel sorry because we cry, angry because we strike, afraid because we tremble, and not that we cry, strike, or tremble, because we are sorry, angry, or fearful, as the case may be.[26]

The little tear undergoes a marked change in James's reversal of viscera and passion. The tear is neither the physical, external manifestation of the emotional, interior change of state nor the posterior expression of some anterior cause; rather, it is the bodily manifestation whose perception produces a subsequent feeling of sadness. Consequently, the tear is no longer a privileged sign of emotionality, but an energetic corporeal state rather like running or striking an opponent, trembling skin or quivering viscera. The tear is external and observable, and because it is not an after-action of some prior cause, it is legible as the motor provocation of "the mental affection called the emotion." This is a significant change, for if the tear is a bodily change whose perception is the emotion itself, then the tear is a haecceity—it is its thisness. While James's account has some conceptual problems—as Jerome Neu argues, it requires that we ignore the fact that "we can be sad without crying"—his dramatic reorientation of causality in emotion is an important moment in the uses of the tear in philosophical and, now, psychological thought.[27]

Our brief history of the tear is now firmly in modernity, and with the shift to the nineteenth century come revolutionary redescriptions of the human, which in turn generate new theories of the tear. The major intervention that marked the changing episteme in which James participated was the treatment of emotions not as true internal states but as external and observable—and, increasingly, as ambiguous, even deceptive. While James's contribution to this shift is the reversal of the order of elements, so that it is not we-feel-we-cry but we-cry-we-feel, Charles Darwin, writing a few years before James, would suggest that crying and feeling, in fact, do not necessarily have anything to do with each other at all. Darwin, like James, focuses on the physiology of crying in *The Expression of the Emotions in Man and Animals* (1872), but, as suggested in his title, he had different aims from the psychological inquiry. While his interest is in explaining questions such as the perennial "Why do we cry?" in evolutionary terms, he is also engaged in a process of distinguishing the two subjects of his title—hence "Special Expressions of Man: Suffering and Weeping," the particularizing title of the chapter that holds our interest. Darwin's hyper-externalized view of the tear finds its visual equivalent in the photographs by Oscar Rejlander that appear throughout his text, detailing in facial close-ups the grimaces and comportment appropriate to each expressed emotion.[28]

Darwin begins his discussion of "low spirits, grief, dejection, and despair" by speaking of *none* of those things. Instead, his inquiry opens by considering the crying of babes:

> Infants, when suffering even slight pain, moderate hunger, or discomfort, utter violent and prolonged screams. Whilst thus screaming their eyes are firmly closed, so that the skin round them is wrinkled, and the forehead contracted into a frown. The mouth is widely opened with the lips retracted in a peculiar manner, which causes it to assume a squarish form; the gums or teeth being more or less exposed. The breath is inhaled almost spasmodically.[29]

The most remarkable aspect of this description for Darwin—and the universal trait of criers of all ages (save, however, our Marion)—is the tight closing of the eyes. His explanation for this shuttering is that the compression of the eyeball protects the eye "from becoming too much gorged with blood."[30] (Beckett's version of this law: "the human eyelid is not teartight [happily for the human eye]."[31]) The protective mechanism unlinks crying from the various motivators for the excitation that has led to a profusion of blood flowing into the eyeball; the cause of the excitation is less important than the resulting evolutionary compensation to protect the vulnerable orb. Indeed, Darwin notes that very young infants do not shed tears at all; like the acquisition of a wet vocabulary, tears need a dry run or two. "It would appear as if the lachrymal glands required some practice in the individual before they are easily excited into action," he supposes, "in somewhat the same manner as various inherited consensual movements and tastes require some exercise before they are fixed and perfected."[32] Thus, weeping, that most basic and common of emotional expressions, that essential testing ground for philosophical theories of sentiment, is for Darwin a habit that must be acquired, that must be rehearsed and developed.

Darwin rightly notes the strangeness of this developmental necessity precisely because of the assumed legibility and immediacy of the tear: "the fact of tears not being shed at a very early age from pain or any mental emotion is remarkable, as, later in life, no expression is more general or more strongly marked than weeping."[33] Despite the evolutionary protective quality of tears—lubricating the eyes, flushing out irritating particles, keeping nostrils damp—Darwin is also highly aware of the habitual and social dimensions of their expression.[34] He differentiates, for example, the "passionate cry" of the child from wailings of grief; argues that men in Western cultures soon lose tears as an expression of bodily pain; describes the insane as notorious for giving way to their tears at the slightest whim, and so forth. To weep requires practice; tearing must be perfected or its skill can be lost. Thus, despite its evolutionary value, the tear comes, over the course of Darwin's analysis, to seem increasingly unnatural, habitual, cultural, even contingent. Crying is structured, we might say, like a language.

When Darwin attempts to explain why an evolutionarily motivated defense can come to be associated with the abstract movements of emotional thought, he brings together his emphasis on habituation with a meditation on will: "when complex actions or movements have long been performed in strict association together, and these are from any cause at first voluntarily and afterwards habitually checked," then proper conditions can produce an involuntary performance of the complex actions.[35] Thus, tears may be secreted despite age, culture, gender, habit, or any other attempt to fight or avoid that secretion. For an example with the additional utility of invoking the aesthetic, someone who reads "a pathetic story" may twitch or tremble imperceptibly and may not show any outward movements associated with tearing, but "it is almost certain that there would have been some tendency to transmit nerve-force in these same directions; and as the lachrymal glands are remarkably free from the control of the will, they would be eminently liable still to act, thus betraying, though there were no other outward signs, the pathetic thoughts which were passing through the person's mind."[36] The tear, then, is ambiguous for Darwin: habitual and developmentally mutable, yet sufficiently independent of the will that it can betray the thoughts of the moved reader to an outside, scrutinizing world.

What makes Darwin's treatment of the tear quite remarkable, in addition to the emphasis on its cultural variability and its learned practice, is the way in which he wrenches the tear away from the affects altogether. The origin of the tear is muscular, not emotional: "it is an important fact which must be considered in any theory of the secretion of tears from the mind being affected, that whenever the muscles round the eyes are strongly and involuntarily contracted in order to compress the blood-vessels and thus to protect the eyes, tears are secreted, often in sufficient abundance to roll down the cheeks. This occurs under the most opposite emotions, and under no emotion at all."[37] Darwin's account takes the affective ambivalence of the eighteenth-century philosophical tear to an extreme. While the first half of his conclusion is striking and Humean—that tears of joy and despair are equally possible—it is that second "and under no emotion at all" that wrests the tear away from its philosophical lineage altogether. Indeed, despite the suggestion in the title of Darwin's chapter that weeping is a special expression of the human, a long aside on the tears of the Indian elephant makes it clear that the tear can no longer even stand in for the judgment or emotional raptures of man as distinct from beast. This de-emotionalization of the tear reduces it to its brute physical necessity and evolutionary function. That spasms of the musculature in wild laughter or wild grief, heaving vomit or violent coughing, a painful strike or bracing cold equally require protecting the ocular organ through tightly closed eyes and lachrymal flow suggests that it is no longer possible to regard the tear as an unmediated production of interiority, an expression of the secrets of the soul, or even a sign of emotion's presence (either prior or imminent) in the subject. The tear at this point in its narrative, in fact, can signify nothing more than that it cannot signify anything essential or obvious at all. It is its wet appearance and reveals nothing more.

With this voiding, we arrive in the twentieth century, armed to approach a paradoxical set of treatments of tears. What the next two accounts share is a demand that tears be read and interpreted, for not only are they not pure expressions of the feeling self, they are fundamentally not to be trusted. What these thinkers differ on, however, is the very nature of the tear. For Jean-Paul

Sartre, emotion will now be described as an action on the world; for Sigmund Freud, it will be a symptom, a sign of nonaction and a displacement or repression of energies. The utility of reading Freud and Sartre together, despite a span of forty years between their accounts, is that both discuss the tear in relation to the analytic encounter, which is marked from Freud's earliest writings—indeed, is cause for and result of the psychoanalytic injunction to speak all—as one involving deception, partial truths, and necessary falsities. No longer merely linked to paradoxical states of feeling, the tear is now a performance; it is now essentially *suspect*.

As if invoking the psychological version of Darwin's lachrymal cleansings, Freud treats tears as defenses. In "Hysterical Phantasies and Their Relation to Bisexuality" (1908), Freud writes of a patient plagued with tears that offer no immediate clue to their origin or relation to emotion but that must be interpreted to produce meaning:

> She told me that on one occasion she had suddenly found herself in tears in the street and that, rapidly considering what it was she was actually crying about, she had got hold of a phantasy to the following effect. In her imagination she had formed a tender attachment to a pianist who was well known in the town (though she was not personally acquainted with him); she had had a child by him (she was in fact childless); and he had deserted her and her child and left them in poverty. It was at this point in her romance that she had burst into tears.[38]

The significance of this anecdote is twofold. First, the unconscious fantasy produces abundant tears that are sudden and seemingly without cause; thus, tears no longer require the mediation of judgment or conscious processes. And second, the context for the motivation of these tears is shrouded in mystery until it is hermeneutically apprehended through analytical archeology. The tear functions as a semiotic block, what must be read and cannot be understood immediately or without interpretation; tears, that is, do not mean by or in themselves. The tear, rather, testifies to a lost sincerity, announces that nothing is what it initially seems to be; revolting against notions of easy bodily legibility, these drops impel a mazy process of unearthing and wonderment. And when interpretation finally takes place, the tear does not signal a deep longing or private expression of the heart, but an unconscious fantasy ambivalently expressed as a symptom.

If Freud's treatment of the tear as a defense that must be read is striking, it is nevertheless of a piece with earlier accounts in that he continues to locate tearness in matters of the body (while adding to that body the domain of unconscious fantasies). But Sartre, forty years later, treats the tear and emotion in general as a largely non-material matter. His argument in *The Emotions: Outline of a Theory* is that all emotion is action in and on the world. Thus, against Darwin's insistence that the tear can function against the will, betraying the unwitting feeler, and against Freud's emphasis on the wash of tears that catches his patient by surprise in the street, Sartre de-passifies the passions, refiguring them as active, chosen attempts to transform and act on the world in which the subject finds herself. In this way, he starkly rejects James's version of emotions as instinctual, visceral reactions over which one has no control. The dilemma of the free subject thrown into the world ("left alone, without excuse," as he often puts it) is that that world is a fiercely thorny place in which to live. Emotions offer what Sartre describes as a magical way to attempt to transform that world: "when the paths traced out become too difficult, or when we see no path, we can no longer live in so urgent and difficult a world. All the ways are barred. However, we must act. So we try to change the world, that is, to live as if the connection between things and their potentialities were not ruled by deterministic processes, but by magic."[39] Such voluntary transformations of the world (or attempts at transformation) are strategic efforts at evading the consequences of the existential subject's freedom. But if emotion is "the seizure of new connections and new exigencies," which Sartre does admit, it is also a practice of regarding the world that is imbued with bad faith and an evasion of will.[40] Despite the fact that emotion is action, it is not like other actions in that "it is not *effective*"; the emotive behavior attempts less to exercise agency than to confer on the acted-on object "another quality, a lesser existence, or a lesser presence."[41] Contra the Freudian reading of emotion as bound up with repressed desires and the unconscious, Sartre posits that "in emotion it is the body which, directed by consciousness, changes its relations with the world in order that the world may change its qualities. If emotion is a joke, it is a joke we believe in."[42]

Sartre's examples are telling partly for their repetition of scenarios also found in James and Darwin. However, his reading of physiological responses is markedly different, as a behavior of escape not from the object of fear but from responsibility for the frightening world:

> For example, take passive fear. I see a wild animal coming toward me. My legs give way, my heart beats more feebly, I turn pale, I fall and faint. Nothing seems less adapted than this behavior which hands me over de-

fenseless to the danger. And yet it is a behavior of *escape.* Here the fainting is a refuge. Let it not be thought that this is a refuge *for me,* that I am trying to *save myself* in order not to *see* the wild animal *any more. I* did not leave the unreflective level, but, lacking power to avoid the danger by the normal methods and the deterministic links, I denied it. . . . And, by virtue of this fact, I did annihilate it as far as was in my power. These are the limits of my magical action upon the world; I can eliminate it as an object of consciousness, but I can do so only by eliminating consciousness itself.[43]

Unlike James's reading of an almost identical scenario, in which the physiological experience of swooning produces the emotion of fear, for Sartre such a faint is a feint, an attempt to magically transform the world into one that does not pose a threat. Likewise, Sartre reads melancholy's "behavior of oppression" (turning away, tucking into oneself in the darkness of a quiet, empty room) *not* as the profundity of one meditating on sorrow or grief, but as an evasion of the world's insistence that we act in it and engage the potentialities of life ("tasks *to* do, people *to* see, acts of daily life *to* carry out").[44] The conscription of the depressive's physical space mirrors the truncation of her hodological space, and the ethical consequences of this affective abdication are absolute: "sadness aims at eliminating the obligation to seek new ways, to transform the structure of the world by a totally undifferentiated structure. . . . In other words, lacking the power and will to accomplish the acts which we had been planning, we behave in such a way that the universe no longer requires anything of us."[45] The emotions under consideration here are ways of "setting up a magical world by using the body as a means of incantation" (with echoes of Freud), and for that reason they are aligned with a retreat from the world, its potentialities, and our freedom to act in and on it.[46] Emotions, for Sartre, involve deploying the body in the evasive action of dodging the proper use of will.

When Sartre turns to the tear, he does so in the context of a patient of Freud's contemporary (and fellow student of Charcot), Pierre Janet: "a sick girl comes to Janet; she wants to confide the secret of her turmoil, to describe her obsession minutely. But she is unable to; such social behavior is too hard for her. *Then* she sobs. But does she sob *because* she cannot say anything? Are her sobs vain attempts to act, a diffuse upheaval which represents the decomposition of too difficult behavior? Or does she sob precisely *in order not to say anything?*"[47] The "abyss" between those two possible interpretations of the girl's tears is the difference, for Sartre, between his new account of the emotions and all prior ones. Unlike the first, mechanistic view, the second reading—that the girl sobs not as a loud profession but in order to remain silent—theorizes emotion as organized behavior, means aiming at an end. But what that emotion-behavior aims at is precisely deception, delay, and an evasion of difficulty. Emotions, then, are not windows into the soul; rather, they are "a particular subterfuge, a special trick, each one of them being a different means of eluding a difficulty."[48] The truth of emotions, for a Sartre who sounds here like Nietzsche, is that they are masks—not of some other or prior truth, but evasions through and through, active deceptions in their essence, masks all the way down. While Darwin's tear is a defense, and Freud's tear is a symptomatic eruption, Sartre's tear is a refusal. The lubricatory effusions involve a use of the body to carry out a substitution: Janet is to be affectively moved by this display in a displacement of affect that distracts and detracts from the original stakes of the intimate conversation. Sartre concludes this reading of Janet's patient by figuring the tear as an agent of motor purgation, though not in the sense of Aristotelian catharsis: "by putting herself into a state which made confession impossible, she cast the act to be performed out of her range. Thus, as long as she was shaken with tears and hiccups, any possibility of talking was removed."[49] While psychoanalysis will increasingly listen to the body in the interpretation of symptoms, Sartre figures this deception less as a truth that must be analytically mined than as a successful circumvention of confession altogether.

The advantage of reading Freud and Sartre at the end of this record of the tear—(or, there is no "the" tear, but this record of many tears)—is that a noticeable shift occurs between the earliest and latest stages of theorization: where a tear's legibility or artlessness was unquestioned in earlier accounts, here the tear is unquestionably deceitful, suspect for its illegibility. As opposed to standing in for the immediacy of interiority, the tear by the twentieth century solicits probing, if not outright hostility, suspicion, and doubt. The Romantic insistence that the moved, sentimental body is the site of a privileged truth—as in the commonplace that tears say more than words, avowed equally across the centuries by both poetry and pop (e.g., A. W. Schlegel's "In Praise of Tears" and Radney Foster's "Never Say Die")—is replaced with the sense that the body is imbricated in beguilement, refusal, hedgy falsehoods. The tear is now indeterminate and indeterminable, exterior and observable—but observable in a way that does not reveal its truths or its emotional cause or judgment thereof. The tear demands interpretation, but that reading does not point inward toward the depths of the soul—it remains a surface reading always, a tracing of the bodily production of the sign that signifies only its refusal to reveal itself.

In other words, the tear is no longer regarded as purely expressive, purely mimetic, purely osmotic, purely emissive. It is something else altogether. No longer the spontaneous expression of, or physiological anticipation of, any determinate, determinable emotion, the tear is physicalized and materialized with increased indifference to interior states; it is but an opaque rendering (even a dismantling) of those interior states. The tear has lost its obviousness, is bad evidence. Finally, as opposed to the true solitude brought about by tears in Augustine's *Confessions,* tears by the twentieth century have traversed a line ending in lies, untrustworthiness, and doubt *in their address to an other.* Instead of Adam Smith's fantasy of a world in which sentiment enables inter-subjective moral sympathy, the tear now stands for the unbridgeable break between self and other, that what it is to encounter an other is to deploy the body to lie about or through sentiment itself.

It has been said that tears are universally viewed as the sole bodily excretion that is pure and clean, but this idiosyncratic history has demonstrated that tears can take on the qualities so long endured by shit, urine, vomit, blood, and pus. They can be made filthy, put in the service of deception, Baudelaire's "*vils pleurs*"—all of them tears that are not legible as tears.

TEARS WITHOUT BODIES

Consider, then, the shower scene in *Psycho,* after it has all come and gone. What is the status of that drop welled in the corner of Marion's magnified duct; what is one to do with that tear that is not necessarily a tear, that craves a reading, that may deceive, and that refuses all obviousness? In many ways, Hitchcock's 1960 film is theorizing the tear after modernity, after the tear has been placed under suspicion, for if *Psycho* could be redescribed as a treatise on the oils orbs can spill, then Marion's limpid droplet is the recto of a verso evoked earlier in the film by Norman Bates. As the doomed figures take dinner in the motel's study minutes before the shower scene's burst, Norman violently rejects Marion's suggestion that he put Mother Bates "someplace." He spits, "People always call a madhouse 'someplace,' don't they?" and continues, de-spite her protesting apologies, to storm, "What do you know about caring? Have you ever seen the inside of one of those places? The laughing and the tears, and the cruel eyes studying you? My mother, there?" Norman's pas-sionate appeal to the passions offers a strikingly different account of wild tears from the opaque, illegible drop glimpsed later on the bridge of the nose of the carcass on the floor. His accusation is most striking for its reflexive evocation of the inside of a movie theater—another "someplace" marked by laughing, tears, and cruel eyes that study. The institution at stake in Norman's horrified description slides: from madhouse to art house, from mental institution to cinematic institution. The cruel eyes studying "you" become the eyes studying the very figure speaking these lines; thus, even before the shower curtain is ripped through, infamously puncturing the safety of the fabled fourth wall, Norman's accusation strikes at the heart of representational security, calling on the audience of *Psycho* to attend to its own affective work during the film—to ask what sort of tears it sheds or fails to shed. These tears he evokes (eyewater) are also tears (cleaves), rends in representation, pointing reflexively to the jolted, affective audience to Hitchcock's text. However, in addition to this reflexive disclosure, the evocation of the tears of the mad pluralizes *les pleurs*, introduces into the text the possibility of different modalities of tears: the tears of the mad and the tears of the dead.

Marion's tear is the inverse of all that Norman's tears stand for. It figures, instead, after the possibility of laughter is annihilated, as a lifeless or stillborn tear or a tear that in fact may not be a tear at all. Instead of being linked to cruelly studying orbs, it is sworn and bound to a lifeless eye, as though trapped for eternity in a Cartesian optical experiment: *And if, taking the eye of a woman recently dead...* [50] Its photographic equivalent is Man Ray's 1932 *Larmes* (*Tears*), sometimes called *Glass Tears* in honor of the visual pun of the piece: five tiny transparent beads set precisely on a fragmented section of a woman's face, perfect, cold and still, unmoved, unmoving. Hers is emphatically not the tear of the affective film audience, not jerked out of the productive, expressive body as at a melodrama. Marion's tear is marked by *what it is not*. It is not expressive of the emotions of a subject, not an external production of an internal state; it does not speak to either its emissive past or to its judged emotional future, and it is ripped from, and sits only ever so gently on the surface of, the body. The clear leak neglects to reveal its embodied history and must be read for the potentialities it may or may not offer to the world. It comes from nowhere and advances nothing. Silent tear, it rejects Barthes's claim: "if I have so many ways of crying, it may be because, when I cry, I always address myself to someone. . . . By weeping, I want to impress someone, to bring pressure to bear upon someone."[51] This is a bead that brings pressure to bear on nothing, rests lightly. If one striking example of the tear that addresses in an emotional pedagogy is Heather's famous and oft-mocked close-up implorations of dripping tears and snot in *The Blair Witch Project* (1999), or any number of weeping heroines in classical cinematic melodramas, jerking out of the spectator's responsive body a pathetic movement in kind, this tear by contrast does not solicit or instruct an audience to mirror, mime, or repeat it. In short, this tear is neither *from* Marion nor *for* us.

These negative accounts still have not answered the question of how to grapple with this tear that is not immediately and vividly legible as a tear. The most striking aspect is this drop's insistent exteriority. It is so much a figure of the outside that its historical relation to an inside (the secret of its secretion) is refused entirely. (Is there such a thing as a tear that appears without ever having been wept?) Moving further, even still, from theories that emphasize the visceral physiology of the tear, Marion's tear is indifferent to perceived or judged emotion altogether, linked as it is to the lifeless finite post-conscious subject. But importantly, it is nevertheless the case that this tear exists: although it is ambiguously a tear, it falsely answers the dilemma posed by the tear simply to assert that it is *not* one. In an otherwise exemplary essay on *Psycho*, George Toles, for example, does away with the tear in his effort to trace the evacuating metaphors of the eye across Hitchcock's film (infecting, rather than amplifying, connections in what he describes as a dead metaphoricity). Toles writes of the shower scene, after it has all come and gone, "In a culminating extreme close-up, this eye contemplates us with the alert fixity of death while a false tear, formed by a drop of water on Marion's face, announces that emotion (of any kind) has no further part to play here. The tear might as well be a fly: nothing is but what is."[52] Toles's dismissal is not quite right, either, for it is the nature of the ambiguous drop that it refuses to disclose its relation to truth. In fact, the drip discloses a non-relation to truth: it cannot be said to be a "false tear," for there is no true tear preserved elsewhere on some other plane of metaphysical verifiability. Toles can no more know the falseness of this tear than Rothman can aver its truth, for this drop is not not a tear, but neither is it a tear. It remains, even in attempts at definition, a tear that is not a tear.

Let us recover a history of the tear as strange.

The tear by modernity, I have claimed, forms a hermeneutic demand. That interpretive imperative, however, should not be limited to semiotics, as in so many accounts of melodrama (trickles of pity, of pathos, of loss, of satisfaction), but should be pressed to deliver an account of the tear that takes the full measure of its wet pulse. In other words, if the tear is an action on the world, or habitual or ambivalent; if the tear is defense, symptom or lie—if, in fact, we do not know what a tear is without engaging in the difficult, slow process of interpreting each individual tear—why limit ourselves to the narrow portion of reading that asks what any given textual tear *represents*? The tear is an empty frame, not essentially or necessarily attached to bodies or to emotion or even to meaning. Why not then *really* read the tear? It is, after all, also: a visible shape on the face; a distortion or culmination of pattern; a heaviness or a lightness of weight; a texture;—it is a method of reflecting light. Once the tear is unlinked from emotion, from expression, from interiority, from subjects—even from life and vitality—it is liberated to be read for the exterior structures it takes; the ultimate culmination of the tear placed under suspicion is the dehiscence of tear from sure recuperable substance. The tear is freed to be a glassy orb or plastic bead, a series of curves, a theory of time. In other words, these stark little stars are given and taken as having form. And that form is not determined or determinable in advance, is not paraphrasable or summarizable, essential or given, is not immediately perceptible. Rather, that form must each time be read for.

Once the tear is a structure rather than an emotional expression, new possibilities for reading signs of affective disturbance are set loose. But one loses control of reading; that is its infinite promise. So let us go further: if the tear is a formal element, then why should not every other formal element, other curves, other theories of time and light, also be opened up to being read for their relation to affect? This argument so far has moved in one direction: formalizing the tear. It will ultimately also move the other way, affectivizing form itself. One of the central claims of this book is that film-theoretical accounts of the nexus of terms "emotion," "feeling," and "affect" have not strayed far from the dominant Western philosophical models for thinking about interior states or the passionate movement of subjects. Film theory is thus ill equipped to theorize the tear that is not a tear or the tear placed under suspicion; hence the accounts of *Psycho* described earlier, which ascribe the tear to the oldest metaphysical binary in the West—a true tear; no, a false tear. Plato's choice. In such a strict oppositional logic, there is little room for the tear that is not legible as a tear but must be read in and for its ineluctably specific complexity. As in Nietzsche's critique in *Beyond Good and Evil* of the metaphysician's faith in binary values, we need to move beyond the false true tear–false tear choice. Nietzsche's chosen word for this getting beyond was *jenseits,* an opening up of perspectives, an introduction of the *außer-* or extra-, a reckoning with the potentiality provided by the thing that breaks down the binary by which it was formerly described. This is the generative productivity of the tear that is not legible as a tear: it is not a passive brute mute bead but an opening, a possibility for reading for something beyond (or that resists, even that obscures) its own self-evidence.

Marion's tear is delinked from all of the familiar figures that it has acquired over its long philosophical trip: purgation, will, judgment, interiority, expressivity, address, defense, habit, symptom, action, and emotion. To the extent that its very isness is unverifiable, it also unlinks the classical philosophical categories of ontology and epistemology—it unravels, in other words, the ways in which the world is apprehended and verified and, thus, in some small, wet way, undoes the world itself. What takes the place of these historically dense terms is something new. When the tear no longer functions as a pointer—to the secrets of the heart, to cathartic release, to interior states—it is no longer possible to regard it as an entry into knowledge of a subject. Equally, the tear can no longer be deemed a way to acquire knowledge of the body, the unconscious, the will, or even the tear itself. What *Psycho* gives us in its second theory of the tear is a pure exteriority of the sign of emotionality. In the absolute refusal to let the tear function as a deixis, what fails to communicate is not only this tear but all tears as stand-ins for emotion itself. The tear here not only voids its relation *to* interiority, so privileged in Western thought, but is itself voided *of* interiority, losing both its inside and its deep meaning. In the sense of both substance and corpus, *the tear no longer has a body*. In this exteriorizing of the tear, in place of the wet pointer to some other scene hidden in the soul, the tear points only ever and again to itself and to itself as an exteriority that has form. In other words, Marion's tear does not drop;—it folds.

In his book on Michel Foucault, Gilles Deleuze insistently reads his compatriot through architectural and topological forms. In particular, Deleuze emphasizes the folds (*replis*) that constantly mark Foucault's thought as he "continually submits interiority to a radical critique."[53] That recurrently replayed critique in relation to knowledge, power, and thought does not involve privileging an outside in distinction to an inside, but requires putting under duress the very binary of interiority against some knowable, fixed exteriority. Deleuze's explanation, rife with the language of forces that marks all of his work, figures Foucault's philosophizing in the language of perpetual foldings: "the outside is not a fixed limit but a moving matter animated by peristaltic movements, folds and foldings that together make up an inside: they are not something other than the outside, but precisely the inside *of* the outside."[54] Thus, interiority (of thought, as the unthought; as finitude, as the ground of subjectivity) is brought to the surface, made exterior to constitute a new topography of the subject, the body, and knowledge in the process. The crux of Deleuze's reading: "the inside as an operation of the outside: in all his work Foucault seems haunted by this theme of an inside which is merely the fold of an outside, as if the ship were a folding of the sea."[55] Although Deleuze's appeal to peristaltic movements evokes the clenching waves of the digestive tract, these foldings do not produce or successfully digest anything at all—*all ileus,* they remain in undulation, in the heaving kinetic gesture of perpetual folding.

A similar logic and anti-epistemology of the fold is at work in *Psycho's* second theory of the tear. The film follows the bend that Deleuze ascribes to Foucault's thinking and relocates the inside or interiority of emotion as an operation of the outside, as the exteriority of *visible form* in the ambiguity of the clear contours of the shape of something like a tear. The logic of the droplet here fails to conform to the metaphysics of inside matter; that is, it does not point to a content or future in which it places itself in significatory or temporal relation. The relation to itself, rather, "assumes an independent status," as Deleuze writes of the Greek care of the self as articulated in Foucault's later work. "It is as if the relations of the outside folded back to create a doubling, allow a relation to oneself to emerge, and constitute an inside which is hollowed out and develops its own unique dimension."[56] But if the relation of self to self, or of force to force, replaces the relation of interior to exterior, then that relation is not affectively neutral, either—(it would be incorrect to say that Marion's death signals the death of affect for a poor anhedonic cinema). Instead, "what comes about as a result is *a relation which force has with itself, a power to affect itself, an affect of self on self.*"[57] Although Deleuze here is speaking about a Greek conception of the self as a form of practice, the relation of an "affect of self on self" provides a vocabulary for thinking the exteriority of the tear independently of its relation to interior meaning or the interiority of a feeling subject. Deleuze summarizes this self-relation as an "auto-affection," which constructs "an *inside-space* that will be completely co-present with the outside-space on the line of the fold."[58] In place of a line of the fold, we have the curve of the plica here, a gentle heavy sweep in the shape of a tear. This tear that does not drop but folds manifests in an emotional economy in which wet shedding is no longer the expression of an interior state or property of the classical subject but an affective exteriority, an ectoaffect—a formal affectivity of shape, structure, duration, line, light.

This turn to the exterior and to the tear that folds instead of drops accompanies another turn, from the word "emotion" to the word that will be used henceforth in this book: "affect." As in Deleuze's reading of the priority of force on force, the word "affect"—far more so than the often taken synonyms "emotion" or "feeling" or "sensation"—is redolent of a topology that de-privileges interiority, depth, containment, and recovery. While the etymological trajectory of emotion gestures at moving out, emission, and migration (*e-movere*)—and therefore evokes a communicative, transferential relationship—"affect" etymologically allows for a proliferation of concepts related to forces that act on themselves. Derived from the Latin *affectus* (a completed action) and the verb *afficere* (to act upon), "affect," according to the first definition in the *Oxford English Dictionary*, is "the way in which one is affected or disposed; mental state, mood, feeling, desire, intention."[59] "Affect" thus invokes force more than transmission, a force that does not have to move from subject to object but may fold back, rebound, recursively amplify. The semicolon in the OED's definition indicates the double bind of affect—action or the capacity to be acted on, which leaves open the lively and forceful dimension of the word without reducing it to a transference between agents—and interior states, such as mood, feeling, or desire, which is the sense in which it has been evoked most often in the history of philosophy.

Deleuze, reacting to a set of philosophical predecessors that includes Spinoza, Leibniz, and Nietzsche, defines affect as a relation of force irreducible to the affections perceived by any individual subject. He returns to Spinoza's *Ethics* to formulate an account of *affectio* as "the trace of one body upon another, the state of a body insofar as it suffers the action of another body."[60] Affects for Deleuze are not feelings, emotions, or moods but autonomous potentialities, pure "possibles" that are linked to a complex series of highly specific terms, such as "sensation," "becoming," "force," "lines of flight," and "deterritorialization." Art, for Deleuze—literature in *Essays Critical and Clinical;* painting in *Francis Bacon: The Logic of Sensation;* film in *Cinema 1* and *Cinema 2*—is imbricated in the extraction, production, and prodding of affect [*affectus*].[61] Thus, for Deleuze, affect is not linked to an interior state or individuated subject, as "pure affects imply an enterprise of desubjectification."[62]

My argument in this book is indebted to this initial gesture of shedding the subject for affect. Like the Heideggerian avowal that we do not speak language, language speaks us, we might say that Marion does not shed her tear, her tear sheds her. But that process, in turn, produces her self as a non-self, as a de-subjectified subject also figured as a folding process of the outside. This is where Deleuze and I part ways. While his definition of affect is an important precursor to the intervention made in this book, Deleuze loses the subject only to hold tight to the body—or, rather, following the pluralizing impulse of a figure such as Nietzsche, *bodies*. Thus, Deleuze and Deleuzian criticism retain—and, in fact, insist on—the role of bodies in thinking affectivity after the subject. This has led to a host of work on the potentiality of a visceral aesthetics, with an emphasis on new modes of spectatorship, and that is a very different take on affect from the sense in which I will employ it. Affect, as I theorize it here, has fully shed the subject, but my argument goes a step further and also loses for affects the body and bodies. This book regards any individual affect as a self-folding exteriority that manifests in, as, and with textual form. Under the pressure of the encounter between forms and affects, each tear loses every body, and affect loses its tight bond with tears. These losses entail, however, many wild recoveries. Cold white tile is not only a place where vitality drains away.

TWO

Film Theory's
Absent Center

When the history of film and media theory in the 1990s and 2000s is written, it will turn out to have been the long decade of the affect.

Although the affective turn is often referred to in the singular, there were in fact several turns to affects, affectivity, and affection in the discipline's broader early-1990s trans-theoretical revisiting of matters of corporeality, physicality, the visceral, and the material. Deleuze's work on the autonomy of affect began to influence film theory around the same time that cognitivist film theorists began seriously considering emotion, phenomenologists and feminists engaged in a rethinking of the role of hapticity and the body (from the "film body" to the specificity of different bodies), and cultural theorists advanced the need for attention to the multiple senses, moving criticism away from the hegemony of the visual and sonic. One could even persuasively argue that work not theorizing affect was theorizing affect in contemporary film studies, for simultaneous with these rotations was the "historical turn" of Tom Gunning, Miriam Hansen, and Mary Ann Doane, who traveled various returns to Walter Benjamin's interest in the sensorial shocks and corporeal agitations of modernity. The persistent concern in media studies with the rise of the digital (and the correspondingly avowed end or "death" of cinema, as though it, too, were an animately existent being) has also formed curious connections to scholarship on affect to the extent that digital cinema's effects are said principally to appeal to skin and body to agitate the corpus in new and exclusive ways. Each time a turning toward affect has taken place, it has demonstrated one thing above all: the intellectual seductions of this very call. An insistent need to attend to whatever constitutes each subdisciplinary investment in affectivity figures the very notion of "affect" as a placeholder for the unthought of this (or of any) discipline.[1] What animates brings things to life: the affective turn is not only directed toward an object of theoretical inquiry; it is also, quite literally, an affective, affect-laden turn, passionate in its insistence that a new approach is required in the study of representation, providing, above all, analytical vitality. The turn to affect thus has been more operation than curve, and what it has generated primarily is a series of polemics for its own tropistic gesture, a repeated insistence that the humanities direct new and urgent attention to the previously ignored concept of _____.

EMOTION, FEELING, EXCESS, AFFECT

Turning to affect provided film theory with a nodal point around which multiple threads of scholarly work from otherwise irreconcilable camps could coalesce, bringing together thought inspired by Deleuze's philosophy with cognitivism, feminism, queer theory, cultural studies, and phenomenology. These disparate positions came together around a shared investment in thinking the embodied experience of cinematic spectatorship and a reluctance about (if not outright hostility toward) an apparatus theory committed to reading for form and ideology, meaning and sign.

Although the recent polemical theorizations of affect (from the likes of Marco Abel, Giuliana Bruno, Lisa Cartwright, Steven Shaviro, and many others) provide the local context for this book, it is important to note that their work is not the first disciplinary consideration of the subject of perception or affection.[2] A great deal of pre-1970s film theory was interested in, even obsessed with, the question of affect, although earlier theory may have used the words "emotion," "feeling," or "sentiment." Hugo Münsterberg's work on film's psychological effect on emotions and perceptions from 1916; Jean Epstein's ecstatic account of the cinephile's sublime pleasures of *photogénie* in the 1920s; Siegfried Kracauer's work of the late 1920s on *Zerstreuung*, mass culture's seductive assaultive distraction; and, in the 1930s and 1940s, Sergei Eisenstein's polemics for the shock and agitation of the spectator, in addition to his work on ecstasy and enthusiasm, are only a few examples of a long-standing disciplinary investment in the passions.[3] More recently, affect has been central to studies of particular genres taken to have especially strong connections to emotional intensity in relation to the presumed, desired, or actual reactions of spectators: the "body genres" of melodrama, pornography, horror.[4] Here, an affective taxonomy provides a generic taxonomy: if it does not make you weep, it cannot be a weepie; if it does not raise the hairs on the back of your neck, it is not a *horrere*-grounded horror film. We might say that film studies has been haunted by the question of affect since its inception; it has always taken seriously how spectators are moved at the movies. However, the work on affect and emotion from the past two decades that constitutes the "turn to affect" in film studies is novel in its shared sense that 1970s film theory, with its grounding in psychoanalysis, Marxism, and structuralism, lost its way, engaged diligently in the forgetting of affect by remembering too well how to read.

Instead of relegating affectivity to the ghetto of body genres, most contemporary participants in the affective turn in film studies, despite their philosophical divergences, begin with an aggressive suspicion of the disembodied, immobile, textually-positioned spectator imputed to *Screen* theory, which, while known formally as "apparatus theory," is as often these days called "affectless theory." For an example as useful for its early and thus influential polemicism as for its succinct objections, consider Steven Shaviro's *The Cinematic Body* (1993). There, Shaviro declares war on a theory intent on reading for depth, arguing for the importance of accounting for "visceral, affective responses to film, in sharp contrast to most critics' exclusive concern with issues of form, meaning, and ideology."[5] He positions his work explicitly against psychoanalytic accounts and in favor of a turn toward the alternative canon of Bataille, Benjamin, Bergson, Deleuze, Foucault, and Guattari. Rejecting the ways in which percept and affect (defined following Deleuze) have been "subordinated to textuality and the Law of the signifier," Shaviro instead insists on attending to the "immediacy and violence of sensation that powerfully engages the eye and body of the spectator."[6] Shaviro's text has had a sizable impact on post-*Screen* film theory, and his more recent *Post-Cinematic Affect* (2010) continues this project for a new media world. He shares with theorists such as Brian Massumi the sense that intensities are necessarily and utterly divorced from all that signifies. Shaviro's "not that, but this" model of theoretical argument is repeated with striking frequency by most parties in the turn to affect, from Elena del Rio to Giuliana Bruno, Anna Powell, and Lisa Cartwright: beginning with a list of the forgettings of apparatus theory, the theorist then proceeds to insist on another method of approaching film.[7] From the beginning of this recent turn, affect has been theorized defensively—as an omission, a forgotten underside to film and media theory.

While numerous theoretical claims were made for the specificity of a Deleuzian or phenomenological treatment of affect, "post-theory" film research was not indifferent to matters of corporeality or emotional provocation. Cognitivist film theorists participated in a simultaneous return to the problem of feeling at the turn of the most recent century, generating a large body of work on emotional responses in (largely narrative) film, reaching back to Aristotle's theory of catharsis to argue for the role of judgment and belief in emotion.[8] Despite the philosophical differences between the cognitivist and Deleuzian or phenomenological film theorists—they, for example, repeat a twentieth-century analytic versus continental philosophical split—there are important points of connection between the two groups. First, cognitivists shared with Deleuzians a penchant for positioning themselves against psychoanalytic theory as a corrective disciplinary endeavor. Second, both camps used the word "affect," which may be surprising, given that "emotion" and its cognitive associations since Aristotle certainly inform this post-theory school. Assuredly, their use of "affect" is not in the Deleuzian-Spinozan sense of *affectus*. But Noël Carroll defends this choice to write "affect" because "the ordinary notion of *emotion* can be exceedingly broad and elastic, sometimes ranging so widely as to encompass hard-wired reflex reactions (like the startle response), kinesthetic turbulence, moods, sexual arousal, pleasures and desires, as well as occurrent mental states like anger, fear and sorrow."[9] That is, the use of the word "emotion" or "affect" does not function as a theoretical tell, coded to lead a reader back to the philosophical orientation of the thinker.

While the "not that" model is de rigueur in much academic criticism, it is particularly virulent in the case of theorists of feeling in their approach to psychoanalysis. Giuliana Bruno, for example, figures her work most aggressively against the Lacanian-informed film theory of the 1970s, which for her left the unpleasant legacy of a frozen spectator, unmoved, in its unmoved, unmoving theory. In that tradition's emphasis on the gaze, she writes, we are given only the spectator as a voyeur; her revision will account for the film spectator as a *voyageur*, traveling and mapping but also moving and being emotionally moved.[10] In fact, numerous accounts deploy the very language of psychoanalysis that they seem to so despise in order to pathologize affect's omission from psychoanalytic film theory. In her Silvan Tompkins-inspired approach to affect, Lisa Cartwright damns those who remained silent, writing, "Feeling is a suspect area of research for media and film scholars, who, since the time of Brechtian distanciation and Althusserian apparatus theory, have worked to institute models that allow us to resist the seductive pull of the medium as it moves us to feel for the other."[11] Given that Cartwright's argument is that affect allows us to develop what she calls a "moral spectatorship," she is accusing structuralist and psychoanalytic film theorists not only of instituting models that frigidly stave off the seductions of the medium, but also of working actively to avoid feeling for the other. This is not merely a theoretical-historical accusation; it is also an ethical one. At stake in Cartwright's insistence that affect was forgotten is a parallel insistence that its forgetting had a principled, purposive coldness and cruelty. Like Shaviro's designation of psychoanalytic film theory as "phobic," there is an aggression in the turn to affect, as though writing on affectivity compelled linguistic force in its own theorizing.[12] The disparate theorists and post-theorists in film studies—these strange and otherwise hostile bedfellows of Deleuzians, cognitivists, psychologists, and phenomenologists—have united through the shared suspicion that 1970s film theory led the discipline astray by omitting a serious consideration of sensation, embodiment, and materiality. The net result, though, was that in rejecting *Screen* theory in favor of immediate seductive feeling, these theorists severed discussions of affect from any consideration of textuality. The affective turn in film theory perhaps recovered the visceral, but only at the expense of reading. Anne Rutherford goes so far as to advocate for her notion of an embodied affect by claiming that the aroused body is "the underside, the suppressed underbelly of film theory, lost for decades in detours about the formal, the signifier, the subject, desire."[13] That *formal* meditations would be positioned as a disciplinary *detour* suggests the heart of the turn to affect's evasive take on close reading: it constitutes a wrong turn, a digression off-course, a temporary roadblock, too circuitous.—It is what is not the point: *des-* (aside), *tourner* (to turn). The theoretical map is penned clearly here, routing the turn to affect on a track that travels brusquely away from the formal.

On this there is no debate: *Interpretation is indeed the long way round.* Tarrying with a text's specificities is, in a manner, nothing but restless detours, strange delays, awkward encounters, and endless alternative routes—a constant possible going otherwise that traces the unpredictable path of what is unexpected.

This concept of "affect" that is all formless-feeling/what-is-not-structure thus has become a general term for any resistance to systematicity, a promised recovery of contingency, surprise, play, pleasure, and possibility. It is therefore a concept that functions today much as "excess" did for film scholars of the 1970s and not unlike what cinephilia was to theorists such as Paul Willemen: a flexible abstraction that "doesn't do anything other than designate something which resists, which escapes existing networks of critical discourse and theoretical frameworks."[14] That affectivity is what has been taken to have been excluded and rejected by hegemonic film theory, and the renewed polemics for attending to "X" (emotion, feeling, excess, affect), suggest that it is the exuberantly generative nature of this negative term more than positive formulations that has mobilized a renewed interest in affect for the past thirty years in film studies. "Affect" in this general sense is the negative ontology of the humanities.

AFFECTIVE FALLACIES

The poster described above currently faces me, hanging on the wall above my computer, drawing me into a zone of proximity with its prominent face and the affective charge it forcefully exerts on me.—Marco Abel, *Violent Affect: Literature, Cinema, and Critique after Representation*

How can I write about sadness, about my cinematic griefs?—Tim Groves, "Cinema/Affect/Writing"

While the use of the word "affect" in place of "emotion" and the aggressions against 1970s film theory are two points of connection among contemporary theorizers of affect, there is a more significant *point de capiton:* these divergent treatments of affect have insistently linked emotion to concerns about spectatorship and spectatorial experience. The affective turn in film and media studies has produced repeated versions of the reification of the passions: films *produce* something in the audience, or, sometimes, in the theorist, or, sometimes, in the theorist all alone. It is often *her* felt stirrings, *his* intense disgust that comprises the specific affective case study. These accounts, whatever their philosophical orientations, insist on the directional property theory of affect: that it is intentional, that it is effective. Affect is taken as always being, in the end, *for us.* The theoretical consequence of this assumption is an approach to writing theory that emphasizes the personal experience of the theorist. Because of the polemical agitations of much work in the turn to affect, there is a performative dimension to the theory that repeatedly traces spectatorial movements, ruptures, rumblings, and passions—but this performance is also always a solipsism. As a result, a great deal of contemporary work on cinema and affect relies on an excessive use of "I" expressions in relation to experienced emotions or personal narratives of sensorial disequilibrium (as in the epigraphs above). The turn to affect thus risks turning every film theorist into a phenomenologist, each critic a mere omphaloskeptic.

However thrilling it may be to write and even read the personal accounts of any theorist's tremulous pleasures and shudderings, it is a signature of work on affectivity that must be resisted, for it tells us far more about being affected than about affects. Ironically, in accounts of affect that attempt to focus on the immediate, visceral, and corporeal, such an introspective style retains a notion of classical interiority merely redescribed as the interiority of the feeling theorist, even as the written theory attempts to reject and move beyond that metaphysical framework. Perhaps the greatest danger of this approach is that it emphasizes the successful *consumption* of affect and thus makes theoretical accounts of each private feeling experience complicit with the explicit marketing of feeling from the commercial side of film production. One suspects, from these furiously recorded diaries, that the theoretical qualification for such work is to be a better consumer of feelings; if affect does not need to be interpreted, just recorded, then the most affected theorist wins. After Foucault, should we not be very wary of exactly such confessional models as standards for philosophical truth-bearing?

Even in the most subtle theoretical treatments of affect—for example, Jean-François Lyotard's aesthetic injunction to provide a *compte rendu d'affect*—a report of the affect provoked by the work of art, a report that must transmit and not merely objectify or describe the affect—there is nevertheless a reliance on the assumption that what affect is must involve provocations.[15] Ironically, given that many of the worst offenders of the intentional affect model are otherwise mired in poststructuralist theory, the effect is to preserve a kernel of humanism in any discussion of affect. Thus, despite their claims to radically revise approaches to representation, even Deleuzian treatments comfortingly assume that affectivity has something to do with warm bodies in the theater. Take, as just one example, these lines from Marco Abel's *Violent Affect*: "the problem is that we, as spectators, are not privy to the actual, but to us invisible, forces that impinge on the body." The question he regards as posed in the films of the Coen Brothers is "how to make *us* sense these invisible forces, or how to actualize what is merely virtual in the frame."[16] The typographical emphasis is in the original, and it makes clear that when all is said and done: this affective stuff, it tolls for me. What matters in even the most radically anti-representational accounts of affect and violence is what it all means for a body's sensation, what intensity it actualizes directionally and intentionally for a viewer.

The consequence of this tendency to devolve into brute and final description of one man's movements or one woman's felt pressures is the compromising of the speculative etymological roots of *theoria*. This loss of generalizability is no secret; some theorists celebrate it. Shaviro, for his part, insists that "the consuming obsessions of writing theory . . . cannot be separated from the bodily agitations, the movements of fascination, the reactions of attraction and repulsion. . . . I am too deeply implicated in the pleasures of film viewing . . . to be able to give a full and balanced account."[17] Instead of positioning an exploration of affect as a mind/body problem, such writing makes affect a *my mind/my body* problem. With the loss of theoretical generalizability comes a loss of new readings and new questions or problems. So the methodological issue remains: how is scholarly dialogue to engage with accounts of affective shudderings that are particular to the writer/experiencer? For those who insist that we are after- or post-theoretical, this will not feel like such a loss. But for those who care deeply about speculation (of which I am one), these accounts are ends, not beginnings, of theoretical inquiry.

Like many debates in film studies—and the discipline ignores this at its peril—this one has its origins in far older debates in literary studies. New Criticism famously argued for an "intentional fallacy," highlighting the way in which authorial intention was wrongly said to offer privileged insight into a work's meaning. These days, we have (and must subject again to scrutiny) a new version. This intention is not authorial but Husserlian—"intentional" in the sense of that philosopher's theory that consciousness is always consciousness *of* something and that objects of consciousness are intentional themselves. Like the phenomenological contention that each mental act is of or related to an object, this new intentional fallacy suggests that each instance of cinematic affect is of or related to a spectator, that affect by definition represents or gives over something as some thing to an other. In other words, this fallacy assumes that spectator or theorist (it matters little which) is *noetic* (the experiencing) and that affect is *noematic* (that which is experienced). My critique of "intentional affect" argues not against the idea of affect as authorially purposive (although I would resist that, as well) but against the idea of affect as intentional in this second sense. Affect, as I will argue in this book, is nonintentional, indifferent, and resists the given-over attributes of a teleological spectatorship with acquirable gains.

It is worth resurrecting a bit of New Critical history to recall that the seminal "intentional fallacy" was one of a pair, although the influential takedown of Authorship certainly would receive the greatest share of subsequent critical attention. This second fault was W. K. Wimsatt's charge in 1946 of an "affective fallacy," an error of assuming that a text should be judged as having (or failing to have) value for its emotional or affective effect on a reader. The target was a Romantic criticism that focused on the subjective impressions and unrepeatable assertions of the critic, a criticism that confused what a poem is (New Criticism's target) with what it does: in other words, "a confusion between the poem and its *results*."[18] Wimsatt called this "a special case of epistemological skepticism" that tried to derive criticisms "from the psychological effects of the poem and ends in impressionism and relativism."[19] The poem as a unique, objective object of critical judgment disappears in this attention to readerly movings. This criticism is as appropriate today as ever: "the report of some readers . . . that a poem or story induces in them vivid images, intense feelings, or heightened consciousness is neither anything which can be refuted nor anything which it is possible for the objective critic to take into account. The purely affective report is either too physiological or it is too vague."[20] One does not have to accept entirely Wimsatt's claims of an "objective" criticism—certainly the most vulnerable and troubling spot of such an assessment—or make the assumption that reading itself is unproblematic to want nevertheless to take to task the way in which subjective, vague accounts of a reader's or critic's feelings shut down critical inquiry instead of opening up avenues for thought and investigation. In particular, note the charge that such critical readings are irrefutable: while one can reject tout court a theoretical model that argues for reading against signification and for particular, visceral experiences, it is not the case that subsequent claims can be challenged, as they are purportedly the record of some theorist's or spectator's kinesthetic strivings and pleasures. Film theory on affectivity has confused the two fallacies: it has surrendered to the affective fallacy in relation to the theorist's spectatorial responses, and it has done so under the expanded meaning of "intentional." That is, today's theorist of affect errs in reporting the emotional jolts of the film and errs in doing so via the assumption that emotional jolts are definitionally, necessarily, and essentially intentional in aim, direction, and effect. They always land, without fail, let us say in the lap of the awaiting critic.

Does an analysis of tone or mood get us out of this bind? In *Ugly Feelings* (2007), Sianne Ngai considers aesthetics and politics in relation to affects in order to theorize "aesthetic emotions" or "feelings unique to our encounters with artworks."[21] While the text has been most influential for its interest in minor emotions (such as envy and irritation; I am less inclined to agree with her grouping of anxiety and disgust under the banner of the "minor"), the strength of *Ugly Feelings* is also its greatest limitation. Ngai's argument centers on a theory of mood created through formal techniques, "a literary or cultural artifact's feeling tone: its global or organizing affect, its general disposition or orientation toward its audience and the world."[22] However, despite Ngai's promise to read for those minor, "weaker and nastier" feelings through formal techniques ("exhausting repetitions and permutations" in the case of bored shock; first-person subjective shots in film), she commits to the minor and to the affective but remains firmly on the side of experience. The value of forms ultimately resides in how "these affective values [can be regarded as mean-ingful] to how one understands the text as a totality within an equally holistic matrix of social relations."[23] Thus, forms are attended to solely insofar as they explain the ugly feelings felt by a reader or spectator. (And reading for form is further put to work for the sake of the political critique of the minor that brackets the book.) Those "exhausting repetitions" and subjective shots, in other words, are mere formal means to felt affective ends. Similarly, although Jennifer Barker writes that attention to "the sensual aspects of the experi-ence" of film does not involve an attendant dismissal of "narrative, theme, psychology, and history," she insists that "those aspects of a film cannot be separated from—indeed, are conveyed and understood through—our sensual, muscular experience of the films." In the case of Buster Keaton's comedies and action films, "We *feel for* Keaton's earnest characters and the frantic heroes of chase films precisely because we *feel with* them."[24] Although Barker's *The Tactile Eye* is replete with references to specific films and specific shots or scenes in specific films, its emphasis on "muscular empathy" and the visceral exchange between film body and spectatorial body puts those formal traits to work for this sensuous relation, for that "we" who feels. As with Ngai and Barker, though under the sign of Deleuze, Abel routinely enlists form to serve affectively an affected spectator. In his reading of the mise-en-scène of the Coen Brothers' *Miller's Crossing*, he notes that due to the "intense presence of thick layers of brown . . . we, as spectators, sense Caspar's sensation."[25] Such a tautological claim, and the argument it supports, tells us little about, and pushes back not at all against, the notion of muddy tawny overtones. One could find many more examples in the literature of putting form to work for a spectator who feels, senses, or is affected—the choices of Ngai, Barker, and Abel have the advantage of demonstrating that political, phenomenological, and Deleuzian commitments equally take this approach. These deployments of details to support readings that emphasize the exchange between cinema and spectator use a bit of form to argue for sensation, but use does not constitute thought. The instrumentalizing of form to privilege affective experience is an utterly different approach from a reading that lingers with the many questions posed by textual form itself.

READING FOR AFFECT

I charged in the previous chapter that the second (stillborn) tear in *Psycho* is indifferent to its *from* and indifferent to its *for,* and therefore is inscrutable to existing work on affectivity that would return that wet fold to the legible interiority of a character, a narrative or thematic expression, a mimetic instruction to a viewer, a force that moves a spectatorial body, or that would deny altogether that this drop might be a tear and rend it from affectivity to settle the argument. It is the central claim of this book that theorizing affective *replis* involves thinking a construct that can never be returned to the thinker in its for-me dimension: a *repli* that does not reply. I will therefore treat affect not as a matter of expression, not as a matter of sensation for a spectator—in fact, not as a matter of spectatorship at all. Thus, not only is this book not offering a contribution to theories of spectatorship; it should be regarded as a de-contribution to spectatorship studies, an attempt to dethrone the subject and the spectator—and attendant terms, such as "cognition," "perception," "experience," even "sensation"—for affect theory. Rejecting accounts that regard affective displacements as a property of the film given over to another, a thrilling little gift to the spectator, a theorist's private buzz, this book treats affects outside the expressivity hypothesis. In place of affect as a matter of expression, communication, address, spectatorship, experience, or sensation, affect will be regarded as a fold, which is another way of saying that affects will be read for as forms.

Treating affects as having and inhering in form does not require that affect be read through the lens of neo-formalism as defined by cognitivist film theorists, as in David Bordwell and Kristin Thompson's use of a taxonomy of visual strategies meant to guide a spectator comfortably through narrative straits. Indeed, one advantage of treating affect as a problem of form is precisely in how it demands the total redefining of formalism in and for film studies. Specifically, given that Bordwell explicitly positions neo-formalism against what he terms "Grand Theory," my approach to affect recovers and reintroduces the insights and problematics of continental theory in dialogue with form instead of necessarily opposed to it.[26] Not neo-formalism but *radical formalism.* This I mean quite literally: heeding its own etymological *radix,* radical formalism returns to roots, presses on what is essential, foundational, and necessary in formalism itself. A radical formalism in film and media studies would take the measure of theory for form *and* take the measure of form for affectivity; this vital formalism, in the sense of what is both affective and urgent, returns to the roots of formalist analysis, and extends their reach. One wager of this book is that affect is the right and productive site for radically redefining what reading for form might look like in the theoretical humanities today. First and foremost, this approach requires beginning with the premise that affective force works over form, that forms are auto-affectively charged, and that affects take shape in the details of specific visual forms and temporal structures. Reading for form involves a slow, deep attention both to the usual suspects of close analysis that are so often ignored or reduced to paraphrase in recent work on affect—montage, camera movement, mise-en-scène, color, sound—and to more ephemeral problematics such as duration, rhythm, absences, elisions, ruptures, gaps, and points of contradiction (ideological, aesthetic, structural, and formal). Reading for formal affectivity involves interpreting form's waning and absence, and also attending to formlessness.

Specifically, this book makes two moves regarding form: *reading for form* is the methodological strategy, and *reading affects as having forms* is the theoretical intervention. Reading for form enables the specificity, complexity, and sensitivity to textuality that has gone missing in affect studies and is sorely needed to defend the theoretical stakes of the second move. Reading affects as having forms involves de-privileging models of expressivity and interiority in favor of treating affects as structures that work through formal means, as consisting in their formal dimensions (as line, light, color, rhythm, and so on) of passionate structures.

It is the conviction of this book (and a fervent one at that) that arguing for affect as having form and reading for affect as it inheres in form does not empty the word of its forceful, striving meaning; it does not deflate or de-passify passion or weaken its kinetic lure. The myth of asignifying affective immediacy offers the fantasy of superficial flashes of brilliance and insight, but its very antithesis to the durational mediations of reading inevitably leaves it with no specificity that might durably ground its affective claim. Affect is thus left a mere shiver, a tingle, the capacity to find brute responsiveness to flashes of light, loud noises, startling surprises. If affect as a conceptual area of inquiry is to have the radical potential to open up ethical, political, and aesthetic avenues for theoretical inquiry, then, quite simply, we have to do better than documenting the stirrings of the skin. My argument is that *it is only because one must read for it that affect has any force at all.* The intensity of that force derives from the textual specificity and particularity made available uniquely through reading, the vitality of all that is not known in advance of close reading, the surprising enchantments of the new that are not uncovered by interpretation but produced and brought into being as its activity.

My rethinking of the relationship between affect, form, and reading diverges radically from previous work on affectivity and formalism in film studies and critical theory. As part of this departure, I contend not only that a serious treatment of affect in film does not require repudiating the philosophical roots that informed 1970s film theory, but that the problem with that theory was that its provocations were not taken far enough. Since the harangues of Bordwell and Carroll in the late 1990s, the cognitivist rally has been under the sign of "post-theory," but we should be wary of taking this historical moment as an after, end, succession, triumphal beyond. Like Lyotard's critique of the prefix as it appends "modernity," we should regard post-theory as a moment for the reconsideration of theory, for looking again instead of feeding into a chronology of what is lost absolutely. The preferred prefix in Lyotard's work changes the play: "the 'post-' of 'postmodern' does not signify a movement of *comeback, flashback,* or *feedback,* that is, not a movement of repetition but a procedure in 'ana-': a procedure of analysis, anamnesis, anagogy, and anamorphosis that elaborates an 'initial forgetting.'"[27] This redescription is instructive here: for this book, a turn to affect is not part of a post-theoretical moment (or does not have to be), but is an ana-theoretical exercise that extends rather than repudiates the most valuable insights of structuralist and poststructuralist thought, recollects and re-creates that theory instead of imagining it has all come and gone.

This revitalization of both theory and affect is especially urgent at this moment, arriving well into the era of the turn to affect and at the early days of a series of aesthetic turns. The necessity for this intervention now is that, although the turn to affect was meant to be a radical reinsertion of forgotten matter(s) into film studies, the hostility toward form and reading that marked the turn has netted little more than a reassuring uselessness and generality whereby every film comforts for doing and being affectively the same intense thing each time. As a result, as of this writing, the turn to affect is making the final lap of its historical journey, coming to a turned close, as it has not engendered the potentialities that it claims the object of its theorizing necessarily put forth. Instead of producing new readings and new questions, the turn to affect has largely been a series of reminders that the movies move some "us." The only course of action is to tie affect to a process of reading and rereading, returning, and rethinking. The name for that process is the ever-speculative theory. Thus, affect cannot answer a question posed by apparatus theory; it cannot be a mere plug in a historical hole. Affect's potential is in pointing out the non-questions and non-answers at play in any theory. Treating affect as a form is another way of demanding that we read for and speculate on these non-answers.

We may well be at the beginning of what will eventually be called the twenty-first-century "return to form" in the humanities. There has been a growing sense of frustration and disenchantment (affects both) with textual digest, the banality of tropes (hegemony, power, the other), and a lack of interest in formal processes. Calls in the past decade for a return to reading in literary and cultural studies, and recent growing interest in work on aesthetics from philosophers such as Jacques Rancière, suggest that after a long historical stretch of criticisms, disparagement, and outright hostility, we are ready to get back to texts, forms, closeness, attention, specificity.[28] But reading for form does not involve a retreat from other theoretical, political, and ethical commitments. As Ellen Rooney wonderfully words it, all that is required for taking formalism seriously is "refusing to reduce reading entirely to the elucidation, essentially the paraphrase of themes."[29] To the many advantages to reading that Rooney describes for literary studies, I would add that reading affect for form allows a richer language for describing the concept (beyond violences or frenzies or intensities); avoids the tendency of thematizing affect; and allows for a nuanced articulation of the ineluctable specificity and complexity of individual texts and individual affects as a way into something new and not as a confirmation of prior, static models. Of especial value in her polemic is Rooney's insistence that reading for form does not involve a retreat from theory: "rather, the renewal of form as an operation intrinsic to reading enables literary and cultural studies fully to take the pressure of those interventions."[30] To this list of interventions better taken stock of through the renewal of form I would add work on affect, despite its penchant for being defined as intrinsically the antipode to form or structure.[31]

If the project of theoretical speculation is to tackle affect in such a way that it remains open to the surprises attendant on reading a specific film without succumbing to one theorist's intimate record, then affect must be regarded not as a matter of spectatorship but as a problematic of form in a text, which is another way of saying: as a problematic that cannot be determined in advance of or outside of interpretive labor. This book's approach, while a polemic, is also a panic. The danger in ceding the specificity of affects or the generalizability of theory or the persuasiveness of textual interpretation is potentially to risk both the loss of disciplinary rigor brought about by 1970s film theory and the critical insights of that theory. Some readers, certainly, will not regard this as a risk but as the fitting death throes of continental philosophy's grip on American academia. But for those who share my concern with protecting theory's insights, methodology, and hermeneutic suspicions, it is imperative to rescue affect for theory in advance of the realization that the heralded turn has come to a whimpering close.

It will almost certainly be objected that my reading of affect with and in form has a central problem, which is that the turn to affect in film theory was undertaken specifically as an attempt to think the sensory, material body back into a discipline that, under the sway of sign and structure, had "forgotten" the (heavy, lived, real) body. Thinking affect as a form does not obviously offer insight into meat and corporeality in the same way that a phenomenological or Deleuzian turn offers, and thus I am appearing to act in ignorance of what motivated these polemics in the first place. It could be argued that this book is ignoring precisely the value of a turn to affect: that it reintroduced the excessive, irrational, corporeal dimensions that a cold, dry analytic of ideology shunted aside. In a sense, this objection is fair: taking affect away from spectatorship studies, positioning affect as a matter of aesthetics, form, and structure, undeniably removes corporeality, experience, physicality, viscerality, and skin shudderings from the discussion. However, that objection cannot be the final word on the matter, for it assumes one great thing: that in advance we can know what the terms under its objection are; that we have already determined that forms and bodies have nothing to say to each other; that the question cannot be posed whether form can inform what it is to be, have, or fail to be or have a body. In other words, to assert that treating affect as a form ignores the body is to refuse to question what forms and bodies might mean to each other, what form might cause us to rethink about bodies, that form might deform matter or our theory of skin in productive ways—or whether, indeed, the body itself is a kind of form. Because form and affect have been taken as antonyms in the post-1970s battle over the discipline of film studies, this book will insist from the outset that *we have not yet asked enough of form;* that we do not know what forms are capable of; that in the strident pulling apart of form and affect, it hitherto has been undetermined what the body can do to form and even what form can do to a body. Those matters become provocative only under the pressure of specific encounters between particular affects and distinct forms, which is to say, only through— and, yes, its labor involves detours, departures, unpredictable wandering—the unfoldments of close reading.

MISE-N'EN-SCÈNE: FORMALISM AFTER PRESENCE

The approach taken here, to link affect with textual form, is not without dis- ciplinary precedent. However, to see this requires recovering a history of the study of affectivity that leaps back to before the "turn to affect" proper. Take V. I. Pudovkin's account of his most famous "experiment" with Lev Kuleshov, in which identical close-ups of the actor Ivan Mozzhukhin with the same im- passive face ("quiet close-ups," says Pudovkin) were juxtaposed, in turn, with a plate of soup, a dead woman in a coffin, and a little girl playing, each of which in turn was praised by an audience for the emotional nuances of the actor's expressive faciality.[32] As early as these trials in the 1920s, emotion in cinema was unlinked from classical tropes of expressivity and communication, dis- placed onto the expressivity inherent in the plastic processes of montage. One could argue, indeed, that the entirety of Soviet montage filmwork and film theory was organized around an affective center: the enthusiasm and passion for montage itself, an affective *technē*. Nevertheless, Soviet montage retained an interest in examining how montage, in its juxtapositions and productive connections, acted on and worked over spectators. Eisenstein's theories of emotional intensity and film likewise retained an interest in exploring how affective jolts could be wrenched out of spectatorial bodies and minds.

Although amid Romantic views of the sentiments in film theory's brief history one can find treatments of affect that undermine the expressivity hy- pothesis, it is not until the insights of structuralist and, later, poststructuralist thought in film theory that its treatment takes the question of the subject out of the equation altogether. In 1970s film theory, attempts were made to consider affect independent of a subject under the guise of the theoretical concept of "excess." In some ways, this concept is a precursor to the idea of a formal affect. The term can be dated to Roland Barthes's treatment of *Ivan the Terrible* in "The Third Meaning." There, Barthes found that even when he had done away with the informational/semiotic level and the symbolic/ signifying level, "I am still held by the image."[33] This third meaning, "evident, erratic, obstinate"—linked so idiosyncratically to "a certain compactness of the courtiers' make-up"—exceeds generalizability and meaning, and yet it is there, compelling "an interrogative reading."[34] This excess is the theoretical precursor to Barthes's late work on the pleasures of the text and his final work on the photographic punctum in *Camera Lucida*. Exactly as "affect" does for theorists such as Shaviro, what excess undoes is a certain approach to theory; it remains with the stubbornly contingent "I," and what it "disturbs, sterilizes, is metalanguage (criticism)."[35]

The concept of excess spoke to the ways in which a text's contradictions, ruptures, and non-coherences could be more important to a reading than its apparent seamlessness. Although film theory, not unlike Barthes, moved between structuralist and poststructuralist phases, this insistence on the too-much dimension of films, the always-beyond quality that cannot be reduced to coded narrative structures, is a central poststructuralist problematic. In the history of film theory, one shorthand for this switch to poststructuralism would be the shift from codes-in-texts to texts-in-process. One could find multiple versions of this move in this large body of theoretical work, but Stephen Heath's was foundational and remains representative: "narrative can never contain the whole film which permanently exceeds its fictions."[36] Heath, influenced by the Barthes of *S/Z*, writes of the displacements of textual play, its shifts, processual slippages, and inevitable losses or failures. Such slidings produce gaps, rends, holes, contradictions, and an excess that works against organization, homogeneity and motivated representation—works, in other words, against the codes taken to systematize and order classical cinema. The excessive terms of a text are precisely those that lie outside of its unified structures, and thus it is with the turn to excess that film theory moved squarely to a decentered poststructuralist mode of reading. When I argue, then, that my project does not repudiate 1970s film theory but ana-theoretically returns to it, reexamines it to take it further, it is in part because the motivating principles of concepts such as excess can be put in productive dialogue with contemporary scholarship on affect. Theories of excess, however, were not without their problems, not least that they failed to generate inventive questions after the heyday of *Screen* theory. In addition, one can glimpse in excess theory the seeds of solipsistic or idiosyncratic reverie that would germinate into the full-blown indifference to theoretical reach in contemporary work on affect. "Excess," like "affect," was also routinely invoked in the singular, general, universal as the capacity of a text to fail in relation to structural systematicity. Thus, simply returning to excess cannot solve the problems borne out by affect today.

Of course, there has been some work on emotion in film studies that inter-twines with formalist concerns. In his influential "Tales of Sound and Fury: Observations on the Family Melodrama," Thomas Elsaesser focused on melos and pathos in relation to mise-en-scène. Although he is certainly a product of the ethos of 1970s film theory—attentive as the essay is to the Marxist and Freudian dynamics in the genre—Elsaesser is particularly sensitive to how the "dynamic use of spatial and musical categories" plays the spectator's emotions in a "subtle and yet precise formal language."[37] It is precisely work such as this that makes untenable any neat opposition between pre-affect film theory and pro-affect film theory, for it is not simply because his subject is the emotionally laden genre of melodrama that Elsaesser turns to emotion. Like more recent work on affect, Elsaesser approaches the melodramatic as having a resistant or disruptive charge against the more formal signifying material. His interest was in how melodrama functions as "a particular form of dramatic mise-en-scène," whereby style can puncture signification. Nonetheless, Elsaesser maintains the spectatorial assumptions of affect, writing of the "direct emo-tional involvement" and "identification patterns, empathy, and catharsis" of Hollywood cinema.[38] Thus, even in his productive attention to the importance of form for producing emotional effects, he does not take the next step and ask how form might imbue itself with intensities that are not teleological in their aim of moving an emotionally involved spectator. In the end, Elsaesser's interest was more in how ideological contradictions play out in the formal mise-en-scène than in how mise-en-scène might play out the forms of affects.

More recently, Anne Rutherford has attempted to cross the bridge between formal analysis and embodiment and affect. At first, she seems to move away from any intentional or humanist view of emotion when she writes of Theo Angelopoulos's *Ulysses' Gaze* that the "affective power of the film is neither equivalent to, nor dependent on, empathy."[39] But her objection is less to the communicative model of emotion than to its mental empathic organization; thus, she pulls affect back into a matter of spectatorship but relocates it in the corporeal self: "affective intensity is . . . diffracted, dispersed across all of the available sensory registers; it is not detachment that ensues, but a more embodied engagement."[40] To make this argument, Rutherford rehabilitates what she regards as the lost conceptual treasure of mise-en-scène analysis, unearthing in some of its earliest theorizations a richly affective emphasis. She extends, for example, Alexandre Astruc's understanding of mise-en-scène as "a conceptual process," quoting Astruc on how what seems to involve a fixity or determination (what is placed into the theatrical scene) actually involves "interrogation and dialogue."[41] Astruc's materialist mise-en-scène entails "a certain way of extending states of mind into movements of the body. It is a song, a rhythm, a dance"—thus, its affective expressivity is not the movements of a mute collection of investments but itself an expenditure of energy and potentialities.[42] This kinetic engagement is ultimately aimed at an embodied viewer for Astruc—"the *mise en scene*: to make the spectator feel the moment of disequilibrium where everything suddenly falls apart"—thus, it does not move us far from the goal, aim and direction model of emotional intensity.[43] (Indeed, there is something in this account that calls into being three decades later the Deleuze of the *Cinema* books; when Astruc writes that mise-en-scène "is a look which forces people to act," he sounds a great deal like the philosopher of immanence and the sensory-motor schema.[44])

While Astruc's late-1950s model is an innovative reinvigoration of a concept taken for bruteness; while Elsaesser's early-1970s reading of style for its relation to emotion productively asks how form matters to feeling; and while Rutherford's early-2000s scholarship compellingly links together embodiment, affect, and an embodied, mobile mise-en-scène, each remains beholden to a model of emotional intensity that assumes its energetic vector leads to an energetic spectatorial sensorial reaction. Despite the value of these various turns to cinematic form, they remain invested in a functional and instrumentalized notion of it: as outwardly affective, spectatorially bound, and productive to analyze only insofar as it leads us to insight into how texts affect, move, displace, jerk, tear at, mimetically instruct or unnervingly unsettle bodies or subjects. Thus, even when form and affect have been considered together, the marked stubbornness of the theoretical interest in how form affects spectators ultimately has made the study of *affects* in the history of film theory into little more than the study of *effects*.

These accounts across half a century have one further shared problem: their treatment of mise-en-scène. It remains bound to sets, costumes, props, lighting, the battery of theatrically derived things-put-into-the-scene that passes for much visual analysis of film. Despite Astruc's interesting redescription of the term as processual—and despite Rutherford's analysis of "sounds, rhythms and colours" in relation to temporality—the turn to affective intensities has not troubled the logic of mise-en-scène as fundamentally a logic of *presence*. Form itself has not been sufficiently treated to a poststructuralist logic, form itself has not changed conceptions under the pressure of its encounter with affect, and what it is to read for form is taken for granted. If affect and form are to be ana-theoretically considered, one must attend to how the terms speak back to theoretical modes of reading, change each other in their encounter, and even compel a grappling with things gone missing, with aspects of film that do not hold forth in advance and disclose their secrets as surface appearance or immediate impression. Mise-en-scène as a logic of presence is one powerful, pervasive way in which film theory remains on the side of metaphysically dominant terms. Accordingly, one sub-argument of this book is that the encounter between form and affect is a productive site for a critique of the metaphysics of film theory. One way that that critique takes place here is through a dismantling of presence as the founding given of formal analysis. Derrida's famous rereading of the absent origin in his critique of metaphysics suggests the new possibilities thusly afforded: "as a turning toward the presence, lost or impossible, of the absent origin, this structuralist thematic of broken immediateness is thus the sad, *negative,* nostalgic, guilty, Rousseauist facet of the thinking of freeplay of which the Nietzschean *affirmation* . . . would be the other side."[45] This joyful critique asks us to think the absent center as something other than a loss, think loss as something other than an absence, and take seriously the creativity generated by affirming the undoing of presence. The critical imperative is a positive one: to imagine how new readings, and new possibilities for readings, are opened up by dismantling and expanding the terms by which an analysis of form may take place.

Though its appearance in this text is now long gone, the body cleaned and dried, the droplet lost in the shuffle of the cover-up: regard, one last time, the shower scene in *Psycho* and the tear that is not quite a tear. This tear that does not disclose its origin, aim, or ontology troubles, even refuses, the available models for thinking about affect in film theory and the theoretical humanities. Such a tear that does not drop but folds points to a subjectless affect, bound up in an exteriority, uncoupled from emotion, interiority, expressivity, mimesis, humanism, spectatorship, and bodies. It stands to reason that such a bead of resistance would press back not only against theoretical approaches to affect but against methods of cinematic interpretation as well. We must reconsider the plural ways one might read for cinematic form, refusing to assume that mise-en-scène holds to metaphysical logics. Mise-en-scène may be the foundational unit of formalist or neo-formalist analysis, but it is not the ground of radical formalism.

Freud taught us how to take grammar seriously. In his theorization of the *unheimlich* as naming what was once familiar and is now strange, he writes, "The prefix '*un*' is the token of repression."[46] In a similar fashion, in order to interrupt and complicate the assumption of formal analysis for presence, I will insert the sign of negation into the building block of cinematic analysis: a little *n*. In bringing together form and affect, this book will read for what I am calling *mise-n'en-scène*. This phrase is a grammatical impossibility; it is an error in French. Fittingly untranslatable, the term is useful less for what it represents than for the possibilities it sets loose. Mise-n'en-scène suggests that in addition to reading for what is put into the scene, one must also read for all of its permutations: what is *not* put into the scene; what is put into the *non-scene;* and what is *not enough* put into the scene. Formal affects, affects with and in forms, affects after interiority and after spectatorship—these trouble the very philosophical binaries that hold apart presence and absence, interiority and exteriority, self and other, excretion and reception. It is only fitting to follow the logic of the fold into one that upsets a reading method that has only ever looked for presence and so often only found what it knew it would see. One critical pressure that affectivity in particular brings to bear on form is in the way that negative affects exert negative stresses on, even distentions of, cinematic construction, undoing grids, schemas, orderings, all aesthetic plans. The genealogy of non-unities written by an attention to the mise-n'en-scène is a fitting anti-narrative for an approach to form that reads for its impersonal impresence and structural destructurings.

Solitude

We began with a tear. And as the tear folds, so we will end with a tear. When Derrida eulogizes his friend the philosopher Jean-Marie Benoist, he tells us about a tear that nourishes. Offered in the title of the sad homage "The Taste of Tears" is a drinkable wetness, a shared experience between the thinkers, a salty exchange. As an epigraph to his text, Derrida gives way to the words of the now departed other: Benoist's account in *The Geometry of the Meta-physical Poets* of the punishment of the imprudent who "drink the tear and wonder about the strangeness of its taste compared to one's own."[1] Derrida's answer cannot answer these words of the dead but repeats them. His ethics of friendship is on display in *The Work of Mourning*, a collection of eulogies for fellow theorists and philosophers; it takes its title from Freud's notion of the *Trauerarbeit* and takes the work of mourning as the practice of witnessing.[2] In each of the pieces in that collection, Derrida writes of the other in the self and the promise of *philia*—the vow to go before the other and to remain and write in the wake of that going. This logic of interiorization does not, in Derrida, produce catharsis: it is in-terminable, in-complete, im-possible, and yet required.

The promise of friendship is a debt for the future payment of witnessing the other's absence, a debt Derrida made good on in his tributes. "To have a friend, to look at him, to follow him with your eyes, to admire him in friend-ship," he writes, "is to know in a more intense way, already injured, always insistent, and more and more unforgettable, that one of the two of you will inevitably see the other die."[3] The promise of friendship is to open up the world to the existence of the other, an opening that will not fail to confront the pains of finitude on either side of its rend. "That is the blurred and trans-parent testimony borne by this tear, this small, infinitely small, tear, which the mourning of friends passes through and endures even before death."[4] But it is not the tasting—even less the wondering at its difference—of which Benoist and Derrida write. The latter on the former, instead, suggests, "He does not teach us that we must not cry; he reminds us that we must not *taste* a tear. . . . Therefore: not to cry over oneself. . . . One should not develop a taste for mourning, and yet mourn we *must*."[5] Thus, one must not taste the tear and return with a newly poignant love of the self; rather, every grieving tear must remain from and for the other. The taste of the tear is a sensory displacement, a tingle of the chemosenses making gustatory Levinas's ethics of encountering visually the face of the other. One must always cry, and always cry not for the self but for the other; one must find a way to drink tears without tasting them, like a practiced ageusia.

The tear testifies to the exchange of the futurity of finitude—that "you will inevitably see the other die"—and thus it is a tear that begins from the two, a tear that wetly speaks to the more than the one alone. The tear passes between friends, friendship passes between its crystalline edges. Marion's somewhat-tear is not of this world of others to be eulogized. Wet, plain, her tear is not saturated; it is undrinkable. The tear that is not immediately legible as a tear is marked by its resistance, and by its intense solitude. And in the end, this is the only kind of mark that leaves its trace. It does not ex-press but im-presses; hers is a tear of the one all alone, failing to communicate inward with the nuances of the judging mind, or with the skin on which it rests, or with the world that would mirror it and feel alike in turn. The extraordinary solitude of the tear that does not drop but folds is the ethical consequence of its extraordinary ontology. *The bead waits to be regarded with curiosity.* And forever lost in the fold of perpetual exteriority is any logic of ingestion and exchange. That Marion's droplet speaks to no one and is spoken nothing in turn is a funda-mentally different tear from the mourning daub of Derrida's eulogy.

No one dies in just the same way; *Psycho* presents the loneliest death in cinema. Here, the end is not finitude's witness (as for Derrida) but a duration of folding and unfolding evacuations without end. Marion's tear is withdrawn from the very categories by which it can be known: a wasteland of meaning, as wasted as the muddy water that foretold it. Fittingly given form in a clear bead through which nothing can be seen, which magnifies nothing, distorts no emplaced world—death is figured as an undialectical moment, responsive to nothing and to which no thing is responsible. In this solitude without end, Marion cannot be mourned. The form of that single opaque grain, the secret of its secretion, its silence that addresses no one and nothing, is a droplet that will not transform—will not resolve itself into a tear, or into what is not a tear, or into meaning that makes sense of what has just taken place at night in the cruelly flat motel. The form of the tear, this tear, any tear, cannot be dried or casually wiped away—every tear a glass tear, each can only, and infinitely, and bitterly, be read.

grieve, v.

Etymology: < French *grever* < popular Latin **grevāre*

(see grief adj.) = classical Latin *gravāre*, < *gravis* heavy,

grave adj.

a. *trans.* To press heavily upon, as a weight; to burden.

Only in *pass. Obs.*

b. To make heavy. *Obs. Rare.*

—OXFORD ENGLISH DICTIONARY,

2nd ed., s.v. "grieve."

💧

The Illumination

of Light

My heart grew sombre with grief, and wherever I looked
I saw only death. My own country became a torment and
my own home a grotesque abode of misery. All that we
had done together was now a grim ordeal without him. My
eyes searched everywhere for him, but he was not there
to be seen. I hated all the places we had known together,
because he was not in them and they could no longer
whisper to me "Here he comes!" as they would have done
had he been alive but absent for a while. I had become a
puzzle to myself.

—AUGUSTINE, *Confessions*

Quo dolore contenebratum est cor meum, et quidquid aspiciebam mors erat.
(Read: This misery is a misery of light.)[1]

Grief darkens, it blackens; dim eyes, dusky heart—all such hurt is stygian. The opening line of Augustine's lament for his friend is a reworked condensation of Lamentations 5:17: "*propterea maestum factum est cor nostrum ideo contenebrati sunt oculi nostri*" (for this our heart is faint; for these things our eyes are dim). The torture room of this mournful confinement is suffused with darkness and blindness. Augustine's haunting avowal participates in a longstanding Western philosophical and theological tradition of figuring suffering in relation to loss as a problematic of vision and visibility. The plaintive motif can be found throughout the Bible: "my eyes fail because of tears" (Lamentations 2:11); "my eye has also grown dim because of grief, [a]nd all my members are as a shadow" (Job 17:7).[2] Mourning's pain is figured as a matter of waning, dulling luminosity and troubled representation: Augustine's sorrow slides between grief and darkness, suffering and blindness, material absence and absolute visual foreclosure.

Death deprives one of the vision of the other who is lost and, in a larger sense, deprives one of the illuminating possibilities of light, visibility, and untroubled vision. New eyes seek and find only the presence of absence, not instructing a self on the approach of the other but speaking the opposite of "Look, he is coming." (That opposite is not the affirmation, "Look, he is not coming." Its language of visual presence resists negation; it is something closer to a mathematical negative than a grammatical one: "Unlook.") In blackness, one regards only death (*et quidquid aspiciebam mors erat*); thus, it is not a matter of the elimination of seeing, or the absolutism of a sensual truncation, but, rather, the muting of light's approach to the eye in favor of a visibility based in and of darkness, a vision that now *sees nothing*. This is the optics of Milton's Hell: "from those flames / No light, but rather darkness visible." In other words, grief at the death of Augustine's dear friend rewrites the physics of optics to no longer demand or require the entrance of light-avowing presences, creating a seeing that neither instructs one on the world nor deploys the senses as epistemological vouchers. The visual field, in mourning, is reduced entirely to its blind spot.

Eyes seek (a) being, but they do not see—for *being is no longer there to be seen*. This visibility involves nerves that recursively hunt for the impossible presence of nonbeing; as though standing apart from the anguished body,

plucked-out orbs turn in an endless left-to-right rotation of desperate sur-
veillance. Grieving, which involves the ontological loss of the other, figured
through the sensual loss of the vision of the other, culminates in a radical
transformation of the possibilities of a vision based on illumination and presence altogether. The pain at the death of the other *necessarily* involves this
reconfiguration of visibility, the paradoxical vision of an absence that seeks
out what can no longer present itself to the senses except in its refusal to self-
present. In loss, there is simply no more of the object off which light could
bounce. Every loss of being is thus fundamentally a loss of light, including, as
Augustine insists, the transparent, well-lit, comprehending self. Grief refigures
seeing as envisioning without enlightenment: spectating in the darkness on
a retinal other scene. Looking through dead eyes into which no light can be
taken, on which no image can imprint its rays, *dolore* dampens the optic possibilities of a sensual encounter with a present existent world, like an affective
cataract.

Augustine's account details a very particular and complex visual scenario
whereby suffering takes the form of a kind of blindness, and yet blindness
through this association takes on a strange and specific sense, one that requires
a history of the signifier for its relation to grief to emerge. "Blind" derives from
the etymological bases *bhlendh* (to glimmer indistinctly, to mix, confuse) and
blesti (to become dark). Blindness as an obstruction of sight is a relatively
recent usage, dating to around the early 1500s (and thus well after Augustine),
but the original sense of confusion, not sightlessness, is better suited for understanding the eye-dimming consequence of loss.[3] For what is confused in
Augustine's dirge is both the classical epistemology of vision whereby "Look!"
involves looking-for, in an intentionality that assumes the objectal presence of
the imperative's target, and the self-comprehending self that no longer finds
its bearings in space, light, and vision (the newly riddled, hard-riddled self).
The confessions of grief in *Confessions* are confessions of confusions. What
glimmers indistinctly in this passage is neither the lost absent nor the remaining present but the indeterminate fact that avows the bewilderingly stubborn
existence of one in the wake of the irrefutable nonexistence of the other. If
blindness were to be redescribed as an affect, it would be the affect of a stricken
disorientation.

In Augustine's account, visual confusion, epistemological confusion, and
the felt experience of sorrow are blurred together in their own muddled super-
blindness. The affective anguish and the confusion of visibility are themselves
one and the same. Although this book tightly conscribes grief to matters of the

twentieth century, to technologies of vision (photography and cinema) that modify any consideration of illumination and visibility, this stubborn binding of sorrowful pain to confused blindness, grief to dimming eyes, persists. If sorrow interrupts and confuses illumination and enlightenment, it cannot fail simultaneously to interrupt and confuse the enlightened subject—as goes vision, Augustine tells us, so goes the unriddled self. Tracing the figure of troubled light for grief, I will pass through Freudian mourning, Roland Barthes's meditation on photography, and a film by Michael Haneke to argue that the structure of grief manifests in visual form as a cinematic tableau that puts on display its own conditions of illumination, being, and representation. Instead of working against the tremendous pain of loss, this formal affectivity commits to the raw affective state of the death of the beloved and organizes the image around the heaviness of grief. Likewise, instead of commuting the negativity of mourning into a productive new state, the stasis of the cinematic tableau fixes on light in order to present an affective state that does not transform, but that bends illuminated form to its particular mode of pain.

LIGHT, THE PECULIAR

The self-evident is a heavy burden. —Georges Bataille, quoted in Jacques Derrida, "From Restricted to General Economy: A Hegelianism without Reserve," in *Writing and Difference,* 1978.

What we know about grief: it, from a loss. This is largely all we know of grief. That loss might be material (your body I adored), sensual (the sight she once had), geographical-historical (the home he had to leave), ephemeral-ideational (the ideology they saw fail). This, too: the affect of grief is a uniquely painful suffering—("No worst, there is none. Pitched past pitch of grief, / More pangs will, schooled at forepangs, wilder wring"), and it is painful because the lost thing was valued highly—wanted, needed; it sustained; it defined; it was loved.[4]

Any thorough history of mourning would linger with the extensive theorizations of—and performances of, sculptures depicting, calls for—grief and mourning in Greek philosophy, literature, and drama and would trace the development of a rigorous sentimental aesthetics of loss in the Romantic tradition, but this is not such a history. The aim of this chapter and the next is to consider affective pain related to loss in relation to visual culture in modernity. Thus, grief and mourning will be frozen for first consideration at the moment of their most influential treatment in the twentieth century: Sigmund Freud's essay "Trauer und Melancholie" (Mourning and Melancholia) from 1917. Freud's treatises on grief have been explored extensively in the humanities, in particular his strict opposition between mourning and melancholia, a duality that, like most of his binary oppositions, comes to collapse into a murky unity. However, I want to return to these well-known texts to recover and illuminate a different story about psychoanalytic thinking on loss, for Freud, echoing Augustine, treats painful grief as an affect bound up—vitally and intimately and essentially—with light.

Freud famously distinguishes "the normal emotion" of mourning from the pathological form of depressive melancholia.[5] (I will remain with these two poles for now; however, a third term, "grief," will soon insinuate itself, and much hinges on their distinction.) The loss that compels mourning can be of a loved person or a valued abstraction; Freud's examples are "fatherland, liberty, an ideal," which is one reason that theorizations of nostalgia (*nostos* [to return home]; *algos* [pain]) are so reminiscent of those of grief. In *Trauerarbeit* (the work of mourning), the mourner tests reality to ascertain that "the loved object no longer exists," and ultimately, in labor that is both processual and durational—"the task is carried through bit by bit, under great expense of time and cathectic energy"—the libido withdraws its cathexes from the missing object potentially to redirect the energies of that attachment elsewhere.[6] While Freud speaks of the great pain of loss, it is nevertheless the case that the throb of mourning has an expiration date. Mourning work ultimately sets one free.[7]

The conceptual treatment of mourning is squarely binary in the 1917 essay, and that reductive opposition frames debates about mourning to the present day. While grieving is certainly unpleasant and "involves grave departures from the normal attitude to life," Freud regards it as a non-morbid, comprehensible disposition, and he assures the reader that "after a lapse of time it will be overcome."[8] By contrast, melancholia is the pathological, morbid, problematic version of mourning. One of the most significant differences between the two terms is in their relationships to temporality: melancholia takes an expanded duration, it persists and continues indefinitely, adhering to time; mourning, by contrast, because it can and will be overcome, has a finite future. The analysis of time in relation to mourning and melancholy is so crucial to Freud's account that Jean Laplanche reads psychoanalysis as suggesting that "the dimension of loss is probably co-extensive with temporalisation itself."[9] For Laplanche, mourning is "the work of memory" and "an affect with a duration (*Daueraffekt*): it has a beginning and an end, it occupies a *lapse* of time."[10] Laplanche's reading of Freudian mourning turns on the figure of Homer's Penelope, weaving and unweaving as a case of performative mourning that also, for Laplanche, is the very motif of psychoanalysis: "unweaving so that a new fabric can be woven, disentangling to *allow* the formation of new knots."[11] Thus, if mourning is a figure for the entire analytic process—and, furthermore, is the work of memory in a discipline famous for its obsessions with psychic and cultural pasts—mourning and melancholia function as metonymies for the whole of psychoanalytic philosophy.

Unlike the overcoming of mourning, which is achieved through work and over time, Freud describes melancholia as a "state of grief"—endless, undifferentiated, a state in its most precise sense, involving stasis and "profoundly painful dejection, abrogation of interest in the outside world."[12] In addition to the mournful attitude toward the missing person or ideal, the melancholic adds a supplementary loss in a subsequent depletion of "the capacity to love" and an inhibition of vitality and engagement. Freud's metaphoric language is telling in this regard. He writes, of melancholia, that it "behaves like an open wound, drawing to itself cathectic energy from all sides," a figuration that makes open wounds hunt, suck, gravitationally drain.[13] The melancholic's strange and sad etiology is due to an energy glitch. In Freud's economic theory, the libido's attachment to the now missing object is not withdrawn and redirected elsewhere, as in mourning; instead, the libidinal investment is taken into the self (first introjection), and the melancholic identifies his or her ego with the missing object (then identification). This narcissistic melancholia, as opposed to "normal grief," is due, for Freud, to an ambivalence about the missing other. In his famous summation of the difference, "In grief the world becomes poor and empty; in melancholia it is the ego itself."[14] While the mourner is a productive laborer (he *does*), the melancholic is a frozen, horrible statue (she *is*). And that interminable stasis is total: Freud argues that the cathectic investment in grief for the melancholic is so profound that little psychic energy is left for other purposes or attachments. Melancholia, in a sense, just uses the self up.

Freud avows the irreducible difference between mourning and melancholia through a figure that recalls Augustine's grief-caused darkened eyes. Let us return to the beginning. The opening line of "Mourning and Melancholia" is, "Nachdem uns der Traum als Normalvorbild der narzißtischen Seelenstörungen gedient hat, wollen wir den Versuch machen, das Wesen der Melancholie durch ihre Vergleichung mit dem Normalaffekt der Trauer zu erhellen" (Now that dreams have proved of service to us as the normal prototypes of narcissistic mental disorders, we propose to try whether a comparison with the normal emotion of grief, and its expression in mourning, will not *throw some light* on the nature of melancholia).[15] Of the normal pain of mourning, "It never occurs to us to regard it as a morbid condition."[16] The key word in the German is *erhellen* (to light up, illuminate). Grammatically, melancholia is illuminated through or via the differentiated *Normalaffekt* of *Trauer*. In language that is metaphorically resonant with Augustine's lament, Laplanche rereads this opening line by saying of mourning, "It is that which sheds light, and thus that on which there would be no light to be shed: how could light be illuminated?"[17] Mourning, in Laplanche's ventriloquizing of Freud's opening line, is the originary spotlight beyond which no source of illumination is possible, casting hunting rays over the field of inquiry, trying to capture and reveal that morbid shadowy stealth, melancholia. As though it is the enabling condition of representation itself, mourning is the transparence to melancholia's opacity; the transcendence to the other's immanence; the self-comprehending self to the other's dark, hard riddle.

Light as such, because it contains no atoms and thus can reflect nothing, cannot be illuminated; Laplanche's question rightly ends on an aporia. But at the same time, of course, light's *effects* or reflections can be illuminated. Simply stand in the umbra. It might be said that this is precisely what the profession of psychoanalysis does: in Freud's account, the rays of analytic truth-seeking wash over the dual objects of light-casting mourning and brightly lit melancholia. How else could light be seen, if not illuminated? Via a prism that splits it apart into its constitutive elements, or through refractive or diffractive lenses that manipulate and distort the light; or by tracing the visible radiation emitted when an object is illuminated with invisible ultraviolet light. Of course, light is metaphorically illuminated as an object of knowledge if we escape the opticentric altogether to consider that light exerts force in the world, that it displaces objects in its path, or that it has a speed, that it can leave traces.

How *might* light be illuminated? It would seem as though the technologies of vision of the nineteenth century and twentieth century exist in part to ponder and grapple with this question. The etymological breakdown of photography, a word dating to 1839, adapts the German *Photographie*, from the Greek *phos* (light) and *graphos* (writing). Photography as light-writing, or light-recording, though, is an ambiguous, hybrid term, evocative of both *writing by light* and *writing of light* (the same way that the cinematograph is a writing *of* movement and a writing *by* movement). If it is precisely through the mediating capture of photographic technology that both writing *by* light and a writing *of* light is possible, then, in a sense, every camera obscura is also a camera lucida. Perhaps the answer to Laplanche's question—the invisible assumption that makes visible the guiding methodology of Freud's essay—is that light *cannot* be illuminated except by its framing, storage, and capture in a medium dependent on its inscriptive power. Put another way, in the terms of casting and the casted-on, another response to Laplanche's question is that light cannot be illuminated while standing on the side of illumination. Light must be put on display from the other side of its display, from the murk, the inky darkness against which luminosity is measured.

Cracks vein Freud's foundational opposition, and as from water soaking into stone, they expand and eventually cannot hold the edifice on which the theoretical structure is built. The year before the publication of "Mourning and Melancholia," Freud wrote "On Transience," a quiet meditation on decay and the beautiful. It opens with Romantic Freud recalling a summer stroll in the countryside with friends: "the poet admired the beauty of the scene around us but felt no joy in it. He was disturbed by the thought that all this beauty was fated to extinction, that it would vanish when winter came, like all human beauty and all the beauty and splendour that men have created or may create."[18] Here, the loved things that will eventually go missing are Nature and Art in the sentimental tradition. Freud resigns himself in this story to playing the realist, maintaining that immortality, permanence, or non-mutability is the height of wishful retreats from the painful truth of "the transience of all things." He insists, though, in an aesthetic version of the economic argument for compensations, that far from depleting our enjoyment, transience is itself what produces pleasure. Freud's interlocutors remain unmoved by his argument, and he hypothesizes, "What spoilt their enjoyment of beauty must have been a revolt in their minds against mourning."[19] The thoughts of the losses to come were interfering with the enjoyment of his friends' otherwise attractive objects. Thus, Freud attempts to grapple with mourning. He immediately, however, runs into a roadblock that would seem to suggest precisely the opposite of his speculation only one year later. "Mourning over the loss of something that we have loved or admired seems so natural to the layman that he regards it as self-evident," he states. "But to psychologists mourning is a great riddle, one of those phenomena which cannot themselves be explained but to which other obscurities can be traced back."[20] In "On Transience," mourning is self-evident to the layman but a "great riddle" to the analyst; in "Mourning and Melancholia," mourning is self-evident to the analyst, but melancholia has become the great riddle whose nature requires illumination from the self-evident phenomenon. That mourning is that to which "other obscurities can be traced back" makes mourning the concept much like Freud's later description of melancholia the open wound, drawing to itself obscurities on all sides. It is not merely that Freud's first division is between opposing methodologies of reading, while the second is between objects of speculation; it is that in order to make that move, mourning has to switch from being the riddle to being the self-evident standard against which riddles are measured, and the light by which caliginous riddles are illuminated. The essay of 1916 and the essay of 1917 are thus like a photograph and its negative: each shaded area now illumined in its other version, each patch of light now dark.

Although Freud's revisions to his own work are legendary, the slipperiness by which mourning and then, one year later, melancholia comes to occupy the position of the riddle anticipates the muddying of the neat distinction between the two on which "Mourning and Melancholia" insists. While it could be that what Freud calls "mourning" in 1916 is what he will call "melancholia" in 1917—and thus that the underlying structure of the argument remains unchanged—it is precisely because both terms can plausibly occupy the position of the riddle for the analyst that we should be wary of assuming their purely antonymic relation. Furthermore, in "On Transience," Freud writes that mourning, "however painful it may be, comes to a spontaneous end." Thus, even if some of mourning's traits in that piece are reminiscent of what will be called melancholia one year later, the terminus of mourning here suggests its similarity with its later usage. Any neat distinction between the terms is preemptively troubled in the earlier essay and continues to complicate Freud's attempts to hold the normal and pathological forms of suffering at bay.

The two late, revisionary texts that cause the greatest difficulties for reading Freud's earlier work on mourning are *The Ego and the Id* (1923) and *Inhibitions, Symptoms and Anxiety* (1926). Each troubles the primary metaphysical division our light-language requires: What is illuminating, and what remains shrouded in darkness (necessitating the other's light-casting)? The final section of *Inhibitions, Symptoms and Anxiety* is titled "Anxiety, Pain, and Mourning," and in it, after concluding that "anxiety comes to be a reaction to the danger of a loss of the object," Freud asks, "When does that loss lead to anxiety and when to mourning?" As one attempt to clarify those different reactions, Freud acknowledges that the great unknown of mourning is "ihre besondere Schmerzlichkeit" (its peculiar painfulness).[21] This specific affective void in the study of mourning is readily acknowledged in earlier works. In "On Transience," he writes, adding to the riddle the quality of a mystery, "But why it is that this detachment of libido from its objects should be such a painful process is a mystery to us and we have not hitherto been able to frame any hypothesis to account for it."[22] Stated ignorance of this mysterious pain is repeated in *Inhibitions, Symptoms and Anxiety* when Freud notes in an aside, "Incidentally, it may be remembered that in discussing the question of mourning we also failed to discover why it should be such a painful thing."[23] That "peculiar painfulness" of grief calls attention to a problem that plagues the illuminating first principle of suffering related to a loss: its self-evidentness *and* its simultaneous mysteriousness. Of mourning (in 1926) Freud writes, again: "This was its peculiar painfulness. And yet it seems self-evident that separation from an object should be painful. Thus the problem becomes more complicated: when does separation from an object produce anxiety, when does it produce mourning and when does it produce, it may be, only pain?"[24] What remains in darkness, what does not easily come to light, is the peculiarity of pain, what belongs uniquely to it all alone.

In his inimitable way, just as Freud holds out this question to the light, he withdraws it, staging a performance of the course of libidinal attachments and withholdings. "Let me say at once that there is no prospect in sight of answering these questions," he writes, resolving the matter by writing mourning out of the discussion.[25] In the last lines of *Inhibitions, Symptoms and Anxiety,* mourning's pain is given account as a separation that hurts due to the "high and unsatisfiable cathexis of longing which is concentrated on the object by the bereaved person during the reproduction of situations in which he must undo the ties that bind him to it."[26] But notably unsaid at the end of this passage is whether this unsatisfiable cathexis of longing (an economic disappointment or insufficiency) accounts for the peculiarly painful tonality of mourning to which Freud continually returns. Unsatisfiable cathexis is a long way from the rawness of the aching word "pain" (*Schmerz*), and that shift marks the text's own inadequate reading of the most intense form of suffering related to a loss.

The insufficiency of Freud's account of that "peculiar painfulness" of mourning necessitates a return to Laplanche's question about optic impossibility that frames the opening of "Mourning and Melancholia." Recall that Laplanche writes of Freud's positioning of mourning: "it is that which sheds light, and thus that on which there would be no light to be shed: how could light be illuminated?"[27] What is striking about Laplanche's description of Freud's opening move is that the two halves of his account on either side of the colon fail to perfectly match up. Mourning is, in the first clause, "that which sheds light"; melancholia is then the object receiving the illuminating rays.

Mourning, in this sense, is a source or point of origin for the understanding of the other term in the dyad; it is a condition of illumination or a cause (even a first cause) of illumination. However, being that which sheds light does not make something light itself; being the cause of illumination does not collapse mourning into illumination. If mourning is the origin or point of illumination, conveying or transferring the evidentiary power of its self-evidentness, then logically it could have light shed on it as a source or cause independent of that which it generates. What to make, then, of the consequence on which Laplanche insists: that mourning must become "that on which there would be no light to be shed"? If we take Laplanche at his word, take as true the material after the colon as a consequence of the material before it, then in a way he appears to remain highly faithful to the Freud of 1917, to the economic model of compensations, libidinal withdrawal and redirection. In this view, light would be a finite resource that, once cast on a concept, is used up entirely, unable to cast light elsewhere. As a result, it is because there is simply no more light after its first casting that mourning cannot be illuminated. It does not share its evidentiary power; it *gives away* its evidence, and with it, its self-. Mourning would thus be that on which there *would* be no light to be shed—not that on which there *could* be no light to be shed.

Laplanche effectively reverses his terms at the site of the colon, and light is figured as the sticky melancholic: once attached to melancholia as an object of speculation, it cannot be withdrawn or redirected elsewhere and thus can never illuminate its source. Light would constitutively be an introjecting element that uses itself up and thus cannot mirror back illumination, because like the suffering depressive, it has withdrawn entirely. The melancholic, while illuminated on the level of the signifier for Laplanche, is, on the level of the signified, a black hole, absorbing light and foreclosing illumination. But if this is the case and melancholia is figured as an absorptive that can cast no light outward, that hungrily consumes all of the illumination in this closed model, then Laplanche's final, cryptic question—how *could* light be illuminated?— applies equally to both terms in Freud's title. Mourning is shrouded in prohibitive darkness because it casts the light that illuminates the system and is thus that on which no light could be shed, and melancholia is shrouded in an absorptive light because it consumes entirely the light that illuminates the system and reflects nothing in turn. The gamble of Freud's first line (the speculative venture of *erhellen*) is that light *can be cast at all* on the painful matter at hand. Laplanche's rereading of that risk suggests that beams have both a direction and an object, but that the target of this peculiar beam forecloses an examination of its very source. Melancholia's inability to reflect back the light cast on it by mourning means that both terms exist at the antipode to literal and philosophical illumination.

What Freud's remarks about the "peculiar painfulness" of mourning suggest—along with his continual placing of its agony as, variously, a riddle, a mystery, a peculiarity, and yet, simultaneously, self-evident (*selbstverständlich*)—is that mourning, far from casting unreturnable light on melancholia, casts its originary beam on the discipline of analysis and is thus external to the system that interrogates it. Mourning's self-evidence is not an obviousness contained *within* the discipline of psychoanalysis but an evidentiary promise visible only to and within itself as a logic. What replaces the never-arriving account of mourning's peculiar and unique pain is ultimately a negative *textual* affect: Freud's frustration about mourning's stubborn opacity and resistance to thought. Thus, the "peculiar painfulness" of mourning is transformed or displaced into the peculiar painfulness of the failure of psychoanalytic meta-language (a kind of disciplinary grief). Mourning remains the unanswerable question of analysis, the blind spot around which the discipline's questions of and to loss are organized. At the same time that mourning's self-evidence paradoxically appears to make it less illuminated for psychoanalysis, melancholia's quality of being a morbid introjection of the lost other comes to seem less pathological (better lit) in the texts of late Freud. While mourning's pain is increasingly shrouded in peculiar darkness, melancholia comes to contemplative light, fulfills the promise of being illuminated from above, and takes on a certain lightness of ordinary ego-introjecting being. By the time of *The Ego and the Id,* Freud's description of the object-cathexis with a withdrawn or forbidden sexual object choice is explicitly likened to the work of a melancholic: "when it happens that a person has to give up a sexual object, there quite often ensues an alteration of his ego which can only be described as a setting up of the object inside the ego, as it occurs in melancholia."[28] This process is constitutive of attachment itself and becomes, in this revisionary text, a non-pathological mechanism for identity formation as such. In late Freud (and the tradition indebted to it), the normative subject is constituted through attachments to losses; consequently, melancholia's introjective logic seems almost self-evident. Thus, as mourning moves into disciplinary darkness, a mothy melancholia inches toward the flame. Henceforth, the light-caster becomes more and more of a riddle while that which originally required theoretical illumination becomes more and more obvious, transparent, even lucent.

Much happens to mourning and melancholia in the decades after this shift in Freud's thinking—notably, the increasing rehabilitation, normalization, and de-pathologization of melancholy (ending with its valorization) and the increasing confusion over mourning as a separate category in relation to loss (its *self-evidence* deprived of both the reflective referring hyphen and the claim of evidentiary value).[29] The seeds of this transition are visible in Freud's texts, in particular when he notes that the depressive "has a keener eye for the truth than others who are not melancholic." The bleak subject resembles the mystic when it is wondered of the former, "For all we know it may be that he has come very near to self-knowledge; we only wonder why a man must become ill before he can discover truth of this kind."[30] (In the visual logic of Laplanche's formulation, it is as though the melancholic after Freud casts the brightest spotlight on her own suffering, a sort of self-lighting light, a bioluminescent firefly of a subject.) These lines have been taken by many readers of Freud to find in melancholia a dialectical relationship between creative or philosophical insight and depressive introjective pain—a reading that plays on a very deep and ancient association of black bile humors with artistic creativity. But it is crucial to recall that Freud is speaking specifically of the depressive's self-accusations and self-criticism and not to all truth or creative insight in general. Nevertheless, this revelatory dimension of melancholia later in the twentieth century overtakes its painful, affective dimension (becoming all *Schein* and no *Schmerz*). Although the "work of mourning" is Freud's term for the processual labor involved in directing libidinal attachments after a loss, in the humanities of the twenty-first century it seems as though (all) that (dull) work is contrasted negatively with melancholia's productive play.

Freud's insistence in 1917 that in melancholia there are "countless separate struggles" over the lost object has made it a contemporary figure for an ongoing, never-ending negotiation or relationship with some missing thing.[31] The culmination of this trend can be seen in the anthology *Loss* (2003), edited by David L. Eng and David Kazanjian, in which melancholia constitutes "an ongoing and open relationship with the past—bringing its ghosts and specters, its flaring and fleeting images, into the present."[32] This specific collection crystallizes a broader tendency in contemporary thought in its forthrightly polemical conviction regarding the positive potential of melancholia; the editors' stated goal: "to impute to loss a creative instead of negative quality."[33] In this celebration of the formerly pathologized term, though, the problems of illumination, mysteriousness, and affective pain detailed earlier are set aside; as a theoretical rehabilitation, it entails a great forfeiture. In *Loss,* melancholia is redescribed as a rich site for rethinking losses both individual and collective in a non-pathological, non-narcissistic manner. "This attention to remains," insist the editors, "generates a politics of mourning that might be active rather than reactive, prescient rather than nostalgic, abundant rather than lacking, social rather than solipsistic, militant rather than reactionary."[34] Melancholia's ongoing struggle with the lost object, its ambivalent negotiation of the relationship between the loss as an object and the loss as part of the self, its refusal to relinquish its libidinal attachment and its tacky stickiness to the missing make it a rallying point for an entire politics and ethics of not forgetting. No longer a private psychic experience, melancholia in this school of thought is figured as what founds collective politics and remembrance.[35] Not least among the problems with this argument, in the wake of Nietzsche's analysis of dolorous, injury-oriented *ressentiment,* there should be something particularly unsettling about figuring melancholia as the grounding disposition of the political.

This shifting meaning of melancholia means that one key trait of its definition—its fundamental *difference* from mourning—is blurred. Melancholy comes to take on every positive conceptual attribute previously denied it: as a projective reach into the historical totality that precedes an individual or society far from the introjective ambivalence and solipsistic suffering of Freud's earliest treatments. Problematically, this move tends to view classical mourning's libidinal withdrawal and reattachment as implicitly placed on the side of forgetting, non-commemoration, even the apolitical and ahistorical. An entire post-Levinasian discourse of bearing witness is deployed in this move to suggest that the melancholic is the seer of historical trauma and scripter of compensation and transformation. Thus, all mourning that wants the mantle of "ethical" and "political" becomes defined normatively as taking the melancholic stance of non-detached, ongoing negotiation with losses; prescient and transformative mourning becomes definitionally melancholic. In a way, this tendency extends Freud's own inability to hold the two forms of loss-abreaction at bay by taking melancholia, and not mourning, as the standard-bearer for all forms of relation to loss. Melancholia is now regarded as that which casts light on historical, collective, and personal losses and is the politically self-evident theoretical term. Indeed, the contrasting words of Freud's title, which suggest an absolute alternative, no longer seem appropriate here. Perhaps the best description of this object of contemplation in contemporary discourse would be something akin to the hybrid *mournincholia.*

A doubled form of melancholia is deployed throughout *Loss:* the one, a lingering sadness and recursive loitering in the past; the other, active, transformative, and oriented toward future possibilities. Although haunted by its depressive other, melancholia is figured in the collection as precisely that which can overcome its other, peculiarly painful form. Indeed, as framed by the editors, "The politics of mourning might be described as that creative process mediating a hopeful or hopeless relationship between loss and history."[36] What should give us pause in this theoretical project is that word "mediating" in the editors' summation of the politics of mourning. For melancholia in Freud's version of 1917 is the anti-mediating: its stickiness to the past is precisely a recursive loop of painful attachment that cannot renounce, that never synthesizes, that is temporally pathological for its expanded affective duration without end or change. It does not transform, and it is not transformative. Thus, a "politics of mourning" that involves mediation requires a dialecticizing of that which is unmediatable in the original treatment of mourning. In one sense, this is fitting, for Benjamin, and not Freud, is the true philosophical touchstone for this theoretical shift, and Benjamin's approach to mourning in the *Trauerspiel* is suffused with recuperative dialectics.[37]

Judith Butler's "Afterword: After Loss, What Then?" summarizes the stakes of this broad intervention and symptomatically performs the corresponding risks. Her final paragraph, which functions as the conclusion to *Loss,* notes, "Many of the essays here refer to the sensuality of melancholia, to its form of pleasure, its mode of becoming, and therefore reject its identification with paralysis. . . . The rituals of mourning are sites of merriment; Benjamin knew this as well, but as his text effectively shows, it is not always possible to keep the dance alive."[38] Butler is correct that the revalorization of melancholia deploys terms such as "sensuality," "play," and "change." As a figure for an ongoing, engaged struggle with the past, as a mediating figure that transforms mournful passivity into potentiality as a mode of becoming new, melancholia indeed is now marked by forms of pleasure. But if mournincholia involves a risk of the living, and one that everywhere resembles a kind of redemptive compensatory enjoyment, then why was it ever grouped with the negative affects, and what value would it have to speak of mourning's intense suffering, its pathos, its outright and forthrightly "besondere Schmerzlichkeit" (its particular, peculiar, special ache)?

Contra Freud's view of the 1917 melancholic whose cathectic totality is bound up in grief and whose ego becomes "poor and empty," the melancholic of the 2000s is the historical materialist artist and scholar, her grief enabling an engagement with remains that "generates sites for memory and history, for the rewriting of the past as well as the reimagining of the future."[39] This is a melancholic any of us might want to be. (Indeed, this is the theorist of melancholia as the ideal melancholic, for she is truly the curator of historical losses.) Because of these ongoing struggles with the potentiality of the past, the melancholic (or a de-subjectified melancholic hermeneutics) is in a unique position to imagine the world otherwise, to speak to (or for) and grapple with the new. This shifting stance on loss is a recurring trope in contemporary critical theory: in *Stanzas,* Giorgio Agamben likens "the specific ambition of the ambiguous melancholy project" in Freud to "what the ancient humoral theory rightly identified in the will to transform into an object of amorous embrace what should have remained only an object of contemplation." This embrace confers on the unobtainable object of contemplation "the phantasmagorical reality of what is lost."[40] More than generating the new or unearthing the potential imbued in the already absent past, Agamben figures melancholy as the opening up of a space for the unreal as such, for magically transforming the loss that grounds it, for making possible the category of the imaginary.

No phantasmatic without melancholia suggests that its particular struggles with losses produce the very condition for the fictive and performative, the transformations on which all functions of the spectral imagination are based. This newly active melancholia is superlatively fecund and remarkably creative. When the editors of *Loss* write that "avowals of and attachments to loss can produce a world of remains as a world of new representations and alternative meanings," it is as though melancholia generates not only the ego but also different representations, new meanings, and from there to meaning as such or to representation itself.[41] Indeed, Marc Nichanian avows that "there is no art without mourning."[42] In one sense, this is true: representation supplies a supplement or repetition of presence in the wake of an absence. Immortality or a totality of presence would not require representation, and thus art generally necessitates grappling with absence and loss.

But if mourning is taken in its broadest possible sense to suggest a negotiation with depletions of presence, or a long slow tango with the negative, then it becomes a useless or dead concept, stretched beyond recognition to cover the entirety of the problematic of ontology. In a similar vein, the repeated theoretical appeal to concepts such as traces, residue, excess, and memory suggests that melancholia may well stand in for the slippery yet generative work of the signifier or for the flexibility of signification as such. Mourning thus becomes the nodal point of a theory based on lack. While a negative ontology has much to recommend it as a displacement of positive, often theological, grounds for subjectivity and signification, it is also the case that supplementary losses attend the generalizing of mourning to structuration by absence. If this mourning stands in for a negotiated relationship to lack as foundational, then mourning's particularity as a matter of suffering related to a beloved loss is extended to a plane of irrelevant thinness. One need not refuse *in toto* the many compelling examples of political and ethical productivity suggested by a struggle with the past in place of a completed "working through" of historical traumas to nevertheless feel that this melancholia bears little resemblance to the melancholy of psychoanalysis and that something important has gone missing in the translation.

This specific theoretical loss is the death of that "peculiar painfulness" of mourning on which Freud insisted. The dirty secret of mourninocholia is that it principally has to do with remains, not losses; the living, not the dead; and the pleasure and potentiality of ongoing struggle in place of breath-strangling anguish when objects or lovers go missing. In place of an attention to the affective dimensions of pain, contemporary work on loss is largely directed toward illuminating what remains, who remains, who can establish a relation between what remains and what has gone missing, and who can speak that relation. This transformation of loss into an ongoing negotiation with the missing involves an endlessly productive dialecticizing of mourning. In fact, the association between mourning and dialectics is so ingrained in contemporary work on loss that one critic can write of Benjamin's notion of divine violence that it is "the experience of a pure destruction, of an infinite loss, without mourning, without dialectic."[43] The inverse of that final repetition is clear: that which would be foundational, from which law could be derived, would be *with* mourning and *with* dialectics. The problem with this approach is that it fails to imagine a mourning that is an experience of "pure destruction, an infinite loss." (That, however, is much closer to what Freud imagines as the peculiar pain of suffering related to loss, the strange self-evident anguish that bedevils psychoanalytic comprehension.) Mourning-work has thus come to resemble Hegel's *Aufhebung,* the "lifting up" or sublation that is the synthesizing force of dialectics: a negation that is a conservation, a surpassing that maintains. Part of the motivation for the theoretical shift epitomized by *Loss* is a resistance to simplistic models of pain as passive, subjecting, and mute— hence, the turn to dialectics, active engagement, remembrance, and ongoing dialogue. But erasing the painfulness of pain does not re-theorize pain. It only sets aside the question of negative affectivity to be considered at a later date, one that is put off indefinitely.

A dialecticized mourning has the same problem as all dialectical structures, which no one has ever summarized better than Kierkegaard: that the paradox of mediation cannot be mediated. In its relentless economy of the total, *Aufhebung* can be made to profit from anything. Even death for Hegel, as Dennis Keenan puts it, "is productive insofar as one appropriates it"— witness tragedy's privileged position in Hegel.[44] Likewise, in *Loss,* death's affective aftershocks are politically, ethically, and aesthetically productive insofar as one appropriates melancholia's generative negotiation with losses. This mourning machine simply runs too well. As in Derrida's deconstruction of Hegel's speculative dialectics, everything negated can be recuperated, each speculative investment preserves unity and totality; the consequence is that "this transition, produced by the anxiety of the infinite, continuously links meaning up to itself."[45] From this new model of loss nothing goes missing and every loss can be made through mourning work to become meaningful through those continuing negotiations; *Trauerarbeit* guarantees a return on its cathectic investment.[46] A dialectical mourning is easily illuminated and seems very unpeculiar.

The problem with placing mourning within a restricted economy is that the "peculiar painfulness" of mourning is neutralized in the very act of being put to work, for the peculiarly painful is also the peculiarly purposeless, that which does not work (for a subject) and is not an example of terminable or successful (analytic) work. Freud's crucial word "peculiar" derives from *peculiaris,* from one's own—specifically, from one's own property. The German *besonders* has the same resonance, suggesting the opposite of what is common or shared or universal (cognate of *sunder,* it denotes what stands apart, what is marked as separate). In all appropriative dialectics, mourning's self-regarding painfulness, the painfulness that is the private emotional property of mourning, is put to work *for the other;* it *brings together;* it *can be shared;* and it builds, it makes. This model of mourning does not merely lose the peculiar pain on which Freud insists; it actually gains every conceptual attribute denied to what is *besondere Schmerzlichkeit.* The affective register of suffering and the enigmatic, non-recuperable dimension of mourning are elided in a dialecticized loss. Whether sentenced to labor for a community, a politics, or even the aesthetic, the restricted economy that makes mourning meaningful attempts to co-opt (and thereby own the rights to, put to work in its name) its peculiarity. Grief's pain is thereby purloined.

In place of the "peculiar painfulness" of mourning, it is now a peculiar *painlessness* that centers post-Freudian discourses of loss: mourning made melancholia, or mournincholia, has been dialecticized, and it has been anesthetized, deprived of the intensity of its affective force. The opposition that is therefore now required is no longer between two forms of mourning—one normal and self-evident, the other pathological and mysterious—but between a mourning that stubbornly adheres to its "peculiar painfulness" in the affective wake of a loss and a mournincholia marked by its productivity, creativity, sensuality, even pleasure. I propose, then, that we need a word for that kernel of "peculiar painfulness" that Freud cannot demystify, and given that both "mourning" and "melancholia" have become so oversaturated, I name that other thing *grief.* Grief will be the term for that which resists the relational dimension of loss; the form for that suffering of a general economy in which not everything can be made to mean and things escape systematicity without return, labor guarantees no profit. As the peculiarly painful dimension of loss, grief resists mediation and ongoing processual struggle. It takes a different form altogether, and it is undialectical.

GRIEF WITHOUT SUBLATION

Just as with mourning and melancholia, treatments of grief and mourning routinely blur the distinction between the two terms. Take, for example, Judith Butler's *Precarious Life,* which explores which lives are deemed worthy of commemoration through public mourning and suggests the moving idea that we are who we grieve. Her emphasis on grief as maintainable and her argument that it brings out "relational ties" suggests that "grief" here swears fidelity to the dialectical form of "mourning" described earlier.[47] Throughout, Butler employs identically structured phrases, often within the span of a few paragraphs, substituting grief and mourning for each other. Within the first two paragraphs of the preface, she writes in parallel of "cause for fear and for mourning," anticipates "reasons for both fear and grief."[48] In a passage that summarizes her project, the signifiers slip without remark: "and though for some, mourning can only be resolved through violence, it seems clear that violence only brings on more loss, and the failure to heed the claim of precarious life only leads, again and again, to the dry grief of an endless political rage."[49] Context suggests that, while occasionally deployed as synonyms, more often Butler uses the terms as inverted forms of interior affect and exterior expressive displays.

This division of labor between "grief" and "mourning" is an old one, in which grief would be the private passion (feelings, sentiments, experiences) and mourning the public manifestation of that interior state to the outside world (rituals, customs, shared beliefs). In this usage, grief involves emotional, cognitive, and physical responses to loss centered around affective reactions such as anger, rage, anxiety, fear, nausea, hysteria, numbness, and denial. Mourning, by contrast, is often figured as formalized or ritualized responses to death: funerals, eulogizing, memorial services, and burial habits. But this distinction is not always insisted on and often appears to matter little in the literature, even for those to whom it would seem critical. For example, Tammy Clewell argues in the *Journal of the American Psychoanalytic Association* that "mourning names an experience of grief."[50] Likewise, consider the parenthetical at the beginning of a sentence in John Archer's *The Nature of Grief,* "Of mourning (i.e. grief)."[51]

The very different etymologies of "grief" and "mourning," however, *are* productive for articulating the unbridgeable gap between the two concepts. "Mourn" is the older word, with the *Oxford English Dictionary* noting instances back to circa 888. Its roots suggest *morna* (to pine away); *mornen* (to be anxious or careful, evoking Freud's query about when loss leads to anxiety and when to mourning); and in an obsolete form (but one that evocatively suggests the ululations of keeners, weepers, and wailers), "mourn" means a murmur or murmuring sound. The connections between "mourn" and "to be anxious" may come from *smer-* (to remember) or from *mer-* (to die or wither). (The influence of the root *smer-* fittingly anticipates the emphasis on recollection, memorializing, and historicizing seen in the contemporary culture of endless, engaged mourning.) The first definition of mourning in its current usage is "to feel sorrow, grief, or regret (often with the added notion of expressing one's grief)," tellingly muddled for its identification of mourning with grief and subsequent separation of the two as a quality and an expressive activity. Most important, there is no contemporary substantive form of "mourn"—rather, one *mourns,* it is what one does, what one effects in the world. To mourn is always mourning, mourning is definitively in process, caught in the linguistic act after its work has begun.[52]

Grief, by contrast, is a hardship or suffering, "hurt, harm, mischief, or injury"; it is a wrong, a feeling of displeasure, even umbrage or offense. It is a bodily injury, a physical pain or discomfort—and all this before its very late definition of "mental pain, distress, or sorrow. In mod. [modern] use in a more limited sense: Deep or violent sorrow, caused by loss or trouble; a keen or bitter feeling of regret for something lost, remorse for something done, or sorrow for mishap to oneself or others."[53] Grief is derived from *grever* (afflict, burden, oppress), from the Latin *gravare* (to cause grief, make heavy)—hence, the etymological intimacy of *grief* and *gravity*, both from *gravis* (weighty). The sense of mental pain and sorrow dates from about 1350. The older sense of weightiness is one key to a grief that has gone missing in contemporary accounts of loss and whose remembering points to the felt experience of heaviness, of being weighted down, of pushing and pressing, as on one's sternum in sighing, choking breaths that do not fully arrive. The etymological archeology of "grief" is clear on this matter: it begins with a pressure on the body, a dragging the body down to earth like gravity, a vector of invisible force pulling down and down further still. The contemporary forgetting of grief—through the dialecticizing of mourning and the anesthetizing of sorrow's special pain—participates in a theoretical occlusion of the formal force, the heavy, gravitational weightiness, of the affect.

Occasional meditations on loss resist the lure of figuring grief and mourning as slippery synonyms or as a public–private dyad. Powerful, if rare, attempts are made to wrest the two concepts apart or to tarry with this singularly strange and heavy agony. One wrenching case is Joan Didion's memoir about the death of her husband, *The Year of Magical Thinking* (2006). Didion's narrative is committed to fine distinctions between affective states; in an early passage, she marks the deaths of her parents late in their lives as producing "sadness, loneliness (the loneliness of the abandoned child of whatever age), regret for time gone by, for things unsaid. . . . I had been expecting (fearing, dreading, anticipating) those deaths all my life."[54] Grief for her husband, however, is of a different order; when it arrives, it is "nothing we expect it to be."[55]

In the wake of the sudden absence of the witness to one's life, she writes these clipped lines:

> Grief is different. Grief has no distance. Grief comes in waves, paroxysms, sudden apprehensions that weaken the knees and blind the eyes and obliterate the dailiness of life. . . .
> Tightness in the throat.
> Choking, need for sighing.[56]

Captured in Didion's impressionistic account, itself rolling in partial phrases like a spasm of bad affect, is a choking, sighing grapple with that "peculiar painfulness" Freud also found to be somehow otherwise, without distance. Her insistence that "grief is different" points to the affect's peculiar, separate, apart aspect that is opposed to all that is common, shared, or shareable. Likewise, her reference to the blinding of the eyes is a descendant of Augustine's self-surveilling account of the dimming of vision in the wake of loss's trauma. Freud's peculiar pain and Didion's different grief are updated versions of the claim in Robert Burton's early-seventeenth-century *Anatomy of Melancholy* that this particular suffering is at the top of the affective hierarchy: "every perturbation is a misery, but grief is a cruel torment, a domineering passion. . . . [W]hen grief appears, all other passions vanish."[57] For Didion, all of these quiet aftershocks are in the hours and days after the simultaneous violence and banality of the dying of the body—as is the title's "magical thinking," a holding open of the possibility of the departed's return; later, the catastrophe commutes its sentence.

Grief gives way. In the daily rhythm of daily doings, many months later, Didion describes the return of clearer eyes, a dispersing shadow. "That I was only now beginning the process of mourning did not occur to me," she reports. "Until now I had been able only to grieve, not mourn. Grief was passive. Grief happened. Mourning, the act of dealing with grief, required attention."[58] The narrative progress detailed here is familiar: from darkness to the light; from the fogging pain of riddled confusion to the active deployment of attention. Although Didion retains a teleology of loss in which mourning as working-through temporally supplants the knee-weakened confusion of immediate grief, her earlier insistence on the marked difference between the two suggests a shift of orders instead of a slide along an inevitable and therapeutic continuum. Grief's passivity, as contrasted with mourning's demanded attentiveness, evokes not an event and its unknotting but an event and, then, after, another, different event. Didion does not relinquish the entire constellation of the disorientations of grief; if its obliterative dimension is somewhat steadied, materiality restocked and cartilage thickened, nonetheless it sighs through her writing, chokes out the final revelation of finitude's curse as an "unending absence that follows, the void, the very opposite of meaning, the relentless succession of moments during which we will confront the experience of meaninglessness itself."[59] Resolution fails to arrive, and against a receding chaos, "no clarity is taking its place"—no illumination, no brightness at the end of the year in a calendar in which time will now be measured by time since he went missing, a calendar by which everyone in love agrees to someday abide.

In the end, Didion reaches from the private, individual case to reflect on all of them, the so many bloodless:

I know why we try to keep the dead alive: we try to keep them alive in order to keep them with us. I also know that if we are to live ourselves there comes a point at which we must relinquish the dead, let them go, keep them dead.

Let them become the photograph on the table.[60]

Letting the dead become photographs on the table—this is a moving conclusion and transmutation of the magical thinking of the promise of the dead's return. Beyond its loveliness as a line, I am invoking this formulation, this total acquiescence to the permanence of finitude, in a spirit apart from Didion's. I want to suggest that one way to theorize grief as irresolvable—undialectical, unproductive, a bad investment, and peculiarly painful—precisely involves letting the dead become life-cluttering photographs. Far from ameliorating the affective pang, the becoming-photograph of the dead materializes the untransformative and untransformable dimension of loss's pain. Redescribing grief in relation to the materiality of photography figures the loss of being's peculiarity, what is its uniquely alone, as a problem of the transmission and capture and staging of light. It is through attention to the photographic and cinematic presencing of illuminated luminosity that we can rediscover the irreducibly painful, untransformative, weighty pain of those who would weep themselves to death.

Light is what ultimately gives us a theory of grief worthy of a Longest Night Service.

Grief and the

Undialectical Image

November 30: Don't say *Mourning*. It's too psychoanalytic.
I'm not *mourning*. I'm suffering.

—ROLAND BARTHES, *Mourning Diary*

In *Camera Lucida* (1980), Roland Barthes's meditation on his mother's raw, recent death and his last writing before his own untimely (but they all are) end, the photograph is not the sign of a waning or muting of blinding, knee-quaking grief—as in Didion's promise to let the dead still in the captured light of their material luminosity—but, rather, the very form of the peculiar unending pain of loss. It is in this text of Barthes's that we are offered the fullest picture of grief as something radically different from mourning, as non-relational, as a non-labor that does not profit, and as fundamentally undialectical. Barthes's theory of this suffering *as* a photographic structure prompts a thinking of grief outside of the grieving subject, grapples with mourning after subjectivity. A consequence of figuring grief as undialectical is that grief does not limit itself to a model of affect based in and of individual psychology or phenomenological experience. Rather, it inheres in material objects, takes shape in an exteriority and in formal structures bound up intimately with light. For Barthes, it is not the knee-weakened self who grieves but an undialectical form in which *gravis*-derived grief *pulls weightily down, forces its force* on visual form. It is through grief—and neither mourning nor melancholia—that we can grapple with that crucial question inaugurated by Augustine's visually-confused blindness and articulated by Laplanche in the previous chapter: How could light be illuminated?

The full, original title of Barthes's last work, *La chambre claire: Note sur la photographie,* gestures at one approach to an answer.

MA MORT INDIALECTIQUE

La chambre claire was given for an English title the Latinate *Camera Lucida* and, as Derrida notes, "*La chambre claire,* the light room, no doubt says more than *camera lucida,* the name of the apparatus anterior to photography that Barthes opposes to *camera obscura.*"[1] (What more it says is left unsaid by Derrida, that "more than" perhaps a problematic of the visible and not of the sayable at all.) *La chambre claire* is a fragmented assemblage of forty-eight meditations in two equal parts, each of which begins with a story about vision, the photograph, and finitude.

[Part 1]:

One day, quite some time ago, I happened on a photograph of Napoleon's youngest brother, Jerome, taken in 1852. And I realized then, with an amazement I have not been able to lessen since: "I am looking at eyes that looked at the Emperor."

[Part 2]:

Now, one November evening shortly after my mother's death, I was going through some photographs. I had no hope of "finding" her, I expected nothing from these "photographs of a being before which one recalls less of that being than by merely thinking of him or her" (Proust).[2]

The similarity between these two opening salvos is striking—and in the original French, their repetitions of language, placing, and time are even more apparent: "un jour, il y a bien longtemps, je tombai sur une photographie du dernier frère de Napoléon"; "Or, un soir de novembre, peu de temps après la mort de ma mère, je rangeai des photos."[3] The pastness of each account gives a fairy-tale quality to the telling, as does the contingency of the solitary private happening on each telling photographic object of the dead who were once alive (with the important caveat that the photograph of Napoleon's brother materializes Barthes's amazement in contrast to the hopelessness of a failed encountering in the second story). Taken together, these two deaths in two narratives of encountering two photographs make up the totality of a single day (*un jour, un soir*). They also form one of the many sets of oppositions that organize the text: the studium (the general commitment of cultural interest in a coded image) and the punctum (a detail, resistant to critical language, that breaks into the *studium*); the unknowing "I" of wonderment and the knowing "I" of writing; the "cynical phenomenology" Barthes disavows and the affective phenomenological ethics with which he writes that disavowal, and so on.[4]

Like the illuminated twin to Descartes's dark-enshrined doubter in the *Meditations,* the opening of *La chambre claire* frames a thought experiment on the body (on the eyes) of the scripting, wondering philosopher. In fact, Gary Shapiro reads *Camera Lucida* as though it were a novel in the first person; this "narrative of an ontological quest" is marked by its "distinction between a naïve 'I' who does not yet know where the journey will lead and a more knowledgeable, sophisticated 'I' who has completed it."[5] The epic quest materializes photography's own relationship to preservation, memory, and historicity but also foreclosure. In turn, the permutations of the knowing/unknowing "I" designate photography as a discourse moving between the self as an object (of mediatic capture, of knowledge) and subject (of vision but also desire). Each half of what Shapiro calls this "Cartesian/Hegelian *Bildungsroman*" opens with the narrative of a chance encounter for which theoretical language has not yet been discovered but that carries an enigmatic trace conscripting Barthes's textual avatar to its peculiarity.[6]

The opening line, "Je tombai sur une photographie," brings together the contingency of the event with the coming-upon (*tomber* [to fall, to happen, to occur]) and that which is the most certain event of being, finitude, with the verb's echo of the French for tomb (*tombe*). Nevertheless, a fundamentally different relationship to death and the past is presented in each narrative. The photograph that presents being at a remove (through the mediating relation of a fraternal look that Barthes cannot share) and at a great historical distance is associated with the house of the dead, with tomb/*tombe*—preserved like a body in Les Invalides, enshrined within the very mythology of France. By contrast, the second writing of death and the image does not evoke the *tombe* but *la mort* (*de ma mère*). This photograph is marked not by preservation or distance but by the immediacy of an event that has just taken place and is not yet buried. The first photographic encounter is with the ossuary, a death transmuted and transformed into something symbolic; the second death is an event that does not suggest another possible form, that is not placed into a history or a meaningful narrative (—and, indeed, may never be).

One of the most crucial debates in twentieth-century philosophy is played out in Barthes's text. At stake: is death a meta-phenomenological event, figured in relation to Being, as always the (future) finitude of the self? This is Heidegger's position, as when he insists, "By its very essence, death is in every case mine, insofar as it 'is' at all."[7] While one can die for another as a sacrifice or displacement, "*No one can take the Other's dying away from him,*" in Heidegger's philosophy.[8] Derrida's formulation of this impossibility makes clear the objection: "death's dative (dying *for* the other, giving one's life *to* the other) does not signify a substitution (*for* is not *pro* in the sense of 'in place of the other')."[9] Or, by contrast, is death fundamentally a non-ontological matter, related to ethics in place of Being and always the (in advance) death of the other? The latter revision is from Levinas's philosophy, which objected to Heidegger's privileging of "his own death" above all.[10]

Barthes seems to align his theory of photography with Heidegger in this continental dogfight. In the earliest passages in *La chambre claire,* the "terrible thing" in every photograph is the "return of the dead," but also the futurity of the dead (self) as when a photographed subject "feels he is becoming an object . . . : I am truly becoming a specter."[11] The singularity of one's own certain, irreplaceable, unsubstitutable death is present in Barthes's textual anxiety about the photograph's ability to announce the shaded self in advance of one's ever-arriving death: "it is because each photograph always contains this imperious sign of my future death that each one . . . challenges each of us, one by one, outside of any generality (but not outside of any transcendence)."[12] At the same time, however, there is a strain of that Levinasian insistence that "I am responsible for the death of the other," that responsibility as the force and form of ethics is derived from the vulnerability of the other. One glimpses this especially in Barthes's care for the return of the dead materialized in the photograph, a regard that is a *regard*—a look, a light, and a recognition. "*This will be* and *this has been,*" he whispers. "I observe with horror an anterior future of which death is the stake. . . . In front of the photograph of my mother as a child, I tell myself: she is going to die: I shudder . . . *over a catastrophe which has already occurred.*"[13] This double quality of the death of the self (unique and ineluctable) and the death of the other (every photograph a catastrophe that calls my regard) makes photography, for Barthes, both a problem of ontology and of ethics. What the photograph is *not* is also telling, for it is not a matter of aesthetics—not disinterested speculation but the most interested fact of the certainty of finitude.

This doubled focus on ontology and ethics organizes the two major sections of *La chambre claire*. The immediate, striking *punctum* is the theoretical target of part 1, but that wounding detail is largely irrelevant to a search for the totality of the mother's missing being in part 2. There, in place of the punctum's telling, crucial specificity—its *peculiarity* a tiny anamorphotic shock of the Real—Barthes instead hunts for "the truth of the face I had loved," a truth that is a totality, that is the anti-detail. Part 2 thus begins with the foreclosure of the possibility of recognition in photographs, evoking "that fatality, one of the most agonizing features of mourning, which decreed that however often [he] might consult such images, [he] could never recall" his mother's features. The first part of *La chambre claire* is a performance of the cynical phenomenology Barthes decries in an attempt to approach the essence of the nature of photography. The second part, by contrast, is less about the essence of photography than it is about grief in relation to one specific photograph. Sorting the images, Barthes realizes, "I missed her *being*, and . . . therefore I missed her altogether. It was not she, and yet it was no one else. . . . I was struggling among images partially true, and therefore totally false."[14]

Barthes ultimately finds what is missing in an image of his mother at five years old in a conservatory with glass walls, the famous Winter Garden Photograph.[15] In reflecting on this specific image, Barthes introduces to his meditation on death a figure of the anti-sublative:

> If, as so many philosophers have said, Death is the harsh victory of the race, if the particular dies for the satisfaction of the universal, if after having been reproduced as other than himself, the individual dies, having thereby denied and transcended himself, I who had not procreated, I had, in her very illness, engendered my mother. Once she was dead I no longer had any reason to attune myself to the progress of the superior Life Force (the race, the species). My particularity could never again universalize itself (unless, utopically, by writing, whose project henceforth would become the unique goal of my life). From now on I could do no more than await my total undialectical death.[16]

Time folds within Barthes's own text. He opens part 2 by invoking an evening right after his mother's death, but here he insists that her death has taken place with the very event of the being of Barthes, as in Hegel's principle that in the education of the child, parents "engender their death. . . . What they give to him they lose; they die in him."[17] Elsewhere, Barthes repeats this law, defining history as "what the time when my mother was alive *before me* is."[18] The future unthinkable event, in other words, has already taken place, is not transformed or transformable, and will not repeat itself in the childless Barthes, who begets nothing for the continuity of the dialectic. In the climactic promise—"Je ne pouvais plus qu'attendre ma mort totale, indialectique"—the historical super-session of the child has been suspended, frozen as though in a photographic pose, stilled and awaiting that "total undialectical death" that will certainly arrive for the self but that involves no transcendence.

Equally resisting sublation is the heavy felt intensity of Barthes's mourning affect. If the writer's future certain death is undialectical, so is the mourning pain in response to the loss of his mother. Alone with the Winter Garden Photograph, "I suffer, motionless. Cruel, sterile deficiency: I cannot *transform* my grief, I cannot let my gaze drift; no culture will help me utter this suffering which I experience entirely on the level of the image's finitude . . . : the Photograph—my Photograph—is without culture: when it is painful, nothing in it can transform grief into mourning."[19] Suffering, motionless, as in the freeze of melancholic stasis, Barthes joins grief to Time's arrest in the form of the photograph itself. Barthes's insistence on grief's peculiarly painful suffering, its resistance to transformation and being put to work for meaning, let alone for a politics, is a far cry from the celebration of mournincholia's laboring play in contemporary work on loss, and much closer to Freud's account of the *besondere Schmerzlichkeit* of bereavement. Like the certainty of his future finitude, in suspense (though simultaneously fully arrived) is Barthes's affective pain at the having-happened dimension of this event. "It is said that mourning, by its gradual labor, slowly erases pain," Barthes writes in a nod toward Freud's theory of *Trauerarbeit*. "I could not, I cannot believe this; because for me, Time eliminates the emotion of loss (I do not weep), that is all. For the rest, everything has remained motionless. For what I have lost is not a Figure (the Mother), but a being; and not a being, but a *quality* (a soul): not the indispensable, but the irreplaceable."[20] The substitution of the contingent, unique detail that defines photographic essence in the first part is here refigured as the irreplaceable unique being or quality of the mourned-for. Refusing any language of labor, transformation, or renunciation, Barthes insists instead on that other account of mourning's pain—writing in the wake of, and binding his grief and the photograph itself to, the irresolvably particular anguish at the absolute loss of light that might ever again announce: Look, she is coming.

Death, *indialectique;* a grief, *indialectique.* Like all incantations, this one will have a third term. The final death of the dialectic in *La chambre claire* brings the text full circle to the explicit subject of theoretical contemplation: the "photo-graph," the writing of light. Barthes argues, "If dialectic is that thought which masters the corruptible and converts the negation of death into the power to work, then the photograph is undialectical: it is a denatured theater where death cannot 'be contemplated,' reflected and interiorized."[21] Refusing any model of the photograph as cathartic, placed into ritual, or in any other way recuperable into systematicity, totality, and meaning, Barthes figures the photograph as the final element in the slowly unfolding series of undialecticals that comprise the fragments of this text. He employs the same language to describe the death he awaits in the wake of his grief ("*ma mort totale, indialectique*") and the refusal of the photograph to accede to transformation, contemplation, and being put to work for meaning ("*la Photographie est indialectique*"). These three formulations bring together finitude's futurity, affect's intensity, and the photograph's essence to suggest that a new theory of being is required to grapple equally with death, with affect, and with the direct capture of light in an image that distresses sublation.

Barthes hints at this new theoretical disposition when he argues early in the text that phenomenology has ignored affect, and yet its power "was what I didn't want to reduce; . . . could I retain an affective intentionality, a view of the object which was immediately steeped in desire, repulsion, nostalgia, euphoria?"[22] He is not convinced that classical phenomenology can adequately speak of mourning, desire, ecstasy—and *therefore* that it thus cannot account for photography. Ultimately, what *La chambre claire* imagines is a revision of the very problem of being. Quietly sympathetic to Levinas's argument that philosophy has erred in taking being as an object, Barthes concludes that photography's evidential power "bears the effigy to that crazy point where affect (love, compassion, grief, enthusiasm, desire) is a guarantee of Being."[23] In place of a phenomenology that occludes affect, Barthes refigures both phenomenology and ontology as suffused with affect, to the point where "*l'affect . . . est garant de l'être.*" This revision of being as *not* an object evokes the problem framed by Laplanche of Freud's mourning thought: that if mourning casts the illuminating light on melancholia, it itself is not caught in a beam—for how could light be illuminated? Laplanche was technically correct in his logic: light cannot be illuminated, for there is no material isness to reflect and be seen. But in light of Barthes's revision of being as guaranteed by affectivity in place of objectivity, a different possibility for reading this paradox emerges: if illumination is thought as a problematic not of matter but of an affect such as grief, then perhaps some light can be shed on mourning after all. The sculpting of mass by light can be rethought as the pressure or force of that sculpting, not for or of being, but for or of an affective visual form.

Presence is materialized in Barthes's theory of the photograph. The return of the dead that Barthes sees in all photographs is not a figural return but an ontological fold: "the corpse is alive, as *corpse*: it is the living image of a dead thing."[24] His realist take on the image relies on the photographic referent being defined as the undeniably and necessarily real object that was placed at a specific place and in a unique moment in time before the lens. This onto-logical adherence of the referent to the subsequent image changes the object of inquiry: photography is no longer a medium like any other but a medium without mediation. And all because of light. The *noeme* "that-has-been" (*ça a été*) is made possible by the technological discovery of the possibility "to recover and print directly the luminous rays emitted by a variously lighted object."[25] The consequence is that the photograph is "literally an emanation of the referent. From a real body, which was there, proceed radiations which ultimately touch me, who am here."[26] What photography thus *graphs* is not just an image enabled by light but that image captured as light in its lightness. The significance of figuring photography as a medium without mediation, wherein rays from the photographed body directly touch a viewing body, is a profu-sion of corporeal figurations, as if touch signaled the final death of dialectics. Hence, Barthes writes of an "umbilical cord" linking the photographed thing to a later gaze and figures light as "a carnal medium, a skin I share with anyone who has been photographed."[27] Insisting on the invisible hyphen in the term "photo-graphed," Barthes reads back into the photograph the materiality of light, a light that moves, at a distance, that emanates but also binds—a light that caresses, that presses, that strains. If the Winter Garden Photograph is a "treasury of rays," it is not a vault or crypt (it is no tomb in which the Emperor would reside) but, rather, an archive in motion; for those rays that are not superadded continually move between bodies seen and seeing at a temporal gap to link up illuminated, reflecting, receptive planes of sensitive skin. (This emphasis on the non-mediating in late Barthes is itself a kind of illuminating surprise after a lifetime of work on semiotics. It also suggests that *Camera Lucida* functions as a kind of magical thinking, a leap or departure—even a point of *peculiarity*—in the history of the narrative of Barthes's own writing.)

This "certificate of presence" of every photograph is its essence but is also its affective mobility: to emanate the reality of the past in light—hence, the title of the work, *La chambre claire* (the light room), the other to the *camera obscura*.[28] Barthes refuses the historical trajectory of photography that plots it as emerging out of dark rooms; rather, the art's ancestry is the *camera lucida,* the "apparatus, anterior to Photography, which permitted drawing an object through a prism, one eye on the model, the other on the paper."[29] This early nineteenth-century optical device, patented by William Wollaston, was a drawing-aid prism; it doubled vision by superimposing an image of the subject for the artist on the surface for the reproduction. With the camera lucida, no image is projected (and no darkroom required); images are multiplied, brought to presence in the real and in the image. Revising Jonathan Crary's argument that the camera obscura is an epistemological model, we might say that the camera lucida is an ethical-ontological model.[30] Its doubling suggests the simultaneously live and dead, past and present, binding of light-emanating visual subject of photographic capture to light-receiving viewer of the image. The camera lucida introduces a supplement to visuality, bringing together in one image the ground of representation and the figure in advance of its being made figural. In both title and theoretical account, then, Barthes answers Laplanche's question by making light a matter for affect and not for matter at all. Light's immaterial being is illuminated when its force is materialized through the exchange of looks with the photographic image. Barthes suggests the heaviness of the force of light when he writes that the photograph should be thought of as the "image revealed, 'extracted,' 'mounted,' 'expressed' (like the juice of a lemon) by the action of light."[31] Not merely force but a heavy force; not merely a light that expresses (some representation) but a light-constituted image that ex-presses, that puts great pressure on, as though to cast in rock, the form of a beloved body.

EXTRA MISSING THINGS

Four paratextual peculiarities frame *La chambre claire:* a dedication, two photographs, and an italicized passage on the back cover. Two function as absent figures: the Winter Garden Photograph of Barthes's mother on which the entire argument hinges, which does not appear in this text littered with dozens of images, and a quotation on the very edges of the book, which goes missing in published translations of the French edition. The two other strangenesses are supplements to the text: a dedication, not to a person but to a piece of philosophy, and a single color photograph inserted in advance of the word, Daniel Boudinet's "Polaroid, 1979."

Beginning at the back: the rear cover of the original edition of *La chambre claire* contains a quoted passage, one that is not cut from the text but added to it as a supplement and that is not reproduced in English editions—which is to say, these lines belong to *La chambre claire* but not at all to *Camera Lucida*. The excerpt is from *Pratique de la voie tibétaine* (A Practice of the Tibetan Way):

Marpa fut très remué lorsque son fils fut tué, et l'un de ses disciples dit: "Vous nous disiez toujours que tout est illusion. Qu'en est-il de la mort de votre fils, n'est-ce pas une illusion?" Et Marpa répondit: "Certes, mais la mort de mon fils est une super-illusion."

Marpa was very moved when his son died, and one of his disciples said, "You have always told us that everything is illusion. Is not the death of your son an illusion?" And Marpa responded, "Certainly, but the death of my son is a super-illusion."[32]

This addition to the physical reality of the book (in a text about the material transmission of the affects of objects) demands the question Derrida poses more generally of "gestures around what we believe to be the essential writing" of any of Barthes's own texts: "how and when did he choose these lines for the back cover where Marpa speaks of his son's death?"[33] This supplement, which tells the story of familial grief, inverts the players of Barthes's sad tale. It is the death of the child, not the mother, that prompts the suffering. Indeed, in his diary entry of November 19, 1977, not yet a month after her death, Barthes enters "[Status confusion]. For months, I have been her mother. It is as if I had lost my daughter (a greater grief than that? It had never occurred to me)."[34] In some ways, these few lines marking the hard border of the book radically condense the affective essence of death's material and peculiar pain—in their starkness, they summarize through the metaphysical leap of the *super-* what Barthes talks around within the text. Neither Marpa nor Roland, however, can present directly the agony itself. Their mutual failures make the one a kind of echo, even a reproduction or print, of the other.

The structure of what is unnecessarily present at the edges of Barthes's text stands in awkward relation to the missing kernel of *La chambre claire,* the Winter Garden Photograph whose visual (photographic) presence Barthes withholds absolutely. It is one of the loveliest mysteries of *La chambre claire* that the presence, or luminous material, of the photograph of Barthes's mother as a child is not reproduced—it is not given over *for us.* This spectre informs the text, however, in the ways in which we might say light in-forms the image:

it impresses itself, it bends the text to its force. One might see its diffracted reappearance in the very title of the work: Mary Lydon, for one, suggests that the photographic room that names the book is a substitute for the room of the missing maternal image. In her taking of Barthes's text as an "elaborate spectacle of sound and light," she reads the absent photograph as a play of light and shadow and the Jardin d'Hiver as "literally a *chambre claire:* that is to say, a *light* room."[35] The camera lucida thus names the luminous space of the Winter Garden, and the missing piece titles the whole, giving form to the text as it grounds it through its absence.[36] Or the notable absence might be displaced, as though in dreamwork's condensation and displacement, into the photo of Nadar's Ernestine, captioned curiously by Barthes "The Artist's Mother (or Wife)."[37] But I prefer to regard *what* goes missing in a text about *who* goes missing in relation to these figures on the periphery of the work itself, Marpa and Sartre and Boudinet but also Marpa's dead son, Barthes's dead mother, all these dim selves guarding (or regarding) the threshold of Barthes's writing.

Barthes's philosophy of the photograph is presented in the name of a work: "*En hommage à* L'Imaginaire *de Sartre.*" It is initially strange that Barthes dedicates his work to a book, not a person, and names Jean-Paul Sartre and not, for example, Henriette Barthes. The *hommage* is thus severed from personal memorialization and instead pays tribute to an intellectual (and national, and philosophical) history into which Barthes's own affective phenomenology must be placed. Sartre's L'Imaginaire (1940) is not simply an abstract or thematic ground for Barthes's later figurations. It is also a model for Barthes's ruminative form. Like the opening line of each of the two main parts of *La chambre claire,* Sartre begins his text *in medias res* with a troubled encounter with an image: "despite some prejudices, to which we will return, it is certain that when I produce in myself the image of Pierre, it is Pierre who is the object of my current consciousness."[38] Structurally equivalent to Barthes's mother in the Winter Garden Photograph, Sartre's friend Pierre appears in the text, which is to say that Pierre affects its line of thought, through his constant nonappearance. Of a mental representation, a photograph, and a caricature of his *ami,* "from beginning to end, the aim is the same: to make present the face of Pierre, who is not there."[39] In the effort to fulfill the desire to make present the absent, Sartre forms an imaged consciousness, but the result "is very imperfectly attained: some details are lacking, others are suspect, the whole is rather blurred." He hunts: while the photographic portrait he finds restores the external traits of the face, "it does not capture his expression." Sartre's version of Barthes's treasured photograph is a caricature: while it distorts characteristics, nevertheless "something that was lacking in the photograph, life, expression, is clearly manifest in the drawing: I 'regain' Pierre."[40] Barthes and Sartre share an intimate faith that representation, which necessarily tarries with absence, can, in certain visual forms, do more than bring to presence the notion or sense of the missing. Certain forms—this caricature, that photograph—go even further and propose nonbeing's return, to regain, see once more, recruit back to presence, the friend, the mother, all of the loved who have gone missing.

Barthes's dedication to Sartre's work also imports to the later text the importance of affects and desire from the 1940 study of the imaginary. Anticipating Barthes's argument that in the photograph affect guarantees being, Sartre argues that "reflection delivers us affective *consciousness.*"[41] In a passage that beautifully and strikingly evokes the Barthes of forty years later, Sartre writes, "If I love the long, white, fine hands of that person, this love, which is directed on the hands, could be considered as one of the ways that they have appeared to my consciousness. It is indeed a feeling that aims at their *finesse,* their *whiteness,* the vivacity of their movement: what would a love mean which was not a love *of* those qualities?"[42] The consequence of figuring affectivity as central to consciousness is that Sartre can define desire as "a blind effort to possess on the representative plane what is already given to me on the affective plane" and therefore that "the structure of an affective consciousness of desire is already that of an imaging consciousness."[43] The quote from Marpa on the back of *La chambre claire* suggests the same tangling of desire, affectivity, and consciousness: What is beyond or above illusion? A parent's love. But this is a love of which Barthes cannot speak—begetting no child, this continuity is denied to him, and again the foreclosure of dialectical thinking ensures only the future total death of the self. Recall that in formulating the undialectical in relation to death and the photograph, Barthes writes, "My particularity could never again universalize itself (unless, utopically, by writing, whose project henceforth would become the unique goal of my life)."[44] Writing stands in place of the absent child; thus, the sad script on the back cover positions Barthes's *La chambre claire* as the utopian site of any valuation beyond illusion.

While the substitution of print for progeny marks the back cover of the French text, Boudinet's "Polaroid, 1979" is set in advance of what is written, appearing before reading takes place. This visual epigraph, like the quote from Marpa, figures beyond the parameters of the work: unmentioned or approached in critical language, it is also in color and therefore unmentionable, critically unapproachable, given that Barthes insists that "color is a coating applied *later on* to the original truth of the black-and-white photograph. For me, color is an artifice, a cosmetic (like the kind used to paint corpses)."[45] The exchange of light between the body photo-graphed and the later looking self is covered up with this superadded (we might say, super-illusory) coating. It is fitting, then, that the singular color photograph in the text should be something *added,* as though later on, to the original truth of the black and white lines of written criticism. Boudinet's photograph is part of a series titled *Fragments d'un labyrinthe,* taken at night before dawn in Boudinet's apartment, using only the light that entered through the window (image of morning thus precedes words on mourning). The image reproduced at the beginning of Barthes's study, "Polaroid, 1979," is of a barely parted curtain through which early light traces textured threads and the corner of an uninhabited bed in a strikingly monochromatic pale cerulean.[46]

One way to read this cryptic image is to put saturation to work, investing the striking color with meaning. Diane Knight does just this, suggesting that the photograph evokes the color of Barthes's mother's bright eyes, which he mentions only once: "it was a quite physical luminosity, the photographic trace of a color, the blue-green of her pupils."[47] However, the context for this quotation is the insufficient, mediating, however beautiful and luminous, photographs of his mother before the discovery of the Winter Garden Photograph. If the anticipation of that luminosity is one tonal affect attached to the image, it is a poor substitute for the missing image that conveys that luminosity directly, immediately, and perfectly. Lydon deploys Boudinet's image for a familial interpretation, reading it in relation to the maternal: "this strategically placed image," produced but not described, is the counterpoint to the image of the mother that is described but not reproduced. Her claim is that, as the "antithesis of *la chambre claire,*" the darkened room functions as a pendant of the missing maternal in the text to come. Perhaps it is the case that this image functions in a relation to the missing one that means only for Barthes: the title of Boudinet's series, *Fragments of a Labyrinth,* certainly evokes Barthes's claim that "all the world's photographs formed a Labyrinth," at whose center he would find the Winter Garden image, not as a substance, but as the thread leading his desire there. However, any reading of Boudinet's photograph as a substitute for the missing image of the mother (or the image of the missing mother) ignores its supplementary dimension in its textual placement: criticism that lets the image function as an avatar for the maternal falls for the lure, in the sense of enticement and trap, of all images, putting this image to *work* for a narrative in criticism, reading it as though it were placed *in* the text instead of above, around, or before it.[48] Lydon, Knight, and Jean-Michel Rabaté (who calls the picture an allegory for birth) treat this photograph, that is, only from the point of view of the *studium:* they study it, derive its nameable meaning, then name it.

Instead, we really should linger with the specifics of light. For this color photograph functions like the reference to the child whose death is a super-illusion on the flip side of the physical text. That is, what this image brings forth is not Barthes's mother but Barthes himself. One should attend to the date in the title: the light captured in Boudinet's image emanated in 1979, the very time Barthes was completing the writing of *La chambre claire.* This photograph *avant le texte* is thus a kind of gift to the reader, a material conveyance of the historicity of the time when Barthes was writing to those who arrive as readers later—and a prophetic trace of his own death that we now know came so soon after the time of the transmission of that very light. (Is the image also thus figuring a kind of retrospective and umbilical bond between Barthes and Walt Whitman, whose name did not appear on the cover or title page of the edition of *Leaves of Grass* published in 1855 and was disclosed only later and only within the text? In place of the name of the electric author, famously, was only a picture. If this is a ligature, it is a converted one: there, Whitman's visage; here, the time of Barthes's writing-light.) Holding the thick, glossy paper of the cyan photograph is one small way to touch, and therefore to mourn, the historicity of the being of Roland Barthes himself. If the conveyance of those rays does not convey a dialectical meaning to that death, it is nevertheless the form of the affect of reading *La chambre claire.* Regarding the Boudinet, the reader grieves R. B. through the exchange of light in advance of a philosophical encounter that retroactively declares that this is what has taken place. That is, the reader grieves both *for* Barthes as a missing (already dead) author and *with,* alongside, Barthes in his grief for his mother, continuing and extending the light-transmitting force of this specific, peculiar pain.

> Grieving in advance,
> call this reading,
> call this love,
> it is all the same.

ACEDIA AND THE POSE

In the wake of Barthes's account, affect can no longer be regarded as a private expression of a subject. Rather, affect has a force independent of being—it, in his words, can be carried to the mad limit where love or grief or desire is itself "a guarantee of Being." Affects bring forth a brutal pressure, and grief's etymological link to *gravis* is here felt in its full weight as heavily untransformable. Against any theory of affect as a thematic (of a photograph) or expression (of an independent being), affect here suffuses the very form of the photograph; it *is* the structure of the medium. The ecstasy of the image can be reduced neither to a trope or aesthetic presence nor to an experience of some independent spectator. It is, instead, the form of the captured light. The question that must follow is whether this theory of the undialectical photograph that does not express affect but is constituted by affect can be thought in relation to cinema. Unlike film theorists who have taken the photographic basis of celluloid as the ground for a cinematic ontology (André Bazin most famously), Barthes insists in *Camera Lucida* that the cinema is irreconcilably apart from photography and that its *eidos* is emphatically not death. (This is part of a larger disavowal of the cinema in his study. The cinema is not only severed from photography, or so parts of the text claim, but the fact that Bazin, the film theorist whose argument is so close to Barthes's that their claims seem almost familial, is loudly never mentioned, makes his name and his ontology of the cinema yet another visible absence in this text, not unlike the Winter Garden Photograph.[49]) The cinema, however, does have one supplementary dimension: comparing the types of technology, Barthes writes that "the cinema has a power which at first glance the Photograph does not have: the screen . . . is not a frame but a hideout; the man or woman who emerges from it continues living: a 'blind field' constantly doubles our partial vision."[50] Barthes senses no beyond or blind field in most photographs ("everything which happens within the frame dies absolutely once this frame is passed beyond"); however, "once there is a *punctum,* a blind field is created."[51] That the punctum endows the image with a beyond suggests that the animating desire of mobility in (all) cinema and photography is the wandering desire to see what is on the edge of vision. Why is it not the case, then, that the photograph that pricks is the cinematified image? Why is cinema not the privileged locus of wounds and stings to which only a subset of photographic images aspires?

For Barthes, the problem for cinema derives from the centrality of the pose to the essence of photographic ontology. The noeme thus "deteriorates when this Photograph is animated and becomes cinema: in the Photograph, something *has posed* in front of the tiny hole and has remained there forever (that is my feeling); but in cinema, something *has passed* in front of this same tiny hole: the pose is swept away and denied by the continuous series of images."[52] The distinction between the *s'est posé* and the *est passé* points to the role of mobility in undermining the fixity of the captured presence that avows the object's once existence. The photographic pose only ever attests to the unmediated certainty of "the body's formality," while the cinema combines "the actor's 'this-has-been' and the role's."[53] The instant of the motionless self-presencing self is thus swept away and muddled by the movements of the cinematograph.[54] So although a cinema of celluloid is based ontologically on photography, phenomenologically they are utterly distinct: while there is a stable photographic referent (each a ghost), the cinema's peculiar mobility causes the referent to constantly shift (zoetic art). Paradoxically, the vitality of film seems to undermine the affectivity of the substrate of its images. The lie of cinema's twenty-four frames per second is the promise of reality's experiential flow; its illusion is the futurity of time, unlike photography's being, as Barthes says, "*without future* (this is its pathos, its melancholy)."[55] The motionlessness of photography is the condition of possibility for its doubled relationship to death: the self's certain future one and the past's certain ones that have taken place. (That Barthes follows this insistence with his description of the photograph as undialectical makes clear that cinema's movement, for him, gives it a relation to futurity and sublation that is denied the static posed trace of the referent in photography.)

However, *La chambre claire* is not Barthes's only meditation on the image.[56] In other texts, his language suggests possible connections between photography and the cinema—in "En sortant du cinéma," he refers to "that festival of affects known as a film," and in "The Third Meaning," his account of the supplementary dimension of the film still anticipates the theory of the punctum.[57] Indeed, like the binary between mourning and melancholia in Freud, the opposition between photography and cinema in Barthes is more tenuous than it appears at first glance. One of Barthes's conclusions in *La chambre claire* is that (classical) cinema is the "domestication of Photography . . . ; a film can be mad by artifice, can present the cultural signs of madness, it is never mad by nature (by iconic status); it is always the very opposite of an hallucination; it is simply an illusion; its vision is oneiric, not ecmnesic."[58] Here it would seem as though the experiences of the film spectator are what fail to be tinged with desire and the fecundity of madness. However, from Barthes's description in "En sortant du cinéma" of the awkward, chilly drowse of the spectator—"limp as a sleeping cat"—we can return to the cinema these hypnotic reveries and dream-like dimensions. One critic reads this spectatorial sleepiness specifically as "lassitude, inertia, torpor; a body become soporific, soft, limp; a loss of reality, a porosity to the strangeness of the world, a hallucinatory vivacity of sensations. A 'very special way of being in the world,' known for centuries of Western Christianity as *acedia*—a state of mortal sin."[59] This description of the "steady drowsiness" of acedia that Barthes reads into cinematic spectatorship opens up a point of (affective) communion between photography and film, for acedia is another word for melancholia; its relation to sloth and the demonic was due to its peculiar penchant for compelling sufferers to wander, lose themselves, become distracted. Acedia, writes a historian of the disposition, resulted from the "affections of the irrational part of man's soul, which originate in sense impressions or in memory and are often accompanied by pleasure."[60] Thus, Barthes's description of film in "En sortant du cinéma" does not move him far from matters of affect or from matters of pain, grief, sorrow, and a resistance to reason.[61] Despite insistences in *La chambre claire* on the irrelevance of the cinema to his theory of photography, Barthes's other writings suggest a bleed between the two media.

A germ of a critique that would extend Barthes's work on grief, the undialectical, affect, and the photograph to cinema might likewise point to the moment in *La chambre claire* when he writes that the photograph "is violent: not because it shows violent things, but because on each occasion *it fills the sight by force,* and because in it nothing can be refused or transformed."[62] This insistence on the non-transformable adheres to Barthes's larger project of severing a link between the image and dialectics, but the added notion of the violence of a sight filled by force leaves room for a theorization of cinema that emphasizes its internal mobility—of force—in place of the substitutive mobility of referents that Barthes suggests annihilates the *noesis* of photography. If this chapter's turn to thinking grief, finitude, the affective, and the undialectical in relation to film is therefore unauthorized by certain figurations in *La chambre claire,* it is nevertheless a move put in critical motion by other fragments of this fragmentary text.

The urgency of thinking *La chambre claire* with film theory is twofold: it enables a new approach to a formal affect, and it engenders an approach to grief that resists dialectics and preserves the "peculiar painfulness" of loss. In place of a limited, aims-oriented model of affect as the psychological experience of any one subject, the presencing of grief through the photograph suggests a theory of affect as a force that takes form in texts. Although Barthes's phenomenological language and methodology emphasize his felt festival of affects in relation to the Winter Garden Photograph, the fact that both grief and the photograph are undialectical—that they do not productively labor but, rather, announce and *regard* finitude—suggests that affect cannot be reduced to the felt stirrings of any singular self. The externalization of affect into the ontology of the photograph forms the ground for a post-subjective, impersonal affect. Thus, it is not a knee-weakened subject who grieves but an undialectical image through which the dimension of grief moves as something that is painful *for form*. As in Augustine, grief troubles presence and light, but instead of being a problem of illumination for a grieving subject, in Barthes grief is a burden on light for the image written by light. (It is also, in the companion work *Mourning Diary*, begun the day after his mother's death and kept on small bits of quartered paper—this material evocation of Pascal's famous scraps embodying yet another Barthesian affection for fragmentation—a vocatory and sonic problem. Note the similarity with and sensory permutation of Augustine's confessed surprise at his conditional *blindness* from loss. "How strange," Barthes inks in his grief journal, "her voice, which I knew so well, and which is said to be the very texture of memory . . . , I no longer hear. Like a localized deafness.")[63] Illumination exceeds matters of representation for a viewing subject to constitute a problem for the form that presses out, that ex-presses, the force of that illumination. The form of this affect is delinked from individual experience and communal politics: this impersonal grief rests in the photo-graphic and resists all dialectics. But a formal grief hurts no less; that affect is tangled up with light lessens none of the cruelty of bereavement's pain. It is only that the image bears this out in place of a subject.

WHERE BEING WOULD HAVE BEEN

Death is not one example of absence among others; it speaks to us of absence itself by naming the most absent of absences, the one that is given by death.
—Jacques Derrida, "By Force of Mourning"

Visual theory is delighted to grieve. For Raymond Bellour and Christian Metz, in particular, film-theoretical labor is animated by mourning, and desire, for the lost cinematic object, that missing target of theoretical speculation. Bellour terms film a *texte introuvable*—unfindable, unattainable, lost—to a criticism that destroys its object (violates continuity) in order to find it (to imagine it is whole, is not lost). The inability to cite film directly—even a still involves temporal and kinetic losses—means that written analysis can only ever capture a "skeleton, stripped of flesh," all film criticism a charnel house.[64] Likewise, Metz's argument for the role of the imaginary in the cinema centers on what he calls "this always absent presence" of the unconscious.[65] But the imaginary is also entwined with the animating desire for the theorizing of the cinema, a desire that everywhere demands that the theorist relinquish the object of study—that he lose it and that he ambivalently mourn that loss. "To be a theoretician of the cinema," Metz declares, "one should ideally no longer love the cinema and yet still love it: have loved it a lot and only have detached oneself from it by taking it up again from the other end."[66] Metz grieves the cinema as corpse explicitly, writing that the projection of film gives pleasure over "its dead body" (*à son corps defendant*).[67] Film theory, in this tradition, privileges—even fetishizes—its relationship to absence and mourning, putting in place its own writerly compensations for the missing object. Deleuze, for example, insists at the beginning of *Cinema 1* that there will be no reproductions from the films about which he writes, because his text will appear in place of their absence.[68] His text not only stands in for every possible but missing film still; it also relocates the promise of being in the generative production of film-philosophy itself. Film theory is only too happy to wallow pleasurably in the suffering wake of loss.

But being's absence *is* traumatic to film form.

The problematic of grief is a particularly cinematic one—or, rather, reading grief in relation to film is not quite like considering any other affect—for, as articulated earlier in relation to Augustine, Freud, Laplanche, and Barthes, grief is irreducibly involved in matters of light, presence, visibility, and representation. This is made clear as early as Leon Battista Alberti's fifteenth-century declaration, "Painting contains a divine force which not only makes absent men present . . . but moreover makes the dead seem almost alive."[69] The force of representation's play with presence and absence derives from this greatest or first absence. Thus, grief, as the affect most tightly linked to the loss of being, poses a unique set of problems for any system of representation predicated on presencing: tarrying with grief requires representation to negotiate an affect that results from a loss and thus requires representation to invent a visual vocabulary for the in-visible absent. When a loved thing or one goes missing in a cinematic diegesis, it is a trauma not only to a psychologically invested character in the film—whose face traces, usually in close-up, the gestural expressions of sorrow—but also a formal trauma to film and its endlessly recuperative ability to make absent things present.

The treatment of grief in film criticism historically has conformed to the dialectical models of laboring and working through critiqued earlier: the very telos of narrative progression in classical film is from traumatic loss to resolution and catharsis. For this reason, suffering in the wake of a loss is a productive (even beloved) thematic for narrative cinema precisely because its form has an intrinsic arc of resolution; mourning demands and brings forth a story. After the attacks of September 11, 2001, a newly ascendant subgenre we might call "griefcore" emerged in Hollywood cinema, resplendent with scenes of protracted emotional pathos and grieving figures—*WTC View* (2005), *Remember Me* (2010), and the maudlin *Reign over Me* (2007) typified the trend—but there are also precedents for this rich trope in melodrama. Grief is classically thought of in relation to expression—of characters, on the screen, in narratives of loss, marking subjective pain through gestures that exteriorize and communicate emotion—and simultaneously to moved spectators who mimetically follow the tragic figures by having tears literally yanked from their viewing bodies (hence, "weepies" as a preeminent body genre, so much wet fat rendered from the spectatorial slab).[70]

The loss that prompts grief is especially traumatic to narrative film, with its compulsive reliance on shot–reverse shot dyads, the duality of the couple, and the drive toward the dialogical; any loss of (a) being is potentially disastrous for such an economy of the two. Grief is usually posed as a problem in film via the paradox of Augustine's sorrow: I looked for presence but saw nothing. There is a habeas corpus drive in the cinema, and when a body fails to appear, film form historically compensates in three ways: the loss is denied altogether; the loss is framed by the environment; or the loss is compensated for with a supplemental doubling. The story of a marriage, but suddenly the man dies, and the film will follow—will skulk about—widowed grief and how she moves on; how moving it will be. That loss is not only hers, though, as the structure of the film will grapple with it on its own terms. So in the one case, the loss might be denied altogether, and the absent one will remain present as an embodied ghost, ruining the second marriage in a comedy, touchingly giving gentle permission for the woman to love again in the drama. The fleshing of the shade is the essence of this form of loss abreaction: from the passionate specter, as in *Ghost* (1990), to the child as horrific crone in Nicolas Roeg's classic *Don't Look Now* (1973). Or, instead, the loss can be framed by the environment, delimiting the missing being by marking out the space of or in relation to objects that that body should properly inhabit—hence, the clichéd images of unoccupied beds and chairs in narratives of loss. *Here is where being would have been,* says the subjunctive tense of this shot. Absence is made present visually to the film by displaying the materiality under or behind any being, replacing the substance of a body with the substance of the environment in which that body once existed. Finally, instead, the loss might be inverted into a doubling. Film abhors a vacuum, and thus in place of the missing being is put a second version of some figure who remains. Most often, this is done through a mirror shot of the mourning one staring at herself, the substantive being and the reflected being caught in the same shot. In *Morvern Callar* (2002), the title character wakes on Christmas to find her boyfriend has committed suicide and is lying next to her in a pool of blood; for a third of the film, there is no problem, as things can be done with corpses: they can be stepped around, covered, kicked, and dismembered. But once the lover's body is finally made absent, into the void of the visually missing being are placed a series of shots of Morvern staring at herself in a mirror, answering the loss with a supplement.

Sometimes, a film will deploy all three strategies to compensate for an absence—even to delimit the representational knot of the problematic as constituting the meat of the central narrative. Thus, in François Ozon's *Sous le sable* (Under the Sand; 2000), Charlotte Rampling's grapple with the sudden disappearance of her husband is presented as a thematic crisis (initially, no body appears, and thus her grief cannot fix itself to the concreteness of finitude; she wanders the beach) that is also a formal crisis, as each of the three modes of absence-presencing are employed, failing to settle on the meaning of this absence. Her husband remains present as a specter, even making love to her at one point; the environment frames his absence in the non-occupied chair to which the image frequently cuts from an indirect non-subjective viewpoint; and Rampling's worn visage is doubled in numerous shots of her staring into a mirror. This exploration of the visual compensations for a missing body links the multiple and irreducible experiences of loss with the possibilities for negotiating cinematic structural loss to share the affect across the modalities of film form, mise-en-scène, and editing. Ozon resists closure, mercurially suggesting a cathartic burial in the sand and at the same time withholding its promise of resolution by having the final shot be a mirage of a man after which Rampling lustily chases without completing that approach to an endlessly deferred presence.

These cinematic strategies for addressing the visual problem of a loss of being are strikingly common and consistent in their compensatory drive: they labor to move film form away from the traumatic loss of presence toward a resolution that redirects that absence into some other scene or being. In a sense, films that employ this strategy are perfect mourners in Freud's sense in "Mourning and Melancholia" of withdrawing cathectic (here, visual) energy from that which goes missing and making it available to attach to new objects of cinematic presence. *Sous le sable* comes closest to a melancholic film form, stickily moving through each compensatory option but refusing to relinquish loss absolutely or give up on its visual deprivations. However, on some level, Ozon's film is still a study in emotion from a classical perspective: as a content or property of a character; expressed from internal to external (visual, facial, narrative, social) forms; and moving or displacing a receptive, feeling spectatorial sense or body. Each of these compensations maintains the supposition that affect is a trope for a narrative, a property of a subject, and potentially an experience phenomenologically available for a spectator. Visual form is brought in only to structurally replace and even annul the loss that undoes structure as well as characters, but affect is treated as a matter independent of that form.

To approach grief as a formal problematic—and to theorize cinematic grief as an undialectical image, following Barthes—requires reading for what the heaviness of loss in grief does to light in form. This is a departure from film theory that puts grief to work as expressive (by characters) or receptive (for spectators). Take Sergei Eisenstein, who opens "The Structure of the Film" by supposing, "Let us say that grief is to be represented on the screen. There is no such thing as grief 'in general.' Grief is concrete; it is always attached to something; it has conveyors, when your film's characters grieve; it has consumers, when your portrayal of grief makes the spectators sorrow, too."[71] The portrayal of grief as a matter for representation does not necessarily align with the evocation of grief in spectators, but the affective intention remains, as Eisenstein notes that "the grief of an enemy, after his defeat, arouses joy in the spectator." This claim is familiar from contemporary work on affect: grief has "conveyors" and "consumers"; it is represented, and it is experienced.[72] My argument is that affect theory needs fewer conveyors and consumers; pairing affect with form suggests, by contrast, that grief requires *readers*.

Pathos, for Eisenstein, is in excess of thematic or compositional elements, and is put in the service of "its affect on the spectator"; this affect is revealed "when the spectator is compelled to jump from his seat. . . . In brief—when the spectator is forced 'to go out of himself.'"[73] The *ex-stasis,* or self-departure, of the spectator "implies a transition to something else." Thus, not only is grief relegated to spectatorship, but Eisenstein's model of grief is also bound to dialectics (as expected, given his political commitments).[74] Eisenstein argues for dialectics in relation to form through his theory of "transfers to opposites" in rhythm, shot length, imagery, and editing: this "fundamental ecstatic formula: the leap 'out of oneself' invariably becomes a leap to a new quality."[75] From Eisenstein's model of dialectical mourning as "A leap. A transition from quantity to quality. A transition to opposition," we can speculate what its opposite form—peculiarly painful, untransformative grief—might look like. The undialectical image fails to mediate, does not transition or neatly move toward opposition. In place of *ex-stasis,* it employs *im-stasis*—in place of departure, there is only the fold. In addition, instead of a spectatorial jolt into emotional state changes that move the subject through dialectical processes, the spectatorial body is made irrelevant to this formal affective image.

The undialectical image is linked to the antitransformative, the nontransformable, and a resistance to the oppositions or permutations of form. Thus, while Eisenstein's privileged form of dialectics and grief was the busy movements and transitions generated by montage, the privileged visual form for an undialectical image is the stasis of the tableau. In place of Eisenstein's restless drive toward the pathetic structure as a unity, tableau is grounded in absence, nonbeing, a quiet, stilling void encircling Freud's "peculiar painfulness" of grief. The undialectical image is the sole way that the cinema can *present* the certainty of the body's formality without shifting the referent in a flow resembling life—that is, the undialectical image is the mode of cinema closest to an account of the photographic as *indialectique.* Tableau is how the cinema approaches Barthes's vision of a "blind field" in photography, where "everything which happens within the frame dies absolutely once this frame is passed beyond."[76] It is photography's absence of futurity that is its pathos for Barthes, its eidos finitude. In the undialectical image, the cinema makes its closest possible approach to this mode where affect is the guarantee of being, grief is untransformable, and form presences the force of grief.

A STILL AND HEAVY PAIN

Michael Haneke is a filmmaker of the pose, an aesthete of the posing of form. His work brings to presence the force of a non-intentional formal affect situated in staging, mise-n'en-scène, and duration. In the midst of the quasi-invasion-thriller narrative of his controversial *Funny Games* (1997), Haneke articulates a structural relation between the agony of parental grief and problems of illumination, visibility, and the direction of rays of an upturned luminosity. *Funny Games* appeared between the early *"emotionale Vergletscherung"* (emotional glaciation) trilogy and Haneke's move to France and collaborations with Isabelle Huppert and Juliette Binoche. It is a film that has been critically approached through the thematic lenses of violence, late Austrian postmodernism, and the decline of the family and bourgeoisie. Curiously, however, Haneke centers this violent, reflexive film on a stunning, ten-minute, spectacular (read, non-narrative) presentation of light. What that light illuminates is the heavy fixity of a body in posed stasis. In place of grief as the expression of a psychologically deep character (no close-up tears in up-close eyes) or a narrative trauma requiring processing, transformation, and resolution, in *Funny Games* form itself takes up the peculiarly painful suffering, gives it shape, weight, intensity, and force. The name for the structure that *is* the affect of grief in this film is the tableau.

Reading grief as a matter of form, composition, and structure requires leaving behind narrative thematics and critical treatments that claim mourning for meaning. Therefore, I am turning to Haneke precisely because of his rigorous avoidance of classical narrative, character psychology, and diegetic affectivity in place of a polemically formalist modernism.[77] Haneke's work exemplifies how formalism might be read as working *toward* affective commitment; his rigorous attention to cinematic structure is precisely what enables a formal affectivity. This is not, however, due to any provocations to the spectators of a Haneke film. One sustained theorization of affect in relation to Haneke is in Brigitte Peucker's argument that his films employ modernist techniques, especially in relation to sound, to violently move spectators.[78] While Peucker's introduction of affect alongside Haneke's work is an important rejoinder to accounts that emphasize the flat coldness of his works (*emotionale Vergletscherung* and all that), making formal rigor a *cause* for affective spectatorship instrumentalizes form for feeling and relies on retaining affect as separate and distinct from formalism. In other words, Peucker's argument that violence in Haneke's postmodern worldview has to escape representation altogether to make itself directly and assaultively present to the senses via affect retains a model of affect as having an aim, direction, and target, and ultimately figures affect as recuperable for meaning uniquely on the level of spectatorship. Haneke's work, on the contrary, is remarkable precisely for the utter *indifference* to spectatorial strivings that it demonstrates. This does not mean that his work is affectless.

Funny Games, like so many horror films, begins as a family leaves the city for a country home, where, ultimately, mother, father, son, and dog will be terrorized, tortured, and murdered by two well-dressed young men whose intrusion into the house is structured by the meta-game of social politeness. The pair play a series of sadistic *Spiele* with the family, ranging from betting that the family will be dead in twelve hours (a wager shared, in a close-up aside and wink, with the audience), to dares involving the mother's undress;

"warm–cold" alternations in a hunt to find the dead family dog; and a vicious hide and seek with the son, who escapes only to be caught and then indifferently shot. The child is murdered off-screen as the camera lingers over one of the visitors making a snack; the father, wounded from the beginning, is casually dispensed with; and the mother, only temporarily eluding the killers, is caught and returned and, without fanfare, drowned at the end of the film as the two unfailingly courteous men approach another family to begin a new set of funny vile games.

Critical work on *Funny Games* has tended to focus on the role of violence in the very violent film (and its attendant forms: panic, anxiety, the torturous games). But one of the most striking formal elements in the film has been largely elided in criticism to date, perhaps because its force derives from components of aesthetic violence isolated from matters of narrative violence. If the film is effecting a critique (about representation, about postmodernism, about collusions between spectators to the film and the diegetic forces of entropy), the very long central scene on which I will focus may appear to be a pause in the forward progress and elaboration of that critique, a digression away (or even an abstention) from the violence that grounds the text. My argument, however, is that this scene of duration is not a caesura in the violence—indeed, it can only be taken to effect a break if violence remains on the side of narratives, bodies, torture. Rather, this exhibition in and of time is the literal and figural center of the film; it poses cinematic representation as a problem for suffering, and suffering as a problem for representation. *Funny Games* is a film grounded on the structure, and not the thematic, of parental grief. As grief is the very form—undialectical, antisublative—that configures the film after the death of the child, *Funny Games* is not about grief or grieving. Rather, it brings to light the force of the affect *as* its visual and temporal form. It would not be a misstatement to say that it is the form of Haneke's film above all that grieves.

The bending of cinematic form to the heavy shape of grief occurs in the wake of the murder of the young boy, the first of the family to go. Although he has won a child's game of pointing, this "win" is misrecognized as a loss by Peter, the denser killer, the most vicious end of life reduced to an inclarity in the rules of the game. Earlier, the son had attempted escape, and now he has been dragged back to the living room (the irony of whose architectural naming begins to appear) along with the gun with which he attempted to gain his freedom and which anticipates the future violence that will be done to him. The editing of the scene before the death is familiar and classical, structured around the duality of the narrative divide between agents of force and bodily planes receiving that force: a series of cuts alternate between the two men on the sofa and their exhausted victims on the sofa opposite, the volleying shot–reverse shot a cinematic realization of the most fundamental spatial relation between victims and oppressors.

The family members have been confined to their first-floor parlor for the first half of the film, and when the intruder Paul leaves to calmly assemble a sandwich, the camera follows him out of that room and into the bright sterile buzz of the kitchen. Over that image, spectators access the missing room only at an aural remove, hearing: a single piercing gunshot; the low, edgy drone of a car race on the television; the mother's muffled gagging; a thump, a struggle, some causeless crash. Is that choking? Breathing? The return to the living room is effected through a hard cut from Paul in the kitchen to a close-up of a blood-streaked television screen under which, as though appearing through the scrim of the body's interior, remains the mobile circularity of an in-process car race and behind which are a series of thin parallel blood lines vertically parsing the wall. Over that image, thickly through its mechanical sounds, the killers voice their intention to leave (—"So: have a good evening . . ."), the rules having been compromised, the timing of the wager ruined. The film comes too quickly to an end, and only one hour in.

The ten-minute scene in question begins when the image of the blood-lined television screen cuts sharply to a long shot of the living room. But it is changed since last displayed, as though refigured under the unbearable pressure of finitude's irreversible certainty. At this cut, the living room is reimagined cinematically as a tableau. There is a split-second silence at the instant of that cut, after which the race announcer's intoning voice returns—as though the force of the cut silences the interminably noisy television, the tableau breaking into and effecting a split within the narrative world and within representation. Right before the murder is a shot over the shoulder of the intruder Peter as he watches the car racing on television: the *mise en abyme* shot is typical of Haneke's work and creates a perfect model for embedded mediation that leads elsewhere, that has a depth and extension in imaginary space. By contrast, the tableau after the murder of the child involves a radical flattening of space, a collapse of the cinematic into the theatrical and a foreclosure of spatial and representational depths that may lead elsewhere. The frame now presents the living room not as one option among many in the house but as a total space unto itself: tight framing on the center of the room leaves aside the methods of entry and departure, does not include the door frame that leads elsewhere into the house, and which has previously framed (and will yet again, later) the killers' foray into the family's privacy. The tight boundaries of the space and the fixed camera emphasize the room's rectangular lines; the image is centered on the intersection of two walls, reminiscent of the visible and neat seam of theatrical sets. The composition of the room is rigidly balanced: three windows, each with matching sets of long white drapes; three seating areas, each of varying lengths but forming a harmonious triangle for conversation. If that balance is slightly awry, it is only due to the bent corpse of the child in the middle edge of the right side of the frame, but the tableau recenters within minutes, setting that surplus just to the edges of the image, restoring visual order to the composition.

The living room is a study in neutrals: taupe sofas, pale yellow walls, a lightly blue-gray carpet against a dark brown floor, and those excruciatingly white drapes around the very dark windows. Most of the tones are gauzily muted, for much of the room is cast in shadow. At the foreground and to the right, the dark brown floor bleeds into blackness, completely bereft of illumination; the bottom two-thirds of the frame are largely without detail, flat planes of vague tones in expanses of fabric and shape. At the exact center of the frame, however, is a violently pure, bright hole of light, its diegetic source hidden behind the thick mass of furniture in the foreground. The bored hole of illumination has a specific forceful shape and direction: the line of its visual demarcation stretches up from the very center of the image to the left in a sharp triangular beam to slowly fade in intensity as that triangle stretches to the upper corner of the frame where, at the edge of the screen, it again returns to dusky darkness. Sitting just to the right of this point of illumination is the mother, bent forward in a slant perfectly parallel to the ascending beam, as though shaping with the pressure of her forward tilt the directional vector that light takes in this space. On the other side, leading off to the voided right side of the frame, is a darker triangle, excerpting the mass of her body but without a shadow's resemblance to the form of the human. Below that darkened, thinner triangle is the assemblage of splayed limbs that were the boy's, when he was alive, but are now mere markers, lines denoting the edge of the stage beyond which no actor may now cross.

It is not a freeze frame; tiny movements of a head and the continuous sound put motion into the tableau, but each pose of each destroyed parent will settle into an approximation of painterly stillness. There are three central framings, each comprising a tableau in miniature and each with an insistent and forceful duration, shocking in the thickness of time they comprise. From the instant of the cut to the room as tableau, it is over a minute of racing

FIG. 4.1. *Funny Games* (Michael Haneke, 1997)

sound and stillness in the image before the mother almost imperceptibly tilts her head; she slowly gets to her feet and, bound, hops over to the television to turn it off—silence. Kneeling by the television, where the camera has panned a bit to continue its framing, the sound of a car recedes into the distance, and the bright spot of centered light is on the left side of the frame, now visibly attached at its source to a knocked-over lamp. Two minutes and thirty seconds into the scene, the mother croaks, "Sie sind weg" (They're gone), and sits, again, in stillness. Her pronoun betrays the complexity of absence: *they* who are gone include the two torturers but also her son. All are gone, one terrible compound of grief (for the other) and solace (for the self). At three and a half minutes, the mother (and is she still one? It is what she was—) struggles to undo the binding around her wrists and, finally, at four minutes in she begins the lengthy, deliberate, painful struggle across the room. The camera follows the wife with deliberate and agonized languor, the *indolent* capture of light suggesting sloth while putting to lie the etymology that supposedly lets a lack of exertion negate the root *dolere* (pain). Panning from the right of the room to the left, the slow camera goes no farther than the edges of the proscenium and does not follow the female body out of the living room, as it had with the intruder Paul. Our image waits, still and patient, reframed on the whole scene as it was in the first cut to the room.

Thus, now, four minutes into the so very long scene, there is a new tableau, an inversion of the first one: the same two sofas, but now on the right side of the frame instead of the left, and an identical armchair, but flipped from the far right to the far left. Three windows in the background remain, but in place of two along the back wall and one on the intersecting perpendicular, now the three windows are along the back long edge of the set. Each framing has focused on permutations of the fractured family as the figures settle into the stillness of minutes-long poses: in the first, the mother is all alone; the second pan to the right frames the mother and the dead son; and the third and final leaves only the mother and wounded father utterly and totally alone, as they always, from now on, forever will be. In the final framing of the tableau, the one that alights four minutes into the scene, the father first appears in place of the tangled limbs of the son in the first framing in a substitution that cannot substitute. (Is that not the pathos of grief—that bodies do not convey?) He struggles to sit up and then poses in a bent slump while screeching sobs occasionally escape on the action of the breath. Once again, the mother's movement and the camera's minor panning adjustments have decentered the light from the first tableau, now on the right side of the frame, nearly left behind just as the boy's body is absolutely left behind in this framing, positioned just outside its borders.[79] Five and a half minutes in, the wife appears in the space again and goes to her husband. The couple is now in the center of the frame, settling into the stillness of this new pose, as halting, choking struggles break the larynx.

Only at eight and a half minutes in do these bodies slowly, so slowly, begin to rise—or, rather, as in some hyper-controlled Butoh performance, they do not rise, do not move, do not levitate so much as they are rearranged. Their figures *are moved* in such a manner as to take up more vertical space in the composition of the image. It takes almost a minute for the forms to become fully upright—and they never quite reach that posture, falling, massively, onto each other, the husband to the right collapsed entirely on his wife's bent back, the composite form an assemblage of weights and heavinesses. Grief is a technique of the arrangement of this burden. The doubled beast slumps forward, shuffles on the woman's broad splayed knees, widely gapped: the movement is less forward motion toward the door just outside the frame than pressures down and shifted halts in lateral mobilities without progress. Their faces down, expressivity is redirected from faciality to the tensile inner lines of thighs under the struggling weight of a failing pace. The mother's shock as she catches a glimpse of the corpse is written into her quaking knees, not her eyes. The figures slouch toward the left border of the frame, edging toward the light just beyond the image, but we do not see them leave the room. (You will have known something like this before, will recognize how the hard act of going leaves its painful trace on spines, as in the rounded bent Masaccio's early fifteenth-century fresco gives to his expelled Adam and his howling Eve.) Haneke's scene ends on the parents' bowed double posture approaching the door; they remain frozen on the frame's and room's edges at the threshold of the world, a still-life pose toward which all light and being is pulled, with no possibility of escape. *Doubled-Niobe: were they, too, cast in stone, they, too, still would weep.* When the scene finally ends its long, long take, and the camera cuts away from these drooped corpuses, it has been more than ten minutes since the last cut on that first image of the tableau. The peculiar pain of grief in *Funny Games* takes the shape of a form with duration, the heavy form of duration.

When the cut occurs that ends this still scene, it is to a long shot of the outside of the house, a strange image that lasts half a minute, with only the ambient sound of the countryside at night. This shot is a literal inversion of the light structure of the tableau: inside the room, the room is barely lit and the windows bracket three vertical rectangles of darkness, the theatrical world composed of what takes place inside the lit space, admitting nothing beyond its edges. The reverse image is of a dark house and environment punctuated by repeated vertical rectangles of illumination. The angle of the house where two walls come together to form a seam figures this other side as the exact place of the tableau, now seen from beyond the limits of representation allowed by the frame in the earlier scene. This shot is completely unattributed: no retroactivity places it as the point of view of the killers. There is no narrative motivation for this shot—absolutely nothing can be learned from it.

Rather, the purpose of this long shot of the exterior of the house is to illuminate and illustrate the visual inversion that it is: the shot of the outside of the house is the photo-graphic negative of the grief tableau. It puts on display the principle of backlighting, stages a drama of presence and absence: a study of light and darkness in miniature, one horrid little *son et lumière*.[80] When, after this shot, the film cuts back to the couple, they have already left the living room. Immediately, narrative progress, a frenzied pace, and all the work of suspense start up again (—in the hallway, quickly, a close-up hand tries the door, they are locked in, what to do next, how to get help). What the shot to the outside of the house covers over in its exhibition of the principles of illumination is the moment that the narrative restarts, the figures' exiting of the tableau (at which point they become characters again), and the resumption of narrative teleology. The shot thus masks the ob-scene, or the exit from the scene, the shift into a new form of representation and the inversion of light and darkness that stands in for the ontological obscenity of crossing the threshold of the tableau. It is a shocking image, and it is done *solely* to illuminate light—to set it off from the other side of the framed spectacle. These twenty-two seconds present the conditions of possibility for visual representation as such.[81] *How might light be illuminated? One must leave the theater, exit the cave.*

Haneke's tableau consists of three scenes set in place by nearly still poses of a cinematically rare duration. If one effect of the tableau is to point to the history of cinema itself—with the long shot, still camera, and rigid frontality, the image evokes early silent cinema before montage broke it into angles and partial perspectives—it is a history overlaid with other visual traditions. The evocation of painterly and theatrical modes of representation within the film, and alongside the blaring television, makes this central scene more broadly a meta-allegory for mediation. Each scene of grief played out in the stasis of forms suggests the impossibility of a cinematic (that is to say, on the side of movement and life) treatment of familial grief. There is a classical form to the room, with a distinct front, middle, and background; a rectangular proscenium as on a stage; balanced composition in the mise-en-scène; and the rigorous, specific movement from right to left across the entire tableau, traversing and marking the borders of the representational world. The set of long white curtains on each of the three windows evokes the curtains of a theatrical stage, taking into the scene the signs of its artifice.

If Peucker is correct that "tableau vivant moments in film—moments of arrested motion, by and large—remind us by contrast that the 'motion picture' is the first medium able to animate visual representation, to make painting 'come to life,'" here the tableau *vivant* is a tableau *mort,* conferring death not through intermedial juxtapositions but through a co-opting of stasis *for* cinema. Peucker explores the tableau vivant in film as both a moment of "arrested action that interrupts the flow of images in cinema" and "the cinematic reenactment of painting" to introduce the problem of the real. She notes, following Diderot, that tableaux vivants are precursors to the "*apothéose* in the staged melodrama,"[82] themselves precursors to the frontal exhibition of early cinema. The tableau that centers *Funny Games,* like the tableau in the theatrical melodrama, is the staging of a family drama. However, melodrama's association of stasis with affective transfixation to produce a stilled gesture at a heightened moment is effected in order to put on display the emotional intensity of characters. (As Paul Coates figures this hesitation, it is "a pause in pell-mell events, it reveals the form's essential stasis.")[83] This stasis is an essential (and formal) point of contact between cinematic melodrama and the unyielding duration of Freudian melancholia: as Coates writes, "The time of melodrama is *endless.*"[84] By contrast, instead of an expanded duration or endless time or arrested motion in forms *vivant,* the tableau at the heart of *Funny Games* involves a scene out of time that presents living pictures refigured as dead pictures, the pose made synonymous with the corpse.

While not an explicit citation to any one painterly representation, the tableau vivant at the center of Haneke's film suggests the light and formal arrangement of a Vermeer or a Rembrandt—though instead of something like Rembrandt's famous light from the left, Haneke's light emerges from the center of the image (in both senses, emerges from its *dead* center). As in the work of the Dutch painters, the image, otherwise dark, is organized around a central point of falling light that both provides materiality and is given its own materiality within the scene. The salient trait of the Dutch painters that is reproduced in Haneke's composition is the centrality of illumination as a feature within the scene. As in one critic's summation of Vermeer's *Girl with a Pearl Earring,* "We are in the presence of the real world of light, recording, as it seems, its own objective print."[85] The cinematic image here offers to the senses an objective print of "the real world of light," going so far as to show its inverse from the other side of representation in the exterior shot of the light-seeping house. The scene of grief sets the image in light, not only reflexively to call attention to the conditions of cinematic representation, but to put illumination itself on display in that bright piercing round, to bring light to presence in the service of the drama of presence and absence that is the nullity of the child.

Once the little boy is dead, light is literally turned on its side. The logics that enable representation are undone by the untimely violence, and grief is this formal fold. Haneke's tableau thus organizes itself as a study in the conditions of the possibility of representation under the formal pressure of grief. A parallel structure likens the body of the dead boy to the knocked-over lamp; they occupy similar positions in each of the frozen settings, each casting something out into the space of the image: a ray of light, rays of blood splatter. The image of the double traumas that occur in the space—the instance of the death of the son and the knocking of the lamp to the floor—are each occluded by the absent camera. Each ob-scenity (the one for matter, the other for representation) takes place off-screen, and the invisibility of the cause of each felling makes each event a figure for the other, makes them, as far as visual composition is concerned, *one and the same event.* Although the moment and happening of each (world) upending is hidden, in-visible, what is subsequently put on display are the visible effects and the effect on visibility. The profusion of white fabrics (the killers' clothes and gloves, the mother's slip, the theatrical curtains framing each window) suggests the ground of representation in a tactile way, as well, evoking at once the painterly canvas and the drapes around a theatrical proscenium, but also the whiteness of projection's light. When the lamp is knocked to the ground, it poses a problem for film form as much as for metaphysics: casting its beam sideways *in* space instead of *on* space, illumination shows itself instead of presencing objects and the world. In this scene of nonbeing, in place of seeing through light, one sees just light.

For all that this form evokes the painterly and the theatrical, its illumination of light's presence evokes the photographic above all. The pose is the photographizing of any display.[86] Barthes makes it central to photography's privileged relation to mediation: "what founds the nature of Photography is the pose" of that instant in which the body faced the camera in the real. Likewise, the play of light on figures adopting fixed postures evokes the attitude Craig Owens reads this way: "what do I do when I pose for a photograph? . . . I freeze, as if anticipating the still I am about to become; mimicking its opacity, its stillness; inscribing, across the surface of my body, photography's 'mortification' of the flesh."[87] A subject who freezes in anticipation of the photographic still to come is equally the subject of finitude grieving in advance of the stillness of being definitively to come. The mortification of the flesh in photography and in mortality, then, are brought together in the adoption of the composite, fraught, tortured pose by the mother and father forms in *Funny Games*. The pose arrests the body in its movement but also in its liveliness; the pose is thus both cause and effect of photographic inscription.[88] The picture does not bring forth the pose; the pose brings forth the picture. Indeed, "The representational force which the pose exerts is so great," Kaja Silverman argues, "that it radiates outwards, and transforms the space around the body and everything which comes into contact with it into an imaginary photograph."[89] Thus, the tableau inscribed within the film is transformed in its play of posture and stillness into the general image of a photographic image. The three aspects of the pose that Silverman identifies are in play in Haneke's tableau: the pose conjures into existence a frame; it generates mise-en-scène; and it "signifies 'lit-upness' in a larger, metaphoric respect, and encourages us to make formal and conceptual sense of the actual play of light and shadows across the other components of the imaginary photograph."[90] Illumination's capacity to make corporeality present *for representation* makes every pose "photographically resonant."

Those figures and their poses are of a very specific nature in the tableau in

Funny Games. Bent. Distended. Slunk in a slow low curve to the earth. If grief's affective force on form involves turning the origins of illumination and thus representation on its side—the literal knocking to the ground the source of light—its affective force on bodies likewise upends and weights down to dust the contour of fleshy materiality. *Gravare: to cause grief, hardship, suffering; to make heavy.* The effect of force as a pull into the stasis of the pose, this weighting on the corpus in bent tense limbs and joints, involves a formal orientation of posture toward the grave. The peculiar painfulness of grief is given its proper *gravity* in the cinematic tableau. This gravity should not be read as an expression of characterization or interiority; rather, the body is turned into a plastic form, made to exhibit the force of grief as a representational problem of line and curve for the arrangement of elements in the tableau. Grief is a matter not of interiority (for a feeling subject) but of exteriority (for a form that takes its measure).[91] The force of grief's gravity equally presses on and distorts the substance of the tableau form and the misshaping of the body's material lines. The tableau's studies in figures and pose, studies in bent posture, studies in weighted materiality assume an aesthetic and corporeal stance of being pulled on. Grief becomes a representational problem of moving figures across space in felt heavy time and the way bodies as lines are weighed down with loss's pain. Staging this movement in a tableau puts on display the materiality of film form weighted down, as well, struggling to breathe under the pressure of a breathless duration without a cut. The image labors to step forward, to re-find the smoothness of cinematic movement free from the heaviness of irreversible mortality.

Death in *Funny Games* is not compensated for with the classical cinematic options that tarry with loss: it is not substantively disavowed, it is not framed substitutively, and it does not produce supplementary doubles to stand in for the now-missing present. The absence is neither denied nor replaced; instead, the form of the film takes measure of the force of that absence, and the film form displays this configuration of everything in the world now being otherwise. For a death that cannot be mediated, for a grief that is untransformable in its peculiar felt heavy pain, the image becomes undialectical in the fixity of a tableau that is opposed to montage. In place of a relation with the grieved-for one (a relation predicated on reasserting the primacy of being), the film form figures itself in relation to light, which is to say that it takes up a non-relation to being by de-substantiating light in the presentation of the tableau. The refusal of editing is only one dimension of the undialectical; the deployment of the pose of the body *in relation to gravity* also presents the formal force of the affective sorrow. Grief, in other words, co-opts bodies for form, makes them materially vulnerable to the image of gravity's effects on flesh. The struggling of the upright forms of beings who can die alongside the proper verticality of the artificial set acutely stands for what it means to be a mortal body—to be weighted down to earth (as every body will be), as a form subject to the forces of *gravis,* as formal bodies that grieve in space more than in time, that grieve as a curved straining line and not as some feeling self.

By organizing the form of the scene around a point of the purest white light (Barthes's term is appropriate here: this is a punctum), the tableau in *Funny Games* centers itself on a paradox: a totality of presence in the literal composition of color in the light, and a totality of absence in the metaphorical composition of the voided hole in the image. Sign of simultaneous plenitude and finitude, the image centered by this circle of light both stages the condition of the possibility of the cinematic medium and, with its vacant center, stages precisely *nothing.* This scene folds on itself: just as the voided circle of light is at the center of the tableau, this ten-minute scene is at the temporal center of the structure of Haneke's film as a whole. The grounding of the image and the grounding of the film are each centered on a locus of strange stillness and a problem of voided presence. If the point of illumination at the center of the image is a hole in the image, a rend in the fabric of the screen, it also evokes the beam of cinematic projection and thus casts light outward *on* the scene within which it is inscribed. Light empties the image and simultaneously creates it, founds the image of which it is its finitude. Perhaps light now must be pluralized: there is *lumen,* cause of light, what gives or lends light to systems; there is *lux,* brightness itself.[92] Or, if not made multiple, perhaps light must accumulate, must draw supplementary dimensions to itself. Light, whether *lumen* or *lux,* is also *levis,* what is not heavy, what is opposed to *gravis* and to weight—nimble, in place of burdened; even trivial or without consequence, as opposed to what is of the greatest consequence, the very essence of the serious. It is what levitates, what lacks gravitational attraction, what synthesizes in dialectics (for the French, sublation is *la relève*). Grief's suffer, what is heavy, felt as a burden, weights one down to soil and gravel, my own, yours, his, is the opposite of all that lifts up; *levis* is what is by definition not *gravis.* This brilliance at the center of representation is the ground of the visual, but it constitutes this ground by absenting itself absolutely, illuminating itself only as matterless light. What is not heavy in the ether becomes burdened with worldly certainty. In *Funny Games,* all *levis* thus becomes *gravis.*

At the end of "Image et violence," Jean-Luc Nancy proposes two forms of violence: the groundless violence of art and the violence of blows that provides its own ground. The former is a "violence without violence [that] consists in the revelation's not taking place, its remaining imminent"; it is a revelation "that there is nothing to reveal." By contrast, "Violent and violating violence reveals and believes that it reveals absolutely."[93] The image marked by violence without violence knows that "there is nothing to reveal, not even an abyss, and that the groundless is not the chasm of a conflagration, but imminence infinitely suspended over itself."[94] The formal upending of representation that puts illumination and the form of grief on display at the center of *Funny Games* is a revelation of precisely this sort: a suspension of revelation in the static freeze of the posed figures in the tableau. The infinite hold of the ever-arriving imminence is the non-forthcoming of that which will have taken place; like the figure of death in Barthes that is definitive but untransformable, it is the ungraspable dimension of the certainty of futurity. In place of making recourse to any number of exteriorities—the space beyond the edges of the frame, suggesting escape and mobility; the recuperative time after which this grief will pass for the parents, and its worked-through catharsis; the intervention of the law and imposition of justice that classical film dictates must take place, and that remains purely imaginary in this text—Haneke's tableau folds the certainty of the terrible thing that has taken place on itself, absorbs the force of the affect into the ground of the image, bending time and light and body to the shape and weight of formal affectivity. What is suspended is both revelation within the mobility of the cinematic signifier and meta-critical revelation that might put this grief to work for meaning. This is what the undialectical image of grief brings forth: the heavy suspension of revelation in the frozen suspension of resolution.

The suspension of revelation puts the nothing into the scene but does not fill it in as the ground of meaning. In place of giving the void, or that central sphere of light, a substance, a signification, a link to totality, Haneke here lets the image play out its formal force without channeling that energy for the productive labor of *Trauerarbeit*. The mise-en-scène of the tableau with nothing at its center, then, becomes a mise-n'en-scène in which *the nothing* is put into the scene. Augustine's lament at the death of his friend requires only the additive revision of a grammatical article: it is not that in the wake of death grieving visuality finds empty absence in place of desired presence—in other words, finds nothing. It is, rather, that in the wake of death grieving sees all too well the non-presencing force of *the* nothing. The undialectical image— the image without transformation, reflection, sublation, or revelation—is not fixed, passive, or the merely unchanging. Rather, the undialectical is given its force, its power and affect *as* the duration of suspended form. Grief does not dialectically trans-form; it inheres in and distorts form. The image thus does not represent affective force but is illuminated by this force, and the image does not represent the form of grief for a spectator but is constituted as illumination by it.

Light has no matter, substance, or being and therefore, it was claimed, could reflect nothing. Laplanche's question was posed with neither answer nor resolution: how could light be illuminated? After Haneke, one answer can be proposed:—It is because light has nothing of its own (no peculiarity) that it can be made to reflect the nothing. Illumination of *lumen* is made possible by redirecting being away from substance and toward the affective intensity of visual and temporal form: light is illuminated only in the frozen suspension in the structure of a cinematic tableau. In *Funny Games,* the force of grief's heavy pain acts on line and light, on curve and composition, and not on psyche. This suffering does not work, does not resolve agony, but is suspended in a revelation without relevation, a revelation that will never take place.

Und ihr sagt mir, Freunde, dass nicht zu streiten sei über *Geschmack* und *Schmecken*? Aber alles Leben ist Streit um *Geschmack* und *Schmecken!*

Geschmack: das ist Gewicht zugleich und Wagschale und Wägender; und wehe allem Lebendigen, das ohne Streit um Gewicht und Wagschale und Wägende leben wollte!

And you tell me, friends, that there should be no disputing about taste and tasting? But all of life is a dispute over taste and tasting!

Taste: that is at the same time weight and scales and weigher; and woe to any living thing that would live without dispute about weight and scales and weighers!

—FRIEDRICH NIETZSCHE,
Thus Spoke Zarathustra

FIVE

Aesthetic Exclusions

and the Worse

than the Worst

The violence of a need to vomit—

> In the long run Bacon's Figures aren't wracked bodies at all, but ordinary bodies in ordinary situations of constraint and discomfort. A man ordered to sit still for hours on a narrow stool is bound to assume contorted postures. The violence of a hiccup, of a need to vomit, but also of a hysterical, involuntary smile. . . . Bacon's bodies, heads, Figures are of flesh, and what fascinates him are the invisible forces that model flesh or shake it.[1]

—is a formal violence.

In his account of the paintings of Francis Bacon and the "violence of sensation," Deleuze zeroes in on the energy of about-to-arrive sick; the distention of Figures; a deformed painterly material that organizes itself around forces acting on flesh and that manifests as visual rhythm; and the energetic autonomy and intensity of fields and flows of color—"regimes of color," he calls them.[2] Suddenly, in the midst of this reading, Deleuze asks a curious question: does Bacon's use of color suggest that his work is in "good taste"? He wonders, "Can taste be a potentially creative force and not simply an arbiter of fashion?"[3] Or, rather, are Bacon's monsters and crucifixions and suicide toilet bowls forever in *bad* taste? The answer Deleuze ventures to give splits the crucial difference.

The Figures are monstrous "from the viewpoint of a lingering figuration," but once they are considered "figurally," they reveal the forces molding them in formal broken tones, and are in good taste once more. "There is indeed a creative taste in color," Deleuze writes, "in the different regimes of color, which constitute a properly visual sense of touch, or a haptic sense of sight."[4]

What is remarkable about Deleuze's turn to the aesthetic question of being in good (or bad) taste is how quickly that philosophical metaphor is rewritten away from orality in favor of promising visuality. Representationally, the paintings are in poor taste; formally—and, specifically, chromatically—they are in good taste, but only if taste is taken as constituting a certain form of *haptic vision*. "Taste" as an aesthetic problematic relies for its metaphorical labor on the lowest bodily sense of tongue-tasting, but it is evoked here by Deleuze only to be converted immediately into the higher sense of touch and the highest metaphysical sense of sight. While it is common enough in the history of philosophy to disembody or allegorize taste, it is peculiar to see it here, given Deleuze's long-standing interest in apertures (oral and otherwise), screams, and vomit. One expects the great philosopher of things that wrack bodies, in other words, to linger with the mouth. But he does not. In this way, Deleuze's philosophical text itself remains on the side of *good* metaphorical-aesthetic taste, failing to stick with the dangerous figure of *bad* embodied-mouth taste, the sort of bad taste a Baconian Figure under the urge to vomit might well sense emerging at the back of the slightly curling tongue.

This chapter and the next continue this book's broader project of reading for a formal affectivity—for the forms of affects and for the way in which affects inhere in textual and visual forms—with the affect marked by its ambivalent relationship to both senses of taste: disgust. Like Deleuze's reading of Bacon's paintings, my argument centers on formal distentions and deformations that ultimately involve the autonomy and force of color. Unlike Deleuze, however, I do not convert taste to hapticity, or tasting to touching, or mouth to eyes, but let "taste" hover between aesthetic propriety and the tongue's work, bridging what is in "good taste" with what tastes good and noting how good aesthetic and literal taste also have an intimate relationship with all that tastes bad and is forever in bad taste. From transcendental aesthetics we move to transcendental gastronomy to see the way in which the negative of good taste (*dis-gust, de-goût*) organizes the field of haute cuisine as much as it does aesthetics. Then, in the subsequent chapter, a film by Peter Greenaway emerges as a text that collapses aesthetics, embodiment, and high gastronomy in its chromatic structure, producing neither a narrative of disgust nor isolatable images of the disgusting, and not provoking the affect from an embodied viewing subject but, instead, constituting a rotting and decaying film form. While in the previous two chapters the privileged form for the stasis of an untransformable painful grief was the frozen tableau, the form of disgust suggests wild movements, and the energetic liberating of qualities manifests its mutable structure and its formal potential. Disgust as I will argue for it is neither immediate nor visceral; ultimately, I will claim that one must read for disgust. For all that it is so often figured as the supreme instance of the negative or excluded or radically nullifying, disgust is in fact one way of speaking about the possible and the new.

PHILOSOPHY OF THE RETCH

A rush of air that chokes, a rush of choking air. Aristophanes's eructating hiccups constitute the most famous bodily discharge in the history of philosophy—at least until the rotting odors that leak from the low and so permeate the writings of Nietzsche.[5] Much has been written about Aristophanes's spasmodic glottal upset in Plato's *Symposium,* the intaking releases so violent that he is incapable of making his speech in the prescribed order of philosophical declamations, and those interpretations are much focused on giving an account in relation to the twin pillars of philosophical reflection: either the cause of the coughs or the effect of the involuntary breaths. The causes range from the indeterminate local one given in the dialogue ("whether he'd been overeating I don't know"; *plêsmonê* [being filled or excess satiety]) to the literary critical reading of the hiccups in relation to satire and irony, narrative deferral, or evocations of Dionysus, who appears through the remnants of gustatory intake in the now disturbed belly of the poet. Because of the hiccups' effect on the reversal of speech orders, criticism has focused on the interplay between Aristophanes and Eryximachus, the doctor whose name literally means "belch-curer" and who takes the gasper's turn while prescribing a cure for the noisy embodied revolt. Due to the disruption, Eryximachus's materialist account of love comes after Pausanias's meditation on shameful versus beautiful Eros, and the gulping poet is displaced to a later spot, now centering the dialogue as the fourth speaker in a group of seven. Over and punctuating the scientific precision of Eryximachus's discussion of Love as a binding and harmonizing force is the absurd spectacle of the facticity of the utterly unbound body: "Aristophanes is holding his breath (sputtering, no doubt, and belching), hiccoughing, gargling, and finally sneezing, generally disrupting the harmony (or 'attunement') of the discussion."[6] Critics inclined to put the hiccups to work for interpretive guidance argue that Pausanias and Eryximachus make a fitting pair of speeches (both focus on good and bad forms of love, a topic that disappears in Aristophanes's speech) and note the pleasant formal irony that "bodily disorders establish the harmonious structure of the speeches of the *Symposium*."[7]

Tellingly, Aristophanes begins his speech by noting that he will begin in a different manner from that of the previous speakers; speaking otherwise philosophically repeats a speaking otherwise of his bodily hesitations, and it is difficult to read Aristophanes's meditation on "*anthropinen physin kai ta pathemata autes*" (human nature and its sufferings), by far the most famous of the accounts given in the dialogue, without recalling the bodily difficulties that delayed this very speech. The emphasis on the original wounding of every being (the navel a reminder of the suffering of being split in two) and the conclusion of his reading of Eros as producing a divided, non-whole self, yearning for completion but failing ("their souls are longing for a something else—a something . . . which they can only give an inkling of in cryptic sayings and prophetic riddles"), lures the critic to read the little coughs' revolts of being in relation to a failed, incomplete, ridiculous material body, the sort of body that fails to keep itself alive without noisily spluttering, leaking, and breaking apart at tenuous seams.[8]

Implicit in all of these accounts is the insistence that Aristophanes's hiccups must *mean* something, and the drive to make them meaningful continues into the twentieth century. Alexandre Kojève reportedly said to his student Jacques Lacan, "You will certainly not be able to interpret *Symposium* if you don't know why Aristophanes has hiccups," a why that Kojève ultimately leaves unspoken.[9] Mladen Dolar's reformulation of Kojève's injunction is the formula "*it means that it means.*" Dolar continues, "This involuntary voice rising from the body's entrails can be read as Plato's version of mana: the condensation of a senseless sound and the elusive highest meaning, something which can ultimately decide the sense of the whole. This pre-cultural, non-cultural voice can be seen as the zero-point of signification, the incident of meaning, itself not meaning anything, the point around which other—meaningful—voices can be ordered, as if the hiccups stood at the very focus of the structure."[10] In Dolar's account, the hiccups function as the nodal point around which signification is organized, as the strangling involuntary gasp at the center of every kind of speech. Occluded in the rush to determine the signification of the hiccups, however, is the episode as such—the expanded duration of what Aristophanes himself calls "an appalling union of noise and irritation."[11] All of these critical approaches make discursive what is, let us admit, a very raucous and irritating, very wet and juicy, very gross and sloppy scene—not least because the Greek for "hiccup," *lugx* (*luzo* [to have the hiccup]) can also mean "belching," even "retching."[12] Written over in interpretations of the philosophical *lunga* is not just the grating gasping sound or image of the body in ridiculous and distended red-faced breath-holding, but the clenching hesitation of a torso's unfulfilled pre-vomits; the faint odor of every hiccup and burp that brings forth airs from the gut; the wet nose-tickled sneezes, each exhalation threatening a bead of viscous snot or hailing drizzle of spit onto the famous banquet table of the philosophers.

Like Deleuze's conversion of taste to touch and sight, the taste, smell, and sound of these retches are converted to images of the body in disarray or the highest faculty of intellection as metaphor for philosophical distaste. Even in a critical account that finally mentions disgust, it is immediately put to the service of the higher faculties: Drew Hyland argues that the hiccups are a symbol of the comic poet's "disgust at the import of Pausanias' speech."[13] Although acknowledging the hiccups as a noisy, smelly bodily revolt, the disgusting dimension of the eruptions is converted into *critical* distaste and the capacity for judgments of conceptual distinctions. The history of philosophy and philosophical criticism generally has assumed that Aristophanes's hiccups and sneezes were dry, polite affairs that could be reduced to their ordinal, satirical, historical, or literary import. But while the philosophers may have decided to avoid excess food and drink for the sake of philosophical reflection, the gustatory returns in the odorous afterglow of digestion's excessive effects on the bloated corpus.[14] The cleaning up of Aristophanes's hiccups—the putting of them to work for meaning and the attendant neutralizing of their odor—is part of a much broader philosophical forgetting of the materiality of the body and simultaneous forgetting (or disembodying or making metaphorical) of disgust and the disgusting. (It thereby also recalls the anesthetizing of grief's "peculiar painfulness" and the putting of mourning to work for meaning's recuperative dialectics.) Even the resistance to the notion that the hiccups must mean something—as in Dolar's insistence that they possess no content or secret signification—nevertheless continues to account for the hiccups in relation to their discursive labor: as the hole in the Real around which signification is organized. Even in Dolar's account, the hiccups remain more voice than entrail.

That the cluster of terms "hiccup," "sound," "smell," "body," and "disgust" are passed over in the dialogue and subsequent criticism is no surprise, given the long-standing hierarchy of the senses in Western philosophy, a ranking structure that elevates the critical faculties above the material corpus, and that privileges senses associated with judging, reasoning, perceiving faculties (sight, sound, and occasionally touch) over those aligned with reproduction, death, decay, survival, and the bestial (smell, taste, and occasionally touch). The creation myth of Plato's *Timaeus,* to invoke one canonical example, famously breaks the body apart at its seams to segment it into zones of propriety. Like a Baconian Figure maximally destroyed for spectacular effect, the body is split to divide interior soul from exterior mortal body, and drawn and quartered to delimit interior boundaries, policing guards, and the physical apparatus of a labyrinthine prison:

> Wherefore, fearing to pollute the divine any more than was absolutely unavoidable . . . they divided the cavity of the thorax into two parts, as the women's and men's apartments are divided in houses, and placed the midriff to be a wall of partition between them. . . . The part of the soul which desires meats and drinks . . . they placed between the midriff and the boundary of the navel, contriving in all this region a sort of manger for the food of the body, and there they bound it down like a wild animal which was chained up with man, and must be nourished if man was to exist. They appointed this lower creation his place here in order that he . . . have his dwelling as far as might be from the council chamber, making as little noise and disturbance as possible.[15]

Aristophanes's hiccups are surely the great reminder of the violability of this divine plan, for it is the rebellion of this place of lower creation that makes as much noisy disturbance as possible at the classical table, not only punctuating but reordering philosophy's critical line. Instead of a myth of the body's smooth, hard perfection, such as classical Greek sculpture posits, in this account the body's sloppy, slippery form takes a series of defensive blockages and inefficient passageways, an Upstairs–Downstairs lure for transgression, for, as with the partition separating women's and men's apartments evoked in the passage, there have always been ways to get around those partitions, and it is just a matter of time before the midriff has to get some sleep.

This partitioning of the upright body may be especially detailed in Plato, but in the twentieth century Freud offered a creation myth of his own, following a well-worn, handed-down map. In a set of two stunning footnotes in *Civilization and Its Discontents*—one of which appears to refer to, albeit without naming him, Aristophanes's theory of the hermaphroditic beings from his creation myth in *Symposium*—Freud famously posits that civilization has consisted of a slow, long diminishing of the olfactory sense due to the reoriented spatial hierarchy of the upright body.[16] From this upright assumption, anal eroticism is repudiated and repressed, and sexual excitation is delinked from the periodicity of menstruation and redirected into "visual excitations, which, in contrast to the intermittent olfactory stimuli, were able to maintain a permanent effect."[17] The compositional body of Freud's text and the upright body in Freud's text depend on the inheritance of the twin tendencies of philosophical thought: a hierarchy of senses that repudiates smell and taste and a hierarchy of the body that opposes the lower (itself aligned with those senses) and the higher faculties. The body's placement remains remarkably consistent in thought in the West: the forgotten corners of the chassis—the corporeal Third World, its subaltern subjects—are not only divided from reason but opposed to it. Bits are partitioned off: an orifice stopped, a region fenced. The blueprint of flesh and frame is forced to name and etch what stays in and what must stay out.

What stays in, time and again—even in philosophers of immanence such as Deleuze—are the aspects of the body that are least embodied, the least sensual senses, the faculties of reason and judgment most tightly linked to explorations of the exterior world and acquisition of knowledge. This ordering and valuation appears in the oft-quoted opening lines of Aristotle's *Metaphysics,* which link sight and the desire to know, and repeats itself in Hegel's identification of sight and hearing as the "theoretical senses."[18] As goes the lower belly, so go the senses linked to the appetitive and the excessive: Freud is not the only thinker to place smell and vision in a zero-sum sense game whereby the diminishment of one is compensated for by the enhancement of the other. Aesthetics and Idealism historically colluded in a suspicion of taste and smell and derision toward the physicality of the body. Unlike the category-making, truth-approaching sense of vision, smell and taste are dismissed as senses that cannot discriminate or produce knowledge about the world. Thus, Étienne Bonnot de Condillac's thought experiment of 1754, in which he imagines endowing a statue with a progression of senses, begins with smell, "because of all the senses it is the one which appears to contribute least to the knowledge of the human mind."[19] The broader Western hierarchizing of the senses suggests that odor, and not blindness, is vision's true other. This is why it is so shocking when, in 1971, Roland Barthes describes vertiginous speech as "subject to remanence, it *smells*."[20]

To the extent that philosophy is a body of work comprised of its sensual metaphors, the dearth of philosophical appeals to knowledge that invoke smell or taste—and, correspondingly, the interior, lower, and appetitive dimensions of the body—is both a cause and a symptom of a philosophical failure to theorize a relationship between knowledge and those senses.[21] In the eighteenth-century aesthetic theory of Moses Mendelssohn, taste, smell, and touch constitute what he dubs "the darkest of all the senses."[22] Vision is ranked at the top of the hierarchy of the senses because of its requirement of distance between the perceiving body and the object of perception; by contrast, as Carolyn Korsmeyer notes, "The proximal senses keep the percipient in a state of awareness of his or her own flesh."[23] A dangerous intimacy between object and body figures even more in the case of taste than in that of smell, for it requires the ingestion or consumption of its object of sense, a blurring of the object with the flesh, even a disintegrating equivalence in the case of taken-in food that, as Jean Anthelme Brillat-Savarin's famous maxim reminds us, literally becomes us—indeed, tells others what we *are*.

As part of the broader critique of metaphysics in the nineteenth and twentieth centuries, there emerged a veritable explosion of work attending to writing the body, its orifices and sticky leechings, back into the body of philosophy. Most famous among these critiques was Nietzsche's corporeal turn, but caught in the net of that arc, if well before it, was Spinoza's sweeping wonderment at all that we do not yet know about what a body can do, repeated in Nietzsche's insistence that "the body is a more astonishing idea than the old 'soul.'"[24] One could also point to the thinking of the body in phenomenology and existentialism; the entirety of the Freudian revolution and the theory of the drives; and much French thought of the twentieth century, including offshoots of surrealism, Lacanian psychoanalysis, and Foucault's historicizing of the disciplining of a mutable body-in-process. "The body" as a category is redefined in this gesture: Nietzsche insistently refers to "bodies" in place of "the body," itself a metaphysical concept, as the excluded other of metaphysics. As opposed to figuring the body as a substance with an essence, as in classical ontology, the move to an immanent philosophy in Spinoza and Nietzsche (and its resurgence in the twentieth-century philosophy of Deleuze) refigures the body as a singularity comprised of force, or as an assemblage of multiple forces. In turn, feminist philosophers participated in a parallel rethinking, including as targets for their criticism the very same participants in the corporealizing of philosophy named earlier. Luce Irigaray insisted that Freud repeated philosophy's privileging of vision over touch; more recently, Kelly Oliver and

Elizabeth Grosz have argued that Nietzsche's corporeal sweep casts aside the feminine body, or opens up philosophy to the otherness of the body so long as that body is a masculine one.[25] Like the needling of gray lard through a slab of lean, the corpus was slowly reintroduced, thickly woven back into and through continental philosophy and theory.

As with a sticky something else stuck to that fatback, simultaneously reinserted into philosophy was a reevaluation of disgust. The affect's eighteenth-century status as a definitionally excluded category of rejection, ejection, repulsion, and refusal is refigured in the nineteenth century and twentieth century as a category to which one must adhere, brought back to the philosophical fold along with its causal agents of rotting odors, viscous substances, and dark, damp regions of the body. While Nietzsche demanded that one engage with, and not merely refuse or reject, the bad smells that signaled a disgust with the world as constituted—what Derrida refers to as the admonition of the "value of learning to vomit" in Nietzsche—Sartre located in nausea both a productive metaphor and disposition toward being, an apprehension of the "disgust of existing."[26] Georges Bataille subsequently moved toward the logical consequence of this revaluation of values in the form of the eroto-ethical imperative: "nothing is more important for us than that we recognize that we are bound and sworn to . . . that which provokes our most intense disgust."[27] The supreme instance of this anti-aesthetic move is Bataille's turn toward the notion of *informe,* the term "serving to degrade things in the world" that command form, substance, propriety, and order.[28] Bataille's theorization of the seductions of the revolting, however, did not radically reposition the affect that remained the excluded, rejected, viscerally refused other—indeed, it was because of its retention of the fixity of those senses that its adherence by Bataille constitutes something novel. The inversion of values in any metaphysical hierarchy does not shake that hierarchy; it is precisely because disgust remains the excluded other that it can be sworn fidelity to by Bataille as counter-aesthetic praxis. It is merely that this anti-aesthetic commits to that refusal in place of the tautology of refusing that refusal. Disgust remains markedly unchanged in this account. Like the threatening stick of a leech, the affect stubbornly adheres to its status as the rejected other.[29]

AESTHETICS' TASTES

Until the eighteenth century, disgust was largely shunted to the dark margins of philosophical valuation. When it finally exploded onto the philosophical scene in the 1750s, it was given philosophical substance in the field of aesthetics through its geographic and architectural dis-placement: as the definitionally, structurally, necessarily excluded. Indeed, Winfried Menninghaus describes the sensation as something more than a powerfully felt refusal, but as "an inability *not* to say no," a grammatical pile-up of undoings appropriate for the affect of abyssal negation.[30] Menninghaus produces one of the most nuanced treatments of revulsion in his genealogy of the terms and concepts of disgust, *degoût, Ekel*—each of which came into philosophical usage only in the past two hundred and fifty years. (Before then, they were assimilated to treatises on humiliation, shame, honor, and theology.)[31] His history of this "strong sensation" centers on an epistemic break in the eighteenth century, a moment in which disgust became "worthy of consideration for the sake of its own (anti)aesthetic and moral qualities."[32] Although Foucault's name does not appear in Menninghaus's text, it is worth noting that the century in which Menninghaus locates an independent discourse of disgust is the same one in which Foucault finds the rise of myriad techniques for organizing and disciplining the body. The disciplining of the body through techniques of power is thus linked to the "disciplining" of aesthetics in the eighteenth century—as an ordering or structuring, as of a body, but also as the making, as in forming, of a discipline as a category of distinct philosophical speculation. To this day, disgust continues to act on disciplines with extraordinary force: Stephen Greenblatt argues that "loathing and disgust" played a key role in the development of the human sciences, linking ethnography to both the experience and the overcoming of disgust, a disciplinary project that reflects and alleviates revulsion.[33] In the counternarrative to *philosophia*'s love of knowledge, it may be that the ordering of knowledge in the academy is structured far more by disgust's boundary-setting and line-drawing. Perhaps, in fact, there is no disciplinarity without disgust.

The "disgust debates" of the 1750s, which produced the separate field of inquiry called "aesthetics," were concerned primarily with the conditions of possibility for aesthetic judgment and the radical exclusion or omission at the center of that system that constituted those possibilities. The inverse of the interest in moral and aesthetic "taste," or *goût,* dis-gust functioned less as a category than as a kind of pock, an excerpted node around which the field of study was organized by figures such as Schlegel, Mendelssohn, Lessing, Herder, and Kant. The founding of modern aesthetics in the eighteenth century, Menninghaus argues, "can be described negatively as a foundation based on [the] prohibition of what is disgusting. The 'aesthetic' is the field of a particular 'pleasure' whose absolute other is disgust."[34] As though rising out of the sticky muck of the aesthetic's pleasures, *Ekel* is first linked to an overindulgence, an excessive sweetness that past a certain point becomes nauseating. The risk of overdosing on surfeit beauty can lead to the sensation of unpleasure, an exhaustion of the senses in what ultimately refuses distance or contemplation—(hence, the subtitle of a section in Menninghaus's genealogical critique of the negative affect: "the beautiful as vomitive").[35] These risks of excess enjoyment are mitigated in the eighteenth-century "rules for avoiding satiation, developed for the pleasures of eating as well as of social and sexual intercourse," extended into aesthetic laws that moderate pleasure through the notion of an unlimited or infinite reflection.[36] The avoidance of satiation through non-finite enjoyment, and the free play of the imagination, holds at bay the aesthetic lure of gorging until one chokes or the finite dimensions of the body's container become overrun. As though disciplining a body through dietary ascesis, aesthetic pleasure as articulated by Lessing and Kant required what Menninghaus summarizes as "an economy of reserve: the retention of open possibilities for intensification."[37] While the radical alterity in the experience of disgust will be conceived of in the twentieth century principally in terms of threats to a feeling subject, it began its theoretical life as a threat to the field of the aesthetic as such that, in its threatening dimension, as the aesthetic's ultimate limit, simultaneously constituted that field. Disgust haunts aesthetics; it not only must be disciplined, but it gives shape to the nascent philosophical discipline. If aesthetics could be spatially reimagined as folding into itself a prohibited excluded threat from without, such a bend might visually evoke an esophageal tube running through the interior of the subdiscipline's torso.

The aesthetic formulation of disgust's law of exclusion, its affective peculiarity, was first articulated by Schlegel: "disgust alone is excluded from those unpleasant sensations whose nature can be altered through imitation."[38] However, its strongest formulation appears in Kant's Third Critique. *Ekel* surfaces in *The Critique of Judgment* in a discussion of the mimetic and the beautiful:

> The furies, diseases, devastations of war . . . can, as harmful things, be very beautifully described, indeed even represented in painting; only one kind of ugliness cannot be represented in a way adequate to nature without destroying all aesthetic satisfaction, hence beauty in art, namely, that which arouses loathing [*Ekel*]. For since in this strange sensation, resting on sheer imagination, the object is represented as if it were imposing the enjoyment which we are nevertheless forcibly resisting, the artistic representation of

the object is no longer distinguished in our sensation itself from the nature of the object itself, and it then becomes impossible for the former to be taken as beautiful.[39]

Ekel is the particular form of nauseating ugliness that functions as the limit for the possibilities of the aesthetic. For Kant, as for much aesthetic theory of the time, disgust figures as an unintegratable aspect of the aesthetic that the aesthetic cannot speak.

Or, digest—as goes Derrida's formulation in "Economimesis," his analysis of the negatively-privileged role of disgust in Kant's aesthetic philosophy. In that essay, Derrida's deconstructive laser is focused on several terms in Kant's logic, in particular the seeming opposition between pleasure and enjoyment, and the titular relation between *mimesis* and *oikonomia,* art and salary. It is to the role of disgust in Kant's aesthetic, but also logocentric, philosophy that Derrida eventually turns—and "turn" (*strephein*) is appropriate here, as disgust is framed as a catastrophe for the philosophy of the beautiful. The mouth as a key but ambiguous term in Kantian philosophy becomes the central site for a struggle over the opposing terms in this reading. As Derrida writes of Kant's oral examples and metaphors, there is "a certain allergy in the mouth, between pure taste and actual tasting [*dégustation*]."[40] Disgust poses the problem of relating the two forms of taste (aesthetic) and taste (tasting) to each other, a relation that will be figured as an irreducible opposition. As the question of orality comes to the fore, Derrida insists on the double sense in which the mouth is taken (and given) in Kant: this mouth no longer "merely occupies one place among others. It can no longer be situated *in* a typology of the body but seeks to organize the sites and to localize all the organs."[41] Place of consumption (sensual: taste) and production (textual: *logos*), the mouth becomes a double fold. Derrida finally distinguishes in Kant between "two means of entering and two means of leaving the mouth, where one would be expressive and emissive (of the poem in the best case), the other vomitive or emetic."[42]

The mouth of Kantian interiorization "assimilates everything to itself by idealizing it within interiority, masters everything by mourning its passing, refusing to touch it, to digest it naturally, but digests it ideally, . . . produces disinterestedness in the possibility of pronouncing judgments . . . governs a space of analogy into which it does not let itself be drawn."[43] *Ekel* functions as the border, limit, and frame of what is "excluded from it and what, proceeding from this exclusion, gives it form, limit, and contour." The gesture of exclusion that Derrida locates is not one that can be reduced to any opposition to ingestion, for it is not a *relation* of opposition that is in play but, rather, another figuration altogether of the negative, the excluded, the limit. Kant's logo-phonocentrism excludes "what does not allow itself to be digested, or represented, or stated. . . . It is an irreducible heterogeneity which cannot be eaten either sensibly or ideally and which—this is the tautology—by never letting itself be swallowed must therefore *cause itself to be vomited*."[44] Vomit is not one excluded figure among many, but is the privileged and organizing, sustaining, essential figure. Its specific "parergonal overflow," argues Derrida, "lends its form to this whole system."[45] Derrida's description of this overflow extends to vomit his theorization in *The Truth in Painting* of Kant's use of the term *parergon*. There, Derrida argues that Kant's term "inscribes something which comes as an extra, exterior to the proper field . . . but whose transcendent exteriority comes to play, abut onto, brush against, rub, press against the limit itself and intervene in the inside only to the extent that the inside is lacking. It is lacking *in* something and it is lacking *from itself*."[46] One crucial aspect of this figure of the supplement is the gestural sketch by which exteriority comes to take on a relation to a lack of the inside. That is, the overflow of vomit is not an excess of its inherent or essential meaning but, rather, a structural supplementarity in the relation of vomit to that "transcendent exteriority" by which disgust is not the opposite of the aesthetic but that which can never stand inside it (it cannot be swallowed) and thus never ceases to be expelled from it (it can only *cause itself to be vomited*). It is not sick's content that is at stake but its supplementary form.

Two things are seemingly excluded from the transcendental aesthetic—the shattering, negative pleasures of the sublime and the figuration of the ugly in the Fine Arts—but, in fact, neither stands outside Kant's system. "Although repulsive on one of its faces," Derrida writes, "the sublime is not the absolute other of the beautiful. It still provokes a certain pleasure."[47] The negativity of the sublime—and that of the ugly, evil, or horrible—is affectively and aesthetically recuperable. The non-recuperable excluded is a singular unassimilable thing, and it therefore forms "the transcendental of the transcendental, the non-transcendentalisable, the non-idealisable, and that is the *disgusting*."[48] Disgust figures as what Derrida calls "*l'exclu absolu*." As the absolute other of the aesthetic, this affect in its privileged figure of the retch poses a problem for Kant's theory of representation: "vomit is represented in advance as forcing pleasure, and that is why it disgusts."[49] The disgusting or revolting is too much of the object that it purports to represent. Recall Kant's language: "the object is represented *as if it were imposing the enjoyment which we are nevertheless forcibly resisting.*" In other words, disgust is the expression of an ugliness that fails to represent, that cannot therefore be reinscribed into an aesthetic or—in a different sense of its failure to represent—political economy; it is a representation that, in Derrida's words, "annuls itself," that fails in relation to the representable, that "forces one to consume, but without allowing any chance for idealization."[50] Disgust just comes too close—it forces itself down your throat and yet cannot be digested, only expelled forever, utterly—hence, "the disgusting can only be vomited."[51] Derrida likens the affect to *jouissance,* a shattering pleasure that confers too much satisfaction unto an equal measure of erosion and entropy. This is the particular perversion of disgust: in giving far too much enjoyment, it eats the conditions for the possibility of pleasure—in other words, and in a formulation horrible for a Kant if acceptable to a Nietzsche, disgust "makes one desire to vomit."[52]

WHAT IS WORSE THAN THE WORST

And worse I may be yet: The worst is not
So long as we can say, "This is the worst."
—*King Lear,* act 4, scene 1

Derrida concludes "Economimesis" with the provocative assertion that the logocentric system can accommodate, consume, and represent everything except vomit. While it might thus seem that vomit as the metonymy of the bad-tasting is the outer boundary, limit, or radical negative of that system, this is not the case. Rather, what stands at the edge of the aesthetic is a single thing further. Citing Kant's claim about the senses, which conforms to the familiar philosophical hierarchy, that smell and taste "are both more subjective than objective" and fail to lead to direct cognition without interventionary media (salts, liquid, air), Derrida notes that, even so, smell suffers a harsher treatment from Kant than taste proper. The eighteenth-century philosopher sniffs, "Smell is, so to speak, taste at a distance, and other people are forced to share in the pleasure [*mit zu geniessen*] whether they want to or not. Hence, by interfering with individual reason, smell is less sociable than taste. . . . Internal penetration (into the lungs) through smell is even more intimate than through the absorptive vessels of mouth or gullet."[53] What is literally disgusting remains on the side of taste, but smell's unsociability, its imposition and forced pleasure (or unpleasure), makes it something even worse. This leads to a paradox whereby something exceeds the hyperbolic negativity of disgust. "There is worse than the literally disgusting," Derrida insists, "and if there is worse, it is because the literally disgusting is maintained, as security, in place of the worse."[54] Because disgust falls outside of any economy, its debt cannot be secured: the absolute excluded designates not a limit or the reaching of a transgression, but the place without placement—the place that cannot take place. This non-place is not an issue of taste (aesthetic or sensual); it is an opening up of the possibility for "something more disgusting than the disgusting, than what disgusts taste. The chemistry of smell exceeds the tautology taste/disgust." What is unnamable in logocentrism (what cannot pass through the mouth) and "which in turn can only vomit it and vomit itself in it" is that which is completely unassimilable to speech. Speaking the word "vomit," Derrida writes, "arrests the vicariousness of disgust; it puts the thing in the mouth," establishing it as the other of taste and, in turn, halting the risk of disgust, which is the ever about-to-arrive unassimilable that cannot be spoken.[55] What disgust names, and the structure that overrides individual instantiations of the disgusting (vomit, the corpse), is what Derrida calls the "something more disgusting than the disgusting," that which is worse than a disgusting that remains on the side of words that misshape the mouth. The form of this affect is thus a structure organized around a process of exclusion and not a content that fills it in or gives it definition, shape, coherence, substance. Disgust names the opening up of something that is *worse than the worst*.

Remaining with the "literally disgusting" (instead of what is *worse* than it; in other words, remaining with what disgusts taste in order to avoid having to think what is *more* disgusting on the level of unsociable smell) has led to a critical tendency to focus on the concrete objects that provoke disgust. It is the lure of disgust to give it content, either substantives to its law or rules for determining that membership. Like Derrida's argument that saying the word "vomit" halts disgust and puts the comfort of a speakable word in the mouth in place of an oral apparatus contorted with unspeakable retching, the rabid critical gesture of taxonomizing, category-making, boundary-drawing and -violating, and determining what is inside and what is outside propriety involves neutralizing the risk of disgust by privileging the object over the affect. The literature on disgust thus normatively begins, as though commanded by its own formal stylistic law, with a detailed lengthy list of objects of the affect's intention: *Imagine a pool of sweetish vomit with a single buzzing fly; tasting the trickle of pus leaking from a rotting sore; the smell that overwhelms the room in which the rotting corp—*. But to the extent that this sort of rabid definition-giving (in the sense of coming into focus or line-drawing) is precisely what disgust conceptually compels, theory should resist the urge to align so squarely with the affect's insistence of an iconography of its own.

If one falls for this lure, disgust becomes but a set of itemized disgusting things. Every critic has his or her own privileged ones. Menninghaus offers the strongest form of disgust specificity in a singular figure, writing that the "decaying corpse is therefore not only one among many other foul smelling and disfigured objects of disgust. Rather, it is *the* emblem of the menace that, in the case of disgust, meets with such a decisive defense, as measured by its extremely potent register on the scale of unpleasant affects. Every book about disgust is not least a book about the rotting corpse."[56] Where Menninghaus places the corpse, however, others will insistently place vomit; others, blood (especially menstrual); others, shit. In turn, each of these claims for the pure, true, singular icon of disgust invokes related senses (touch in one case; smell or taste in another) as the privileged ones for the affect, again falling for disgust's hungry demand for rules of inclusion and exclusion.[57] Even in the structuralist argument for disgust's highly constructed nature (the antipode to the Darwinian argument for innate food rejection), epitomized in Mary Douglas's claim that "there is no such thing as dirt," the impure is nevertheless described, albeit contingently, as the shunned objects that it takes in specific historical and cultural contexts.[58]

Concretizing disgust into particular singular things, images, or icons, however, involves what Derrida describes as making a down payment on something before true disgust, paying out a security in place of disgust as such. It involves identifying (disgusting) objects instead of regarding the form (of disgust as such). The notion of Derrida's "worse than the literally disgusting"— what I call *the worse than the worst*—is a grammatical paradox, the suggestion that the superlative is surpassable, a logical impossibility. But the force from that continual generative opening into a space that language does not allow, that regurgitation without pause, involves the continual negotiation with irrecuperable negation that is the animated structure of disgust. Disgust is a beyond of any singular or objectal thing. It is the promise of worsening, this possibility of something more disgusting than the disgusting. Giving disgust its contents, then, filling in its gut with objectal specificities, avows that the excluded can be known, perceived, bounded, and therefore limited. Each time criticism reduces disgust to a list of things, it is claiming that the worst has been reached, identified, and corralled and that no worse will come into play. Naming the objects of disgust each time puts the cleanliness of the word into the mouth and thus annihilates the other oral activities the affect might compel.[59] Paradoxically, this theoretical move to identify and give form to the excluded is an attempt to move the exterior of thought to the interior of theory (or a theory, of disgust). But to give the excluded substance—to point, as if with a stark deictic arrow and insist, "This is this" or "This is it"—is to avoid having to think disgust by only ever thinking the disgusting.

The form of disgust is the form of the excluded as such—from classical aesthetics' prohibition to Kant via Derrida's "worse than the worst"; Bataille's *informe* and Kristeva's abjection; what Sartre calls "Antivalue" in his analysis of slime, and what Douglas describes as differential dirt. Menninghaus's account of disgust's labor as the anti-aesthetic and the "torment" of the aesthetic is that it is "a *shifter* taking on other values without a pause—and yet, or just for that reason, remaining oddly nonexistent."[60] Disgust is a spatial operator, delimiting zones of proximity that are discomforting versus acceptable, drawing lines in the thick muck. It is the forsaken outside that is nevertheless immediate and too close, a threatening proximity from which one recoils, but never with sufficient spacing, an exteriority without distance. If grief in the previous chapters was a problematic, first, of ontology—being's horrible proximity to nonbeing and the unbridgeable difference between one and the other—disgust is a problematic of geography, or geo-ontology. The map it draws puts objects, qualities, and people in their proper place. Destructive and generative, revolting and alluring, disgust is the inscribing agent of the map and the violence that commands one's adherence to its plan.

The history of disgust, therefore, is not limited to the history of its sensual inscriptions, but is also the story of its spatial metaphors. The mapping of disgust involves two distinctly different models: a three-dimensional plot of relative positions in space in disgust's affinity to notions of nearness or its threat of proximity (linked to what Menninghaus calls its "hyperreality" and to the aesthetician's argument that it fails to leave adequate room for contemplative distance and reflection) *and* a series of points on a line, beyond which one must not pass, the model of disgust whereby it derives from excess. These two spatial models are contradictory—or, rather, they cannot be mapped on the same set of axes, for the one involves a coming-too-close, while the other involves a going-too-far: figured onto a singular site, the pull-me-push-you tension might rip a body apart. The spatio-temporal paradoxes of disgust are fitting for a notion that is less substance than structure: the zero point around which disciplines and subjects are organized; an absent center in relation to which forces bend, contract, and mobilize, like a black hole singularity that refuses reflection, measurable only by the intensity of its displacements.

This dark structure (so evocative of the "darkest of all the senses" Mendelssohn assigns to taste and smell), while highly absorptive and foreclosing reflection or distance, is also remarkably fecund and active: a generation of lines, boundaries, and demarcations (of inclusion and exclusion, but also anti-territorial ones of non-mapping forces). Disgust's movements make it a structure in progress, a system of becoming more than being. This is why it is so wrongheaded to limit discussions of disgust to privileged objects instead of thinking its general form. Those theories that fix disgust in space and time lose not only the movements of disgust as a generative structure, but, in their binding of things to affect, also attempt to co-opt the certainty of positions in space at the expense of losing disgust's speed, velocity, and nauseous rush. Indeed, disgust's emesis compels a reversal of metaphorical energies: less the black hole vacuum of meaning that its zero-point function as the excluded of philosophy might suggest, disgust is far more like the hypothetical white hole, an emissive, productive horizon ejecting matter in place of absorbing it.

Despite its aperient labors and generative forces, disgust has continued to be treated as a zero point or structure of absolute exclusion—it has been taken for the vacuum of the black hole, absorbing anything that can be put into it, the irretrievably archival from which nothing returns. Disgust in these "not that" accounts is available to suck in members of attribution continuously, to take potentially any object into its maw, from which there is no escape. In this model, disgust is a floating signifier of rejection, not-ness, exclusion, into which anything can be placed to disappear into the ravenous hunger of cultural prohibition. But in the white-hole model for which I am arguing, in place of a structure that can only suck things in, disgust continuously spits things out. One might say that disgust continually vomits that which it never took in. What is beyond the horizon of the worse than the worst is not the absolute absorbance of a hungry black hole but energetic ejections. If the black hole's pathos is that it is that from which nothing can escape, the white hole ethos is that it is that which is impossible to reach. Because there is always a horizon beyond which the worse than the worst may be put into play, opening up yet another affective deferral, it is not the case that disgust is distinct, immediate, and viscerally overpresent but that disgust as such is impossible. The worst can be exceeded by the ever worse; it is therefore never fully arrived. Certainly, and ineluctably, disgust advises us that the worst is always yet to come.

Freud cannily opens "Das Unheimliche" (1919) with a disciplinary rejoinder (and justification for psychoanalytic investigation), positing that philosophy has historically excluded disgust as part of a broader refusal to grapple with all manner of negative affects. He writes of the uncanny that "as good as nothing is to be found upon this subject in comprehensive treatises on aesthetics, which in general prefer to concern themselves with what is beautiful, attractive and sublime—that is, with feelings of a positive nature—and with the circumstances and the objects that call them forth, rather than with the opposite feelings of repulsion and distress."[61] One could update this claim perfectly for the field of film studies, which historically has been so bound to the assumption of positive feelings—either the commercial imperative of classical cinema's mass appeal or the cinephiliac pleasures in the avant-garde's innovations—that repulsion and distress, anxiety and disgust, terror and horror have been treated only rarely, only recently, and in disciplinary approaches that tend, first and foremost, to thematize those affects or convert them without fail to positive affects (curious fascination, pleasurable suspense).[62]

The literature on cinematic disgust is an even smaller subsection of the minor literature on negative affects and film; again, one reason for this derives from the assumption that disgust's status as the negative of the negative—(and, perhaps most alarming, Darwin's claim that a turned head and shut eyes are the body's gestural symptomatology of disgust)—makes it a risky commercial bet in a medium that, at heart, does not want to turn bodies or eyes away. Disgust as an affect is therefore constrained largely to treatment in the ghetto of horror film studies—in the cognitivist work of Cynthia Freeland and Noël Carroll, who continue the film-philosophy analytic of thinking disgust as an aesthetic problem, or in Mikita Brottman's work on *cinéma vomitif,* her term for a degraded cinema that, through highly indexical imagery of the repellent (representations of cannibalism, dismemberment, torture, or, as in the case of Ruggero Deodato's *Cannibal Holocaust,* real animal mutilation), produces a nauseated spectator.[63] If disgust is broadened to include the related terms of abjection or the Bakhtinian carnivalesque, as theorized in the work of Barbara Creed and Mary Russo, respectively, it is nevertheless still treated to analyses of representations of the disgusting.[64]

Disgust creates a particular challenge for this book's treatment of affect as having form and inhering in form, and outside of theories or practices of spectatorship. As the affect deemed in the literature to be the most intentional, to immediately impose itself on an unwilling perceiver who recoils, disgust seems to be, far more than grief, an affect bound up with bodies, to implant itself without mediation on a skin or a consciousness, to have a direct target in the repulsed sensorium of its victim. Disgust in visual studies is therefore usually regarded through a double lens: the thing (the image or in the image) that disgusts *and* a disgusted viewer. As the affect taken to be without reflection (as in aesthetics), without distance, and without the capacity for discrimination, it appears to suggest that there is no disgust without a subject. This emphasis on spectatorship and disgust is visible in two very different lines of thought that have shaped horror studies, despite the different philosophical traditions from which they derive: Noël Carroll's cognitivist (read, analytic) *The Philosophy of Horror, or, Paradoxes of the Heart* and criticism indebted to Julia Kristeva's psychoanalytic (read, continental) *Powers of Horror.* Despite their differences, both texts have engendered critical offspring that emphasize the disgusting in place of disgust due to an overinvestment in objectified offensive things; an intentional affectivity that is assumed to move an embodied spectator; and, most significant, a forgetting of form, even when textual form would seem to be the most fitting site for testing their respective theories.

The aim of Carroll's treatise is to provide an aesthetics of "art-horror," his ordinary-language term for the literary and cinematic genre of horror, as distinct from "natural horror" (the Shoah) and the horror that any given work of art might produce (say, Sade's narratives). Art-horror involves an appeal, the "intended capacity to raise a certain *affect*" in a spectator.[65] Carroll's approach is a textbook example of the model of affect as intentional and spectatorial, and his analytic commitments constrain his argument to the interplay between the "attitude of characters in the story to the monsters they encounter" and the spectators instructed in their affective response by the mirroring of these attitudes. "For horror appears to be one of those genres," Carroll argues, "in which the emotive responses of the audience, ideally, run parallel to the emotions of characters."[66] Consistent with the cognitivist approach, Carroll converts the emotional reactions of characters into "a set of instructions, or, rather, examples about the way in which the audience is to respond to the monsters in the fiction."[67] Following Mary Douglas's treatment of impurity as derived from category blurring, Carroll's monster is monstrous if "it is categorically interstitial, contradictory . . . , incomplete, and/or formless."[68] The recognition that the monster is threatening and impure ostensibly mobilizes fear and disgust in the viewer.

The problems with such a theoretical approach are legion. For Carroll to make this argument, characters' emotional reactions have to be taken, as it were, at face value. It is assumed that we can think of characters as *having* emotions, that in advance they are psychologized depth subjects, and further that their emotions do not deceive, are in every way and situation perfectly matched to an ideal (visible, transparent, and immediately legible) stimulus response available for mirroring by a simple spectator who will herself never fail to read the instructions correctly before beginning her emotional project. While Carroll and I agree that there is a need to formulate "an objective, as opposed to an introspective, picture of the emotion of art-horror," he nevertheless reduces this objective picture to the neat parallel lines of emotional call and response.[69] This model is also problematic if we work backward from his taxonomic outcomes. Because Carroll defines horror's affect as deriving from the characters' emotive responses to the monster in their universe, and because he defines a monster as a "threatening and impure" being of mixed ontological categories, he can only come to the remarkable conclusion that Hitchcock's *Psycho* is not a horror film, reducing the scope of his argument to explaining merely why Norman Bates might be classified (by some) as "horrific."[70]

My quarrel with Carroll, and the problem that becomes so acute in the case of *Psycho,* is that his ontological theory of monstrosity as a being marked by category impurity and scientific impossibility requires recourse to Science as an a priori and infallible master signifying system that conveys purity or impurity in itself. In other words, it is scientific boundary-drawing, itself tinged with disgust and theories of the possible and proper, that in advance delimits the lines that Carroll accepts for his taxonomy. *Psycho,* the odd generic exception in his theory, is the master signifier of modern horror, but one of the reasons it so radically revised the genre is the same reason it tears an awkward rend in Carroll's theory: Hitchcock's film has a hole at its center, it voids its central figure of identification and requires a spectatorial inversion halfway through the film. *Psycho* is the horror film that suggests the terror and murderousness of normalcy above all—perhaps *the* central feature of horror films that follow—and it is a film structured around deceptions, including spectatorial deception, the most famous of which is ambivalently resolved at the end of the film. Carroll's film theory requires, ironically, a kind of "good faith" on the part of the horror text: that its characters will have the *right* response to their monsters; their faces will not deceive about these feelings; they will be good teachers to the willing audience; and no response, no character, no center will go missing during the lesson. In the strongest claim for his theory of horror, then, Carroll's model would seem to be the theory that comes to an end precisely with *Psycho*. When he insists, "I cannot be art-horrified by an entity that I do not think is threatening and impure," it reeks of a disavowal of precisely the generative role of deception in the structure of *Psycho* and post-*Psycho* horror films. If nothing else, the inflexibility of Carroll's theory, its inability to shift in relation to this omission, suggests that the forms of specific films speak back to, disrupt, and deceive the very taxonomies that attempt to order and constrain them. *Psycho*'s resistance to horror theory is not the least of its innovations; we might even regard its disruption to theories of its genre as *part and parcel* of its horror work. This suggests, furthermore, the importance of a rigorous consideration of structure in any theory of negative affectivity. Perhaps *Psycho* is not a horror film on the level of a character's ontological impurity; on the level of its split and fractured (impure) form, however, it must be allowed back to the horror fold.

Disgust enters Carroll's argument as the affect of differentiation. It anatomizes, marks dissimilarity, signals the impure or threatening element, and simultaneously effects a taxonomic distinction, providing the affective contrariety that cleaves art-horror from what he calls "art-dread." While the latter is aligned with the uncanny, it is the admixture of disgust and fear that is specific to the horror genre as Carroll particularizes it. Mirroring disgust's philosophical role as the marker of difference between the aesthetic and the anti-aesthetic, disgust is theoretically generative here, operative of taxonomic distinctions as well as being defined by distinction-making. Although one can readily imagine a continental chorus of retching at the claim (Nietzsche and Bataille conducting), Carroll calmly asserts, "In the ordinary course of affairs, people shun what disgusts them. Being repulsed by something that one finds to be loathsome and impure is an unpleasant experience. We do not . . . attempt to add some pleasure to a boring afternoon by opening the lid of a steamy trash can in order to savor its unwholesome stew of broken bits of meat, moldering fruits and vegetables, and noxious, unrecognizable clumps, riven thoroughly by all manner of crawling things."[71] And yet, people go to the movies. Thus, the "paradox of horror" evoked in the title to Carroll's book is the very same performance of surprise made by Hume in "Of Tragedy." Like Burke's meditation on delight's relation to pain, and numerous other eighteenth-century writings on sublimity and terror, in Carroll's formulation of horror's peculiarity the genre "obviously attracts consumers; but it seems to do so by means of the expressly repulsive."[72] Carroll mediates this titular paradox with his conclusion that "the objects of art-horror are such that they are both disgusting and fascinating, both disturbing and interesting, because they are classificatory misfits." The fascination with these anomalies is structured through narrative devices that "enhance and sustain curiosity" about the admixtured beings.[73] If category violations command attention, Carroll avows, then positive feelings of curiosity and absorption compensate for the negative affects of fear and disgust. Despite his overt and titular claims to the contrary, Carroll is not writing a book about negative affectivity; he converts each negative affect to a positive one, supplanting disgust with fascination at the disgusting. In relegating disgust to issues of content and spectatorship, this mode of criticism saves both content and spectatorship for good sentiment. Disgust's *form*, its structural relation to negation or what I am calling the opening up of the worse than the worst, is, without fail, set aside. Freud's plaint remains true to this day: criticism still prefers to concern itself with feelings of a positive nature.

Carroll reinstates the non-disgusting at the expense of the disgusting, insists on film's paid-out compensation for any negative affective debt. Nowhere considered in this treatment is the possibility that form itself might embody disgust, for then where would such compensations inhere? Recall that Carroll defines the monstrous as "categorically interstitial, categorically contradictory, incomplete, or formless." It does not require a great stretch—only the unbridgeable step of theoretical allegiance—to imagine that monstrous form would be interstitial, perhaps generically contradictory, narratively or structurally incomplete, or, indeed, formless. The mise-n'en-scène mobilized in this book—that which is not put into the scene, not enough put into the scene, and put into the non-scene—in fact is precisely the formal and structural language mobilized by the contradictory, incomplete, and formless. Instead of formal compensations for disgust, my treatment of disgust as a form inverts Carroll's argument, setting aside characters' emotions and their mimetic instructions to spectators to argue instead for disgust as a structure of generative negation.

Although film theory derived from Kristeva's account of abjection originates in a tradition divergent from Carroll's, the two schools share an interest in affective spectatorship and figuring disgust as derived from the world of the iconographic. While my issue with Carroll's argument and conclusion is with how he theorizes negative affectivity, the use of Kristeva's notion of abjection to theorize disgust is a more complex matter. Her analysis in *Powers of Horror: An Essay on Abjection* gives shape to abjection, but in the critical tradition that followed, her version of disgust was misread and inappropriately objectified. Kristeva's analysis of abjection—"what disturbs identity, system, order. What does not respect borders, positions, rules. The in-between, the ambiguous, the composite"—is the study not of items or icons but of the structure of the unassimilable to which the subject is nevertheless intimately bound.[74] Abjection is not identical to other theories of repulsion; nor should it be blithely assimilated to traditions that explicitly consider disgust (as Menninghaus does by lumping Kristeva with other scholars of *Ekel*). However, because the abject is "radically excluded" and yet pulls the subject "toward the place where meaning collapses," it does resonate with the structure of disgust as taken in this chapter, and abjection's undoing of any attempt to render it fully other to the subject functions as a kind of proxy for disgust.[75] Kristeva's oft-cited formulation of the structure—"I abject *myself* within the same motion through which 'I' claim to establish *myself*"—bears witness to the process by which the subject expels and retains the realm of the abject in order to constitute a coherent "I," a designation of self dependent for its coherence on the excluded and rejected aspects of self.[76] The abject is not fully other; like the banishment of disgust to constitute the field of aesthetics, the abject haunts the borders of subjective constitution as the expelled.

Uses of Kristeva's theory of abjection in film theory have not concerned themselves with this structure so much as with the emblems or ob-jects of ab-jection: loathsome food (the skin on the milk), the corpse, the pus-filled wound, "filth, waste, or dung."[77] Barbara Creed, most notably, argues that "the horror film abounds in images of abjection, foremost of which is the corpse, whole and mutilated, followed by an array of bodily wastes such as blood, vomit, saliva, sweat, tears and putrefying flesh"; excremental and menstrual bodily overdeterminations link women—and specifically mothers—to the abject and do so through those listed images.[78] This move is also repeated outside horror criticism: in a reading of Milcho Manchevski's *Before the Rain* (1994), Katarzyna Marciniak looks to "images of blood and sounds of vomiting," arguing that these tokens of abjection are gestures at "solidarity with the ones who die, who are . . . brutally expelled out of being."[79] Although both Marciniak and Creed consider their chosen images through the lens of Kristeva's work, the psychoanalyst is actually a very bad witness to call in defense of the iconographic. For ultimately, *Powers of Horror* is a work that writes against "instances of" or "images of," instead figuring abjection as a deconstituting gesture that is continually in movement (and a specific thrownness) and that resists attempts at representation.

Criticism that uses *Powers of Horror* to locate the image(s) of abjection makes a critical error unique to theories of disgust: such work takes vomit for the corpse. In Kristeva, vomit is not evoked as an instance of the abject, and it cannot be assimilated to any ontological theory of abjection—vomit is not the corpse, not the skin on offered milk, and, indeed, vomit as such makes no appearance in Kristeva. Rather, vomit is invoked solely as *vomiting*; it emerges as a movement in response to the abject, a signal of its expulsion and its energy—energy both repelling and rappelling. Vomit is linked to the abject not through any objectal dimension but through the gesture's abjectal dimension, through becoming and flow, reflex and reflux. Vomit is not abject but abjecting. Consider the opening of Kristeva's text:

> There looms, within abjection, one of those violent, dark revolts of being, directed against a threat that seems to emanate from an exorbitant outside or inside, ejected beyond the scope of the possible, the tolerable, the think-able. . . . It beseeches, worries, and fascinates desire, which, nevertheless, does not let itself be seduced. Apprehensive, desire turns aside; sickened, it rejects. . . . But simultaneously . . . that spasm, that leap is drawn toward an elsewhere as tempting as it is condemned.[80]

In these lines, the abject lives. Kristeva is adamant on this point: the abject "is not an ob-ject." It is, rather, "revolts of being" that figure in spasms.[81] When vomiting arrives in name soon after, it is not in the figure of filth or the loathed but in the gesture of loathing proper, in the "spasms and vomiting that protect me." Vomit appears in Kristeva's text in the form of heaving, already begun, already in process, in the tremoring gesture of expulsion. Abjection is an art of gesture: the gagging at the milk skin, the nausea at the proffered signs of parental desire, the "violence of sobs, of vomit" that enacts separations of being, not as signs anterior to or causes of that separation.[82] The extrication of excess from the pre-body in order to constitute the body—and from the self in order to constitute the self—are thus figured through a living of abjection that is always, also, a dying of and into abjection. But that is a very different thing from taking vomit for the corpse.

The lure of objectalizing, ontologizing, and concretizing images of the disgusting in film and media theory has produced a strong association between disgust and proximate, magnified images of isolated terrible details. The absence of distance (for critical reflection) in aesthetic approaches to disgust, and the affect's theorized closeness to notions of the contagious and threatening, have produced a long-standing spatial metaphor of closeness, proximity, and unwelcome nearness that has been translated cinematically to the proximity and unwelcome nearness of the close-up. The discursive closeness of the close-up and the disgusting move both ways: examples given of the power of the close-up often tend toward the viscerally powerful sense of a magnified negative, as in Eisenstein's oft-quoted law that a cockroach in close-up is more terrible than one hundred elephants in a long shot, or appeal to the trauma of the claustrophobic proximity to the bisected eyeball in *Un chien andalou* or the affective intensity of the maggots on the meat in Eisenstein's *Potemkin* (themselves enlarged twice over, through a diegetic eyepiece that magnifies the magnification). In turn, theories of disgust in a non-cinematic context often use language suggesting the singular details of a series of close-up shots. Take, for example, this description of the performance of *Opening of the Mouth,* the composer Richard Barrett's collaboration with Crow and the ELISION Ensemble (and a piece that evokes in its title the seminal aperture of disgust):

> Former acid vats filled with decaying fish heads and skins, tables and cupboards littered with crushed skull-like melons, desiccated peppers jammed tightly together, strange-looking exotic fruits, a metal bowl filled with tar into which carrots were impacted, causing, in the heat of the Perth summer, the tar to bubble up and form a scrotum around the withered vegetables, potatoes crucified with large nails and impacted hard onto shattered red screens flinging a bloody light on to a sand pit masking the tender placement of small candles in the shrine of a burnt-out oven.[83]

The performance piece is described as though experienced through the scrim of the visual close-up: the language of the detail; the lists of isolated objects of singular intention, lacking grammatical articles or joiners to place them in contextual space or time or in relation to one another or to meaning. The detachment of the details in the description evokes Mary Ann Doane's account of the cinematic close-up as "disengaged from the mise-en-scène, freighted with an inherent separability or isolation, a 'for-itself' that inevitably escapes, to some degree, the tactics of continuity editing that strive to make it 'whole' again. . . . The close-up embodies the pure fact of presentation, of manifestation, of showing—a 'here it is.'"[84] Discourses of disgust that emphasize disgusting objects and their effect on spectatorship suggest that the affect can be reduced to a similar squicky showing: *There it is! (gross).* The close-up, however, as Doane notes, is not simply a connotation or presentation of closeness or proximity. Rather, she writes, "Its legibility has always been allied with its scale and its status as a form of magnification. More than other types of shots, the close-up exploits the expanse of the screen—the face or the object filmed cover the screen, using up, exhausting all space."[85] Disgust, in fact, mediates the two senses of the term "close-up," one that in English evokes proximity and in French (*gros plan*) suggests largeness and magnification.[86] Disgust bridges these two senses by being both a threatening coming-too-close (what Menninghaus calls its fundamental schema as "a nearness that is not wanted") and a becoming-too-large, as in the descriptions of the monstrosity of Brobdingnag skin, "hairs hanging from it thicker than pack-threads," in *Gulliver's Travels*.[87] The relationship between the close-up and disgust bears more scrutiny than it receives here. One would do well to consider faciality as a privileged subject of the close-up, and the intimate relation between disgust and the open-mouthed visage, as in Lessing's treatment of Laocoön ("Simply imagine Laocoön's mouth forced wide open, and then judge! Imagine him screaming, and then look!") or Bakhtin's image of the grotesque face as "reduced to the gaping mouth."[88] Disgust is being treated in this chapter not as a container for specific objects but as a structure of the worse than the worst, an opening up through exclusion in process. Nowhere is that form more difficult (but therefore most necessary) to consider than in a film that teases us with the concreteness of various objects, in close-up—a film that seems incredibly amenable to a reading of disgusting objects, abjects, and proximities. David Lynch tempts that line with a film that purports to make the image bear the burden of the disgusting but that, on further examination, leaves open the gap for the possibilities of generating an ever worse as a formal structure of disgust.

LAURA DERN'S VOMIT

If: *You got the smell in this room of puke.*

David Lynch's postmodern romp *Wild at Heart* (1990) is one of his films with the least critical favor (at worst, critics loathe it; it provokes intellectual disgust).[89] In one sense, the film requires, and provides, no plot summary, for it is largely a film of instants, memorable spectacles (the man in the bar who barks like a dog; Nicolas Cage's Sailor Ripley singing Elvis songs), parodic citations (largely to *The Wizard of Oz*), and signs of the Lynchean universe (it appears to be set in both the 1980s and the 1950s, violence erupts under seemingly polite social circumstances, a vague tonal weirdness). At the same time, things do take place in the film—though, because it is a road movie, that taking place is always a displacement of sorts, a taking place in motion's trajectory. The film opens with Sailor fighting and killing a man who has been hired by the momma of his sweetie Lula Fortune (a writhing Laura Dern); violence is introduced asymmetrically as an effect always in excess of its narrative cause. Although forbidden to do so, Lula waits for Sailor to get out of prison, takes up with him again, and runs off to the anti-Oz, a sleepy Texas town where trouble and strangeness persistently follow them, as do the various men Lula's mother has hired to kill Sailor and separate the lovers forever.

It is in Texas that Laura Dern vomits. And as though conforming to Derrida's insistence that one must think vomit and not "the act or process of vomiting, which are less disgusting than vomit in so far as they imply an activity, some initiative whereby the subject can at least still mimic mastery . . . believing that he *makes himself vomit*," the close-up of the disgorged food presents it in its material facticity, well after it has come into being.[90] The vomit arrives, as all good strangers must, from out of nowhere. In the second half of the film, Sailor and Lula bide their time in a motel room, fucking, loving, planning for futures that will be deferred by inevitable scenes of violence. Without warning—and without seeing its coming into being—a scene opens with a close-up of vomit on the grimy motel floor, although it is also possible to fail to identify the contents of the strange patterned stain at all, on first seeing it. The spot is large, wet, with indeterminate pale clumps, dark flies settling unevenly over the strange, ovoid circle. When Sailor soon thereafter returns to the motel room, he sits for a moment or two before asking, "What's that smell?" retroactively conferring an affective solidity to the anamorphotic spot. Lula, lying on a bed, confesses that she "barfed," and then there is, again, a brief shot of the vomit, this time from farther away. The visual relationship to the vomit in the film is comprised of just those two shots, together consuming mere seconds of screen duration. Later, Lula will realize—signaled by a flashback to an abortion when she was younger, a different type of extimate expulsion—that the vomit must mean she is pregnant; later still, when the villainous Bobby Peru (Willem Dafoe) attempts to seduce Lula, he will refer to the smell of the vomit that has lingered in the room. The vomit does not figure more prominently than that in *Wild at Heart,* yet the film turns on it. The spill on the ground is the film's grounding catastrophe.

The parergonal vomit that arrives from without and yet centers and destabilizes the film's world repeats the ejecting physicality of Dern's Lula, a shocking, vibrating twitch of a being. Her contorted poses; pinup citations; distended, tortuous, wringing torsions make of her a walking (mostly dancing), talking (barely) affect on which a body is merely propped. A single arm, inexplicably lifted to the back of her head as a permanent pose, distorts her body into a Figure. It could be said that there is no need to spend film time showing Lula vomiting, because her entire physicality in the film up to that point has been an ever-evicting self attempting to loosen the fragile bond between a body and an "I." This fractured physicality literalizes a structure that vomit constitutively puts into play. As Diderot words it in *Élements de physiologie*, "*Ce n'est jamais vous qui voulez manger ou vomir, c'est l'estomac; pisser, c'est la vessie*" (It is never you who wishes to eat or to vomit, it is the stomach; for urinating, it is the bladder).[91] Dern's arm slithers up through her hair to strain her body in angles and stretches; she is all squirms and wriggles. It is as though the definitive mark of both the cinema of ultraviolence and the road movie—*Bonnie and Clyde*'s famous bullet-ridden ballet—has been elongated and spread out over the surface of Dern's writhing skin. Heaving, shrieking, shivering, panting, twisting, torquing, coming, Lula, despite her clacking red shoes, is not Dorothy yearning for Oz but the goddamn tornado itself.

If violence is, on the one hand, a problem of vectors of energy radiating from the female body, it is also, on the other, an interpersonal (and sexualized) structure epitomized by the rape of young Lula and Bobby Peru's repulsive-seductive molestation of the older, pregnant Lula. The earlier rape is introduced through a conversation in which Lula appears to offer her one and only lie to Sailor: she asserts that her mother, Marietta, did not know anything about her rape at twelve by an old family friend. In a flashback, we see Marietta coming across a bloodied postcoital Lula and attacking the assailant. If the rape introduces the possibility of deception—and lies in Lynch's narratives are often associated with violence, as though force's first disruption is always to the possibility of verifiable speech—it also introduces something unspeakable by Lula to Sailor and in *Wild at Heart* more generally. The ontological status of the flashbacks, whether fantasized or historical, is indeterminate and indeterminable. What vomit structurally designates in *Wild at Heart* as the possibility of a something worse than the worst is the retroactive violence of the rape, an unspeakable act that enters the film without having to be spoken, figured without losing its simultaneous quality of being, in a fundamental sense, unfigurable.

The return to the rape is possible only because this non-place has been granted within the film's present logic. The citation of the rape of young Lula— a figural vomiting of it up into the contemporary narrative—occurs in the infamous rape-seduction scene with Bobby Peru. Dafoe's foul villain knocks on Lula's motel room door one day while Sailor is out working on their car. He asks to use her bathroom and then pisses with the door open, his back to an increasingly agitated Lula. Slinking out of the bathroom, Bobby Peru leers, "You got the smell in this room of puke. You been puking, little girl? You sick?

Pregnant?" In this scene, Dafoe famously corners Dern, grabs her, and says to her, over and over, "Say 'Fuck me.'" Until she does, at which point he jumps back, grinning his gap-blackened maw wildly, yee-haws, "Someday, honey, I will!" and leaves a mortified Lula in his wake. The humiliation of the forced speech is the force of exteriorization more broadly, figured as well in the unseen narrative instance of vomiting. But in place of the vision of that originary moment is this violence of speech wrenched out of the body, and the violence of this force is made possible by a parasensual dimension of the vomit: not its vision but its smell. It is the fetor of vomit that lingers, permeates, mobilizes the violence of, and frames this scene (and this woman)—it is the condition for a non-visual apperception of the status of the pregnant body by Bobby Peru and the revelation of a truth now available for blackmail. Readings of this scene, Slavoj Žižek's in particular, reduce the dimension of exteriorization to a matter of the eroto-violent words spoken, but such a reading takes place under the logic of denial that Lula practices and that makes the violence against her possible: to critically refuse the lingering persistence of the smell of vomit that is the precondition for this very encounter.[92]

Smell, recall, is Kant's account of the unsociable dimension of taste: it forces itself on unwitting recruits to its sensory aspects. It is smell by which Derrida accounts for "something more disgusting than the disgusting," and it is, crucially, not the sight of or naming of but the *smell* of the vomit that cannot be erased in Lula and Sailor's motel room. Smell avows bodily revelation in indifference to language; its trail introduces historicity and the archiving of time in the film. It is the threatening mobility of scents that grounds this scene in a materiality that is of, but also beyond, bodies and that in fact makes the forced utterance of "Fuck me" only a citation of the more unmediated force of the smell of the vomit that already moves between, around, and among bodies. This is not to psychologize the famous humiliation scene as a defense or response to the olfactory trauma. Rather, it is to suggest that vomit's labor is neither thematic nor iconic but structural. What vomit mobilizes is the "something more disgusting than the disgusting" of unbound smell—for in the hierarchy of the cinematic senses, smell is the other of vision and thus of cinema, a sensual prohibition at the heart of the medium. The representational refusal, what is foreclosed absolutely from cinematic logics, is the lingering acidity that tears at the tissues of the nose.[93] The visual materiality of this film, then, cannot be all; designated as centering the film is something that is necessarily, absolutely, and irreducibly excluded from its sensual workings. In other words, in Lynch's film, terrible, unthinkable violence is *smelled* instead of spoken, smelled because it cannot be spoken. Thus, what Kant will deem problematically unneighborly in the easy dissemination of fragrance, Lynch will push quite a bit farther. Smell, in *Wild at Heart,* destroys sociality, undoes worlds and ravages bonds—it is the very lubricious ground of what is violence-enabling.

What vomit introduces in *Wild at Heart* is neither an appeal to an embodied spectator nor a trope nor a thematic subject or metaphorical expression. It puts in place, instead, the olfactory as a force that designates a structural rend at the center of the film and that opens film form up to alterity and barbarity. Smell introduces as a non-inhabitable space the something that is more disgusting than the disgusting, the beyond that taste as the literally disgusting holds as security in place of that something worse. Speaking the auditory signifiers, "the smell of puke," not only puts the word in the mouth but puts the spill into the frame; what remains outside the speakable and visible text is that telling, archivable, stubborn scent. The non-place of the worse than the worst that the vomit in *Wild at Heart* opens is a designation that cannot be filled in by the rape, shown in flashbacks, or by the humiliating seduction shown in the present, but that is the condition that makes the exteriority of both to the film's narrative logic possible in the first place. In place of the close-up of the clumpy pool figuring as the "this is this" model of disgust as overly present, violently imposed on a spectator, Laura Dern's vomit introduces something not given over to any perceiver—something that forces the film's narrative to tarry with its lingering sensual force. In place of recuperating disgust for the visual or interpretable or intentional, *Lynch lets his vomit smell.* The film does not engage disgust in a binary of the beautiful versus the ugly, the unspeakable versus the articulatable, interiority versus exteriority. Instead, it structurally commits to the overflow of vomit—its supplementarity; its position as the absolutely excluded. Vomit, then, is not a metaphor for the other unfigurable violences in the film. Rather, the mobilizing of a foreclosed and lingering smell opens up a position for those violences to enter and disturb the film without entering the cinematic narrative. Violence becomes an event not of the contents that happen to subjects but of the form, organized around a sense not just prohibited but foreclosed within film's optocentrism.

WILD HEARTS, SICK FIGURES

That vomit puts in play formal questions—and, indeed, that the gut and alimentary canal might be subsumed to formal elements—is suggested in work dating back to the very beginning of Lynch's career. His early mixed-media piece of screen and sculpture sometimes titled *Six Figures Getting Sick* or *Six Men Getting Sick* (a symptomatic confusion that hovers between representation and its refusal) is particularly indebted to Francis Bacon's onto-aesthetic project of rending figuration and representation to realign Figures with rhythm, color, and Deleuze's "violence of sensation."[94] *Six Figures Getting Sick* (1967), often cast in criticism as Lynch's Ur-text (if not this, then *Eraserhead* [1977]), consists of a screen sculpted into dimension. It is composed of open-mouthed faces in ambiguous states of frozen expulsion—at once, vomit and the scream or wail.[95] Taking literally Deleuze's notion of Baconian "forces that model flesh," the figures in relief were modeled indexically on Lynch's body. On the left side of the work are three sculptured heads. The most classical bust looks down, head tilted and resting in hand; the middle one parts its mouth as though in the beginnings of speech or a nascent Laocoön; and the final figure is an open-mouthed scream of a being: Edvard Munch on the Odessa Steps. A bifurcated half of another figure is painted as a flat image on the right side of the screen, while projected and increasingly abstracted head-things fill out the grouping over the course of the one-minute loop, set all the while to the piercing wails of a siren's sonic catastrophe.

Moving from left to right in the film version of the installation, as though laying out a text in print, and following the cine-archelogy of the head leader's descent, the three sculpted heads first appear, followed by three projected sketches of figures. Under a numerical countdown the word "Look" flashes, the imperative displacing deixis from the wagging digital to the directed ocular. Though less forcibly deformed than those one finds in Bacon's paintings, the heads are primarily fleshy arcs with hollowed-out holes above squared supportive ledges of bone and weight. Two of the projected heads on the right bleed into each other through the mediation of a gut-like pouch with tubes and hollows, a schematic for a duodenal ethics of intersubjectivity through digestive flow. Each figure is eventually elongated by a slender tube leading to a paunchy round, and in its curved frame appears a graphic spiral. The graphic and the gastric continually swap places in a perversion of the Godardian law of representation: *it's not chyme; it's red*. The piece is organized around the formal labors of the enteric nervous system: esophageal flinches and undulations of the viscera provide the work's halting yet churning rhythms, and the visual language derives from lengths of alimentary interconnectedness, bowls and bowels, intestinal fluidity, fistula and passage, abdominal rebellion. Peristaltic undulations effect both the animation of the body and the animation of the sculpted screen. The inhalations of many swallowings and the exhalations of many heavings culminate in a gastric eschatology in which the six figures vomit copious lines of dripping paint.

Vomit in this early work is coequal with the materiality of the image. The vertical lines that reappear in the final moment as sick appear first as graphic striations behind the projected figures and as the wet drippings of paint supplanting a fleshy torso in the third open-mouthed figure. These earlier pours, at once vein and line, tube and border, the residue of the materiality of the image and of the extended duration required for the wetness of paint to dry, evoke Deleuze's adage on the haptic and the tactile, that "no painter has ever been satisfied with the paintbrush," and therefore also trace the body of painterly movement, an indexical mark of Lynch's corpus as much as his head taken for plaster.[96] For only a part of a second, the screen flashes to a flat bright red in place of projecting its sick men. Only the sculptured heads remain for the supplanting of figure with color—or, rather, the taking of color as a Figure. After a mechanical ballet of awkwardly angled arms and hands in silhouette, the stomachs fill with red, leech white and pink lines, and, finally, a waterfall of copious streaks explodes from the top of the figures, overtaking the forms—obliterating the heads on the right, writing over both projected and sculpted heads in the rush of vertiginous ejections. The gagging pour floods white streaks against a now violet background, the overflow composed of the sum of all colors of light and simultaneously a perceived absence of color. Spills surge the image in a cloudy overtake, this expulsion a return to canvas, a newly wet ground for the image, as though sufficient vomit could produce a slate—blank, but not clean. The end of the loop is the annihilation of the logic of color as presence; vomiting to the point of blankness purifies the image by evacuating its visual material. The heave is a mess that cleans up the image, preparing the sixty-second loop to begin once more.

If the white rush is the cannibalism of all colors, a totality of representational tonality, then its structural parallel is the additive excess of media cannibalized in the piece, exemplified by the ontological paradox of a "sculpted screen," but also signaled in the leader and horizontal lines of dots evoking celluloidal sprockets; the photographic X-ray of a torso; the chaotic intermix of painting, relief, image, sound; stasis, movement, space, surface. This *Gesamtkunstwerk* binges on representational intake, and its additive totality returns in the vomiting up of that glut. The piece's spasmodic form is sick—a sick structure, not content; sick in and as gesture, and not reception. Emesis is not a subject of the work, not an iconographic thisness to be located or critically pointed to, but the animating motion of the entire turbulent text.

Nevertheless, criticism persists in taking the formal for the thematic. One critic posits that the project initiated "Lynch's interest in vomiting, which will be graphically and frequently represented in his paintings as well as in his full-length films." Another claims, "Sickness (or disease) and fire are two themes to which Lynch would return continually."[97] These critical readings of the Figures have persisted in figuring vomit as vomiting and the emetic as a thematic.

Perhaps no critic writes with such spectacular indifference to the anti-narrative formal logics of the piece as Martha Nochimson. In *The Passion of David Lynch,* she insists on reading *Six Figures* as both possessing and being about narrative, figuring vomiting as a narrative act that takes place in the linear piece and as a narrative super-metaphor operative in Lynch's corpus as a whole. Lynch's "love of narrative" is evident in *Six Figures,* writes Nochimson, as "he makes the process of vomiting a Lynchian paradigm of the narrative structure. Vomiting is a brilliant image of the unstoppable narrative compulsion, proceeding relentlessly from the beginning, through the middle, to an end. At the same time, it is a completely involuntary process."[98] In a telling error, Nochimson describes the piece as depicting only five men, postulating that perhaps "the 'sixth man' is the spectator, and the title is a humorous comment on viewer engagement and identification."[99] Of course, this is incorrect. There are six Figures, per the title, in the actual piece, and the spectator does not figure as a supplement to the count. On the one hand, this early work of Lynch's was unavailable for a long time, and many critical accounts relied on second- or third-hand reports of the installation, so Nochimson's mistake is neither surprising nor problematic if in fact she has not seen the film. On the other hand, however, the wrong count reveals a broader critical bias, for Nochimson's insistence on reading Lynch's work as structured by an obsession with narrative compels her to place within *Six Figures* a central corpus in the figure of an engaged spectator, to insert not only a body but a subject into the formal freneticism.

On the question of what takes place in the piece, there is a striking critical agreement on some version of the following: "bright red stomachs dropped down from the chins of the faces. Eventually, all the stomachs appeared to explode into flames. Then all six men seemed to vomit violently."[100] Even when criticism falls short of putting the vomit to work for (the process of) narrative, a descriptive arc is imputed to the temporal ordering and culminating crisis of the piece: There are men; vomiting is something they do. However, a Figure is not a body. These forms are not men. Writing the vomit or the vomiting into the piece as a narrative occurrence or thematic trope involves critics in the ignominious task of fleshing out the Figures, imputing to them a corporeal density, adding exits and entries that must be prodded and poked to ascertain their material certainty. To these newly subjectified, newly thickened figures, the critical arm opens mouths by force, manually clenches muscles it imputed into existence, imagines inducing an uptake for critical cleaning up in the retrieval of meaning from the scene. Criticism functions in this case less as a record or unpacking of a prior narrative occurrence than as so much Ipecac. If this violent mess is a critical production, it nevertheless covers up a darker stain: sanitized in the literature is the messier violence of the spill of paint, the excavation of formal material from the materiality of the form. For the vomitus of a Figure is always and only paint. The six Figures are sick on form. Or, rather, they are not "are sick"—they are getting sick, in process and in movement, animated as sick and animatedly sick. Animation as a technical gesture produces a formal nausea, whose roots in *naus* (ship) suggest the sickness of and from movement, here a sickness on and through the movements of mediated technological representation.[101] In other words, and with more ferocity than the clenchings of any intestine, in Lynch's work the Figures do not vomit; the vomit Figures.

And sick figures as an exteriority: as a formal language of the outside. Despite those repeated attempts to return both vomit and Figure to a language of narrative, interiority, subjectivity, and recuperable meaning, the choking, halting turbulence of *Six Figures Getting Sick* involves the wrenching failure of an impossible separation from the substrate of painterly material. It is important that this exteriorization of form figures through vomit, for esophageal passage—despite often being invoked as the trope par excellence of interiority expelled—is in fact a running-through of the inside by the outside. Foucault describes the madman sent to sea as experiencing a privileged enclosure of the outside, "put in the interior of the exterior"; likewise, vomit is an experience of the force of the outside from within the body excerpted around esophageal tubing.[102] It is thus fitting that in a letter to Einstein, Freud explains a certain resistance or hostility toward psychoanalysis in these terms: "if someone tries to turn our awareness inward . . . our whole organization resists—just as, for example, the oesophagus and the urethra resist any attempt to reverse their normal direction of passage."[103] A disposition of the human toward the outside world maps onto the "normal direction of passage" in gut systems. A turn toward the psyche, analytic speech production, the unconscious, however—the entirety of an apparatus of interiority implied in that "awareness inward"—is resisted in full by a physical organization hell-bent on a proper teleology of digestion. Freud's turn to the figure of esophageal revolt to defend the inward turn of psychoanalytic reflection is apt historically (given vomit's importance in his and Breuer's early work on hysteria) and evocatively (as analytic practice was accused of encouraging a vomitous production of speech in the famous injunction that the patient must speak all). Vomit as a privileged confession of the materiality of the body becomes, in Freud's comparison, a privileged confession of the non-materiality of the body in that inward turn. (His metaphor also strikingly suggests that it is the work of the analyst to finger the patient's throat in a sort of forced bulimia.) At the same time, however, the turn that Freud invokes and affiliates with analytic praxis is an inward turn lacking interiority, a turn toward the unconscious as the site of alterity in the subject—in other words, an interiority riddled through and through by unknowable, unspeakable, unfathomable exteriorities.

In *Six Figures Getting Sick,* against the telos of proper digestion, ending in defecation and a voiding of material through the coursing hollow at the center of the body, the face returns as the site of entry and exit—the mouth the only anus within the schematic—circling back intake in a citational recall as though performing the collapse of what Jean-Luc Nancy calls "all the body's introductory *topoi,*" including "breaching bodies, accesses, excesses, orifices, pores and portals of all skins, scars, navels, blazon, pieces, and fields, body by body, place by place, entry by entry by exit," into one singular site of swallowing and spewing activity.[104] Despite the nod toward a humanism organized around faciality as the site of subjectivity, the body is ultimately parsed, pieced, and dissected in Lynch's work, and the human form is reduced to esophageal length and stomach. This length is not an interior enclosed within the confines of the subject but a running through of the outside that supplants the self, a hollowing out at the core of the corpus. As Michael Gershon figures this excavation, "The space enclosed within the wall of the bowel, its *lumen,* is part of the outside world. The open tube that begins at the mouth ends at the anus. Paradoxical as it may seem, the gut is a tunnel that permits the exterior to run right through us. Whatever is in the lumen of the gut is thus actually outside our bodies."[105] Thus, although vomit is retrofitted to a hermeneutics of interiority and depths (of substance or signification) in Lynchian criticism that thematizes, metaphoricizes, or corporealizes its gesture in relation to some imaginary embodied figure with bowel and shape, vomiting should be regarded rather as bringing to the surface the exteriority of form that does not represent the Figures but that is constituted by them. *Six Figures Getting Sick* is, then, neither about men sickened nor a presentation of vomit as a trope, theme, or narrative occurrence—it is the sickness of and on form. Sickness on paint is also the sickness of paint, and this heaving visual language has nothing to do with subjects, spectators, or Figures made men.

Six Figures Getting Sick and *Wild at Heart* deploy disgust as a formal opening up of something worse than the worst. Disgust, in both cases, troubles a text that has an a priori coherence: the negative affect puts in motion formal agitation or introduces the cinematically prohibited and foreclosed forces of smell so that multiple violences enter the film form without entering the film narrative. In the next chapter, however, disgust names the cinematic logic by which Peter Greenaway goes one step further than Lynch. Greenaway's film, *The Cook, the Thief, His Wife, and Her Lover*, like transcendental aesthetics and transcendental gastronomy, not only banishes this excluded figure but cultivates it as banished, putting it to work for the mutability of form itself. Greenaway's film figures a desecration beyond putrefaction as the obscenity at the heart of the aesthetic. The form of the film is not opened up by or to disgust through the figure of putrescence or rot; rather, the film is constituted by that gesture. Decay is not a theme or trope, nor is it something that happens *to* or *on* a preexisting form, wrecking it, as in the case of Lynch's work. Rather, decay is the name for the way in which the film's chromatic structure comes into existence and persists over time. Nothing preexists rot in *The Cook, the Thief, His Wife, and Her Lover*. On the level of visual form, decay is all there is.

SIX

Disgust and
the Cinema
of *Haut Goût*

The pheasant is an enigma whose secret meaning is
known only to the initiate; they alone understand how
to enjoy it to its full.

—JEAN ANTHELME BRILLAT-SAVARIN,
The Physiology of Taste

As with Lacanian psychoanalysis and Derridian thought, in the violent ba-
roque of Peter Greenaway's *The Cook, the Thief, His Wife, and Her Lover*
(1989), much depends on an *a*. "I shall speak, then, of a letter—the first
one, if we are to believe the alphabet and most of the speculations that have
concerned themselves with it."[1] In the minutes preceding the appearance of
that letter, the scarlet curtains have been thrown open; the heavy majesty of
Michael Nyman's score instated; and, in the darkened lot outside the restaurant Le Hollandais, the thief of the title, Albert Spica, has materialized dog shit
to rub into the yielding canvas of a struggling naked man's skin. Progressing
from left to right, introducing the severe horizontality of the film's four central theatrical spaces, the thief, his wife Georgina and gang of brutes in tow,
marches into the hangar of the garishly green, industrially gray, haute cuisine

kitchen. Parading along with them are the stagehands for the cruel play Spica demands of the classical French chef Richard: a farce of forced protection, extortion, and bullying epitomized by the giant letters bearing his name to be added in neon to the exterior of the restaurant, now his restaurant, now named by his letters. Those blocks of signification placed on high scaffolding, the sneering Spica glances up to note a confusion: they have been written "ASPIC," and he demands a correction. "Now what's that? A-S-P . . . That's nonsense. Spell it right, for Christ's sake," he barks, and the hulking "A" is lifted, to be placed, once more, at the end of the collection, the mise-en-scène of restaurant and film now naming correctly their vile protagonist. All this takes place in the distant and chaotic background of the lofty room, littered with chefs in various states of frenetic rhythmic activity, aurally overtaken by the plaintively sung *Miserere* of the young boy Pup and a nearly constant stream of speech by the homonymic speaker Spica, a monologue in which the errantly ordered letters figure as only a minor interrupting concern.

But much depends on that *a*. For, like a Freudian parapraxis, the error of Spica's misspelled name forms a non-erring sign of the cultural milieu of the kitchen: the universe of haute cuisine to which Spica, in name and flesh, stands in relation, not quite one of opposition but of awryness—one letter off. The "ASPIC" named by the letters in the mere seconds before being rearranged is, of course, the savory (for some, quite unsavory) molded jelly made of meat stock, synonymous with the development of classical French cuisine. (Indeed, Auguste Escoffier writes in his *Guide culinaire* [1903] that jellies may be more important to classical cookery than consommés or stock.[2]) Aspic is a preservative: it prevents bacteria from forming on the objects suspended within, halting the effects of time on the quality of ingredients, and it holds objects in visual suspension, its transparent and glistening clarity a glazed frame in three dimensions. Aspic's mold thus freezes both space and time, halting rot's ineluctable forward progress and presenting and bringing to presence floating and fixed objects for a hungry gaze. And in that sense, its powers are not so very unlike the spatiotemporal suspensions of film itself, the stock for which is, also, made of gelatin.

If aspic is, on the one hand, synonymous with desecrations beyond death—a boiling of animal skins and bones in water to produce the wiggling broth upon cooling—it is also, in its preservative and immobilizing functions, a heralding of immortality, a refusal of decay, cuisine's photograph. Aspic is irreducibly linked to the aesthetic. Used to add glisten and shine to terrines or cut into shapes for the excesses of garnishing, it is synonymous with gastronomic presentation in the address of cuisine to the eyes. Therefore, in addition to its preservative utility, it is aligned with aristocratic pleasures in eating in place of the necessities of brute repetitive nutrition that mark low or ordinary cuisine.[3] Put another way, aspic may be thought of as the distillation of a cuisine less concerned with the (visceral) taste of a mouth machine than with the (refined) taste of discernment. In the language of Pierre Bourdieu's critique of cultural capital, it is associated with the "tastes of luxury (or freedom)" over the "tastes of necessity."[4] Holding fast in its clear grasp, putting suspended objects on display, aspic is a medium and a frame, a preserving and a presenting that not only shows but that shows that it shows. Critical arguments for the modernist reflexivity of Greenaway's film usually note the frontality of the film's four central spaces (restaurant parking lot, kitchen, dining room, and lavatory), or the proscenium delimited by curtains that open and close the film. But this visual naming of "ASPIC" is yet another self-conscious display of the signs of artifice, and one that bridges the representational and the gastronomic concerns of the film. Aspic transgresses the breach between flesh and sense, between tasting and cultivated taste, between hunger and aesthetics, and between the two uses of the tongue: softening bits of intake for survival and pronouncing the complex succor of that which is judged good. In contemplation of the eternal paradoxes of human corporeality and subjectivity, one could do worse than meditating a bit on aspic.

Greenaway's explicit claim that his film critiques Thatcherism in the figure of Spica (invoking Oscar Wilde's quip about "a man who knows the price of everything and the value of nothing") has produced a spate of ideological criticism arguing about whether the film critiques consumerism, or whether it is as "symptomatic as much as analytic" of Thatcherism.[5] But ignored in most of the literature—or invoked as class metaphor in support of the political reading— is the most visible system grounding the film: the formal language, with its themes and variations and strict technical rhythms, of high gastronomy. Haute cuisine is roundly taken in the literature on Greenaway's film as a displacement for a Thatcher-era bourgeois sensibility or a metaphor for class ascension and "tastes of luxury," but never itself as a structure, let alone one that determines the rigorous cinematic configurations of time, space, and color.[6]

The argument I intend to earn in this chapter arrives in three courses. First, criticism errs in taking gastronomy as a theme in *The Cook, the Thief, His Wife, and Her Lover,* despite the fact that the film revolves around cannibalism and the kitchen. Gastronomy is, rather, its form. Then, criticism errs in taking gastronomy's interest in good taste as self-evident; on the contrary, that which tastes good and is in good taste in both gastronomy and aesthetics is constituted around a negative in the form of a revolt against taste, a cultivated decay that appends a "dis-" to the gustatory. Finally, criticism errs in taking rot as a fixed, concrete, knowable thing made available in film as an "image of" or an abject object, as in the various critical traditions described in the previous chapter. Quite the opposite: disgust is not immediate, visceral, or obvious, and decay is certainly not a metaphor for moral declivity or ideological distaste. Instead, putrescence is a structure in process, a textually constituting gesture that must be read for. Disgust does not appear in Greenaway's film in the guise of signifiers of the revolting—despite putrid images of rotting meat, coprophagia, and cannibalism—or as a spectatorial affect that embodies the critique of consumerist excesses. Rather, disgust's form as the worse than the worst allows it to figure as the manner by which the negative is put into structures of "good taste," both gastronomic and aesthetic. The repelling gesture of repulsion—the visceral repudiation of nearness that loathing prompts—does not manifest here in a subject or spectator recoiling from an object, but as the things of the world becoming unbound from their chromatic qualities. Gastronomic logic and disgust logic converge as they shape the visual structure of the film, specifically the way in which color and space are mapped onto each other and, ultimately and irrevocably, decoupled. *The Cook, the Thief, His Wife, and Her Lover* is structured not by a gastronomy-theme but by a gastronomy-form organized around a damp core—a text constituted by the negative of good taste, the figure of disgust in the specific form of decay and rot.

GASTRONOMY ACCORDING TO PETER GREENAWAY

Hollandaise sauce is made of warmed egg yolks flavored with lemon juice, into which butter is gradually incorporated to make a thick, yellow, creamy sauce. It is probably the most famous of all sauces, and is often the most dreaded, as the egg yolks can curdle and the sauce can turn.—Julia Child et al., *Mastering the Art of French Cooking*

In the miniature drama of letters, Greenaway does not figure SPICA as the easy negative of ASPIC but, rather, as its rotation, the one the troubling or deferral of the other. The crude, violent Spica is a problem for aspic and all that it represents: the restaurant Le Hollandais, classical French cuisine, taste as refinement, and the moral qualities ascribed to the aesthetically high. The word "s-p-i-c-a" is a perversion of "a-s-p-i-c" as metonym for the "haute" tout court, just as Spica and his gang, despite their mimicry of color, dress, and arrangement, are a perversion of Frans Hals's mural *Banquet of the Officers of the St. George Civic Guard Company* (1614) hanging in the stately-cum-garish dining room. In matters representational and gastronomic, Spica is held apart from the world of good taste—by just one letter, but one letter is enough. The letters forming "aspic" defer or problematize the naming of "spica" in relation to his place in the kitchen, in relation to the name he wishes to displace with his own: Le Hollandais. The formal problem of relation, of things that can be referred to each other, was central to the development of haute cuisine, not in an abstract or metaphorical sense, but in a historically specific and uniquely gastronomic one.

The relation that determined modern gastronomy was one of union, a binding together fraught with peril—(not unlike other forms of fragile relation, including the marital ones named in the title to Greenaway's film). The development of aristocratic cuisine, beginning in the seventeenth century, relied on what one theorist calls an "increasing technical complexity—centered on the major technical innovation of the modern *liaison* (the use of flour to bind, or vinegar to emulsify, butter and cream sauces)."[7] This seventeenth-century transformation in sauce-making is usually dated to La Varenne's "flour liaison," or binding of melted lard and flour—recognizable, Reader, if you cook, as the development of roux.[8] This culinary innovation led to sauces that "were now suave, velvety, and succulent where they used to be thin and floury in flavor, coarse and uneven in texture."[9] Material liaison as the ground for the codification of the culinary arts is especially visible in the encyclopedic *L'art de la cuisine française* (1833–34), where Carême rejoices in the grand possibilities for texture and flavor brought about by the new techniques for sauce-making. The era of rabid classification as identified by Foucault comes to its most delicious apex in the resulting rubric of mother sauces and their variations. This revolution is emblematized by Carême's famous classification of four families, each with a leading or basic *grande sauce*, "and each indefinitely extendible by playing variations on that sauce."[10] Master sauces and their derivatives are not only the formal principle of the development of cuisine, but also the structural logic of Greenaway's film: theme and variation; repetition with flexible but subtle distinctions. If one substitutes space for sauce, Carême's description of mother sauces maps the grid of Greenaway's cinematic architectural structure: "we must consider as leading sauces the espagnole, velouté, allemande, and béchamel, because with these four sauces we can compose a very great number of small sauces, of which the seasoning differs infinitely."[11] By the time Escoffier writes his *Guide culinaire*, just a few years into the twentieth century, he is able to list two hundred different sauces.

The French sauce family—espagnole, velouté, béchamel, hollandaise, tomate—includes the name given to the restaurant in Greenaway's film, a site that functions as the nodal point around which the Eros and Thanatos of the film's events spin but also as alpha and omega, origin and end of the representational world. The one spatial and ethical departure from Le Hollandais takes place in Michael's bookshop, a site where the gastronomic and formal logics of the film likewise are in a state of exception and the place where the false hope of escape from those structures returns in the form of terrible ingestive violence. "Hollandaise" names a historical and geographic translation: "from Holland," spoken through the French (hence, this mother sauce's dairy richness, unique among the stock-heavy leading ones).[12] But "hollandaise" names something further: an emulsified sauce famous for its difficult and fraught dispersion of one liquid into another with which it does not easily or evenly mix. A colloidal system, hollandaise, like all emulsifications, requires a great deal of "energy, and sometimes ingenuity, for their formation."[13] These sauces are difficult; they fail easily. They require the expenditure of great force— but also aesthetic cleverness; a bit of style along with technique—to come into existence and to remain for a duration in that suspended, nervous form. A great deal of surface tension requires violence on the part of the cook to the liquid that must be dispersed in a hollandaise. In Harold McGee's evocative phrasing, "Its preferred monolithic arrangement must be shattered."[14] Fragile, unstable, emulsions break; they are easily ruined. And only sometimes are those breakdowns reversible—flocculation may be addressed with further agitation; coalescence of the original droplets, however, is irreparable. The deferred simultaneity of Spica and Aspic—that the heavy letters in the mise-en-scène may not name both churl and toque at once—makes of them a liaison that fails, a blending or joining that refuses emulsification. The film does not take place only under the generalized sign of haute cuisine or its metonymic representation in a fragile sauce possible only through a refined technē; rather, the world of the film exists under the name for the most precarious and difficult of bonds or relations, a difficulty so pronounced that we might say that the intimate breakability of hollandaise governs *and determines in advance* the impossible relations of those who make, who taste it. It is the difficulty of the relation of forces to each other as such that Le Hollandais both names and demands.

Greenaway's film is composed entirely of modes of relation (sexual, material, archival, architectural), given form in entrances and exits, returns and overlappings, apprehensions and consequences, couples and decoupling. Even the title names a troubled relation on the level of the pronoun, with its series of relational deferrals pivoting on the uneasy association between Aspic (*The Cook*) and Spica (*The Thief*), then, the intimate possessive adjectives moving from institutional to illicit relating: *His Wife, and Her Lover.* The four central rooms of the film are in a series of spatial relations: coextensive in a strong horizontal linearity, emphasized by the steady and heavy left-to-right, right-to-left movements of the ever-restless tracking camera over the course of each meal. Other "difficult relations" include the intimacies of both lovemaking and eating (forms of emulsion that also threaten to break) and the fraught metaphysical one of reading (in the figure of bookkeeper Michael) against speaking (in the monologuing Spica).

These repetitions have been read as interpretable signs having recourse to the meta-narrative of history, as when one critic writes of the film's repetitions that the entire work "looks like a map of the French Revolution: it is bloody and divided into *journées*."[15] However, the film is primarily organized around repetitions without depth, a series of nearly identical menus, a model following from cuisine's origin in master and derivative sauces, a structure of theme and subtle but iterable variation. Not only is this formal rigor antithetical to recuperation for historical or political meaning, it empties out the very sites of interpretive depth. William Van Wert is correct to note "the way language overall is used in the film: stating, restating, inverting, following assertions with inverted rhetorical questions," the result "antagonistic, obsessive, rhythmic."[16] The effect of this patterning is both to linguistify rhythm and to rhythmicize language, to change it from a signifying system to a pulsing one. The repetitions of speech—indeed, the repetitions of knowledge in Michael's depository of books—become less sites of narrative depth and yet more sites for displays of heavy, weighted repetition and variation as such. One critic's wonderful epithet for Spica—that he is "a language monster"—nevertheless limits this sense to the abuse of language.[17] But he is also a language *monstrator*, displaying its capacity for theme and variation, repetition with neither origin nor end, capacity for endless inventiveness, without recourse to substance, but as a noisy, unyielding, aestheticized deferral of sense. These relations are formal, not metaphorical or thematic. They govern the gastronomic repetitions, the entrances and exits, the pulse and rhythm of the film—hence, the rigorous tracking through the four successive spaces, and hence the sequencing of menu, arrival, dining, fucking, returning, departure, beating, and so forth—until violence figures as a punctuation of that repetition, an ordinal as well as thematic intrusion. The rhythm of the film is echoed within the diegesis on the level of mise-en-scène, as in the repeated color scheme between the Hals painting and the figures in the dining room, the repeated notes of the boy Pup's *Miserere* and the even allegro of Nyman's "Memorial," the limited line of which sonically commands a push through space—the funereal march reimagined as horrifyingly lively in its progress toward the grave.

DISSECTING QUALITIES

In the previous chapter, disgust, *degoût*, *Ekel* was treated from the point of view of transcendental aesthetics. The affect's appearance in the "disgust debates" of the 1750s allowed the concept to come into focus in and for the field of aesthetics through a displacement: as the underside of the philosophical interest in moral and aesthetic "taste," disgust functioned as the definitionally, structurally, necessarily excluded. These debates, which produced the independent subdiscipline of philosophy called "aesthetics," were concerned with the conditions of possibility for aesthetic judgment and the grounding exclusion or prohibition at the center of the system that constituted those very possibilities. As I previously wrote, Menninghaus's genealogy of the negative affect centered on the epistemic break in the eighteenth century, in which disgust was treated primarily in relation to its (anti)aesthetic qualities. Then, from disgust's status as a definitionally excluded category of rejection, ejection, and refusal, in the nineteenth century and twentieth century, a shift returned to disgust as a category to which one must adhere.

Broadly, then, in the philosophical literature on disgust there are these two positions: the prohibitive accounts of the eighteenth-century aestheticians and the revaluations of the twentieth-century anti-metaphysicians. Between these two poles, however, and bridging transcendental aesthetics with the transcendental gastronomy to which this chapter will turn, lies a small treatise written in 1927 by an Austrian phenomenologist that treats disgust as an independent mental phenomenon while placing its distinctness in the context of the negative affects more broadly. Aurel Kolnai's *Der Ekel*, first published in 1929 in Edmund Husserl's *Jahrbuch für Philosophie und phänomenologische Forschung*, methodologically followed from Franz Brentano's work on intentionality as a form of directedness toward an object of mental experience. Kolnai's exploration of disgust, while motivated by a descriptive phenomenological approach, ranges over "psychological issues and with phenomena belonging to the sphere of descriptive aesthetics, possibly even to metaphysics," and thus figures disgust as a nodal point of philosophical speculation itself, not unlike the pivotal role *Angst*/anxiety will ultimately play for psychoanalysis.[18] (In the nineteenth century and twentieth century, philosophers will generally choose between anxiety and disgust. Kierkegaard, Heidegger, and Lacan ally with the former; Nietzsche and Bataille fall toward the latter. Freud and Sartre can be claimed by either team, but the stronger case suggests that their systems wither without anxiety.) Kolnai, in this essay but also in later work on the negative affects he calls "standard modes of aversion" (fear, disgust, hatred), positions *Ekel* as an aversive or defensive reaction. Narrowly constricting the range of objects toward which disgust may be directed, Kolnai argues from the negative that disgust "is never related to inorganic or non-biological matter," leaving offensive ideas to the realm of unease and the morally disgusting to anger or contempt.[19]

Anticipating Noël Carroll's argument that the affects mobilized by art-horror are fear and disgust, Kolnai pairs these affects repeatedly. They share the characteristic of being "simultaneously intentional and conditional," and they have "approximately the same degree of immediacy, and also the character of being in a narrower sense attitudes of defense."[20] The unique character of disgust, however, brings Kolnai full circle to the concerns of the philosophers of the 1750s. Comparing it to its closest negative affect, he writes that "disgust is more aesthetically determined than is fear."[21] By "aesthetic," though, Kolnai does not suggest disgust's relation to the ugly, the prohibited to the beautiful, or even the capacity for judgments of taste separate from the overwhelming impression imposed on the spectator. In fact, although Kolnai writes about "the role of the rejecting judgment of *taste* in the arousal of disgust," he means here literal taste as opposed to philosophical-refinement taste (which, of course, relies for its metaphoricity on a parasitic relationship to mouth-taste). "Aesthetics," instead, as Kolnai employs the term, refers to a relation to the features or qualities of an object.

One of Kolnai's major arguments in his monograph is that the intention of fear is toward the *Dasein* (the being as such) of the object feared (that it exists, in its existence) and the self experienced as being threatened in its own *Dasein*. Fear is characterized by "a certain abstractness and an indifference to the intrinsic nature of things: what is dangerous is there before us only as 'danger,' and one's own self is intended principally as a unity of existence only."[22] By contrast, the intention of disgust is toward an object's *Sosein,* or

PLATES 1-2. *The Cook, the Thief, His Wife, and Her Lover*
(Peter Greenaway, 1989)

PLATE 3. *Six Figures Getting Sick* (David Lynch, 1967)

being-so. Disgust is "concerned more with the minutiae of the object."[23] If fear is the state in which the subject's survival as a being is at stake, then disgust is the state in which the object's "own intrinsic constitution" is posited. While the intention of fear is toward "the existential situation [*Daseinslage*] which confronts us," the intention of disgust is toward "the features of the object, towards a *type of so-being* [*Soseinsart*]."[24] So fear is of the fact that something is (*that* the monster in my closet exists in its existential isness), while disgust is of the being-so that something is in its likeness: the sliminess of the miscreation's surface, wetness of its oozing sores, and foulness of its odor.

One surprising consequence of Kolnai's argument that disgust's intentionality is toward "the object's stock of features [*Soseinsgehalt*]" is the forging of an unexpected disciplinary bridge between a phenomenological sense of intention toward *Sosein* with film theory's history of positioning disgust as intimately linked to the close-up of some isolated quality and the twin moves of magnification and proximity that have over-determined representations of the disgusting. Although this language of *Soseinsgehalt* seems to suggest an intimacy between disgust and the realm of the visible, Kolnai will argue that the privileged sense of disgust is smell and "the intimacy made possible" by that incorporative sense. However, disgust is a synesthetic cannibal: Kolnai also describes the intentional object with the language of the visible and visual, writing of "the graphic character of the object," "a visible character of 'disgustingness,'" and "the image-content of the intention."[25] The negative affect touches hapticity, as well: "it reaches out to the subject peripherally, as it were, along the surface of his skin, up to his sensory organs and . . . to his upper digestive tract and even, with some reservations, to his heart."[26] Failing to reach the subject as a whole in its totality, as in the Dasein-threatening case of fear, disgust does not pervade *as* a unity the unity of the experiencing subject. Instead, the threatening proximity of the object of disgust is minacious in "its will to be near, its non-self-containedness" that forces itself on the sensorium. Rotting digital pointer, disgust "reaches out, as it were, to the subject."[27] Disgust meets a self where it lives, hungrily sniffs one out—it comes to you.

One tradition of thought on disgust emphasizes, even takes as self-evident, a tight bind between disgust and immediacy, the affect's role as a visceral, instinctive, unmediated gesture of rejection, expulsion, revulsion, and "No"-ness. However, Kolnai's account of *Ekel* suggests what an alternative tradition for disgust might look like if, instead of immediacy, disgust involved the critical labors of interpretation and the unpacking of a secreted or veiled structure. That disgust is bound not to an object but to its adjectives requires that a suspicious hermeneutics regard this stock of specific features and qualities, take these particulars apart, study the details of the crucial characteristics. In language suggesting the detection of disgust as a noxious nose-burrowing hunt, Kolnai imagines that method:

> From the very beginning there is shuddering and a turning away from the object, and nausea, either real or intentional. These phenomena may increase in intensity with the continued presence of the disgusting object, and they may get "darker" in tone, but the tip of the intention penetrates the object, probing and analyzing it, as it were, and becoming immersed in its motions or in its persistence, in spite of essential hesitations and a reluctance which may, of course, also lead to a sudden cessation of contact with the object and thereby a disappearance of disgust.[28]

This grim tale, of beauty and the beastly, suggests the intimacy of disgust with its perceiver on a formal level in addition to the contagion and immediacy ascribed to the sensation as such. The object of disgust must be probed and questioned and studied, Kolnai maintains, because it is "connected with something which is concealed, secretive, multilayered, uncanny, sinister, as well as with something which is shameless, obtrusive, and alluring; that is, in sum, to be something which is taunting. Everything that is disgusting has in it something which is at one and the same time both striking and veiled."[29] Disgust involves a temporal lag, what Kolnai calls a disturbance—"a moment of being something which as it were 'flows' from the object's so-being and of obtrusive proximity, yet it involves also a certain reserve."[30] Disgust therefore not only is not an immediate experience of a totality, but it actively involves dissecting and analyzing—which is to say breaking up, unloosening—the attributes of Sosein.

This drive to proliferate a list of qualities, that "minutiae of the object" Kolnai speaks of, is linked to the entire problematic of taste whereby one can only infinitely digress or defer by asking of something: What does it taste *like?* What does it smell *like?* "The lexicon of smell is very limited and usually must work by making an adjective of the thing that smells," writes William Ian Miller in his anatomy of the bad affect. "Excrement smells like excrement, roses like a rose, rotting flesh like rotting flesh."[31] Once again, then, we are left with Roland Barthes's worry in relation to music: "are we condemned to the adjective?"[32] Surprisingly, against the myriad claims made for disgust's visceral intensity and immediacy, Kolnai's detailing of disgust everywhere suggests the critical labors of analysis and the unpacking of a text. Disgust involves a duration of interpretation toward the qualities of an object, a hesitating encounter with distinct features. In this way, Kolnai's account of disgust in the late 1920s anticipates the poststructuralist love of the particular and contingent, from Barthes's work on the punctum to Derrida's attention to paratextual and parergonal textual effluvia.[33] Unlike other modes of aversion, disgust—taken to be the most immediate and visceral of the affects—in fact requires an act of reading. And it involves the act of reading for Sosein: for qualities, singularities, and particularities. Reading for these features is the very opposite of the images-of tradition one finds in the object-abject versions of disgust criticism, for one does not know—it is not possible to know—what those attributes are in advance of grappling with them in any particular given text. Kolnai's demand for "dissecting or analyzing" Sosein means that one cannot point to the corpse on the screen and be done with disgust. If reading for form involves attending to what cannot be paraphrased—in other words, necessitates tarrying with the specificities of any text—reading for disgust likewise cannot be accomplished through an a priori attribution of essential disgusting things (already) in the world. To put this in its strongest formulation: Kolnai's argument that disgust is aesthetic because it involves intentionality toward the qualities of an object suggests that disgust in fact requires reading for the unleashed *details* in the form of any film.

"Detail," of course, is the noun signaling an isolatable quality, but it is also the verb for a practice of careful description and close reading—one that Kolnai assiduously follows as a good realist phenomenologist. But the detail, or detailing the detail, is also a departure from Aesthetics in the Idealist tradition that hitherto has defined disgust as the obscenity of the beautiful and defined aesthetics in relation to wholeness, totality, and unity. As Naomi Schor notes, the contemporary "valorization of the minute, the partial, and the marginal runs the risk of inducing a form of amnesia that in turn threatens to diminish the import of the current privileging of detail. For . . . the detail has until very recently been viewed in the West with suspicion if not downright hostility."[34] Kolnai's argument for disgust's intentionality toward Sosein in place of Dasein, then, links disgust to the aesthetic as a broad category for its relation to qualities, but simultaneously rends it from Aesthetics in the narrow historical tradition that is anti-detail. This is a problem not only for disgust but also for the entire realm of taste. In "Tractatus Logico-Gastronomicus," Allen Weiss offers a robust version of this argument: "the only manner of estimating gastronomic values and origins, of considering the question of taste, is through a 'Proustian' digression: lengthy, sensual, detailed, eloquent, seductive, and most especially contingent."[35] Disgust yet again occupies a conceptual non-space, intimately linked *to* Aesthetics by being continually banished *from* it. Like Spica and Aspic's deferred meeting in the proper teleology of naming, a gap that takes on profound ethical dimensions in Greenaway's film, disgust and aesthetics are suspended in their relation of repellent non-relation; they are a fraught, even dreadful, *liaison,* a forever failing bond.[36]

ROT'S PROGRESS

Of all the typical qualities of objects that provoke disgust—excrement; bodily secretions; dirt, the viscous and the adhesive; crawling animals and insects, especially those that swarm and surge; spoiled food; the human body (an unwantedly near one, one that "makes itself felt too much *as a body*"); exaggerated fertility; disease and deformation—Kolnai emphasizes putrefaction, rot, decay above all.[37] Echoing the Freudian argument for the death drive, and endorsing a tradition that reaches at least as far back as Hamlet's plaints, Kolnai theorizes rot as something that displays the interconnectedness of decay and nourishment, a liveliness gone wild, and also something that reveals "an impatient longing for death, a desire to waste away, to over-spend the energy of life."[38] To smell decay is to welcome into the body the softening of flesh, to touch that softness in the nerves of the nose and to lose any sense of which skin it is that festers. Transitioning, in-betweenness, movements of state changes occur not only between sense-sharing bodies in this case, but also among the qualities of the object of disgust. In disgust, "we are drowned within a material which is already prepared for decay"; the proximity to the decaying figures the experience of the self's qualities as fluid, transitionable, ultimately rottable. In *The Cook, the Thief, His Wife, and Her Lover,* the chef Richard's gastronomic color scheme for menu pricing is accounted for explicitly in relation to this desire: "I charge a lot for anything black: grapes, olives, black currants. People like to remind themselves of death. Eating black food is like consuming death, like saying, 'Death, I'm eating you.' Black truffles are the most expensive. And caviar. Death and birth: the end and the beginning." Consuming death in the logic of Richard's menu involves a formal incorporation: eating a color—the mastering of death through the immoderate intake of finitude's inky pigment.

One of Kolnai's most innovative and disturbing arguments, and the one that troubles the philosophical binary of refusal or affirmation attendant on disgust, is that the disgusting is alluring while nevertheless remaining revolting. Secreted in disgust—Freud no doubt would agree—is "a certain macabre allure." What Kolnai calls "the paradox of disgust" resides in this affective ambivalence whereby aversion to an object is superimposed alongside attraction toward that same object.[39] Disgust's corporeal schematic in "the intention to vomit" verifies this structure for Kolnai, for disgust "presupposes a possible contact with the disgusting object, . . . a possibility of a positive laying hold of the object, whether by touching, consuming or embracing it."[40] The erotic, intimate, and incorporatively haptic dimension of disgust suggests a kind of desire (Kolnai writes *Lust*) for the object that provokes the repulsion. While the opposite of fear is the wish, the opposite of disgust is a craving: a desire for nearness and proximity, not of an experience, but of a thing in its thinginess. In a striking question that departs from the philosophical history of the affect to turn to the (at that point merely decades-old) psychoanalytic one, Kolnai posits that in sexual life one might also "oscillate between attraction and disgust," and he therefore wonders "why the paradigmatic disgust reaction complex should have its seat not in the sexual but in the gastric region."[41] The marvelously worded answer Kolnai provides is that "the antiperistaltically-induced 'no!' motion" of vomiting is absent in the sexual sphere; sexuality's complexity fails to allow for as unequivocal a negative reaction as the gastric realm. In other words, Kolnai not only suggests that disgust has a relationship to reading for the detail, to dissecting and interpreting the qualities of an object, but he makes the categorical gut the better literary critic than the indefinite and uncertain sex organs—which can do many things but are limited by their sad inability to retch. In place of a poststructuralist criticism that writes desire, Kolnai's disgust demands a critical language that takes the gastrointestinal pulse.

As evidence for the coexistence of attraction and revulsion in disgust, and following from his meta-figure of decay, Kolnai turns repeatedly to an example from a non-philosophical and non-psychoanalytic field. His privileged case of the affective ambivalent paradox is *haut goût,* the practice in haute cuisine of cultivating gaminess through a slow, sure rot. Haut goût requires a purposeful putrescence; its high taste—in the sense of strong but also refined, again mediating both senses of "taste"—involves a desirable element of the revolting. The heightened flavor of slight, correctly-timed putrescence excites appetite instead of voiding it, as in the Icelandic dish *hákarl,* shark meat that is buried for many months to become sufficiently decomposed, or in the putrescence of aged roast game, or in the Chinese delicacy of rotten eggs.[42] There is even what Kolnai calls "a delicately equivocal evaluation, what one might call an eroticism of disgust" in "penetratingly smelly cheeses, which undoubtedly contain something that has to be recognized as putrefaction."[43] The intimate interconnectedness between life and rot is what is announced in putrefaction:

"the fact that life *is there*."[44] It works both ways: the very vitality of living material suggests it has already begun to molder.

Cultivating gaminess in the haute cuisine practice of *faisandage* (hanging meat to begin the process of decay) is not a form of negation or erasure; it is not an undoing of the intrinsic goodness of a thing. Rather, Kolnai insists that haut goût instructs us in the fact that slight putrefaction can accentuate the qualities of a material to make its taste and smell even more distinctive. Gentle rot "does not suppress the specific smell and taste of the material in question, but indeed accentuates them to an extent which makes them even more characteristic."[45] Not suppression, but supplementarity. The spectrum of physical and moral flavors that range from the cravable alluring to the nauseating disgusting is a traversable one: attraction and revulsion can spill into each other, and the coexistence is explicitly courted in the case of high meat. This courting of the revolting does not make the disgusting palatable; Kolnai's recourse to haut goût suggests that putrefaction makes certain materials *better*. The paradox of disgust—its blend of aversion and attraction—results in a heightened sensual experience, one that is in the best taste, and that tastes best, by retaining its link to the revolting. Decay accentuates, exaggerates, alluringly brings out characteristics by subjecting them to the force of rot's state changes; decay can bring into existence new qualities—even the vitality of the new as such. To the query, How might qualities become new, become different, become otherwise?—the very question of the possibility for formal innovation—one answer that reading for disgust suggests is that aesthetic fecundity is possible because things and beings in the world rot.

When Kolnai calls the law of haut goût disgust's paradox, he is bringing to bear on philosophy a long-standing concern from another discipline: gastronomy. The most famous treatment of rot and taste is in Jean Anthelme Brillat-Savarin's *Physiologie du goût* (1825), in which he formulates his own version of the strangely intertwined relationship between disgust's negative and the field of good taste; as it was for aesthetics, the affect will shape the field of gastronomy as its dark limit. The transcendental gastronomer replaces the void at the heart of transcendental aesthetics with decay in and for the field of good culinary, gustatory (but also refined) taste. Brillat-Savarin calls the pheasant, for example, an "enigma," a temporal mystery: he insists on the deferral of its consumption until the adequate recognition of the *moment juste:*

> Every substance has its peak of deliciousness: some of them have already reached it before their full development, like capers, asparagus, young grey

partridges, squab pigeons, and so on; others reach it at that precise moment when they are all that it is possible for them to be in perfection, like melons and almost all fruits, mutton, beef, venison, and red partridges; and finally still others at that point when they begin to decompose, like medlars, woodcock, and above all pheasant.[46]

Cooked too soon (within three days of its demise), the bird is unremarkable; at just the right instant, however, "its flesh is tender, highly flavored, and sublime."[47] The process of putrefaction, laid out in great detail and with the textual precision of a recipe, involves the juices and oils of the decomposing feathers becoming reabsorbed into the bird's flesh. "This peak is reached when the pheasant begins to decompose; then its aroma develops, and mixes with an oil which in order to form must undergo a certain amount of fermentation."[48] Brillat-Savarin's instructions for presentation at this stage are crucial for any reading of Greenaway's infamous cinematic conclusion; as though describing the cannibalistic serving of Michael, down to the garnish of choice, *Physiologie* admonishes that when the pheasant is cooked (*cuit*), serve it up "*couché avec grâce sur sa rôtie*" (gracefully reclining on its bed of toast) and surrounded with bitter oranges. These instructions for presentation include a final line of marvelous instruction that is at once gastronomic, moral, and affective: "*et soyez tranquille sur l'événement.*" Have no fear of, in other words, no unease about, the carnal result.

The cultivation of faisandé or gaminess does not result from the free flow of time's effects on material, but requires a precise and correct ordering. One must not partake too soon; nor would it be advisable to consume too late. Decay's enhancement of qualities is a falling that occurs over time and yet is paused at a point. Indeed, in a discussion of "moral haut-goût," Kolnai speaks of the crucial temporal "tonality" of the "no longer [fresh; good]"; the preparation of the decayed game also requires identifying the certain, precise moment at which rot must also cease (whose tonality is thus what is "no longer" improving through putrescence but certainly once was).[49] This emphasis on change over time is a radical departure from the critical tradition that argues for disgust's immediacy, its relation to the instant, the sheer speed of its repellent onset. That the cultivation of faisandé or gaminess involves the desire to master the correct ordering of time, a precise arrangement, an order and ordering of time that is linked to disgust's enhancement of qualities, suggests what Barthes, writing a preface to the tome, discovers in all of Brillat-Savarin. He finds in the transcendental gastronomer's ruminations on

the effects of champagne on the body, for example, "one of the most important formal categories of modernity: that of the *sequence* of phenomena."[50]
The temporal form elaborated in *Physiologie du goût* is concerned, writes
Barthes, with displacements, deferrals, and degrees. (He calls this sequential
disposition a "bathmology.") Another name for this form of time is "taste." For
while taste cannot receive the density of impressions that, say, hearing can,
Brillat-Savarin insists that it "can be double, and even multiple, in succession,
so that in a single mouthful a second and sometimes a third sensation can be
realized; they fade gradually, and are called aftertaste, perfume, or aroma."[51]
The very notion of a wine's finish or the lingering complexity of a confection's
afterglow suggests the temporal stretch, the successive and additive pleasures
in time of taste. The gastronomer's account continually returns to taste's *temporal* possibilities: of all of the senses, taste "gives us the greatest joy" because
its indulgence is not subsequently followed by weariness (the mouth and gut
have no refractory period) or, pending a bit of moderation, regret; it is possible at any time; "it recurs of necessity at least once every day, and can be
repeated without inconvenience two or three times in that space of hours";
and it sustains persistence in the futurity of life, "so that by the mere act of
eating we repair our losses, and add to the number of our years."[52] Not least
of the violations that take place in Greenaway's film is the inversion of this
futurity of sustenance. In Michael's bookshop, violence takes the form of a
gastronomic perversion: the wrong things are eaten (books in place of food),
and the feeding is forced and torturous and bloody—food giving not pleasure
but agony, eating not preserving life but taking it.

Barthes's summation of the entire temporal structure of gastronomic pleasure is that "taste is that very meaning which knows and practices certain
multiple and successive apprehensions: entrances, returns, overlappings, a
whole counterpoint to sensation: to *perspective* in vision (in the great pano-
ramic pleasures) corresponds *sequence* in taste."[53] This association of visual
perspective to sequencing is especially provocative in light of the Hals mural
on display in Le Hollandais, an example of "table painting," a genre that poses
the pleasures and problems of dining as a problem for representation, grappling with the dilemma of the maximum visibility of figures without masking.
It solves this problem with diagonals and staggers in place of retreating depth,
as though taking the sequencing in time of gastronomy and presenting all
the courses at once—anathema to haute cuisine's rules for dining in strict
order.[54] Punctuating the temporal line of these multiple gustatory sensation-
successions are breaks, contingencies, even shocks and revelations of the dif-

ferent, the unexpected, the new. "Temporalized, taste knows surprises and subtleties," Barthes promises. And in one of the more marvelous sections of the *Physiologie,* Brillat-Savarin posits that "the whole merit of frying consists in the *surprise*" in the shock of the boiling fat on the surface of the immersed substance; Barthes shockingly calls this "the rape [*le rapt*] to which the substance has been subjected."[55] Finally, in language suggesting that decay is also a process of theorizing, Barthes writes that Brillat-Savarin "decomposes *in time*" gastronomic pleasures. His "submission of the gustative sensation to time," Barthes continues, allows it to develop "in the manner of a narrative, or of a language."[56] As one example, take the extraordinary story Brillat-Savarin tells of the machinery of eating:

> As soon as an edible body has been put into the mouth, it is seized upon, gases, moisture, and all, without possibility of retreat.
>
> Lips stop whatever might try to escape; the teeth bite and break it; saliva drenches it; the tongue mashes and churns it; a breathlike sucking pushes it toward the gullet; the tongue lifts up to make it slide and slip; the sense of smell appreciates it as it passes the nasal channel, and it is pulled down into the stomach to be submitted to sundry baser transformations without, in this whole metamorphosis, a single atom or drop or particle having been missed by the powers of appreciation of the taste sense.[57]

Barthes's reading of taste as involving "multiple and successive apprehensions: entrances, returns, overlappings, a whole counterpoint to sensation" structures both antinomies—space and time—of Greenaway's film. The two poles of gastronomic temporality invoked in the film follow divergent logics of time: aspic and faisandage. Faisandage is the structural opposite of aspic: while the savory jelly is a form of preservation, a defense against rot, faisandé involves the change of flavor through the fermentation of partially decayed meat. (*Le Petit Robert* also notes that faisandé can refer to the decadence of aristocrats in addition to the gaminess of a meat's flavor or the putrescence of its smell. And in Bourdieu's account of the different temporalities of working-class versus bourgeois tastes, it is the hallmark of the latter that the form of the meal involves sequencing, pacing, and a pronounced "rhythm, which implies expectations, pauses, restraints; waiting until the last person served has started to eat, taking modest helpings, not appearing over-eager."[58] Both aspic in its immortal halting of time and faisandage, with its luxury of waiting for time's laborious effects on meat, operate in opposition to a free, immediate present of the meal taken for need.) Aspic encompasses the realm of preservative or archive, from the book depository to the shellacked prepared corpse, while faisandage reigns over the various states of hung carcasses inching toward decay; wormy crawling meat already in the process of enlivening after death; and the ordering of sequencing as such: the repeated menus, iterated days in series. If aspic and faisandage are the two prevailing mythologies of time in Greenaway's film—the promise of suspense and archival immortality, and the irreconcilable promise of an ever forward and irreversible rush—they are simultaneously two theories of space, the one imagining materiality's suspension and the fixity of representation, and the other positing the motion of difference's force. Halting decay and cultivating rot's progress suspend *The Cook, the Thief, His Wife, and Her Lover* in a paradox that is as philosophically modern as it is cinematic, caught between the stillness of mechanical capture and projection's rush of movement.[59]

ON HAVING AN EXCELLENT PALATE

Once he has defined disgust as aesthetic because of its intention toward the Sosein of an object, rot must necessarily be Kolnai's privileged example of the form of the affect, for decay and putrescence are by definition changes in the qualities of a thing: variation in coloration, often glaring, as in the greening spread of mold; a heightened or what Kolnai calls "reinforced" smell; a texture that takes on a sheen or moist glisten; the softening of edges in the slow fuzzing of matter's hard border against the world. Rot is on the side of the aesthetic because of this totality of forces on the animated qualities of a substance— what Kolnai dubs "the whole phenomenon of turbulence characteristic of putrefaction."[60] Disgust's intentionality toward the features of an object is an intention toward features moving into different features, even non-features or featurelessness. At the instant disgust attempts to direct itself in consciousness toward the Sosein of an object, that very so-being is in flux. Disgust's intimacy with the vital and animated puts it not on the side of death or the corpse (as in Menninghaus) but on that of dying, the corpse-becoming—(the getting-sick of Figures, and not their sick-as-gotten). Indeed, Kolnai's insistence that the non-organic is not itself ever disgusting (nor is fresh meat or the cold hard skeleton) suggests that it is movement as such—dissolution, transition, the *process* of putrefaction—that offends in rot, which is never just rot, but always in the expanded time of the gerund as rotting.

That what horrifies in disgust is movement, change, difference over duration—not the evacuation of meaning in a blank void but the productive dimension of voided corporeality's surplus effects—requires a change in conceptual vocabulary. It is not that rot does something atrophic to a previously conceived brute object but that its labors on features bring into being new qualities (even heightened ones), introduce putrefaction's supplementary colors, smells, and textures. Disgust is not *in* the text in advance or in a locatable object, nor does it open the text up to threatening, excluded elements, as in David Lynch's films from the previous chapter. Rather, for Greenaway, disgust brings the form of the text—its colors, spaces, rhythms, textures—into being. That in disgust we must analyze, or hesitate for a moment of interpretation toward, those heightened qualities suggests that rot as the sheer fecundity of new qualities and details is both what horrifies in disgust and what is essential and alluring in it. For rot is a problem *for the form of the thing.* Decomposing and decaying—etymologically derived from *decadere,* a falling off in quality or condition—are not themes. Instead, they involve the mutability of form as such. Putrefaction therefore must be read for as the obscenity, fragility, and fecundity of the features of a structure, organic or, let us say, textual—and what it is to be rot is not knowable in advance of this practice of reading, this dissecting, this analyzing of formal qualities as they undergo otherwising. Under the guise of destruction—disgust's imagined role as pure negation—rot's progress brings forth the new, decays into a material's potentiality. The termination of life in a non-still death is the unique horror of disgust—that finitude as being's limit is neither calm nor quiet. Disgust's counsel is not that in death we are too little—the lesson that anxiety and grief both teach—but that in death, more than elsewhere, the body is furiously *too much.* The material form of disgust's law of the worse than the worst—the non-occupiable place that the form of the affect opens up—is the possibility for a putrefaction beyond death, or what Lacan calls in his seventh seminar "destruction beyond putrefaction," that there is a beyond to finitude itself, and it churns, it moves, it froths.[61] Rot involves the mutability of organic form as such; it is the obscenity, fragility, and fecundity of the aesthetic all at once. What rot signals as a formal structure governing the isolated spaces and the repetitions of entrances and exits is the capacity of form to change, to de-form, to become blurry, change colors, die into the different. The paramour Michael says at one point in Greenaway's film, in reference to Wim Wenders's *Paris, Texas,* that silence makes anything possible. But silence between the lovers is eventually broken in the film, and therefore all that remains linked to potentiality is the unfurling horror of rot and decay as the origin of the new and the possible.

Haut goût is the formal law governing *The Cook, the Thief, His Wife, and*

Her Lover, a film organized around a generative visual declension: the capacity for form to stir, for qualities to change or shift, become fuzzy or formless, and for features to fall and become otherwise. The specific manifestation of form as a process of rot and decay centers on the autonomy and mutability over time of color. The force of color as an independent formal property in Greenaway is the lifting of rot's progress and promise to become autonomous of the objects that serve as color's ground in the world. In the opening scene, in the pitch of the parking lot set, Spica describes Georgina's dress as black—"Georgie, you got ash on your tits. If you're gonna wear black, don't smoke. You look like a tart in black." To this, Georgina insists of her dress, "It's not black; it's blue." "It's black," Spica growls, and thus proceeds the horizontal parade into Le Hollandais and its increased diegetic light. In the busy din of the kitchen, Georgina walks into the light and appears in a pale gray dress. In the restaurant moments later, it is a dazzling crimson red. Georgina's dress of canvas: in darkness, its color must first be spoken, positing the ground for an argument reliant on change over time. The disagreement—is the dress black or is it blue?—establishes the pure fact of difference, the fundamental role of negation in positing the visual structure. Any color could fill that original position—and importantly, in the darkness of the image, any visual ascertaining of the settled matter of the disagreement is impossible because what is important is solely that that initial state will change. The disagreement about color in the opening scene hinges on the spoken "not"—the force of the negative is inserted into coloration. In place of colors belonging to the mise-en-scène of that which is put into the scene as presence, color is from the outset claimed by the mise-n'en-scène, put into the film as what fails to be put into the scene except as its instability:—what is put into the non-scene of the film as the absence and end of material truth.

Georgina has slipped away from the table to meet Michael in the lavatory. In her absence, the chef Richard presents a plate of special preparations for her alone, compliments of the house, and a different set of ordinary dishes to a petulant Spica. To the whine, "Why haven't I got one?" Richard responds "I doubt, Mr. Spica, if you'll like it. . . . We have grown accustomed to you being a conservative eater."[62] Over the thief's protestations that he is as adventurous as any diner, Richard insists that he will not like the preparation made for the wife, instructing politely, "Your wife has an excellent palate, Mr. Spica. It is always a pleasure for us to serve her." At these spoken lines, the film cuts to Georgina in the white-on-white bathroom, her red dress now an environment-echoing ivory. The changes in the dress color not only map the breach between the film's central spaces—those differences setting up the impropriety of their admixture of uses, as when Georgina and Michael make love in the kitchen or when Spica violently bursts into the ladies' room—but take place over the non-space of the walls separating the rooms from each other. As Georgina leaves the bathroom to return to the restaurant hallway and the crimson dress, the ontological breach of color is signaled over the blackness of the cut between hallway and bathroom: it is at once the architectural infringement of the wall and the breaking of color from dress, but it is also the unsuturable gap of the cinematic cut as such.

Perhaps because the structure is so very visible, exists to be apparent to the eyes as color is wont to be, the changing colors of the spaces and the metamorphosis of Georgina's fashion are surprisingly under-analyzed in criticism.[63] Like any good modernist, Greenaway stresses that in order to escape the arbitrariness of telling a story, he invents structures to evade contingency; in this film, that constitutive principle is provided by chromaticity.[64] The formal system of the film—what the alphabet or numbers do in other of Greenaway's works—is color in a six-part scheme: "blue for the car park; green for the kitchen; red for the restaurant; white for the toilet; yellow for the hospital; and a golden hue for the book depository."[65] While color squares the architectural grid of the film, the nine consecutive meals at Le Hollandais, signaled by menus—an ordering system premised on the theme and variation of coursing courses—order the temporal pacing of repeated instances punctuated by force external to the system in the form of violence.

In place of Bacon's Black Triptychs, Greenaway has his Color Polyptych. Color as an independent and constitutive structure organizes bodies and rooms, maps out zones of happenings; released from objects, color floats to potentially redirect and land elsewhere. Color shows that it is, and shows that it is all that it is, as though the film yearns to affirm Barthes's answer to the question, "But what is color? A kind of bliss. . . . [F]or there to be color . . . it is not necessary that color be subject to rhetorical modes of existence; it is not necessary that color be intense, violent, rich, or even delicate, refined, rare, or again thick-spread, crusty, fluid, etc.; in short, it is not necessary that there be affirmation, *installation* of color."[66] Although he is writing about Cy Twombly, a colorist very unlike Greenaway, Barthes's ethic of color demands only one thing: "it suffices that color appear, that it be there, that it be inscribed like a pinprick in the corner of the eye . . . , it suffices that color lacerate something: that it pass in front of the eye, like an apparition—or a disappearance, for color is like a closing eyelid, a tiny fainting spell."[67] This autonomy of color, its decoupling from objects, derives from a broader shift in twentieth-century painting; but color's specific unmooring from bodies, beings, and meaning—any of which in another film might serve as its ground—frees it in Greenaway's film to appear, to allow it to *be there*.

However, coloration is not limited to the different relations between architectural spaces, and color as a formal principle is not simply one of ordering or mapping. This structure is less one by which coloration formally maps space(s) in the film—a structure in which color *serves* space, as it in other cases might *serve* meaning—than one in which space(s) are plotted by but also severed from color. Color is lifted from objects in Greenaway's cinematic world and autonomously circulated independently of bodies, suggesting the movement Deleuze finds in certain paintings of Bacon's, the point at which "*color-structure* gives way to *color-force*. Each dominant color and each broken tone indicates the immediate exercise of a force on the corresponding zone of the body or head; it immediately renders a force visible."[68] Color here does not follow the model outlined by the chef Richard—in which eating black food involves consuming death in a tasty metaphoricity. Failing to reveal a symbology of the world, tracing a path as unwalkable for criticism as for characters, color instead reveals a structure to the film. Color's delinking from material allows it to show itself as a pure quality—to present itself as Sosein delinked from Dasein. In its lifted autonomy it brings forth the force of difference on the level of features, the capacity of form's qualities to change, to suffer the mutability of their material conditions.

All this at the line, "Your wife has an excellent palate, Mr. Spica"—the utterance that collapses the totality of formal and thematic complexities in the film into a single point of irreconcilable coextensive structures. The film poses one question, framed as a declarative: What does it mean to have an excellent palate? This is the single question that may be asked at once of the gastronomer, the philosopher, and the painter. If the question is unanswerable, it is in part because of its homonymic confusion of the machinery of the mouth with gastronomic refinement with the artist's swath of painterly substrate. *Palate:* the roof of the mouth; the separation between mouth and nasal cavity, a mediation between smell and taste; but also *palate:* taste, discrimination, ability to discern, judge, detect distinctions; and still also *palate:* the flavor of food, beer or wine (oaky, hoppy). At the same time, in the ambiguity of spoken language, the chef's pronouncement also speaks of the painter's *palette*. In his genealogy of philosophical treatments of color, Charles Riley notes of the three organizing principles—the color chart, the palette, and the spectrum—"All three maps are surface arrangements for selection and organization; but the spectrum is a natural order, whereas the palette's main rule of organization depends on usage." The artist's palette is thus strategy more than substrate. It hierarchizes the material of the painting: "the most frequently used color is given a bigger, special place on the palette. . . . A trying ground for color effects, the palette stands as the intermediate stage between the tabular surface of the canvas and the painter's conception of how the work's color should appear."[69] Coloration in Greenaway's film is likewise organized according to usage, and a specific kind of usage: the relation of a space to the nodal point of the preparation of food in the kitchen. Where it is delivered (the black parking lot); where it is prepared (the emerald kitchen); where it is consumed (the crimson restaurant); and where it is voided (the white bathroom). The spaces also exist in relation to their usage in lovemaking: where the lovers glance, whisper, couple, escape, suffer.

The artist's palette is a kind of work in miniature, or a distorted en abyme, like the Hals painting in Le Hollandais. This tabular form of palette not only presents but brings to presence the force and energy of the formal work to come and what has already passed: the palette, after all, is Janus-faced, smudged with all of the traces of previous work but also dried (dead) ground for the mixing of new tones for the next one. Thus, it does not just *represent,* it also "displays the essential performative qualities of color in action."[70] This stained slab both announces and determines the form that it also is in miniature. Therefore, like aspic and faisandage, the palette provides another form of time in Greenaway's film, recalling Barthes's insistence that gastronomic taste involves "multiple and successive apprehensions: entrances, returns, overlappings, a whole counterpoint to sensation." While aspic's preservative drive encompasses the realm of the frozen archive and faisandage reigns over the various states of decay, the palette's form of time mediates these two temporal forms: it represents and preserves that which it also calls into being and unleashes. In showing the residue and traces of previous work, stained into the surface but also calling into being new and possible chromatic relations, anticipating and performing the future mixing of the qualities of color, the palette may be said to be the figure for the meeting of the promise of suspense and archival immortality and the irreconcilable promise of an ever forward and irreversible rush. If it is the case, as Barthes writes, that "the truth of things is best read in the castoff. The truth of red is in the smear; the pencil's truth is in the wobbly line. Ideas (in the Platonic sense) are not shiny, metallic Figures in conceptual corsets, but somewhat shaky maculations, tenuous blemishes on a vague background," then the palette is the coming together of the tremorous forces of form in advance of structure's imposition of order.[71] The palette is therefore the expression and performativity of the origin of formal material as such, form's contingency and its spontaneity. To say, "Georgina has an excellent palate/palette"—to make it impossible to determine whether it is her palate or her palette that is excellent—is to collapse her completely into the visual material of the text and its structure of autonomous and mutable hues. The dense ambiguity of the pronouncement makes her body the selfsame as the possibility and potential of cinematic form.

What is "excellent," then, is at once the fleshy roof of the mouth (Georgina's mouth for tasting, and later in the film, a rising vocalization as she takes over the monological function from her husband, pronouncing, indeed, the film's final word and judgment); the capacity for discernment and discrimination (Georgina's excellent taste in food and Gauthier fashion); the taste of Georgina (her body's flavor—savored by her lover Michael and, perhaps, by the envious Richard, as well, at a voyeur's distance); and the mixing surface of coloration of which Georgina is the figure of change, the movement along the grid methodically established by the interminable tracking camera. And, in that sense, in a final homonymic move, she is also the film's excellent *pallet,* the ground for transporting the force of the differences of color through the spaces and structures of the film. Not only do the overlaid homonymic relations of "palate" map the interior cavities of the body onto the exterior surface of the film's form, and likewise solder the sensual and philosophical problems of the twin senses of "taste," they also figure Georgina as both ground for coloration and agent of its transmutation over the course of the film. Site of the appearance of color as quality, she bears forth the force of formal difference, calling into existence the intensity of the appearance of cinematic features as they form, change, and deform in space and over time.

Flesh and judgment; ground for admixtures and coloration itself—Georgina bears into the world of the film the force of haut goût as an aesthetic principle coextensive with it as a gastronomic principle. She rots the film form from within by her body's exterior gestures through space. This rotting decay is not an action on a preexisting cinematic object. Disgust's manifestation in the form of decay constitutes the text in time—rot brings forth the chromatic qualities that *are* the visual language of the film. Thus, Georgina not only *has* or possesses an excellent series of relations surrounding palates, palettes, and pallets, but she brings forth—she *is*—that excellent convergence of terms, her body the site of the collapse of the aesthetic and the gastronomic. Pulling the force of the film's formal structure through the rooms, her body, all that it both is and does, maps the grid of the palette while constituting its ground. Georgina thus brings the changing of color into the temporality of the text. It is neither the Cook whose hands lay on meats for faisandé, nor the Thief as the figure of violent moral rot, nor even the Lover as the corpse that materially decays in the diegesis, but the Wife who is the force of putrescence in the film. Georgina is the figuring of the force of form: it is through her that form figures as visual qualities ever in the gesture of rotting. If rot is the certainty of the future desecration of the flesh, even after death—the future holding not just finitude but decay—then rot and rotting form is the visualization of time's effects on the features of a textual body as much as on flesh. Georgina does not bear witness to the capacity of qualities to change over time so much as she bears that manifest force forward as her body persists over a duration across the grid of the film. This decay that generates, this negation that brings forth ever further aesthetic intensities *as the form of the film,* simultaneously brings to presence many heightened pleasures. Rot's promise of the new is enacted by Georgina's body in a composition that unfolds as a series of decompositions.

INTERVAL

Formalism and Affectivity

As with Michael Haneke's *Funny Games,* Greenaway's film serves as an important test for this book's central provocation about the relation between
affectivity and form precisely because his highly formalist films are so often
critically read as being utterly devoid of affect. Consider Michael Walsh's argument about another of Greenaway's films, one that is made *mutatis mutandis*
about them all and, really, about modernist film in general. "The framing
arithmomania and supporting taxonomies of *Drowning by Numbers,*" Walsh
argues, "weave through a fictional experience of obsessional desire, suggesting that all of Greenaway's grids, lexicons, and encyclopedias are not simply
affectless (as critics tend to say) but determinedly distanced from affect."[1] My
argument, that in *The Cook, the Thief, His Wife, and Her Lover* film form rots
through the chromatic force of Georgina's many excellent palettes, is precisely
the opposite: that it is *in* the grids, the lexicons, the encyclopedias—to which I
would add: the rooms and menus in sequence, the iterations and repetitions,
entrances and exits, patterns and foldings, colors and rhythms—that affect
saturates Greenaway's work. It is not the case that the more formalist the film,
the more distanced it is from affect: rather, the more rigorously structured the
text, the more affective it is. Disgust, like grief before it and anxiety to come, is
neither immediate nor strictly visceral. The strongest negative affect cannot be

reduced to spectatorial experiences or to images of the disgusting but names the negative in structures of good aesthetic and gastronomic taste that can be discovered only through the act of reading for the changing details, features, and qualities of a decaying form.

What Kant in his prohibition against *Ekel* and Bataille in his admonition for *degoût* agree on is that it is possible to know in advance what disgust is, what loathing means, and how the negative of good taste works. But if rot's labor on features must be *read for* in that disturbing hesitation with a duration, then the prompting and negative-affective result of disgust cannot be known prior to this moment of interpretation that addresses the contingent, particular, formal qualities of any text. It is reading that will uncover what was never expected and what is not fixed or certain or obvious before the time and activity of interpretation. The formal explosion of rhythms and repetitions in Greenaway's film, the color in a six-part language, and the mobile homonymic grid of excellent palettes—these structures neither shield nor obscure the most intimate confrontation with the figure of what is banished from gastronomy and aesthetics. On the contrary, Greenaway's formalism forms a demand, an order to be unpacked. And if it instructs us in anything, what the strongest negative sensation teaches is that what will be found on the other side of that encounter will be an excellent horrible something that is nothing like what we expected. If Brillat-Savarin is correct that the pheasant is an enigma whose secret meaning is known only to the initiate, we might in turn say that disgust is an enigma whose secret meaning is known only to the patient reader.

Following from this is one final import, and it concerns the relationship between (high) formalism and (low) affectivity. I have written this book as a polemic, and thus I have chosen to write about formal affectivity in relation to texts that lure a critical response that ties affects either to narrative (narratives of grief; narratives of terror) or to spectatorial sensations or rumblings (a seemingly provoked disgust). My gamble throughout has been that if I am persuasive that formal affectivity is operative in these texts in which affectivity would seem to be about anything other than form, then it should be even less controversial to read for the structure and forms of affects in other, less contested sites. I have tested this affective formalism in relation to Haneke and Greenaway, exemplars of the claim that a rigorous formalism is flat, glacial, and devoid of affect. But in the next turn to the wilds of anxiety, this book is also moving to the debased realm of an independent horror film. I have insisted throughout this study that highly formalist films are suffused with affects, and the inverse is true, as well: genres taken to be (and, it must be said, often derided as) nothing but affect, such as horror, are themselves governed by a rigorous formalism. It is not so surprising to suggest that a horror film is suffused with anxiety. But like Haneke's mode of a grieving form that puts on display illumination, like Greenaway's mode of disgust as chromatic decomposition, *Angst* will untangle itself from spectatorship, intention, and presence to instead be read for in and as having visual and temporal form.

Nothing to fear, of course. What could be all that distressing about an almost colorless, almost imperceptible, horizontal line?

Psychotherapy cannot remove ontological anxiety because it cannot change the structure of finitude. But it can remove compulsory forms of anxiety, and reduce the frequency and intensity of fears. It can put anxiety "in its proper place."

—PAUL TILLICH, *Systematic Theology*

It is almost humiliating that, after working so long, we should still be having difficulty in understanding the most fundamental facts. But we have made up our minds to simplify nothing and to hide nothing. If we cannot see things clearly we will at least see clearly what the obscurities are.

—SIGMUND FREUD,
Inhibitions, Symptoms and Anxiety

SEVEN

Intermittency,

Embarrassment,

Dismay

On this there is a fragile agreement: anxiety has something to do with the nothing. Or, rather, as in the ontological formulation Kierkegaard posits in *The Concept of Anxiety,* the object of anxiety is a "something that is nothing." Later, the pseudonymous voice of Vigilius Haufniensis repeats this shift from the definite to indefinite article in a form to which Lacan will insistently return, writing that "the object of anxiety is a nothing."[1] Out of the aporia posed by asking, "What is the nothing?" a difficult question that "deprives itself of its own object," necessitating that "every answer to this question is also impossible from the start," Heidegger finds in anxiety something that "reveals the nothing."[2] As for the Sartre of *Being and Nothingness,* the second titular term insinuates itself into the relation between one's future being and one's present being, horrifyingly announcing to the self on the crag that "if *nothing* compels me to save my life, *nothing* prevents me from precipitating myself into the abyss."[3] Over the relatively brief history of anxiety, this *the* nothing or *a* nothing—or simply an objectless, articleless nothing—is linked to the open and the possible, but also to the finite and to finitude. For every account of the being of nothingness, the heavy object it constitutes for anxiety, there is one that insists on its ephemeral non-objectal figuration as nonbeing as such. Enacting vertiginousness on the level of thought, the nothingness of anxiety circulates in a theoretical abyss, never quite settling on what its dizzying isness *is* or fails to be. There is agreement, then, that anxiety has something to do with the nothing, but the final term in that formulation makes for a tenuous and fractured consensus, shaky like a limb in dread's nervous thrall.

Whether anchored to *the* nothing or *a* nothing, on this there is a more robust agreement: anxiety has something to do with the not-yet, and, as such, the nothingness of the future that always has not taken place, but that might, in its not-yet-having-happened dimension, take place, displacing that nothing that it is at the moment it is realized and is therefore no longer, I mean it no longer may be regarded as, the future. Kierkegaard's Ur-account of anxiety and the experience of sin, *The Concept of Anxiety: A Simple Psychologically Orienting Deliberation on the Dogmatic Issue of Hereditary Sin* (1844), ushered the concept into continental thought, where it dominated existential philosophy and psychoanalytic ruminations with tenacity for more than a century. There, he figured the affect's temporal entrapment as the openness of presentiment, even as a "complex of presentiments."[4] *Angst,* in Kierkegaard's famous formulation, is "freedom's disclosure to itself in possibility." Like Freud later on, Kierkegaard saw anxiety as fundamentally different from fear, which must take as its object something definite. Heidegger will follow him in this move, positing that, unlike in fear, one is always anxious in the face of something "completely indefinite."[5] Anxiety's woolly object, that "something which is a nothing," produces a series of surprising theological conclusions in *The Concept of Anxiety*—namely that, because "innocence is ignorance," in the state of prelapsarian calm there is no thing against which to strive; the effect is not only peace but dread, for "this is the profound secret of innocence, that it is at the same time anxiety."[6]

Variously described in Vigilius's account as touching on "the possibility of possibility," the "possibility of *being able*" (Adamic anxiety), and "the selfish infinity of possibility," it is not merely that anxiety is always about (or abuts) the future, but that the very notion of the possible, for Kierkegaard, "corresponds exactly to the future."[7] Anxiety as "the possibility of possibility," then, might be redescribed as corresponding to the futurity of futurity—in particular, the utterly contingent moment and manner of the self's certain future death, a finitude colored by temporality, what existentialism describes as being's awareness of nonbeing. As though temporalizing disgust's structure of the "worse than the worst," Kierkegaard writes, "No matter how deep an individual has sunk, he can sink still deeper, and this 'can' is the object of anxiety."[8] If disgust captures the features of the abyss in the expanded present of a fall without end, anxiety figures the infinitude of such a descent. Disgust: the damp horror qualities of the cavity's wall; anxiety: that one will never find ground.

THESE THINGS THAT CREEP, STIR, AND SQUIRM

Kierkegaard concludes *The Concept of Anxiety* with a surprising player substitution: in place of the fallen Adam of the previous sections is a new and nameless figure, one whose unusual activities constitute his identity.

> In one of Grimm's fairy tales there is a story of a young man who goes in search of adventure in order to learn what it is to be in anxiety. We will let the adventurer pursue his journey without concerning ourselves about whether he encountered the terrible on his way. However, I will say that this is an adventure that every human being must go through—to learn to be anxious in order that he may not perish either by never having been in anxiety or by succumbing in anxiety. Whoever has learned to be anxious in the right way has learned the ultimate.[9]

The Grimm story "Das Märchen von einem, der auszog, das Fürchten zu lernen," translated as *A Fairy Tale about a Boy Who Left Home to Learn about Fear* or *The Tale of the Boy Who Set Out to Learn Fear,* tells the tale of a young man described as stupid, dull, useless, and ignorant. In fact, though, what Grimm's boy is is a poor reader of texts, a failed literary critic, a bad recipient of bad affect. For when his brother and friends tell ghost stories, he finds that they do not move him; he feels no fright. When his father proposes he learn a trade, then, the simple boy muses that since horripilation fails at the appropriate textual events, it must be a skill he need learn. "Oh, father," he announces, "I'd be glad to learn something; if I could, I'd like to learn flesh-creeping; I don't understand it at all so far."[10] Mistaking affection for vocation, he sets off for a series of increasingly ghoulish encounters, each of which leaves him cold and unbothered but that produce, presumably, the missing negative affect elsewhere on the body of the reader to Grimm's story. Taking everything literally and believing his eyes absolutely (no Todorovian hesitation whatsoever), the boy fails to experience the fantastic as anything but a series of odd occurrences assimilable to the everyday. To the boy's repeated plaint, "Oh, if only my flesh would creep! Oh, if only my flesh would creep!" various figures attempt the affective pedagogy, and each fails in turn, including a king whose daughter is the reward for the boy's impenetrable psychic shield against fear. The tale ends by fulfilling the enlightening promise of its title, but with a morphological twist, providing knowledge only after the ostensibly heroic journey is complete and the princess is won. Years after the triumphant wedding, the boy plagues his regal wife by bemoaning that even now affective knowledge resists him, repeating ad nauseam, "If only my flesh would creep! If only my flesh would creep!"

> At last his young wife was vexed at this. Her chambermaid said: "I'll come to the rescue; he shall learn flesh-creeping all right." She went out to the brook that flowed through the garden and fetched a whole bucketful of little fishes. At night, when the young king was asleep, his wife was to pull off the coverlet and pour the bucket of cold water with the gudgeons over him, so that the little fish all wriggled on top of him. Then he woke up and cried: "Oh, my flesh is creeping! My flesh is creeping, wife dear! Yes, now I do know what flesh-creeping is."[11]

This early nineteenth-century tale is astonishing in its anticipation by seventy years of William James's argument that emotion results from stimulus instead of producing it. Enacting James's famous claim that one is afraid because one runs from an attacking bear and not that one runs because one is afraid, the Grimms' boy finally learns fear from the outside in, not as an interior feeling but from the creeping of his flesh.

If this fairy tale involves the generic thrust of the education of a dunce, it concludes remarkably with a schooling for skin in place of sense. The bodily expression gives rise not only to the negative affective state of mind named in the title, but presumably answers for the early inability to "read" affective texts correctly—the crawling fish produce the shudder in place of the capacity for "correct" interpretation. Or, put another way, the ending appears to suggest that a wet, cold shudder is an adequate *affective form* of textual interpretation. The Grimm story to which Kierkegaard refers suggests both that one must learn fear/anxiety/the creeps—that it is neither innate nor protective, neither immediate nor obvious—and that the creeps come from an outside force acting on the surface of the body. This structure is, in a way, the precondition for the argument that affectivity be redescribed as a form of exteriority, that it be relocated from the interiority of subjective feeling to an exteriority in which forces act on each other, a relation, in Deleuze's language, that "*force has with itself, a power to affect itself, an affect of self on self.*"[12]

Although Kierkegaard makes recourse to this story—(and it is not the only time he invokes the Grimm Brothers in his works)—in order to claim that all, like the boy, must learn anxiety, this is no mere anecdotal aside or trans-disciplinary slip. Rather, the literary example constitutes a major philosophical argument: the affective state of fear as articulated in the tale is reducible to a flesh-creeping, wriggling-fish-caused shuddering—a question, in other words, of things that squirm, shift, and stir. Kierkegaard continually positions anxiety in relation to energetic discharge and motor excess—as, much later, will Freud and Lacan. Anxiety writhes, roils, and shudders, makes the flesh creep away from the self in a quick, lively flaying; angst spins in abyssal circulation or projects in thrownness. The theoretical claims surrounding anxiety described earlier—that it is linked to questions of nonbeing or to a "something that is a nothing" and that it is linked to the possibility of possibility, the not-yet-having-happened dimension of futurity—pivot on forms of space and time. Traversing these two poles is the figure of change or displacement that converts time or space to the other. Indeed, for all that philosophical and psychoanalytic accounts of anxiety focus on being and time, the form of anxiety is accounted for with remarkable tenacity as a problematic of motion and forces. Therefore, while anxiety is analyzed in relation to the nothing as a non-something in space and the nothingness of the not-yet in time, this chapter will argue that the affect abuts those figures because it is fundamentally about forms of *movement* as a mediation between these two states. This chapter recovers the history of anxiety as an instance of what Lacan will call "difficult movement." In place of the famous tripartite title of Freud's treatise *Inhibitions, Symptoms, and Anxiety,* my argument takes as its central terms the difficult movements of time as a form of *intermittency* and the difficult movements of space as a form of *embarrassment.* After articulating the ways in which the difficult movements of thought set anxiety in motion in the work of Freud and Lacan, in the next chapter I turn to the contemporary horror film *Open Water,* a film that manifests anxiety in a roiling form and not in its horrible content. Unlike the undialectical image of grief, bound to the stasis of a tableau, the form of anxiety is a structure in process. If anxiety is a something that is a nothing, it is a not-yet nothing that *churns.*

HEKSEBREV

That Kierkegaard means to suggest that anxiety as the possibility of possibility has a dimension of movement is not demonstrated solely by a quick allusion to the Grimm tale about the learning of the creeps. At the end of *The Concept of Anxiety,* where the titular concept is given its most vigorous form, he writes an epilogue to the Grimms' narrative: "so when the individual through anxiety is educated unto faith, anxiety will eradicate precisely what it brings forth itself. Anxiety discovers fate, but just when the individual wants to put his trust in fate, anxiety turns around and takes fate away, because fate is like anxiety, and anxiety, like possibility, is a 'magic' picture."[13] This sentence—which itself spins and turns its signifiers, pivoting on a series of resemblances posited only to be displaced—defers to its end the Danish *Heksebrev,* the "magic picture" or "witch's letter" that one critic describes as "a magic-like set of picture segments of people and animals that recombine when unfolded and turned."[14] The conjured book is comprised of pictures cut in two so that the top and bottom halves can be rearranged and joined to form myriad combinations of hybrid figures. In addition to making change over time visible and suggesting any number of haptic—and playful—novel recombinations, the magic picture not only, like possibility, shifts and turns and becomes otherwise, it also, like possibility, is linked to the bringing into being of the new.[15]

The figure of the *Heksebrev* is also evoked in Kierkegaard's *Either/Or,* in reference to the stoic ethical person who, unmoved, does not permit "vague thoughts to rustle around inside him," and in his fixity "is not like a 'magic' picture that shifts from one thing to another, depending on how one turns it."[16] If to the twentieth-century reader the moveable cut composition of the witch's picture suggests forms of the submerged recombining, as in Freud's descriptions of displacement and condensation in *Interpretation of Dreams,* to the twenty-first-century reader, its appeal to optical multiplicity, variability, interactivity—and requirement of haptic disorganizations of totality—surely suggest something more akin to a proto-history of interactive new media. But in Kierkegaard's text, with its date of 1844, it also cannot help but bring to mind the prehistory of the moving picture and the nineteenth-century obsession with the motor trickery of optical toys. Thus, the figure of the *Heksebrev* not only ushers motion into the concept of anxiety, it also brings forth specific forms of labile movements: erratic, choppy, non-continuous, deceitful, and deceiving—in other words, magical movement. Though the technological inscription of duration that marks the early cinema is missing in the *Heksebrev,* movement, change, the reorganization of the visible into infinite possible combinations—relying on the fundamental instability of the coherence of the image—does evoke proto-cinematic shifts in understandings of the image and perception.[17] To the witch's letter, add flicker fusion and an etymological trace of deception and you have the early animation device of the phenakistoscope.

In his analysis of the stereoscope, Jonathan Crary describes this proto-photographic tool (and in the language of affectivity, no less) as producing "a vertiginous uncertainty about the distance separating forms."[18] In the visual experience of the stereoscopic image, "Our eyes follow a choppy and erratic path into its depth: it is an assemblage of local zones of three-dimensionality, zones imbued with a hallucinatory clarity, but which when taken together never coalesce into a homogenous field."[19] The non-communication between parts and the failure of fractured zones to return to a totality evokes the *Heksebrev* less in its role as a material object than in the sense in which Kierkegaard puts it to use as a philosophical trope for all manner of things that turn into other things. In this sense, the *Heksebrev* takes on the dimensions of manipulation, trickery, deceit, subjective flux, fractured space, and erratic juxtaposition that mark the other toys that usher in modernity and anticipate the moving picture. Like the stereoscope, where the idea is to fuse fragments while retaining their difference, the witch's letter plays on the notion of combination without unity. It evokes, therefore, the form of space Deleuze and Guattari call "pure patchwork" in which (here, they are quoting Albert Lautman) *"the linkage between one vicinity and the next is not defined and can be effected in an infinite number of ways."* This form of space *"presents itself as an amorphous collection of pieces that are juxtaposed but not attached to each other."*[20] This spatial multiplicity, in the words of Deleuze and Guattari, "has connections, or tactile relations. It has rhythmic values not found elsewhere, even though they can be translated into a metric space."[21] Although a smooth space, it is marked by "an accumulation of proximities, and each accumulation defines a *zone of indiscernability* proper to 'becoming.'"[22]

The recombined multiplicities of the witch's letter conform, on the level of a bewitched book's pulpy matter, to these tactile relations of space in this account. The accumulation of proximities in an unfolding process of becoming does not recombine to form a totality, but, rather, "each intensity is itself a difference." The spatial form that marks "the beginning of a typology and topology of multiplicities," also, for Deleuze and Guattari, ends dialectics, and it therefore seems fitting to locate such a concordant historical thread in the great philosophical opponent of the dialectic. Indeed, in *The Concept of Anxiety,* Kierkegaard critiques Hegel for the *form of movement* he brought to bear on philosophical thought: "to have brought movement into logic is the merit of Hegel," but this was ultimately "a merit he disdained in order to run aimlessly."[23] There is a textual connection between philosophical movement and the movements of the witch's letter, for Kierkegaard writes in a buried note of "all the strange pixies and goblins who like busy clerks bring about movement in Hegelian logic."[24] Hegel's transfixed movements, put into the workings of logic, run frantically—they seem to appear without cause, without making visible their means of endless flux.[25] In Kierkegaard's critique, the dialectic with its frenetic commotion seems, above all, to be a kind of ever-shifting witch's philosophy. If the philosophical motor gesture of the dialectic is the roiling negative, which "is used as the impelling power to bring movement into all things," the qualitative leap of Kierkegaard's philosophy is one predicated on the non-continuity with previous states, a presuppositionless movement. (This movement-beyond is the leap into faith, what Levinas calls *dépassant,* and what he will call the surging ground for "Kierkegaardian violence."[26]) In place of a movement that runs seamlessly ever on, the anti-dialectical qualitative leap suggests the structure of Deleuze and Guattari's "accumulation of proximities" in which "each intensity is itself a difference." Philosophy, then, for Kierkegaard, like philosophical history and philosophical concepts such as anxiety, rests on differing approaches to forms of movement, forms that are the energetic experiences of philosophical thought and not mere metaphors for concepts.

Kierkegaard's turn to the witch's letter as the meta-figure for transformation as such—whether a conceptual positive, as in the account of anxiety, or an ethical negative, as in *Either/Or*—and his simultaneous critique of the form of movement of the dialectic pivot on one and the same insistence: that there are different types of movements, and that within the multiplicity of movements is a form that transforms without recombining, a movement that suggests a fragmented and wild accumulation of proximities in place of a seamless, continuous transformed resolution.[27] Despite the singular titular "Concept" (1844) of the text, Kierkegaard is more than happy to multiply forms of anxieties, writing in *Either/Or* the year before of Don Giovanni's "sensuous" anxiety, which is substantial, not subjective (in other words, an objective component equivalent to his life), as opposed to Nero's violent causing of anxiety in others because "his inner being is anxiety."[28] In *Either/Or,* in addition to making anxieties multiple, Kierkegaard anticipates his account of the unstable metamorphoses of the negative affect in his description of Antigone's tragic anxiety, which is, again, cast in terms of flux and movement, now with speeds and rhythm added: "anxiety is the energy of the movement by which sorrow bores its way into the heart. But the movement is not swift like the arrow's, it is gradual. It is not once and for all, but in constant becoming."[29] He continues, folding the multiplicity on itself to create even more subdivisions of unrest: "anxiety has a double function. It is the movement of discovery that constantly touches, and by fingering it, discovers sorrow by going around it. Or anxiety is sudden, positing the whole sorrow in the here and now, yet in such a way that this here and now instantly dissolves into succession."[30] Antigone's anxiety, then, is the enabling force, the movements "in constant becoming" as such, of the totality of the negative affects of tragedy. For all that Kierkegaard's treatments of *angst* revolve around finitude, the nothing, ignorance, and presentiment, ultimately the common bond of these concepts-in-process is a structure that is already and always set in motion. Kierkegaard's form of anxiety is a disquieted form of the nothing put into movement and the movements of the nothing. Kierkegaard, in other words, and across his diverse philosophical texts, *mobilizes* the nothing.

The reference to the witch's letter in Kierkegaard's tract is not often re-marked in the literature on anxiety, save for a curious appendix titled "Beyond Anxiety: The Witch's Letter" in Samuel Weber's *Return to Freud*. In reference to Lacan's aim to bring things "beyond the limit of anxiety," Weber imagines that, were this possible, at the site of all the "other 'beyonds' one might con-ceive, we might well find a witch's letter waiting there to greet us."[31] Such a finding would encounter, of course, nothing, for the identity of the witch's letter is one of mutable flux: at the scene of those compendia of beyonds would be movement and recombination and change itself. In a final twisting fold of the magic picture book, its ultimate movement is a perpetual deferral of substance and, in particular, the deferral of the meeting of any thing and I.[32] Anxiety's ever-becoming movements appear to be the motor counterpoints to its description by Kierkegaard as a pivot or nodal point "upon which every-thing turns."[33] Later thinkers, particularly Freud and Lacan, will echo this claim of Kierkegaard's, will continue overtly to link anxiety to time, space, and nothingness while nevertheless describing it as a problematic of movements slow or sudden, and simultaneously dubbing it the fulcrum of psychoanalysis. The pivot or nodal point, indeed, will continually be threatened with its sub-sumption by the language of mobility: the moveable form of anxiety will be figured as a pivot that itself spins, a solar nodal point around which everything turns that itself is in flux.[34]

This is why Lacan insists in *Le Séminaire X*, "*Il ne faut pas que je l'arrange trop vite*" (One should not come to terms too quickly [with anxiety]).[35] The risk is always in *missing* it.

INTERRUPTION OR THE INTERVAL

It may be the case that the nodal point, pivot, or fulcrum is an imperfect meta-phor for the movements of anxiety because of its implied stilling in any revolving system; anxiety is, perhaps, more like a radiating core sustaining systems of thought. For all that continental philosophy in the twentieth century spun out theories of anxiety's webs, the discourse that took anxiety to heart was psychoanalysis, for which anxiety was not only a pivot but *the* pivot, the organ around which the body of the field was constituted and sustained. By the relatively late date of his *Introductory Lectures on Psychoanalysis,* Freud insists that "there is no question that the problem of anxiety is a nodal point at which the most various and important questions converge, a riddle whose solution would be bound to throw a flood of light on our whole mental existence."[36] Lacan, for his part, will likewise call anxiety a convergence, even the *rendez-vous* where "all of my previous discourse awaits you, including a certain number of terms which up to now may have seemed to you to be insufficiently related. You will see how anxiety is the terrain where these terms tie in with each other and thereby assume more clearly their place."[37] In its earliest treatment by Freud, in which he attempted to cordon off "anxiety neurosis" from "neurasthenia," the very categories of the normal and pathological, ordinary and extraordinary, realistic and neurotic, and even exterior and interior are put in play to define the proper objects of debate surrounding the psyche after the discovery of the unconscious. Weber's formulation of Freud's hesitation between the alternatives posed by anxiety evokes an experience of the suspended psychoanalytic fantastic. The issue at stake is directional: where does anxiety, precisely, come from? "It is precisely Freud's inability to resolve the problem in terms of the alternative already described—Is anxiety functional or dysfunctional? Is the danger to which it responds essentially external or internal?—that constitutes the interest of his discussion," Weber writes. "The reality of anxiety, and of the danger to which it reacts, emerges as neither simply external nor internal, neither straightforwardly functional, nor dysfunctional; the functioning of the psyche is, intrinsically, as it were, bound up with an irreducible exteriority, with an alterity that it simultaneously denies and affirms."[38] Not unlike the paradox for all boys going forth to learn what fear is, anxiety is tangled up with the confusion between interior and exterior states, between some "I" that can or will (or will fail to) feel the creeps, and some exteriority for which cold primordial creatures stand in, that accost the self in bed at night, unexpected wriggling nothings performing their violence out of nowhere.

Between the papers on anxiety neurosis of 1895 and *Inhibitions, Symptoms and Anxiety* in 1926, Freud famously reversed his position on the relationship between repression and anxiety. Although it is rarely described in this language, his revision hinges on a changing theory of the *movements* of anxiety.

In the earlier texts, Freud claimed that obstacles to the discharge of libidinal tension cause anxiety as a transformed form of the accumulated sexual excitation—hence, his expression that repression causes anxiety. In the later texts, however, he figures anxiety as a reaction to a dangerous, threatening, or traumatic situation, which repression is meant to alleviate—thus, the new rule: anxiety causes repression. The reversal was a forthright shift in thought. While in 1894 he wrote, "Anxiety arises from a *transformation* of the accumulated tension," by 1933, in the *New Introductory Lectures,* he indicates that he would "no longer maintain that it is the libido itself that is turned into anxiety in such cases."[39] The separation of the cause of libido and the cause of anxiety derives from Freud's work on danger and trauma in *Beyond the Pleasure Principle* (1920) and is part of the more radical shift that occurred with his structural theory of the mind from *The Ego and the Id* (1923), explicitly manifest in his claims that anxiety is a signal and that "the ego alone can produce and feel anxiety."[40] What substantially and provocatively changes in the late theory is the model of energetic movements attributed to the formation, transformation, and reaction to the affect.

The early theory of anxiety, which holds that repression causes anxiety, relies on what Freud describes as "a metapsychological process of direct transformation of libido into anxiety," caused by some disturbance in the discharge of sexual excitation. "I found that outbreaks of anxiety and a general state of preparedness for anxiety," Freud notes in his history of the conceptual reversal, "were produced by certain sexual practices such as *coitus interruptus,* undischarged sexual excitation or enforced abstinence—that is, whenever sexual excitation was inhibited, arrested or deflected in its progress towards satisfaction."[41] The form of the earlier theory of anxiety was interrupted progress marked by breaks, the breaking off of activity, the cessation of movement to thwart a teleological aim. The halt in movement is followed by a conversion of the tension of the suspension into different movements of anxious motor response, the transformation of libido constituting a displaced version of the movement prematurely hindered in its movings. The premise of this theory of the movement associated with anxiety is that the negative affect results from a blockage in the forward progress of energies, from movement's energy now gummed up. It relies on a model of movement as *interruptible,* as something into which a stop can be successfully placed, that temporal and motor advances can be broken off and transformed into something else. This model is grounded on the assumption of an anterior state of plenitude in movement, at which the negative is inserted in the external form of an interruption or stop that breaks in on and disturbs the wholeness and continuity of the advance. Movement is fundamentally regarded as potentially successful and continually progressive unless or until disturbed by an interruption from without (Newton's first law of coitus: *a body in motion . . .*). But the central characteristic of this form is that the interruption is regarded as an absolute breach; it is its cessation as a firm stop that sets in motion the anxious structure. For all that interruption appears, then, to be about a pause or halt in time of movement, Freud's model of the transformation of libido into anxiety suggests, rather, a spatial model of the transfer of energy, as though the abrupt interruption of coitus causes an embarrassing pile-up at the scene of the sudden stop as in any motor crash—interruption means there is nowhere now to *go*. The interruption that transforms libido into anxiety is a spatial blockage in which dammed-up energies redirect elsewhere after the surprise of the halt.

As though performing in miniature the broader swap in modernity of categories of time for categories of space, Freud's later revaluation of anxiety in relation to movement hinges less on the notion of an interruption to a continuous progress or a spatial damming of energy than on a model touched by the temporal language of the interim. Instead of coitus interruptus setting anxiety in motion, by the time *Inhibitions, Symptoms and Anxiety* was published in 1926, Freud had become concerned with what he calls the isolation and interpolation of an interval, a structure that enables a new kind of movement in the form of repetition. In his revised theory of anxiety, that is, Freud shifts from a model of anxiety and movement predicated on *interruption* to one centered on *intermittency,* and it is this shift that will persist in defining the form of anxiety in Lacan and that will reappear in the next chapter in the horror film *Open Water.* Instead of the rhythm of suspension, the revised form of anxiety in Freud's later work revolves around the force of restriction: in place of halts or breaks or blockages, anxiety is linked to pressures squeezing time and choking the possibility for a forward progress that nevertheless persists. As opposed to an interruption that calls movement off, movement is given over as troubled movement, strangled, frayed, worked-over movements.

Freud's one specific reference to the form of anxiety and time in *Inhibitions, Symptoms and Anxiety* perfectly follows Kierkegaard's claim about presentiments and the affect. The psychoanalyst writes that anxiety "has an unmistakable relation to *expectations:* it is anxiety *about* [*vor;* before, in the sense of both facing and prior to] something."[42] In the process of arguing for his broader claim that anxiety causes repression, however, Freud theorizes repression in relation to two techniques of movement that depart from his theory of movement as interruptible in the earlier text. Specifically, in a discussion of the varieties of repression, Freud posits two core techniques for the enactment of neurosis: "*undoing what has been done* and *isolating.*"[43] In a curious textual echo of the *Heksebrev,* which is constitutively a process of undoing what has been done on the level of homogenous visual form, Freud calls the former technique "negative magic," an attempt to dissolve or "'blow away' not merely the *consequences* of some event (or experience or impression) but the event itself."[44] In place of a logic of substitution or erasure, however, the attempt through a second act to cancel out a prior one does not reach its aim: "it is as though neither action had taken place, whereas, in reality, both have."[45] Subtraction, in other words, takes place through the additive; negation produces a supplement. Repetition functions through this double move of erasure in the heightened action of a preservative: "when anything has not happened in the desired way it is undone by being repeated in a different way."[46] In other words, this model of anxiety suggests that as it was unthinkable that something had taken place, it would have to take place again.

The second technique of symptom formation is isolation, which Freud also links to the motor sphere. At the unpleasant or traumatic event, the subject "interpolates an interval during which nothing further must happen—during which he must perceive nothing and do nothing."[47] In the case of an experience that cannot be forgotten, "instead, it is deprived of its affect, and its associative connections are suppressed or interrupted so that it remains as though isolated and is not reproduced in the ordinary processes of thought."[48] Motor isolation ensures that those psychic connections are interrupted and broken apart. In a marvelous reading that fleshes out his language, Freud ultimately links this prevention of associations in thought to the taboo on touching (thought A is prevented from nuzzling too close to thought B). While inhibition is a failure or suspension of movement, and the symptom is a displaced or transformed movement, anxiety is ultimately refigured as a constricted or awkward movement.[49]

Together, these two techniques for symptom formation—undoing/repetition and interpolating an interval—suggest a radically different model of time in relation to the affect theoretically encircled by Freud's discussion. For the interpolation of an interval is not an interruption. The interval, which averts or inhibits contiguous thoughts and associations, puts a gap into continuity instead of breaking it off absolutely. And though described in the language of space and touching, it is also a fundamentally temporal problematic: the interval is put into place that "nothing further must happen," an interval, in other words, that is meant to not take place in ordinary or eventful time. The desired content of that interval—in which nothing more happens—is another form of Kierkegaard's description of the quintessential state of anxiety: the calm nothing of the ignorance prior to original sin and therefore prior to a conception of duration. If the obsessional neurotic desires to put into time a space for nothing to happen, this is not merely an abstention from time but an attempt to introduce into the continuity of time a discontinuity marked by the placement of *the* nothing. The desire is not for a plenitude of movement, space, time, or continuity but for the finitude or inadequacy of the forward progress of futurity. Intermittency is introduced to punctuate time itself, not to halt movement as it takes place in a homogenous field of progression. Because movement does not break off—as in all activity *interruptus*—a new form of it persists in repetition. The interval enables, in other words, a new form of carved-up, iterable movement.

To summarize: in Freud's first theory of anxiety, within the good of the continuous progression of coitus is the danger of an interruption that disturbs continuity and the completion of activity—anxiety derives from an interruption to or absolute breach in that system. By the second theory of anxiety, however, what is desired is the possibility of interpolating an interval into which the nothing is placed to ward off further happenings—anxiety derives from the *failure* or inability to interrupt a system. Instead of the discontinuity of time, there is a saturation of time in the form of repetition through the additive gesture of "undoing what has been done." If movement is a plenitude that may be interrupted in the former case, by the latter, movement's horror is that it cannot be punctuated, that the plenitude of an extirpated interval from time is ultimately impossible. The earlier model is a violence of finitude; the later one recalls the claim made equally by philosophers and vampires that more horrible than death is immortality.

Following from Freud's second form of anxiety, which involves the interpolation of an interval so that nothing further may take place, one may correctly say that Freud's 1926 text is a theory *of* anxiety, not merely about but constituted by precisely these failures, intervals, repetitions, and punctuations. Freud's language everywhere performs a series of slips, failures, and—more than in most of his texts, many of which are marked by such aporias—a persistent sense of having missed the object of his inquiry. The text, in a manner, does not take place.

In fact, one difficulty in locating this shift from a structure of anxiety's interruption to anxiety's intermittency in the undulating lines of thought in

Inhibitions, Symptoms and Anxiety is that Freud continually leaps to and from each of his titular tripartite terms, making anxiety's appearance in the essay itself intermittent through a text that continually interrupts itself in the completion of its psychoanalytic aim. As though evoking Crary's description of the stereoscopic image as "an assemblage of local zones of three-dimensionality, zones imbued with a hallucinatory clarity, but which when taken together never coalesce into a homogenous field," even the tripartite title of *Hemmung, Symptom und Angst* assembles terms that do not form a unity. (As Weber notes, the title "establishes a sequence but not a conceptual or totalizing synthesis."[50]) The title relies on linkages marked by catenation or proximity instead of necessary continuity. In fact, Freud renounces synthesizing altogether at one point, writing of his desire for a new procedure in the text: "I propose to assemble, quite impartially, all the facts that we know about anxiety without expecting it to arrive at a fresh synthesis."[51] The multiple addenda at the end, some of which contain Freud's most explicit statements on anxiety—such as the claim that anxiety, unlike fear, takes no object—contribute to the sense of threads of thought that fail to resolve into a totality of psychoanalytic speculation. Erratic movements of thought *about* anxiety mirror the concept under analysis. "Anxiety is not easy to grasp," Freud admits at one point, recalling the wriggling, flesh-creeping cause of the Grimms' little fish. If, as Freud writes of one form of neurotic anxiety, "the complex which we describe as a state of anxiety is capable of fragmentation," then *Inhibitions, Symptoms and Anxiety* is in a persistent state of anxiety, fragmented and pieced, interrupted and parsed.[52]

The structure of the entire text fails to unify or cohere, but is marked by fits and starts; its language likewise provides no antidote but wanders adrift, continually slips away from itself. Weber describes the argument in *Inhibitions, Symptoms and Anxiety* as following "a seesaw movement of self-revocation not unlike that described by Derrida in his reading of *Beyond the Pleasure Principle* in *The Post Card.*"[53] Continually in a form of motor paralysis, following the back-and-forth of coming into focus only to toggle, blurry, out again, the object of anxiety has no proper place in Freud's later text—or, its place takes place in the continual placing, in its deferral of place or installed non-place that is its continually shifting ground, like a psychoanalytic *Heksebrev*. Thus, Weber's evocation of Derrida's reading is only partially apt. Derrida writes of *Beyond the Pleasure Principle*, "Is what we have retained . . . anything other than a rhythm, the rhythm of a step which always *comes back* [*revient*], which again has just left? What has always just left again?"[54] If Derrida's reading of the rhythm of Freud's text follows the meta-structure of the *fort/da* in "what has always just left again," the wrist of *Inhibitions, Symptoms and Anxiety* does not register an identical pulse. The cadence of that text more perfectly matches Freud's description of anxiety in hysteria as "motor paralyses, contractures, involuntary actions or discharges, pains and hallucinations" in a tempo of "cathectic processes which are either permanently maintained or intermittent."[55] The anxious text, in other words, is not rhythmically organized around a step that returns but a step that misses, a hitch, a tic, a difficult movement that does not rock smoothly in its repeated parting but that stutters, that trips, that can neither return nor leave (let alone return only to leave) because it cannot, fundamentally, get started, and because of this, this hitch, this tic, this hesitation and failure to start, this text also cannot or does not (it refuses to) end, it can only repeat. It will only repeat.

The form of the writing bears this out. Chapters begin with circlings back and hesitations of thought—"To return to the problem of the ego"; "Let us go back again to infantile phobias of animals"; "Time has come to pause and consider"—and will end with failures.[56] The false starts of the early theory of anxiety lead Freud to, precisely, nothing. In the eighth section, two-thirds of the way through the essay, he writes as though starting afresh, "Anxiety is not so simple a matter. Up till now we have arrived at nothing but contradictory views about it."[57] The text, however, self-consciously passes judgment on these failures. Thus, the fourth section of the essay ends: "When coitus is disturbed or sexual excitation interrupted or abstinence enforced, the ego scents certain dangers to which it reacts with anxiety. But this takes us nowhere. On the other hand, our analysis of the phobias seems to admit of no correction. *Non liquet.*"[58] The final explicit (literal) verdict on the sentence—the Latinate "It is not clear"—takes the anxious form of incompletion, pleads guilty to an inability to follow the line of thought to its successful resolution. *Textualis interruptus.* The Latin announces the ambivalence the text will experience as it attempts to grapple with a something that is a nothing, a nothing determined in the failures of the text and as a positivity of the nothing put into the motion of thought in the text. Lines of speculative flight will diverge but lead to no end or conclusion. The work will multiply its failures, even incorporating and cannibalizing the irresolutions of other works. "Incidentally," murmurs the final line of the seventh section, "it may be remembered that in discussing the question of mourning we also failed to discover why it should be such a painful thing."[59] The final two chapters labor not to posit a claim but to drain the text of its contents, putting forward a series of increasingly abstracted questions that pose the question of Freud's entire disciplinary endeavor. If the late speculative work of Freud often contains such detours, and ends on notes of wonderment (*Civilization and Its Discontents*) or a poetic appeal to the slow advances of knowledge (*Beyond the Pleasure Principle*), *Inhibitions, Symptoms and Anxiety* nevertheless appeals to the non-productions of the text in a particularly exaggerated state. The penultimate chapter pivots from anxiety to pose the riddle of psychoanalysis itself as a riddle of time and space—we might as well be at the beginning; we ultimately have not gotten anywhere.

> Why does the affect of anxiety alone seem to enjoy the advantage over all other affects of evoking reactions which are distinguished from the rest in being abnormal and which, through their inexpediency, run counter to the movement of life? In other words, we have once more come unawares upon the riddle which has so often confronted us: whence does neurosis come—what is its ultimate, its own peculiar *raison d'être*? After ten years of psychoanalytic labours, we are as much in the dark about this problem as we were at the start.[60]

While the normal process of mourning was meant, earlier in this book, to cast light (*erhellen*) on the abnormal reaction of melancholia, here anxiety functions as a shade, intercepting illumination: instead of revealing or manifesting psychoanalytic truth, it cloaks any theoretical or disciplinary enterprise in frustrating forms of shadowy darkness. Tracks of thought lead Freud nowhere, and the text is a record or inscription of these inhibited, blocked, failed, and insufficient insights into anxiety. The essay, at this point, and in a figure that will become significant in the next chapter, is simply treading water.[61]

When Freud revises his theory of anxiety, the organ linked to the affect of dread likewise shifts, and despite the analysis of writing's blockage, with the move to a form of anxious intermittency in place of anxious interruption, Freud likewise leaves behind the organs of coitus. Instead, the revised theory emphasizes that anxiety's bond to specific physical sensations is linked to the respiratory system and to the heart. If these motor enervations were, in the early theory, a displacement or transformation of the more primarily erotic break, here they take on an independent status as the primary corporeal components of anxiety. For Freud, like Nietzsche before him, places great emphasis on the etymological link between "anxiety" and its root in *angustus* (narrow) and *angere* (to choke).[62] Anxiety, *Angst, Enge*—derived from narrow straits, a place that chokes, a choking place—is etymologically linked to confinement and a resulting strangulation. This is why both Otto Rank and Freud link anxiety to birth trauma. While philosophers bind anxiety to finitude, for psychoanalysis it is not that we die too soon but that we are in fact born too early. The predicament of the human subject is not that temporality conditions finitude but that we are thrown into worldly time before the proper moment, in what Freud calls "a less finished state" than other animals.[63] In the coitus interruptus days, Freud's account of the breathlessness and fluster of anxiety's motor manifestation was part and parcel of the theory of the transformation of libido; where copulation's vigor was disturbed, the body displaced the energies elsewhere. By 1926, these were no longer transformations but motor repetitions of the traumatic experience of the danger of birth, following the broader Freudian claim that any and every affect "is only a reminiscence of an event."[64] While insisting that anxiety is a reaction to danger, or a signal of it (hence, repression, which attempts to mitigate that feeling), Freud does not accept Rank's argument that anxiety is an abreaction of the original trauma of birth and that the most intense neurotic anxiety results from those whose birth trauma was particularly strong.[65] He does, however, retain the notion that birth is a prototype of the affective structure of anxiety, writing in *The Ego and the Id* that birth was "the first great anxiety-state."[66] While birth is an event for Rank, for Freud it is a form of restricted expression, delimiting the characteristics of motor constriction, breathlessness, and frenetic palpitations that mark the chokings of the straits of the throat in anxiety. Birth *formalizes* the affect's etymological dimension of narrowness, strangulation, and the yearning for breath and escape.[67] Given that Freud accepts Kierkegaard's formulation of anxiety as linked to presentiment, confinement and constriction should not be regarded as relegated to a closed tight system; we might reimagine anxiety as linked to the confinement of that which is exposed, the claustrophobia of the open. A lack of breath not from being shut in tight, but from, perhaps, choking on too much space—the expansive exposed space, even, of the wide open water of the sea. This is the sort of gaping space that one could drown in.

Inhibitions, Symptoms and Anxiety, with its stutters and starts, fits and hesitations, suggests what a theory might sound like when it is gagging, choked, trapped in narrow straits and ultimately strangled—(or, alternatively, when a theory is being violently born). Freud, for all that his new account of anxiety appears to be about time and repetition, ends up performing in place of a theory only the difficult movements of the shallow breaths of thought. The inhalations of the text are asphyxiated ones, and the form of Freud's writing, with its failures and humiliations, its attempts to start over and its frustrations at dead ends that lead to nothing, is a structure of formal suffocation, an essay garroted by its own subject. With the shift from interruption to intermittency, Freud's account of anxiety makes an attendant shift from suspension to restriction: the motor brunt of that shift is nowhere more felt than in the degree of pressure and force and the squeezing of breath that marks psychoanalytic thought about anxiety. These repetitions are the obstructed difficult movements of a thought that cannot take (its, a) place, but only repeats in the horrible manner of an anxious panicked gasping for air that will not arrive, that will not be sufficient or *enough*. The form of anxiety, then, is a form-in-process or a gesture of difficult movement, a choking movement, a movement that does not take place and that does not-enough arrive.

ESMOI, ESMAIS, ÉMOI

These are also, however, repetitions that embarrass. The anxious structure and language of Freud's text not only introduce the theoretical and formal dimension of intermittency to the study of anxiety but also frame the analysis of the affect under the guise of something related to shame. The epigraph that appears before this chapter occurs halfway through Freud's text, apologetically centering the essay: "*Es ist fast beschämend, daß wir nach so langer Arbeit noch immer Schwierigkeiten in der Auffassung der fundamentalsten Verhältnisse finden, aber wir haben uns vorgenommen, nichts zu vereinfachen und nichts zu verheimlichen*" [It is almost humiliating that, after working so long, we should still be having difficulty in understanding the most fundamental facts. But we have made up our minds to simplify nothing and to hide nothing].[68] Humiliation, as with humility, brings things down to earth, makes low the lowly (and in the eyes of others). *Beschämend*, with its evocations of shame and the shameful, is a particularly evocative choice for a Freud who as early as *Three Essays* linked shame to repression. Shame's oft-cited etymological link to covering and concealment suggests a bodily exposure in the history of the letters; what is humbled in Freud's account, what is shamefully exposed to his reading public, is the embarrassing, mortifying stuckness of thought that has not yet transformed into clarity, has failed to become illumined through psychoanalytic reflection. If the structure of Freud's text seesaws, as in Weber's account, this central passage is its blushing fulcrum. Just as anxiety is the nodal point around which psychoanalytic thought is organized, humiliation as the failure to arrive in thought, in turn, is the nodal point of anxiety. The revised theory of anxiety involves the interpolation of an interval that enables repetition and therefore takes the form of *intermittency*, but this temporal problematic is intertwined, even in Freud's account, with *embarrassment*. It is not until Lacan that these divergent threads in Freud are given their full interrelated elaboration, for Lacan's tenth seminar will unify intermittency and embarrassment in his theory of anxiety as a form of humiliating difficult movement.

Lacan's *Le Séminaire X, L'angoisse* (1962–63) grapples with Freud's claim, made in an appendix to *Inhibitions, Symptoms and Anxiety,* that while fear takes a specific object, anxiety is diffuse, with a "quality of *indefiniteness and lack of object.*"[69] Lacan's formulation of his disagreement with Freud's explicit statement on anxiety takes the peculiar grammatical form of "It is not without an object," a statement that Joan Copjec notes is in the form of a litotes or understatement, the expression of an affirmation through the negation of its opposite.[70] The understatement suggests the strongest version of the claim that it is not only the case that anxiety has or takes an object, but that it is centered on the certainty of an object through "the insistent affirmation of a negative contrary."[71] The object that anxiety takes for Lacan is the privileged remainder, the *objet petit a,* an object not like all other objects and what he describes as contributing to the possibility of "an irreducible" and radical type of lack.[72] The little bit of the Real is given in *Seminar X* in the formula, "Once it is known, once something of the Real comes to be known, there is something lost; and the surest way to approach this something lost, is to conceive of it as a fragment of the body."[73] The task of psychoanalytic work is to hold fast this little missing piece, "*ne pas manquer au manque*" (not to miss the lack).[74] This lack or absence is one that cannot be filled by a symbol. Thus, one of Lacan's main arguments in this seminar is that this *a* is not the *a* of the mirror stage; it is "non-specular, it is not graspable in the image" (this *a* is the cause of desire, not its aim).[75] This seminar therefore represents a radical shift in Lacan's thought away from the imaginary to the problems of the symbolic and the Real. What *Seminar X* puts into Lacanian psychoanalysis is the notion that there is a level not reducible to the signifier, that a remainder (what Lacan calls the "not-all") emerges in relation to the Other. It is therefore the seminar in which the first hazy image of "late Lacan" appears, representing a cut or break in his thought that mimics anxiety itself, not unlike the way in which Freud's language plays out the hesitations and temporal breaks of the affect.[76]

The lack associated with anxiety is a lack that the symbol does not, cannot fill. This is why Lacan calls Kierkegaard's identification of anxiety with the notion of the *concept* "audacious." (As Jacques-Alain Miller says, we should more correctly say it is anxiety *or* the concept because anxiety, not of the order of the signifier, is "what comes in the place of a concept."[77]) Anxiety is a cut "without which the presence of the signifier, its functioning, its entry, its furrow in the real is unthinkable."[78] It opens up what Lacan calls, in an evocation of the strangeness (or stranger) of the *unheimlich,* "the unexpected, the visit, the piece of news, what is expressed so well by the term presentiment which is not simply to be understood as the presentiment of something, but also the 'pre' of feeling, that which is *before* the birth of a feeling."[79] This opening up has a temporal rhythm to it, a rush or suddenness of breaking into a structure that will become significant in the following chapter in the temporal labors of cinematic sharks. Recalling Kierkegaard's description of Antigone's anxiety as abrupt, Lacan writes, "'Suddenly,' 'all of a sudden,' you will always find this term, at the moment that the phenomenon of the *unheimlich* makes its entry!"[80] Anxiety, Lacan says, is mistakenly linked to temporal states of expectation, preparation, warning, and anticipation. Rather, "there is no need for this expectation: the frame is always there! . . . Anxiety is when there appears in this frame something which is already there much closer to home."[81] *Seminar X* is famous for several of Lacan's almost aphoristic pronouncements about anxiety—primarily that it is "not without an object"; it is always "framed"; it is "what does not deceive" (because it is not of the order of the signifier); and it appears at the "lack of lack."[82] While Freud provides the form of time for anxiety in his theory of the interval and intermittency, Lacan sets in place its spatial form, treating anxiety as a problematic of the bar and speaking of the (shameful) exposure of the subject.

In the first meeting on *l'angoisse,* Lacan informs his audience that he will "work without a net," that the tightrope analyst will not begin with his familiar return to Freud, for "what is to be seen in connection with anxiety [is] that there is no net, because precisely as regards anxiety, each mesh, as I might appropriately put it, has no meaning except precisely by leaving the void in which anxiety is."[83] Speaking of anxiety by leaving open the nothing, Lacan continues, "In the discourse, thank God, of *Inhibitions, Symptoms and Anxiety,* everything is spoken about except anxiety."[84] So Lacan does not speak. Instead, he draws a graph (figure 7.1). And the graph that he writes at the opening of the year-long seminar takes as its perpendicular axes two terms derived from Freud's repeated turning to problems of the motor in relation to the affect. Where the lines intersect is the origin (0, 0). The arrow is a sign of the amplification of the name given to each axis. Therefore, plotting Freud's three titular terms on the graph in their relation to movement (enabled or foreclosed) and difficulty (which is related to blockage and the putting into place of obstacles), he places the paralysis of inhibition at the stopping of

DIFFICULTY

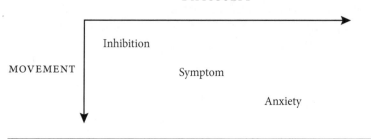

FIG. 7.1. A horizontal axis of difficulty and a vertical axis of movement, based on a graph from Lacan, *Le Séminaire X*.

movement, the symptom at the center of the structure, and anxiety at the point of excessive enervation.[85]

When Lacan fleshes out the Difficulty/Movement graph, he moves beyond the terms of Freud's title to plot a more curious set of points (figure 7.2). Let us remain with the top row. Inhibition, Lacan argues, is one degree removed from impediment (*empêcher*), and while he does not make explicit the link between the root for shackling the feet and the lame-footed Oedipus, one readily sees why he might figure impediment above and near the psychoanalytic symptom. While being impeded is a straight-up symptom, inhibition is "a symptom that has been put in the museum," both for the evocations of framing and putting things on display and for the involvement of what might be preserved in amber or stilled in tar, a structure of ensnaring and binding. *Impedicare*, Lacan posits, "means to be caught in a trap," and the dimension of locomotor difficulty suggests something that "entangles" (*empêtre*) and what happens to the subject "under the form, under the name of anxiety."[86] At the far right, the logic of inhibition taken to its most difficult conclusion is brought forward in a new term, but one that, as I wrote earlier, is anticipated in Freud's philosophical humiliation on the level of the failures of his text. *Embarras* "is very exactly the subject S invested with the bar" from the etymological root *inbarrare* that evokes the bar (*bara*). The putting in place of the bar evokes "the most direct lived experience of embarrassment." In perhaps the only phrasal connection between Lacan and Burt Bacharach, anxiety creates a situation "when you no longer know what to do with yourself."[87] Embarrassment is the experience of the bar, but a flimsy or segmented barrier behind which one cannot barricade or block oneself, a bar or obstacle put into place, but

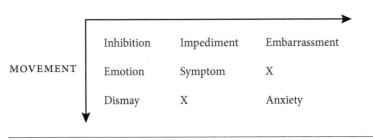

	Inhibition	Impediment	Embarrassment
MOVEMENT	Emotion	Symptom	X
	Dismay	X	Anxiety

FIG. 7.2. A horizontal axis of difficulty and a vertical axis of movement, based on a graph from Lacan, *Le Séminaire X*.

not enough to prevent shameful exposure. Of the first row from left to right, Lacan explicitly links the final terms with the topic of the seminar: "so there we are for the dimension of difficulty. It culminates at this sort of slight form of anxiety which is called embarrassment."[88]

Everything starts at the origin of Inhibition. Moving to the vertical column: emotion's etymological link to movement (*emovere, émouvoir* [to move, stir up, displace]) places it below inhibition (*dis*places it there) as a more mobile figure of "throwing out . . . of the line of movement, the movement which disintegrates, the reaction which is described as catastrophic."[89] Adjacent to the symptom, this movement of emotion is linked to the "catastrophic reaction" of anger or "hysterical crisis." In the dimension of amplified movement, the final term in that first column—which, like embarrassment at (3, 1) is here (at 1, 3) on the level of anxiety, or levels with the affect—is something that "in the dimension of movement . . . responds precisely to the stage of anxiety," and that is *émoi* (dismay). Dismay derives from *émouvoir* (to move, to affect) and thus might appear to be a more mobile form of *e-movere*'s emotion. This is not the case, Lacan insists: *émoi* has nothing to do with the moving-outward quality of emotion.[90] Rather, the series of variations Lacan traces—*esmayer, esmais, esmoi*—suggests *troubler* and *se troubler* (to disturb or frighten and to show disturbance, respectively). Sliding along the signifiers until he reaches *exmagare* (to make [one] lose one's power, one's energy), Lacan figures dismay's cluster of map work as surrounding the notion of discouragement, formal disturbance, even *esmager* (to crush). He concludes by casting *émoi* as "perturbation, collapse of power" (with all that its political tones also suggest).

Framing anxiety, then—which, recall, is always framed, according to

Lacan—are embarrassment and dismay, albeit at the distance of a spatial interval put into the graph. While anxiety does not deceive, this graph does. Its trick, as Miller notes, is that the etymological circus makes one "believe that signifiers can envelop anxiety." It is a *net* made to "trap the fish of anxiety," when, of course, "this is not truly how the fish will be caught."[91] (The film to which I will turn ends with an identical feint.) "Dismay," Lacan delivers, "is the most profound form of being disturbed in the dimension of movement. Embarrassment is the high point reached by difficulty."[92] Moving across the graph to the right, the highest point of difficulty, and a form of anxiety, reveals the barred subject exposed with no barricade behind which to hide the self sufficiently. Moving down the graph, the highest motor disturbance is the draining of one's power, the depletion of the possibility of energetic acting in and on the world, an absolute collapse. Both are forms of anxiety, and both, fundamentally, involve a subject in a formal disturbance of either space or time.

That is all for the graph in the opening of the seminar, and, of course, it leaves two spaces blank and open: the two points most proximate to anxiety, the two points that converge on anxiety. (If dismay and embarrassment constitute a broad frame for anxiety, its more intimate [3, 2] [2, 3] frame—the frame that traps it for the duration of the seminar—are these Xes, these non-points that await the futurity of being filled in but that for now occupy and are inhabited by precisely nothing. In time, in this book, we will follow a murky X again, but there in relation to joy. Do remain somewhat held by all these Xes.) Lacan leaves those gaps in place in their non-place for most of the long year of the tenth seminar. The graph appears twice more in its present form, ultimately filling in those gaps, and twice in a changed, awry form. The next instance of what Lacan calls not an arrangement of Freud's title but its slouching "derangement"—a diagonal staggering toward anxiety—produces the final terms in the matrix as a matter of the orientation of the subject toward the Other (figure 7.3). Embarrassment is on the etymological order of a "too much," a too-muchness of the signifier, while dismay's depletion is on the order of the "too little," a power that is exhausted and lacking.[93] Therefore, the final display of what Lacan dubs "moments" in the table maps the relation toward the Other in their too-muchness or too-littleness. Because anxiety involves an orientation toward the desire of the Other, to its left near the too-little of dismay is acting out, marked by behavior that "shows itself," and what it shows is "the orientation towards the Other of every acting out."[94] Closer to the site of the bar is *passage à l'acte,* which is on the side of the subject, involving her

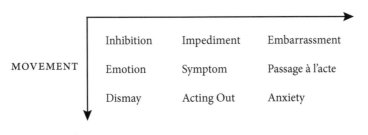

FIG. 7.3. A horizontal axis of difficulty and a vertical axis of movement, based on a graph from Lacan, *Le Séminaire X*.

"in the phantasy in so far as she appears effaced by the bar to the maximum extent." This intermediary term between embarrassment and anxiety involves a transformation: "it is at the moment of greatest embarrassment that, with the behavioral addition of emotion as disorder of movement, the subject . . . precipitates herself from where she is, . . . essentially she topples off the stage."[95]

In this final articulation of the graph, Lacan will call dismay "nothing other than the *o* [*a*] itself." Summarizing the chart before demolishing it altogether, he writes, "This reference to dismay is henceforth that through which anxiety, while being linked to it, does not depend on it, but on the contrary determines this dismay. Anxiety finds itself suspended between what one might call the prior form of the relationship to the cause, the 'what is it?' which is going to be formulated as cause, embarrassment, and something which cannot hold onto this cause, since primarily it is anxiety which literally produces this cause."[96] This dense passage—which performs the slipping away of cause (of desire) in its difficult language that moves toward some (theoretical) cause that cannot be grasped—is given in a more succinct form in Lacan's conclusion that the desire of the Other is what provokes anxiety, because fundamentally, "I do not know what object *a* I am for this desire."[97] Anxiety is suspended between the what of the desire of the Other as its prompting cause (What am I to you?—go the sad songs of lovers; What is it you want of me?—so Thorwald poses to Jeffries at the end of *Rear Window*) at the same time that the affect produces this cause in its repeated address or plaint to the Other. The very act of asking, in other words, to determine the cause produces the cause in its formulation of the *a* of the desire of the Other. As Alain Badiou writes, anxiety ever "is *vor etwas*, confronting something."[98] Anxiety, for Lacan, to finish his loving dogfight with Freud, is "not without an object" because it involves an intimate confrontation with *this* object—the central object of Lacanian thought—en route to the remainder, to what is not on the order of the signifier.[99]

Anxiety involves the skids of thought, an embarrassment or bar put into thought that exposes something, that has nothing behind which one might shield oneself. Thus, though Weber describes anxiety as allowing "the hitherto somewhat disparate membra disjecta of Lacan's terminology to come together and take their proper places," this place is an exposed place, one that allows no space for that concept to hide.[100] The paradox of anxiety is precisely the nature of this place; for all that Lacan describes anxiety as a point or plottable terrain—a "passageway" to lead the analyst, as Lacan puts it, "beyond the limit of anxiety"—this passageway, like a trail in a fairy tale, must exist in order to be followed and simultaneously must disappear in order to take on what is past the limit it lines. The place of anxiety, therefore, is a place that is demarcated only to be deserted, set in place but incomprehensibly and inadequately; one is abandoned there—left behind by, say, a ship's distracted crew—only to have to depart from it. Anxiety involves, then, not a place proper, but what Weber calls the "interval between space and place."[101] This interval suggests a claustrophobic, tight gap one can imagine being trapped in and by, a humiliation of space—an interval, in other words, that is a very narrow, choking strait.

TREADING RED BLUE WATER

Joan Copjec uses the treadmill's nowhere as a simile for anxiety's stuckness: "it sometimes happens, however, that thinking does grind to a halt, stops moving, becomes inhibited. At these times movement is reduced to agitation, a kind of inexpedient-tentative running in place."[102] While this image of kinetic purposelessness articulates the motor dimension of anxiety and the embarrassment of being trapped, arrested, in a non-transformative space, I am going to get this figure wet. The difficult movements of anxiety—its choking, strangling aspects—commuted to the dimension of form resemble nothing so much as a kind of treading water. The advantage of this moistened metaphor is the dimension of threat, danger, and risk added to the embarrassment of repetitious, inexpedient motor discharge: running in place does not convey the urgency of finitude posed by the form of anxiety in the site to which I will now turn. For what treads water in Chris Kentis's independent horror film *Open Water* (2003) is neither figure nor character but form itself in its temporal and spatial manifestations. This argument has been made before in this book:

that the forms of affects instate themselves in and as cinematic structure and neither through psychologized characters who express emotion nor through corporealized spectators who consume it. The difficult movements of form produce a double structure in *Open Water:* one marked by intermittency on the temporal level, a form that is punctuated but persists in time, toward a certain time, and the embarrassment of form on the level of a visual language that ends up stuck in place, treading water—a form that does not transform but that is caught, trapped in the openness of its radically limited visual material.

Anxiety is the difficult movement of form, a form that begins to choke, that is strangled and restricted, has nowhere to go, moves in motor iterations that do not displace or enact change but return in a flailing stupid repetition—a form marked by such punctuations and failures, purposeless repetitions, such that no event is sustainable from within its logic, no event can place itself or find itself in formal place. The structure of anxiety, in other words, involves the stuckness of a form in which nothing can or will take place. It is the difficult movement of intermittent (temporal) form and embarrassed (spatial) form—a movement that sets form adrift and into which no event can be placed other than the place of the event itself. A choking form is one that gasps on itself, fights for a breath that is insufficient, finds it is not enough and therefore can only gulp repetitiously in a humiliating attempt to produce what is constitutively depleted in substance. The limit of being and thought in this dismayed structure is rendered as the limit of form to transform, to instate the event, and to take place. I argue that *Open Water* makes present—frames and puts on display—the drowning of form: that a bar is put in structural place solely to be visually transgressed, and that duration is marked out solely to be punctuated and made intermittent. While intermittency names the temporal form of the film through the formal operator of the shark, the spatial form of the line of the sea at which the film takes place is marked by a formal embarrassment, when form no longer knows what to do with itself, when it fails to find anything behind which to barricade itself but is exposed, like a body under threat. It is the visual and temporal structure of *Open Water* that is subject to the limits of being and that manifests the brutal impediments of anxiety.

EIGHT

Nothing/Will Have

Taken Place/But the Place:

Open Water Anxiety

The independent horror film *Open Water* (2003) is not the story of an event so much as it is a frame around the heavy time of waiting for certain imminent death. That duration *is* the ontology of the film—a film that does not even serve in its materiality as a compensatory living monument, as does, say, the video remainder or documentary corpus left behind in place of bodies in horror films such as *The Blair Witch Project* or *[REC]*. Rather, *Open Water* is the pure taking place of its various drainings and voidings. The film is correlated fully to the mode of its manner—in a disciplinary leap, it is not unlike Kierkegaard's formulation of man's involvement with God: "the *how* is the *what*."[1] Although the narrative is easy enough to summarize, any synopsis will miss how fundamentally opaque and restricted the material of the film is, for what is compelling and curious about *Open Water* cannot be reduced to the chronology of suspense or even the enumeration of paltry plot points or things-that-happen. Remarkable, really, how limited the textual material is: no meta-narratives of politics, community, history; no grand struggles between beast and man, land and sea. Not even a proper singular villain in some individuated selachimorphic other à la *Jaws*. The film is structured around a trite, banal opening—from which one learns nothing about the two central characters aside from the sketchiest of married yuppie clichés, all cell phones and tight stress—followed by this frame around bounded time, this finite waiting for assured aquatic death.[2]

The film begins under the textual sign of self-conscious verisimilitude, pronouncing that it is "based on true events" over an image of lapping ocean waves at dawn.[3] After the brief opening sketch, the central couple, Susan and Daniel, arrive at a generic Othered island for a needed holiday, obligatory tourist tchotchkes and tropical merriment. Though the first quarter of the film gestures at some narrative significance or metaphorical depth in scenes of sex refused, marital sighs, and the small disappointments of vacation, the effect of the jerky digital camerawork, stilted dialogue, and awkward acting is to reveal nothing about these characters: no sense of the dynamic of the couple; no attempt, even, at a history for them individually, dyadically, nationally, or professionally. The pronounced vacuity of the opening suggests that those first minutes do little more than defer the structural focus of the work, put in place a gap to put off a bit longer the scene of the title and the horrors it works out therein. (The violence will arrive soon enough, regardless of any textual reluctance.) The opening scene can be shallow, poorly acted, and narratively inconsequential because its formal labor is solely in interpolating a delay; its content is irrelevant. One review connects this vapidity, the "unflattering videography" and "attractive actors mouthing stilted dialogue," to the aesthetics of pornography, but rather than doing so to suggest that pornography itself works as a form or frame, the reviewer suggests it is compensatory for "the scenario's inherent sadism," a sadism, let it be said—because this *is* the scenario—of the march of time itself.[4] The opening is a critical lure, but a poor lure, bad bait, that fails to reel in any substance or revelation from the depths. The first depletion in the film, then, is of critical frameworks for the soothing meta-narratives that might anticipate or explain away the corporeal rips to come.

An ordinary diving trip turns nightmarish when the boat crew, through a counting error, leaves Daniel and Susan behind in the field of the title. A third of the way through the film, the couple surfaces, realize they are alone, and alternate between rational attempts to solve the terrible problem and hysteria and panic at the pure fact of their abandonment. Amid the little lies couples tell out of love to quell panic—"We'll be fine"; "What a story to tell our friends"—(that never do), they bicker, they mull; they bargain; they wonder and whine; piss, cry, and vomit; drift—and then, the sharks come, he is bitten, suffers, dies, and, eventually, so does she. After a terrifying night of extinguishing in inky darkness, the first light of the second day of dying sees Susan release Daniel's corpse. Then, in a long shot on which more will be written, she slips off her vest and sinks into the sea. The film opens with the uniquely golden peachy light of dawn and image of open water devoid of figures, the very tone of light that arrives after the deaths and closes the main part of the film. Therefore, on the level of the sky's flush, the film opens after the main figures have already died, or they have always already been dead, died in advance only to repeat those deaths again in a loop. Chromatically, the final shot poses the fold of the film as the shape of a wave returning and cycling through its period: *riverrun, past Eve and Adam's, from swerve of shore to bend of bay . . .*

Open Water is a frame around the time of these two deaths, and it is nothing more. It is equivalent entirely to its conceit, which is why the most negative reviews were also, in a sense, the most insightful. In calling the film, for example, a "stunt" or a "gimmick" (as many critics did) the critical derision hit the crux of the matter—the film is its event, its activity exhausted in the attraction of its occurrence over time. It is, therefore, a film that collapses into its frame—or, really, is little more than its frame—a dare or a challenge, not unlike the gesture of open water diving itself. This charge of mere device often was levied to suggest the mitigation of affectivity (or its quick extinguishing): "*Open Water* is simply a stunt—hopelessly literal-minded and cheap in every sense."[5] However, in this critical refrain, the etymological intimacy between gimmick and magic is overlooked or disavowed. Not unlike anxiety's *Heksebrev,* a gimmick involves the motor activity of flux, change, and changeability. One definition of a gimmick is a device that makes a fair game crooked, a method of cheating; in this sense, the film is absolutely a gimmick. What it makes crooked is not only a game of chance in which the cards are stacked against the two unsuspecting divers, but the form of the film itself, its spatial and temporal material made crooked, askew, put awry in the dangerous commission of the cinematic stunt. Nothing happens in this film. However, while that formulation constitutes the repeated critical plaint (one review begins, "Question: What's so scary about watching two people float around in the ocean for an hour or so? Answer: Nothing."), in an important sense, in the gimmick of the film, that is itself its power and horror—that nothing happens, that *not enough* takes place.[6] Even still, though, two beings die. *Open Water* shallows and yet depths.

SOMETHING OR NOTHING

If *Open Water* is in part (and correctly) a gimmick, what it is *not* is an allegory. The counterpart to reviewers' dismissal of the stunt is the critical effort to put the central conceit of the film to work for some grand significance. This rush to produce meaning tends to fixate on the status of the couple, to assimilate the film to a horror genre's take on the hegemonic Hollywood trope of romance and marriage. Consider, for example, Walter Metz's claim in *Film Criticism* that despite the realist, seemingly explicit digital images, *Open Water* is in fact "a 'couple's video,' a study of the intimate contact between two lovers," an anti-pornographic diary of the constitution and dissolution of a marriage.[7] Metz assimilates the horror to its generic cousin, calling the film "an absolutely brilliant couple's melodrama, detailing with few words but beautiful character tensions, the collapse of Daniel and Susan's marriage."[8] Among the many problems with this critical move is that Metz's argument requires a massive disavowal of much of the text, including an eye willfully turned away from the form of the image organized around tensile water patterns far more than tensions between characters. It further requires a heavily front-weighted interpretation, extrapolating from the first ten minutes of petty arguments and bedroom negotiations a framework that metaphorizes in advance the violences to come. (The only close reading in Metz's article, tellingly, is of a high angle surveillance-like shot of the couple in their hotel room the night before the dive.) The majority of the film's duration is subsequently interpreted in relation to the initial displacement read into the film by the critic: the essence of the film is that "the marriage will crumble around the hyperbolic stress produced by having to survive all alone in a shark-infested ocean."[9] This is a reading that refuses to take the film at its word—or, rather, deploys critical language to mobilize anything other than what is seen in the frame. If the cinematic crisis is the state of the marriage, then the narrative of strife must accordingly contort around a villain. Metz's figure of dissolution is the sharks, gutted and hollowed out as at the end of the film to be filled with the critical content: "the sharks become an allegorical force for the attack on Daniel and Susan's bodies, a metaphorical pornography in which the deterioration of the bodies due to the phallic strikes from the sharks gives voice to their collapsing marriage."[10] Metz reaches an extraordinarily unearned conclusion that bends film to critical will: "while they do both die at the end of the film, I think the point is that, as a fictional couple about whom we care, they died back on land, in the sex scene that never was."[11] Filling in the gaps and silences of *Open Water* with a narrative written by critic and not film, producing a continuous narrative of bickering and complaint in order to make the case for a narrative arc for psychological characters, Metz not only writes over the film's form of time but essentially writes out the image and the place.

Question: Why *is* it a problem, or why should we not accept, the making metaphorical of the sharks? (Or, and, in turn, the deaths, the adriftness, the water—) Answer: because reading is a form of investment, and the critical positing of metaphor takes the nothing that takes place in the film and attempts to profit from and erase that nothing, invests in the film solely to the extent that it demands a return on that investment. *Open Water* casts out the lure of just this sort of reading (—but one should not bite): the body of the film ends with the image of dawn and water, having previously introduced a rescue story only to interrupt and abort it. Over the final credits, after the break of a black frame, is a brief scene of disembodied voices and a dead shark being gutted and emptied; revealed in its bowels is the yellow camera that Daniel holds but releases early in the film, before the attack. To the odd final line of the film addressed off-screen by an unknown figure, the query about the camera, "I wonder if it works?" the critic who fleshes out the film answers this question, and posits always and every time: Yes—It works.—The film does some thing, shows some thing, means something; it must not do nothing. However, this camera does *not* work in that sense: it is dropped and lost before the attacks and is therefore not a monument or testament of the waiting for the deaths. The camera avows solely that someone existed at some point in the sea; it fails to capture (or record, or testify to) either the pacing or the pathos of that being's disappearance. Because it has been released into the sea by the time of the deaths (and possibly eaten, although there is no way to know), even if the camera works, it captures only nothing—or, rather, it captures nothing of the event but bears witness, if at all, only to the namesake of the title. The little box records just that blue open blue open blue.

Yellow plastic camera, you are fundamentally patient and *there* in the frame, ever present at Daniel's side, floating as he floats, waiting as he waits. When, however, the event for which this couple has been waiting occurs—the violence a dreadful letter cast the moment they are forgotten and that, as expected, finally arrives at its destination—in the chaos and agitation of the attack you are dehisced from your owner's side, the above-water version of the bits of flesh likewise torn and discharged from the leg below the sea surface. Go on, then.

At this departure, the camera that floats away—assisted by a wild kick from a fin—is marked as insufficient; it fails to be present to document the violence, the bleeding, the dying, these deaths. While the photographic camera does not suffice here as the sign of the possible representability of trauma, the cinematic (digital) one does. There is also, however, a third apparatus for documenting vision, neither photographic nor cinematic, and it is a look called into service at the instant the photographic eye is killed off. When Daniel is bitten, dragged under the water, Susan says, "I'm going to go look," and dips her masked face under the water. Her look confirms the tear; and to his question on her return, "My leg is still there, right?" she attests it is, it is bleeding, and so forth. Susan's eyes function as the intervening mechanism between Daniel's meat and his understanding of his body; his eyes no longer serve as that bridge, and she replaces the photographic medium with an embodied intermediary, a visual channel through the channel of water. This curious relay of looks suggests that among violence's many denaturing forces are those that upend self-knowing. Daniel's feeling of his body does not provide epistemic certainty, which now can come only through the vision of another. If Susan is now a medium in the interventionary sense, she is different from the photographic medium that was previously dropped in one crucial way: she is an anarchival kino-eye, a seeing apparatus but not a preserving apparatus. Her capture—the look for Daniel that ascertains that his leg is still attached to his body—is an immediately erased and an unconveyable image. The ephemeral camera she stands for is one that cannot document or archive what it is about to see—if a witness, she is a finite one whose mediatic work cannot leave traces or a record of the violence still to come. This embodied mediation becomes a pathetic corpo-realizing of the marital promise of being a witness to the life of another. Here, Susan's witnessing becomes of the death and dying of the other, and then when hers comes, the final long shot of the camera means that the audience does not substitute for that missing marital attestor. The losses redound; the deaths merely accrue. Any critical attempt to likewise bear witness to the deaths, to imagine itself in the water alongside Susan, Daniel, camera, and shark, places itself in the position of those in the water without being in the water, offers the supposition of witnessing without adopting the vulnerability that each witness in the film bears out. It is therefore the worst witnessing: a false imagining of shared knowledge at the removal of all risk.

Metaphors—the allegorical sharks, metaphorical forces of flow—attempt to posit an infinitude of meaning to mitigate the anxiety of the finitude of form. Such an approach reappropriates Susan's and Daniel's deaths for critical lan-guage, attempts to speak and stand in the place of the missing in order to stave off the fundamental destructions that constitute the film by subsuming them for meaning's presence. The critical move exemplified by Metz's argument and the broader impulse to suggest that the recovered yellow camera *works* (in other words, attests, signifies, documents) is, therefore, on the side of a kind of violence: complicit with the forces of destruction in the film—like a shark, like the entropic sea—it obliterates and swallows up the materiality of the bodies, but also now the materiality of the form, for its own ends, hungry for the film to give up its substance for the sustenance of the critical mouth. The error, in other words, is to imagine Susan's and Daniel's deaths as thanatosis, apparent and feigned adaptive deaths to an observer that belie continual liveness. But the defense of tonic immobility has at its heart a fundamental avowal of immortality, a phobic attempt to hope that an imitation of finitude is sufficient to make the real thing lose interest and just swim away.

A critical reading predicated on meaning, metaphoricity, allusions, and psychological depth for characters is ultimately an attempt to ensure that *something* persists in this film in which *nothing* persists. My claim is that it is not possible to theorize the nothing, to reckon fully with this frame around the time of waiting for two deaths—and nothing more—in a criticism that figures itself as preserving life for the two central figures by suggesting that their deaths were fundamentally about something other than finitude. This anxious criticism imagines that Freud's first model of time in *Inhibitions, Symptoms and Anxiety* is correct: that interruption is possible; that the endless movement toward the nothing can be halted, paused, frozen, and arrested in a persistence of presence that lives, means, breathes. By contrast, instead of feeding off the film, a critical sensitivity to the form of what takes place requires, in the end, relinquishing any desire for an interpretive investment that promises some return. One must write in the wake of a voiding of beings and a place where the event has failed to take place, without writing over that nothing with a metaphysics that ensures that presence prevails. The critical reappropriation that ensures that no meaning will go missing attempts to figure the nothing not as a place of loss, but as a recuperable site of plenitude. It is therefore always an attempt to reappropriate death for life, an effort to produce a critical afterlife and thus avoid having to write (about, from within) a film formally organized around a finitude that does not extend, but that is a bad investment, that requires an investment of bad affect and will give back to the viewer—nothing. Because anxiety must be read for—as must all of the affects in this book—the task is to read for the form of the nothing without obliterating it, to read with loss instead of reading to fill loss.

A SHARK IS A FORM OF TIME

Spectatorial and critical "investment" in *Open Water* is first and foremost an outlay of precisely ordered duration. The approximately eighty-minute film is structured around seven twelve-minute blocks of time, with crucial events and corresponding shifts in rhythmic pacing at each break between segments. As with the fragments that the previous chapter explored, from the *Heksebrev* to Freud's tripartite subtitle, the ordered juxtapositions in the sequence of *Open Water* do not resolve into a totality or synthesis, but remain an assemblage of temporal concurrences that fail to meld into one grand (meta-)narrative, and remain only that "accumulation of proximities" characteristic of anxiety's intermittency. The seven twelve-minute blocks and their precipitating breaking events plot as shown in Table 1. As though a perverted form of the classic Kübler-Ross stages of grief—denial, anger, bargaining, depression, acceptance—and posing the question of whether terror is a form of grieving in advance for yourself—the form of the film follows something like denial, strategizing, anger, incomprehension, *and then the violent attack,* which in the telos of the former stages substitutes a bloody ripping apart of the body for the role of the calm resolve of acceptance. On the one hand, the form of the film is a series of drainings—first the stuff of the body in a progression from urine to vomit to blood, then pieces of the body in skin and limb, to the final corpse let to drift and Susan's sinking release. But it is simultaneously an affirmative positing of the name of the film, an increasing filling of the frame with the open water that flows to fill those vacuums and to comprise what *is,* what remains and persists, at the end of the film.

Through these durational segments, time in the film is a force of the form of violence. The temporal structure of these seven blocks involves time's pressure on the text, the compression of the correspondence between screen and real time until they approach each other, suffocating the film form, recruiting real time to the logic of cinematic time. When the boat and its safe inhabitants pull away, the film cuts to an image of Susan and Daniel underwater, floating alone, backlit shapes in a field of blue. Over an image of the sky, the first temporal marker appears: "10:25 A.M." it reads against the clouds, and then—only then—does the couple surface. The temporal marker predates the surfacing and the surfacing realization, as though the mark of temporal specificity called them, now abandoned, up from the depths, recruited their bodies to the above-air time of waiting and counting down. The digital markers of diegetic time do not indicate additive progress; rather, they descend on the moment of death. It is time, and the way in which temporality conditions finitude, that knocks Susan and Daniel around, throwing them from one block of time to the next with a hard hurting jerk. Thus, while adrift in the open water, jolted by the bruising collisions with the toothy fish below the sea, they are also pushed around, contused, by the force of the shifting blocks of twelve-minute intervals.

TABLE 1. Open Water Plotting

SEGMENT	DURATION	NARRATIVE ELEMENTS AND EVENTS
1	0.00–0.12	Home, prior to leaving; on plane; arrival; beach tourism; night in hotel
2	0.12–0.24	On boat; safety lecture; the dive; underwater images; boat departs — 0.25, first time marker, "10:25 A.M."
3	0.24–0.36	Surfacing; realization of abandonment; waiting — 0.31, first appearance of a shark; camera dips under line of the sea — 0.35, next time marker appears, "1:30 P.M." (three elapsed hours correspond to ten minutes of screen duration)
4	0.36–0.48	Struggle and strategies; discussion; boredom; lies told out of love; nausea — 0.49, first violent, disturbing appearance of a shark
5	0.48–1.00	De-coherence; breaking down; rage, blame, and silence — 0.59, the duration marker stretches, "6.45 P.M." (two elapsed hours correspond to fifteen minutes of screen time)
6	1.00–1.12	Shark attack; blood; reddening sky; rescue attempt; dawn and death — 1.12, Susan releases Daniel's body
7	1.12–1.24	Helicopter surveying; removal of vest; open water; credits and gutting — 1.16, Susan drops away

Into this time, the figure of the shark bears the force of intermittency, but not in any dialectic of appearance–disappearance. Specifically, the sharks do not bear anxiety *into* the film as punctuations of surprise or as a narrative locus of probable bodily danger; nor do the sharks bear anxiety *out* of the film as relieving punctuations of the endless free-floating suspense of waiting. Anxiety has neither to do with the appearance of the sharks as threat nor with the disappearance of their absence. To Susan's question, "I don't know what's worse: seeing them or not seeing them?" the film is coldly indifferent to the answer. Instead, it is the pulsation of seeing and then not seeing, not seeing and then seeing, that constitutes a form of time that is intermittent. The sharks put in play a form of temporality marked by fits and starts in a progression that does not, will not, end or pause; they repeat a rhythm or pulse of visible time in the film, introducing structures of discontinuity and disjunction. The apex predator is sudden, bursting, a mode of *quick* time. If there is a stuckness in and to time—the relentless forward rush toward death—there is also a structural embarrassment in how being is exposed as stuck in time, stuck with those specific named times, treading water with nowhere to go while time advances. *Open Water* formalizes this stuckness, organizes itself around this relation between intermittency and embarrassment. In order to make present this structure, the sharks break up time, provide form with its pulsing breaks. Thus, the brutal marine fishes bring forth the structure—and not the sense—of anxiety. They are not feeding machines; they are formal operators. Sharks in this film are the very form of predatory time.

On the one hand, time is cruel and implacably violent in its movements—ever forward, progressing toward the certain instant of annihilation, unstoppable, and fundamentally stubborn. As in Freud's revised theory of anxiety, in which it is not movement's interruptibility but its *inability* to cease that provokes dread, it is the fact that time is what moves forward that constitutes the unique form of violence of the progression in the bounded temporal frame of *Open Water*. But on the other hand, time is also given a formal quality in excess of its characteristic of being that unstoppable, undifferentiated force that ineluctably and necessarily presses on. That formal quality is the *number*. The time markers of the extra-diegetic flashing—first 10:25 A.M., then 1:30 P.M., 4:40 P.M., 6:45 P.M., the horrible 11:30 P.M.—pause time's forward rush in the formal instant of an inscribed and particular series of numbers. If the numbers are, in part, relevant when read diachronically to mark the forward movement of time—otherwise undifferentiated save for the natural signs of dawn, noon, dusk, night—they also ground the abstraction of the undifferentiated visual field of water and sky in their specificity and quality of being only a few minutes apart on the clock from the previous marker. They are markers with a questionable ontology, for the desire to order, represent, structure, and concretize time, if one defense against natural time, is no antidote to the narrative terror experienced by Daniel and Susan. One argument for the textual appearance of the digital time signature might be that the marking of successive instants of time exists solely as an address to the film spectator to mark out the parameters of limited time in which the suspense of the attempted rescue will generically take place. Another claim might insist that the two modes of time suggest the metaphorical impasse of professional couple against the acultural violence of the ecosystem into which they will (pay to) plunge with homo-entitlement. First, a clock time that is objective and ordered, repeatable and predictable, structured, certain, cyclical, and concrete, an image of measurement and mastery in an attempt to bypass the fundamental problem of time, that, in Kant's language, it "yields no shape."[12] And then, opposing that, there is a second, countervailing, natural time that is diffuse and linked to the color of the sky's light. For either argument to, forgive me, hold water, however, the clock time would have to portend, would need to represent or be read as representative of, a cluster of meanings attributed to the signifier "time": the formal appearance of the hour would have to be given some content or substance bypassing its textual appearance as instant of abstract measurement. I have made the argument that coming to terms with the structural role of the nothing and finitude in *Open Water* requires resisting the implantation of metaphors—for the sharks, for the water, for the violence, and for the deaths. Nor can the temporal markers be reduced to their significance *as a something else,* as a theory of time and pacing or as a way into understanding the psychology of either spectator or drowner. One must not occlude the form of the clock; one must take seriously clock logic as nothing but the inscription of numbers.

The time markers are numbers repeatedly put into the diegesis at intervals to delimit the film's structural segments—neither more nor less than that. Numbers, in this film, do not mean or point to meaning. They are purely formal. But as I have argued in previous chapters, it is in the formal that the work of grief, disgust, horror, terror, violence (and later, joy, but not yet) takes place. Numbers, in fact, are what kill Daniel and Susan. If contingency is continually blamed in order to give an internal logic and cause to what has taken place—"You picked the dates," one accuses; "I wanted to go skiing," the other responds; "We were too late in surfacing"; or "We were in the wrong place," and so forth—there is in fact a concreteness to the cause of the violence, a numerical logic that damns the couple well before the sharks arrive. On the boat, the proximate source of the abandonment is a counting error. Commotion before the dive: a brusque paragon of First World privilege has forgotten his mask. All hyper-aggression and rudeness to the locals staffing the boat, he blusters, interrupts, and pouts at being denied the dive—until, that is, two other divers come back prematurely, and he bullies his way to a plunge with one of the returning partners. Amid his noisy cajoling, the returning two are tallied but the two new departures are not, and so is set in motion the counting game that our central couple will lose. These mere numbers—on the boat, clustered ticks in groups of five lines; later, the specific integers of an irrelevant extra-diegetic clock—set the cause-and-effect chain of violent consequence in motion. If the violence to the concreteness of the named time of the death frame results in part from the violence accidentally put in play from counting gone awry, this is a formal operation of the numerical that sets in place the anxious structure of the film.

Despite attempts by Susan and Daniel to pin the cause on time and pinpoint a correct time against which their times were wrong ("You were *late* in surfacing"; "You picked the *dates*"), it is not time in its meaningful or contingent content but time in its numerical analogue that is the guarantor of future death. It is the ordering of time that hurts, insofar as concretized time is reducible to a series of numbers in sequence, as in the temporal markers. It is in the counting that things go wrong. Formalizing violence as a problem of numbers, however, does not mitigate the force of violence. It is tempting to cite Barthes's formulation in *Mythologies* that "a little formalism turns one away from History, but . . . a lot brings one back to it."[13] For the rude man on the boat regards it as his prerogative to dive. Unwilling to wait for *another* time, he demands to act and presses to dive *this* time, which is, specifically, the time of tourism: an expanded, planned, determinate but finite now that insists, "I am here, in this place, to act as I want at this concrete moment." It is this relation to time as a form of demand, and the refusal of waiting, the pressing on time that constitutes tourist privilege, that puts the count off, that wrecks the match between numbers and beings and that therefore guarantees Susan's and Daniel's future death. No time of rescue and suspense can catch up to the initial displacement caused by the assertions of white tourist privilege as a form of the autonomous shaping of one's (leisure) time. The form of the counting game does not preclude an ideological critique of this—or any other—text. Violence may be a numbers game—here; perhaps always—but that does not mitigate the affectivity of the formal anxiety. Indeed, what better *form* of violent entitlement could there be than the fact that a man is, quite literally, counted twice so that two others do not count at all?

A SHARK PUNCTURES A LINE

A smooth, amorphous space of this kind is constituted by an accumulation of proximities, and each accumulation defines a *zone of indiscernability* proper to "becoming" (more than a line and less than a surface; less than a volume and more than a surface).—Gilles Deleuze and Félix Guattari, *A Thousand Plateaus*

The antinomies of *Open Water* involve not only the rigorously patterned and structured forms of time—violent, formal, numerical, churning—but also a visual field of space that is remarkably limited and as scrupulously plotted. After Daniel and Susan surface, the visual field generally alternates among four types of shots, each containing similar visual elements arranged differently in space and scale. Like a mobile Rothko canon, the interest in the variance of the shots is in the proportions of each element: the sky to the sea to the scale of the bodies alternately lost in, or filling against the horizon, the frame. The privileged medium shot takes a balanced composition—heads, shoulders, and a bit of torso of each party, centered in the frame horizontally and vertically, against a water-heavy third of sky to two-thirds sea; a longer shot of this version has a greater watery expanse-to-sky ratio. There is an overhead shot that has no horizon, just cranial orbs bobbing in blue. Finally, there is an ostensible point-of-view shot form—(though I, and the film, use this term loosely, refusing to concretely fix whose vision it is providing)—in which the horizon is obliterated continually by the cresting water levels rising over it, lapping and heaving, blocking and obfuscating vision. This shot without figures is a sight that reveals nothing but waves, and not even waves or crests but their motion, and not even their motion but the rising heave of the sea's displacements and the idiosyncrasies of wind. It is, therefore, less a point-of-view shot predicated on presence than a point-of-non-view that organizes the mise-n'en-scène of the film. This shot is of the failure of visibility, one that serves neither to provide privileged psychological or subjective truth nor to reveal a privileged position, except the privilege of blocked vision that is the sole and final right of heads bobbing in the water. The repeated shot-types are minimally different from each other, which causes minor fluctuations in scale and tone to take on the status of absolute and substantial markers of change: shots contain figures or are figureless; they portray varying hues of blue, gray, white, and black; they reveal positions in space, even variation within the minimally useful grid of sea against horizon, or conceal them in an abstract grid of contextlessness.

There is a claustrophobia, even a visual boredom or vacuity, in the limited material of the field of any given cinematic shot of the sea. Because of this, *Open Water* pays homage to the form of restriction and visual limitations in Alfred Hitchcock's famously tight *Lifeboat* (1944), that film of anti-expanses, the radically narrow setting limited to its title and nothing, no place, more.[14] The paradox of the sea, its expansiveness that restricts or its space that binds, is given complementary treatments in the two films: the delimited constraint of the sea in Hitchcock's film, the horror of the unmoored non-place of only that expanse in Kentis's. Donald Spoto's description of Hitchcock's film could *mutatis mutandis* apply as well to *Open Water*: "the ultimate terror generated by *Lifeboat* derives from its setting rather than from any specific action within it. With no music (except under the opening and closing titles) and with no sound but wind and waves, the film conveys a horrific sense of endless floating, with no sure port."[15] But note well: the crucial difference between a film like *Lifeboat* and *Open Water* is that the former metaphorizes drift as an ethical slippage; the "infinite water" of which Spoto speaks does the narrative labor of visualizing and concretizing the moral quagmire in which the group members find themselves, replete with utilitarianism's greatest hits in the form of rationed supplies, malevolent deceit, and Nazis. Against the backdrop of war and a series of debates about ethics, killing, violence, and responsibility in a community, *Lifeboat* opens up its claustrophobic scene to the expanse of wide-open interpretation. *Open Water,* by contrast, is named not for the objects within its expanse but for the expanse itself, and in turn it neither desires nor provides any political or ethical frame in which to read either its violences or its spaces. In this film, a visual analogue for human finitude conditioned by temporality is the visual finitude conditioned by the conceit of being stuck in place, of treading water in the narrowest portion of space and the smallest, but most crucial, rise above the surface of the sea. This visual form does not transform over the course of the film—How could it, with these sad beings having nowhere to go? Instead, it laps and rolls, returns and repeats like an oceanic cycle or the feeling of floating and buoyancy.

The one constant in the minimal variance of the shots named here is that all take place, all figure vision, on top of the water, at or above the line of the surface of the ocean, at the undulating level that divides absolutely the segments of worldly space. The visual field is so radically limited that it suggests as its correlate something akin to Kazimir Malevich's *Black Square,* the ground zero of form, which Slavoj Žižek describes as a structure in which "meaning is reduced to the minimal difference between the presence and absence of meaning itself."[16] The spatial organization of the medium shot at water level, the signature and grounding image of the film to which all framing deviations and variations return, takes place at and frames, puts on display, the minimal difference between the presence and absence of water. The line of the sea surface level, the line that compositionally divides the proportional horizontal expanses of the shot, does neither more nor less than divide Above from Below; the bar separates realms and splits the frame and its subsequent capacity for either opacity or possible visualization. A line—and above the line, below the line, and that is all there is. The signature shot of *Open Water* at the level of the boundary between sea and air makes present the minimal difference between the relative abstractions Higher and Lower. The difference between those realms is, however, let us admit, one on which human life literally hinges.

In the midst of this limited visual iteration of above-sea-level shots, the sharks appear. I have already made the argument that, far from being sleek metaphors for marital dissolution or even a proximate narrative cause for character discord, any shark functions as that-which-is-not-constant-but-sometimes-appears to interpolate intervals into the temporal structure of the film, to punctuate and organize the film around the form of intermittency. The sharks also function as a disturbance in and to the field of vision, for the force of the sharks is less on skin than on the pattern of visual and temporal forms. In the period after the abandonment by the boat, the first image of the shark as threat is seen in the image-type that corresponds to the water-level point-of-non-view. That image is not of a shark as a totality but of its infamous metonymy in the dorsal fin, which, with its triangular jut out of the water, points, like an arrow, like a sudden deictic shock. The effect of this initial appearance is to make the triangular upward-pointing vector itself the form for the shark, the pointing to the breach that it constitutes through its slicing gesture in space. In other words, the shark is made nothing but arrow, the arrow marking the break in the line that the fin itself makes. Spatial punctuation, the sliver of body points to its extremity as event: here, look, this. Just as the sharks as problems for the continuity of time interpolate an interval to structurally introduce intermittency, they likewise figure visually as a break in the composition of the image. A shark breaches that absolute formal line between Above and Below.

A minor digression—it does not drift far. In his genealogy of perception,

Stephen Jay Gould lingers on the shifts of the nineteenth century, focusing on the passion in the 1850s for the aquarium. As Gould notes, this invention does not mark the first time aquatic creatures were displayed and domesticated, but what shifted at midcentury was the defining feature of the glass tank: "a *stable community* of aquatic organisms that can be viewed, not from above through the opacity of flowing waters with surface ripples, but eye-to-eye and from the side through transparent glass and clear water."[17] The stable community, unlike the "temporary display" of the fishbowl, persists with a duration, sustains itself without disruption in its balanced, self-correcting environment.[18] The aquarium and its predecessor, the terrarium, were affectively charged innovations, spawning notions such as "Pteridomania," the "fern craze" of Britain in the 1840s, and what a naturalist at the time dubbed the "aquarium mania" of the 1850s.[19] Gould argues that a direct legacy of the mid-nineteenth-century passion for aquaria is a permanent shift in modes of seeing and, in particular, drawing marine organisms. Today, one draws "such scenes in their 'natural' orientation," in an "'eye-to-eye' or edge-on view, where a human observer sees marine life from within—that is, as if he were underwater with the creatures depicted, and therefore watching them at their own level."[20] Such a mode of seeing emphasizes context and the ordinary behavior of the marine environment. This orientation is in marked contrast to the pre-aquarium perspective, in which marine organisms were drawn "either on top of waters (for swimming forms, mostly fishes) or thrown up on shore and desiccating on land (for bottom-dwellers, mostly invertebrates)."[21] The image in this language of illustration was shown from above, from "a terrestrial vantage point" with a firmly entrenched anthropocentric perspective. It is what happens to water in this pre-aquarium perception that is most remarkable, however, for the organisms must appear "on top, or out of, the waters," in some illustrations even flying in the air above the ocean. For this aesthetic of marine life, in other words, the water must be removed, either receding from the image or with the living organisms yanked from its wet security to strangle on land. It is therefore a mode of seeing marked by violence and a visual anxiety about the obscuring role of water.

Instead of its later role as transparent frame for the environment of the subject, pre-aquarial approaches to water figure it as a blockage to vision, a force of shade—all water dark water. The ocean is emptied, its inhabitants vomited up to reappear in the dry violence of the air, fixed, dead, and still for the eye of the artist. If the shift in modes of seeing with the advent of the aquarium, then, promises an eye-to-eye view in place of a top-down perspective, it also returns water to marine illustration as a medium for vision in place of an impediment to vision. The aquarium is properly a vivarium; while water, Gould writes, "is usually muddy and largely opaque in motion," the new perception clears water, pauses it in its clarity. While the frame in pre-aquarium images is often provided by the subjects themselves in a garland of creatures ringing the image, afterward the water itself becomes a frame. The pre-aquarium perspective is divided between air and land; the post-aquarium perspective, however, is tripartite: air, land, sea (and under the line of the sea). And in place of desiccated, washed-up organisms, marine subjects come back to life in a visual logic of undeadening. Water, in other words, was a block in the pre-aquarium model (a problem solved only by the violence of excerpting and killing off the aesthetic subjects); then it was a frame (presenting the subjects only by obliterating itself, by becoming a medium through which they were seen).

Open Water traces these different historical possibilities for aquatic illustration, moving from a land's-eye view to a diver's perspective. One has to therefore wonder whether the film figures as one final stage in this chain of forms of perception, so marked as it is in production, image, and aesthetic by the ethos of digital video. Does the mobility of the digital camera housed in Ikelite permit one to be in the water while looking locally on the water: does it make water, in a sense, opaque again? The digital represents another shift in illustration techniques, a post-aquarial visual logic in which water is neither block nor frame but now line—and only line, the line at which the digital camera can hover without committing to falling fully or only above or below that marker. If so, then this film is also a field of anxieties about perception and its possibilities or limitations and the attendant problem of exposure— technological, photographic, and also of course material to the elements, body to things that prey on bodies. The relation between human and sea, but also between sea and its creatures, is one that involves proximity without synthesis: closeness and juxtaposition that do not resolve into a totality. The sea is a fractured space in which shark and figure are near but not unifiable. There is a break between them as strong as the one between hierarchical vertical realms, a separation that constitutes the line at which violence takes place.

The appearance of the shark's pointed appendage is the appearance of a visual break at the moment of the puncture. The fin ruptures the firm but also, we come to find, vulnerable separation between registers of space that have been demarcated in the level shots in the ocean. Despite the orienting line of the horizon, there is relatively little visual interest in the receding depths of the screen; the blue block forms constitute a flat image invested in textures and surfaces without depth. Thus, what the deictic fin points to is the breach of the line between spatial types; its target is that minimal difference that the visual distinction of the edge of the sea supplies. The puncture of the fin transforms the rectangle at the bottom of the flat projected image into a space marked as having depth, containing a "below." That crucial fin, in other words, brings into being the openness of the depths.

The break in the line of the sea is the visual analogue to the capacity of material to transgress that separation: that the floor is a surface; that the tension is vulnerable to puncture; that it does not support or hold or ground a permanent separation; that for all the frame marks out proportions of flat expanse, bodies can and will fall under that dividing line that cuts through the image. In the epigraph to this section, Deleuze and Guattari describe a space marked by "an accumulation of proximities," a space that I suggested in the previous chapter is in play in forms of recombination without unity on the level of critical form. This line that is put in place only to be broken is this assemblage of accumulated proximities and forms, not quite line, not quite surface, but hovering amorphously in the space that it simultaneously marks out and defines. The rigorous patterning of shots of the sea, horizon, and sky likewise evokes (in a completely different context) Noël Burch's description of the representation of interior spaces in Japanese film, that domestic spaces in, say, a work by Ozu are *cellular subdivisions of the screen-surface,"* rather than recessing elements with and within deep space.[22] These cellular blocks in *Open Water* reduce sky and sea to variably framed rectangles, what Burch calls "the purest expression of the concept of two-dimensionality."[23] This composition of flatnesses and surfaces, this study of accumulated proximities of shape and blue, is what is broken into and broken up by the visual force of the violent darting appendage. The threat of death is made present through a *formal* possibility: finitude's risk occurs at the commutation of expanse into well, the spatial translation when two-dimensional blocks of blue become three-dimensional depths into which bodies may sink. Resisting a reading of the sharks as metaphors, villains, or symbolic embodiments of anxiety involves redescribing fins as visual elements. And rethinking fins as graphic elements enables the speculation that it is the rupture of a visual divisor—a rupture to form and not to muscle—that opens up this scene to death.

Some breaches cannot be unbroken, some wounds are unsuturable. The visual forms of the film never return to a state of horizontal wholeness after the sharks wreck the demarcation by puncturing a line now rendered a broken series of dashes. In the wake of the fin's infringing cut, the visual form established prior to its appearance is radically disrupted, as though the initial fissure in the minimal difference between registers of hierarchized space caused the world of the film to, for a moment—but the image bears this out—turn on its head. The sharks, in other words, puncture and put pressure on—and are a force external to, which wrecks—the visual schema as such. There is perhaps no purer form of their violence in the entire film. Right before the first appearance of the fin, the image voids itself of figure to display solely an almost colorless study in white on gray. The position of the horizon line shifts with the rise and fall of the water, but the line of demarcation is barely visible: the screen is almost perfectly divided, as though the image, in advance of being turned over, were itself reversible or invertible. At the crucial bolting cut—the deictic fin—this breach causes the waves to repeat the punctuation of the fin's disturbance. The fin disappears as quickly as it appears, but the rhythmic reverberance on the level of a wave traces a more diffuse version of the triangular surprise.

Then, the eruption of a new shot type: a wave flows over the camera lens, and the film for the first time since the couple has risen to the surface dips below the level of the water. The shock of dark blue replaces the empty whites of the cool sky as coloration registers the more substantial shock of dipping below the line that is supporting breath and life. Although an ontological break in the sea-surface line has been signaled in the appearance of the fin that rips through it, the breach's more radical form involves the camera dipping under water in an unattributable shot, an image completely delinked from even an approximation of a character's (limited, partial) vision. The sharks' visual disturbance is not only to line, then, but also to space, to the field of open water, now rendered a depth instead of an expanse. In the (literal) wake of the violence-causers' appearance, put into the field of vision is an inhuman technological gaze associated with the camera that rends image from subject. Strictly subjective shots in film are a rarity, point-of-view shots themselves associated with a cheat over the shoulder, and this film is composed of numerous shots—overhead shots, long shots, extreme close-ups—that are in no way attributable to the point of view of a singular figure. Thus, the significance of this moment when the water rushes over the lens, filling the frame, is not per se that it breaks a connection with an ostensible viewpoint of a character. Rather, it is because the language of the film editing and the narrative result suggest that the image of the fin is correlated to what Susan sees that the impossible-to-place shot under the water—which cannot be attributed to her vision—collapses her into the viewpoint of the camera. In other words, the film drags the eye of "Susan"—this is a linguistic figure here—below the water line with it, pulls that figure under, fills the hybrid woman-camera eye with blue, an image that, if the eye is given a nose and mouth, is the very image of suffocation and drowning.

Formally, the film posits a line only to break it, establishes a surface for the inevitable puncture. Once this structure is set in motion and the energetic effect of shark on wave collapses Susan's eye into an impersonal video gaze that dips below the horizontal divider, the film plays its visual consequences out explicitly in a remarkable sequence. Following the first appearance of the sharks, Susan announces, "I can't stand not knowing what's under me. I'm just going to look, OK?" She places her diving mask on her face and dips her head below the line, repeating but inverting the gesture made previously by the shark fin (and anticipating the gesture she makes later in the film when Daniel is bitten). This breach beneath the line does not limit its effect to the ontological break at the bar that centers the image and world above the surface; it is also a temporal cut. For when Susan contravenes the demand of the line—which is the demand of every line, that it not be crossed—the break causes the film to formally break down.[24] What follows is a one-minute immersion in the potential abstractions of space, time, and image that involves the film falling out of the time of the narrative, dropping into the unattributable and uninhabitable space of six studies of line, shape, and blue. (For a film so insistent on its verisimilitude, from the opening textual pronouncement of its source, to the vérité jerkiness of the digital camerawork, to the extratextual production details, this escape into abstraction is as shocking as the appearance of any shark.) First, the rushing of watery surface: all sensuous ocean line and light; thin horizontal shadows and dark; a rich warm racing, shimmering navy. Then, a different surface—or the same, a different time, years apart or minutes—gunmetal cool with tight compressed ripples, faster like the ridges of a paved road close up, uneven, shorter, bits of wave jut and pulse. A velocious tracking rush to the right for the third shot, routed waves pushing as though constituting the violent wake of a missing marine cause. The fourth image caresses one long, slow swell like the curl of a foamy meringue billowing to a singular diagonal flourish. Violently vertical, the fifth supplies luminescent Kleinian blue cords and threads, wreathing ultramarine wriggles. What a wave is is energy and not substance; it is force, not water, that moves across and along the surface of the ocean. These wave studies submit to vision patterns and rhythms of energy, make present the many possibilities for different forms of movement across a screen.

Finally, after this long minute of abstraction, the sixth study explores the

cruelest space, which is to say announces the depth of those depths in a forward insinuation through the wet shimmer, ending with an under-the-sea
shot of the surface now made skylight to the bluish belly. The camera travels
quickly up and then breaks the surface, this time from the underside; the film
returns to figures and white air, to a certain point in space and time with the
new marker of specificity, "1:30 P.M.," and to Daniel's voice speaking. "OK," he
says. That "OK" is a preliminary to a strongly coded temporal gap—time has
passed since a masked Susan looked down, and his vocal joiner participates
in a new conversation that has taken place in that gap of time behind the
abstractions on the screen. While Susan's "OK?" at the look under the water
presses the film into the studies of rhythm, tone, and line, Daniel's "OK . . ."
responds to her unanswered question, bookends the breach to reestablish
continuity and pull the film back to the narrative world of characters, scenario,
suspense. The effect is to bracket those helixes and loops, to let the pealing
spirals and undulating coils stand apart as though conversation could—and
did—carry on over and indifferent to them.[25] Susan's look under the water—to
which those images are in no way retroactively attributed—introduces a visual
form that emanates from the sensibility of the film, from the aesthetics of
water space. In other words, her dip under the line sets loose the force of an
impersonal aesthetic of speeds and tones, rhythms, lines. It is because that bar
is transgressed that abstraction is called up into the field of the film.

The essential visual form of *Open Water,* then, in its barest articulation,
involves the positing of a horizontal divisor, which is then broken upward by
a punctuating fin, then broken downward by Susan's masked visage. While the
duration of the film is little more than the framed time of waiting for imminent
death, the visual structure involves putting in place a bar and then tracing
the spatial transgressions of that bar. If the film were plotted as a series of
drawn gestures—if, say, Marcel Broodthaers were to reduce the film to its bare
graphic structure—this resulting line with its arrows up and down, its breaks
rising and falling, would look a great deal like the plotted motion of a wave.
The ticks that pull up then contract the firmly held but labile line that divides
above from below reach into, then contract to retreat from, the very possibility
of space. As though giving visual form to Levinas's claim that anxiety is "the
supreme instant from which we can only depart," the structure of the film is
the repeated formal-motor gesture of draining, a series of departures from
a form that is posited solely in order to be transgressed.[26] Lacan's form of
embarrassment was as a blockage that nevertheless does not let one hide—its
cinematic form is this line that is instated but that is not absolute, does not

shield or hide one from the exposure to that which crosses the bar. There is a bar, but it does not support a subject; there is a line, but it can be crossed. Duration exists and is marked out in the film by the cruelty of numbers so that the shark function of appearance–disappearance punctures it, renders time itself continuous and progressive toward death but simultaneously riddled and intermittent. Likewise, the signature shot of the film at the level of the sea surface is delimited so that its bar can be crossed upward then downward, setting in motion the increasing abstraction of the film, a voiding of figures in place of lines and blues.

In short, *Open Water* sets its form in place solely to depart from it. And as for those bodies whose misadventures in space end with their deaths, they are retroactively determined by the film not to have been bodies in space but disruptions to form for which their deaths constitute a mere departure—under that line, again. No revelation is forthcoming from these departures, and the form of anxiety is the end result that nothing but the place of the title will have taken place, that no meaningful event will have instated itself or made itself realized over the course of the cinematic depletion. If an event takes place, it can be read into a narrative of history, unpacked for a meaning that persists; that nothing but this site for emptying will have taken place writes into the film the void of the deaths without assuredly filling that void with significance. The event of the two deaths is a fugitive, elusively escaping the taking-place of the film but also the taking-place of critical reading as event. In turn, the film puts critics out to sea, as well, fails to settle interpretively but continually drifts.

DEATH IS A TURN OF THE COLOR WHEEL

In the same way that the formal structure of a line that is broken is the condition of possibility for death (that the line is breachable, that a surface may be transformed into a depth), the other formal condition of finitude is the substitution in the field of color of red for blue. When Daniel is attacked one hour into the film, a sudden formal shock: an overhead shot of a muddy red stain surrounding the two bodies and rapidly overtaking the steely field in an expanding circle. In *Open Water*, finitude is: the tiniest dip below a line and the other side of a color wheel. As though in agreement with Goethe's claim that when "blue deepens very mildly into red," it "may be said to disturb rather than enliven," this red overtakes blue—and that is enough.[27] (Marvelously, Goethe also notes, "This unquiet feeling increases as the hue progresses, and it may be safely assumed, that a carpet of a perfectly pure deep blue-red would be intolerable."[28] And, indeed, it is.)

To Daniel's moan, "This can't be happening," the late sky matches the swatch of the body's emptying and turns from its tones of blue and gray to ominous ones of red and orange, a chromatic shift that not only maps the trauma of the color-wheel violence to the top third of the screen but also signals the temporal progress of the day toward the certain but unspecified time of their future deaths. Black line horizon, fiery air, the film repeats the establishing shots of ocean and sky as though to put on display the absolute reorientation of the chromatic world of the film, as though to redescribe the totality of the difference of a world in which the space around one's body is red, not blue. Night brings formal terrors: an obliteration of the grounding divisor of the horizon, a punctuated vision against an indifferent and unmarked field of duration, unmoored in time and space. If the night involves a breaking down of cinematic elements to their barest form in the flashes of lightning that toggle visible presence on and off, it is also simultaneously a saturation of the visual in the totality of tones of color. The ocean at night is rendered a series of vertical columns consisting of short horizontal white lines against black expanse, with no sense of cinematic or cartographic scale. This rendering of lunar light and rippling water as a series of dashes evokes, turned on their side, the hash marks made in error on the boat, the entire world collapsed into the counting game that, off by just two marks, the couple has now certainly lost.

Daniel dies overnight, over and under this commutation of blue to red to black, of divided expanses into indifferent horizonless field, of waves and moon to countable rows of line. Under the pulsing of the storm's light, the slightly delayed punctuation of the thunder, the loss of position in space and time and the undifferentiated whispers that fail to attach in knowable ways to bodies, muffled rumbles felt more than heard, amid the pain and prayer and moans, against the ineffectual pleadings of love and the horrible request not to leave his wife alone, the pinkish blue light of dawn arrives too late, or on time, but arrives definitively after his death has taken place. In the pale light of dawn, Susan holds Daniel's body, holds her dead lover, balances thick weight on her arms. She floats, holding him fast. She holds and then releases his corpse (and the body becomes a corpse, in a manner, at this letting go). With its specific form of lovers parting at daybreak, this image evokes the very old literary form of the *aubade,* suggesting that the final chromatic stage of the film, after blue then red then black, is nothing but white (from *auba* [dawn], from *albus* [white]). Radically diverging from the Hollywood meta-narrative of the formation of a couple, the film ends with an unfolding form of uncoupling and decoupling; in place of the lovemaking that precedes the aubade's separation of partners, Susan and Daniel's night contained only the thrashing spasms of a wounded body's bleeding to death. Dawn's emergence, meant to be a beginning or a starting over—a first appearance of white light— here signals only disappearance and the eventual decline of both bodies into the depths of the sea.

Susan asks a question about the sharks earlier in the film, "What's worse: seeing them or not seeing them?" It is an unanswerable question, for, as I have argued in relation to the structure of intermittency, the sharks are that which is seen and then not seen; their appearance cannot be parsed into one or the other—anxiety, formally, rhythmically, is this both/and-ness. Likewise, after the slow letting go of Daniel's corpse, the film ends with a strange long shot of Susan, alone now, alone in the wide open water. Far away, so far that her head appears as a small blot in the field of the early light expanse, we see Susan take off her diving vest and slip under the line of the sea, little more than the smallest vertical displacement, like the breath or bump of an inconsequential crest. Critics, mirroring Susan's question that poses as alternatives a total structure, have debated this opaque shot: does Susan give up, exhausted and beaten, or does she claim some autonomy from the scenario, from the sea, and own her death in a suicide? One way to reformulate this question is that critical disagreement has centered on how to read the time of Susan's death: did she determine that the time of death would come *early* but certainly, or, in a victory for the sea and for time itself, did her certain death arrive *on time?* The difference is figured as significant and signifying: one critic, for example, reads Susan as owning her death discursively in the form of purposeful suicide.[29] It is a difference that is generally given a great deal of weight because suicide is not the same as any other form of death for what it means; as Maurice Blanchot figures killing oneself, "It accuses and it condemns; it makes a final judgment."[30]

But I would argue that the death that takes place with the figure of Susan is not the death of a body or person but that, in fact, of a distinction—of this distinction. The death that takes place is not elevated to the status of an event. The spatial interval put into place by the long shot, the insistent refusal of interiority or psychological depth, ultimately precludes reading this scene as suggesting either exhaustion or ownership. How Susan dies, like the other figurations in the film, does not *mean;* it renders no final judgment. Reading the death for substance—any attempt to suggest that the death is not abso-

lute or final, that it persists in meaning for someone, after the event—fails
to account for the most radical effect of finitude: just that no more goes on.
What the cinematic image gives us in death is neither more nor less than the
modulation of the image, the effect it has on the formal organization of the
frame. The effect of the dying is to pose the question of the event in relation
to the space with which the film ends: the open expanse of the sea now made
proportional blocks of surface again. In the end, nothing will have happened
in this place: neither a suicide nor a collapse. Because the death cannot be
recuperated for the persistence of meaning, nothing but this field of space
will have taken place in the film. The film makes present the not-enough of
the image; the interval of space that holds one apart at the moment of greatest
assumed revelation organizes the mise-en-scène of the film not around the
(or a) nothing, nor a (or the) non-scene, but around an insufficient scene, a
scene that is, does, and reveals constitutively not enough.[31]

If *Open Water* involves the death of a philosophical distinction, the not-
enough of the mise-en-scène, now a riddled mise-n'en-scène, and a formal
restriction of time and space that does not extend infinitely through critical
allegory but that takes the structure of finitude, then what remains at the end
of the film? If the film consists (entirely) of its series of formal and material
drainings, violations of a horizontal line, the commuting of blue to red to black
to white, and the unremarkable and unremarked disappearance of two bodies
from the frame, then what *can* remain at the end of this film? Nothing but the
place where things have not enough taken place. All we are left with is briny
open water. The title of the film thus puts into play a series of correspondences
between space, place, and the nature of the non-event that, like the tripartite
title of Freud's work on anxiety or the other forms of juxtaposed spaces in this
and the previous chapter, do not and cannot synthesize into a totality.

Open Water: the naming of a space, but also a particular kind of non-space,
an expanse, a space without depth written in the surface cover of the ceiling of
the sea as far as visual reach permits. "Open water" is also a particular kind of
affective space, marked by characteristics of dangerous exposure, a lack of obstruction and the quality of being unprotected. Always at a distance from the
shore, open water represents the opening of water, its unmooring from land
but also safety. It is also, however, a space composed only of depth: the depth
open and available for diving under, a place without boundaries that enables
diving—and is also, therefore, the corresponding name for the certification
for these Open Water Divers. (Does it also, with the addition of a punctuation
mark's minor curve, suggest the possible imperative: Open, Water—and swal-

FIG. 8.1. *Open Water* (Chris Kentis, 2003)

low up these bodies, the traces of this event, even the possibility of the story in your wet murky depths?) *Open Water*, in naming a form of diving certification, points to the condition of possibility for the event—because they are certified, they are *there*—and to the name of the site of the event where nothing but that site, that place, will ultimately take place. The name of the film thus folds on itself its cause, condition of possibility, frame, and this flat expanse of open sea that is all that is left, the site the only remainder and reminder of the violence that is now over, leaving behind just a watery stretch. The event contains within it this flat non-eventness: this pure place, this ephemeral line at which nothing will have taken place but this terrible open expansive space.

NOTHING BUT THE PLACE

If this supreme naturalness, this sense of events observed haphazardly as the hours roll by, is the result of an ever-present although invisible system of aesthetics, it is definitely the prior conception of the scenario which allows this to happen. Disappearance of the actor, disappearance of *mise en scène*? Unquestionably, but because the very principle of *Ladri di Biciclette* is the disappearance of a story.—André Bazin, "Bicycle Thief"

Well, then. Recalling the epigraphs to this section, to return to Tillich's care but Freud's concern: have we finally put anxiety in its proper place?

If, in the wake of the disappearance of the bodies in *Open Water*, what is left behind is nothing but the titular field, that place would principally be one in which a disappearance took place: of beings, of a story, of the event, of disruptions to a formal logic. Not unlike Bazin's curious description of the quintessential neo-realist film as operating around a series of *disparitions*—curious because his privileged cinematic mode relies precisely on the ontological promise of visible, avowable *appearance* in the photographic image—*Open Water* puts anxiety on display in a place in which things fade, drain, waste, withdraw. (And, crucially, Bazin's "disparition," while it recalls visible disappearance and vanishing, also suggests what goes missing, what is removed, what dies out, what dies.) *Open Water* not only consists of, or is made up of, these wasting disappearances; it actually constitutes the ruining of appearance as such. The film puts anxiety in *its* place, but that place is one in which nothing will have taken place save for the openness of place itself.

This formulation, and the title for this chapter, are taken from Stéphane Mallarmé's *Un coup de dés jamais n'abolira le hasard* (1897), though not because the white-space poem nominally posits the question of what has happened "*du fond d'un naufrage*"—it is not in the traces of terrible things that happen in waters that the poem and film speak to each other. Rather, their quilting point consists of the tiered capitalization, distributed across multiple pages in the complex literary space of Mallarmé's poem: "RIEN / N'AURA EU LIEU / QUE LE LIEU." This avowal, "NOTHING ... WILL HAVE TAKEN PLACE ... OTHER THAN THE PLACE," is an insistence on a suspension of an event, a relegation of an event (in the poem, a shipwreck) to the traces it leaves behind. In meditation nineteen of *Being and Event,* Alain Badiou reads the poem's production as being of an undecidable event suspended "from a hesitation which is itself absolute."[32] While Badiou takes the form of the poem as concerned with the indecision of the event, and another critic figures the poem's formal hesitation as enacting "the intermittence of meaning and non-meaning," this watery wavering also recalls the temporal intermittency and the difficult movements of anxious form that the sharks as violence operators bear into Kentis's film.[33] Mallarmé's dispersed pronouncement, then, which cancels the violent eventness of the event of the shipwreck to replace it with "QUE LE LIEU," is the same form as the stage on which *Open Water* plays out Susan and Daniel's disappearance—a cancellation of the events (or eventness) of the deaths by their in-visibility, subsumed by the agony of the visibility of the open place where these desertions took place.[34] If the bodies fade so that the field of the title can come into visibility, then what is representable or made present in the film is the staging of the blocked visibility of the disappearance of the event and the calm return of the original site of water in early milky morning light.

As Badiou says of Mallarmé's poem, one must recognize that "place is sovereign, that 'nothing' is the true name of what happens."[35] We are thus back to Kierkegaard's account of anxiety from chapter 7: that the concept of the affect is a something that is nothing, that the nothing, or a nothing, is the true name for what happens in the anxious form of this film. Place is sovereign—the open place of open water—but it is a place brought into formal being through the modulation of visual elements that *necessitates* the elimination of the formal disruptor that Susan and Daniel's presence in that place constitutes.[36] Badiou likens the Mallarméan enigma to "an empty salon, a vase, a dark sea"—all figures of catastrophe and void—and accordingly we might posit the *Open Water* enigma as: a counting error, a disrupted line, a vertical dip. Minor marker traces, all. Susan's flesh sinks below the line that sustains the film and the event disappears with her, leaving only the field of open but deep space that was the condition of possibility for the event. The effect of the bar that is commuted from line to ceiling, put in place in order to be crossed and given depth in *Open Water,* is to give shape to the isolation and restriction of the stage on which the event of these deaths takes place. But they sink without record. And neither reconstruction nor archive is possible in the wake of this total disappearance; what is framed, what remains, is this primacy of nothing but the place. As with Bazin's account of the disappearance of the story in *Ladri di Biciclette,* what takes place in *Open Water* is the disappearance of the event into the pure contingency of the place as once the site of a counting error.

It is not only, then, that Susan and Daniel do die. For film form to rearticulate the primacy of place (or its sovereignty, in Badiou's formulation), Susan and Daniel *must* die. The anxious form, the terrible privileging of place, is thus in collusion with violence and not its mere vehicle for representation. *Open Water* sketches the bodies disrupting the line of the bar as their future anterior omissions from the field of the title: human life is that which will be made to have not taken place in the place of the expanse. Their deaths are not events that take place or happen in or at the site but the unpresentable contained within the place, retroactively named by their certain disappearance from it. Reading for a formal affectivity reveals here that a rigorous attention to form does not preclude other theoretical commitments, including ethical ones. Indeed, we might more broadly consider whether horror is the genre in which the body is formalized, given textual shape only to be subjected to the bare destruction of its form. In the case of *Open Water,* redescribing negative affectivity not as something a character or spectator feels but as a struggle that form itself undergoes has broad implications for taking horror seriously as a site where motor complication is a structural problem; where drained vitality involves a mere but absolute shift from blue to red to black to white; and where death happens on the level of, and because of, a resolutely broken line. The film posits that finitude itself can be redescribed as an iteration of the modulation and then destruction of form. It is not only that a formalist reading of *Open Water* reveals or produces this strain, but that such an account of finitude in the film is impossible without reading for form.

If we follow Badiou's formulation that "the paradox of an evental-site is that it can only be recognized on the basis of what it does not present in the situation in which it is presented," *Open Water* qualifies as a version of this paradox on this basis: the entirety of the film's structure takes variable forms of the not-enough dimension of form outside of the language of presence—what this book has called a problem of mise-n'en-scène. The film does not make present a continuous form of time, fails to put in place a visual bar that functions to demarcate registers of space, and figures the deaths that might ground or center the film only as blocked: first Daniel's behind the cut of blackness in the non-space and non-time of night, and then Susan's in a long shot with such an unbridgeable distance put into place that no meaning can be generated from this act, which is not even act, but gesture, and not even gesture, but mild vertical dip with the consequence of the absolute. The eighty-minute unpresentation of the film is one that is constitutively not enough, a visual language at the greatest point of what Lacan calls difficulty—riddled with blockages and stoppages in the form of embarrassment, a structural stuckness that does not know what to do with itself to *be enough*—a film trapped in and by the openness of its not-enough forthcoming. Finitude, for this reason, is not the pathos of the material end experienced by figures in the film but the radical limitation of film form, its insufficiency in relation to putting an event in place as something that happens. Finitude as a limit of being is here rendered finitude as a limit of becoming—the capacity of form to transform, to cease treading water and to launch meaning, to *take place* as some event. That failure, that structural humiliation, constitutes the void at the center of the film. *Open Water* names this anxiety as the form that is exposed as that in which nothing will have taken place but the movements of a difficult emptying out that retains nothing but the place of the title. Anxiety, in other words, is the form in which bare form has nowhere to hide.

Instead of catharsis, Open Water just depletes, drifts, and then it ends. But the formal structure of this then-it-ends dimension should be distinguished from the disappearance of beings that signals Susan's and Daniel's mortal end as those-who-end within the film. Heidegger makes a useful version of this distinction in Being and Time between things that happen to humans and things that happen to things, and accordingly, he posits two types of ending: "properly dying" (Tod [death] or eigentlich sterben [actually dying]), which is the dying proper to beings (uniquely what a human can do), on the one hand, and, on the other, "perishing" (verenden) or stoppage or "the ending of anything that is alive" (perish, from perire [to leave, disappear, as in transpire, to go beyond a limit]).[37] Heidegger's distinction between death and perishing, though for him bound up with the specificity of Dasein and how it takes its demise, has broader implications for thinking about the ways in which Open Water plays out a cinematic form that perishes and the ways in which the beings Susan and Daniel experience eigentlich Sterben. If one were to argue that the film plays out perishing in order to tell a story about "the proper dying that is unique to beings," then that would be a matter of form mirroring theme—or, put another way, form serving theme—and a re-privileging of those "actual deaths" above all else. The dying proper to beings would be preserved as the site where critical meaning takes place, and the specificity of that dying would be maintained as the privileged form of demise in the film. However, my argument makes exactly the opposite claim. Open Water actually plays out eigentlich Sterben (the deaths proper to beings) in order to put on display the transpiring of a visual distinction, the devastation of a line, the perishing of form.

And this reversal is, I contend, the more radical engagement with finitude.

For once the nothingness of anxiety becomes redescribed as a resolutely formal problem, bodies in Open Water no longer point to subjects, characters, narrative agents, or spectators. Bodies, rather, are essentially vanishing terms, which register only the traces of some event—its meaning, its taking-place—not by their presence in the scene but by their removal from it. The corpus is there solely to come to not be there. Susan and Daniel, therefore, are entirely equivalent to the visual bar set in the middle of the frame: put in (that) place in order to, at some future possible point, vanish from it. Place as site prevails over event that takes place, and nothing that could make open water signify within the logic of the film, nothing that could put the deaths into the trajectory of a narrative of the event, remains—nothing that could give the utter contingency, the couple's terrible horror in the darkness of that punctuated night, meaning, is possible. What is left as the organizing vanishing term of the text is the difficult movement of film form, suspended by hesitations and rhythms and blockages at the level of time and space, a form that traces as its event the place where marked out is the insufficiency of any saying: Yes, you died for *this*.

ANXIETY has been described in the preceding chapters as the structure-in-process of the difficult movements of form, a churning mise-n'en-scène in which, in the end, nothing but the place will have taken place. Thus, although anxiety involves the futurity of the future, it is a future humiliated by its insufficiency, exposed in the horror that what its form brings forth is not enough. *Open Water* puts the potentiality of form on display in its most raw, naked, and stuck state: at the minimal difference of space and time, where a logic of form is exposed as churning around nothing, treading water and having nowhere to go, nowhere to hide. If the pressure of formal negative affectivity is this restriction that renders the structures of space and time not-enough, then how might the form of the affect work at the antipode of anxiety's nothing? What might form do, how might the potentiality of form transform, liberate its motor restrictions, and involve the future not only as a space of the possible but as a space of the certain, where the event as the event may instate itself? This pure form of the positive where *things take place* in form—let us call it joy.

NINE

To Begin Again:
The Ingression
of Joyful Forms

A gaud, a ribbon, a dead flower, something

—OSCAR WILDE, *The Duchess of Padua*

There are at least three ways of bringing joy down to earth. One could, as in Robert Creeley's "Joy," frame the exuberant possibility of infinity as immanent and certain:

> JOY
> I could look at
> an empty hole for hours
> thinking it will
> get something in it,
>
> will collect
> things. There is
> an infinite emptiness
> placed there.[1]

In the broken line "it will / get something in it," all possibility is contained, not as mere possibility but as a possibility that *will* take place, a future state of certain having taken-placedness. There *is,* Creeley writes of the great infinite, not there might be. Or, the joyful could crash and land to the tune of Nietzsche's famous "Drunken Song" affirmation in *Thus Spoke Zarathustra,* "'Was *that*—life?' I will say to death. 'Very well! Once more!'" [*War Das—das Leben?' will ich zum Tode sprechen. 'Wohlan! Noch Ein Mal!*].[2] The "Once more," like Creeley's "There is," suggests joy's simultaneous link to the infinite and to the immanent, its capacity to stick to or suck on this very world and that which takes place (in Nietzsche's inimitable style, joy "bites into *itself*")—that of which we can say there *is* and that of which we can say *Again!* to what *is*.[3]

Then, finally, in an etymological dance, joy via *joie* via *gaudia* could reach back, descend to graze the certain things of the world, some specific and concrete objects therein. *Gaudere* (to rejoice) is that from which we also derive *gaud* (a grammatical doublet for joy), gaudy, and jewels or ornaments, for it was gaudies, the beads on the rosary, through which a joy not tethered to the Earth, a mysterious joy of the Joyful Mysteries of the Virgin, took place.[4] Cognates in Romance languages (such as *joya* in Spanish) also mean "jewel," precious stone, and in diminutive forms a valuable trinket; *gioja* in Italian is both a jewel and joy or mirth. (This link to ornament and bead also sutures joy to other forms of surface and artifice: from *gaude* also derives a trick or jest, which would constitute, perhaps, a fourth way of bringing joy down to earth, but a mischievous joy, this.) While a feeling of great pleasure or delight, a sublime awe, or, as in the Greek for "joy," *chara*—the very notion of grace or the divine—joy is simultaneously marked by its intimacy with faceted gems, angled objects that reflect light, break it down into its constituent parts (what is valued in a diamond is precisely this working-over of light, its treasured and cultivated dispersion, scintillation, and brilliance). While *elation* and *ecstasy* lose or loose the self on the level of the signifier, and happiness tethers itself to the ill or good fortune of what happens to some someone (*hap-* being their common root, so that happiness, happenstance, and what happens to a self ultimately are all the same), joy's merriment hovers in the pleasure or gladness in the glittering surface of *things*.[5] The light-reflecting/refracting qualities of joy bind it to the material objects of the world, the specific, certain, and concrete, the jewel that reflects and breaks up light, but also to the bibelot, the bauble or the trinket, to a gaud, a ribbon, a dead flower—something.

To the immanence of a joy brought down to the surface of the world—the *there is,* the *once more* to life, the thinginess of the gaud—Nietzsche's contribution to the history of joy adds one more crucial dimension: an affirmation that takes the form of a repetition of that immanence. The structure of joy, then, is bound not merely to the shape or surface of the glittering specific something but to the certain repeatability of the certain something. This phrase as written here is mostly adequate, but Nietzsche's formulation of joyful repetition would correct with an important qualifier: joy, for him, involves the repetition of *every* (not *a*) certain something, a joy predicated on a totality in repetition. His specific formulation for it in *Human, All Too Human* is "joy in the actual and active of *every kind*" (*Lust am Wirklichen, Wirkenden* jeder Art).[6] His famous thought experiment of the "eternal recurrence" (*ewige Wiederkehr*) involves a repetition for joy that itself affirms every instance for eternity:

> Woe entreats: Go! Away, woe! But all that suffers wants to live that it may become ripe and joyous and longing—longing for what is farther, higher, brighter. "I want heirs"—thus speaks all that suffers: "I want children, I do not want *myself*."
>
> Joy, however, does not want heirs, or children—wants itself, wants eternity, wants recurrence, wants everything eternally the same.[7]

The totality of "joy in the actual and active of *every kind*" extends the field of the most positive of the positive affects to include (all) instances of tragedy and great suffering—the "every kind" of the actual—but also indeterminate instances, moments of flux and becoming—the "active," even as it comes to be, or, more provocatively, even as it fails to come to be but *might* come to be or *could* come to be. Nietzsche's insistence that *Lust* is inseparable from *Verlust* (loss, bereavement, casualty), this intertwining of joy with suffering, this demand that joy in the actual and active encompass its negation, makes Nietzschean joy, in one critic's formulation, "tragic, Dionysian, and pessimistic," as opposed to "linear, idealistic, and optimistic."[8]

Nietzschean joy is also an ethic, for he is explicit on this point: the eternal recurrence is not a strict return of what has taken place only, but also a beam cast out on the future. The ethical stance of joy involves an avowal that one will will that which one will will might return, that one will refuse to affirm a weakly willing of the just-once—this ambitious jubilation deriving from what Deleuze calls Nietzsche's loathing of "little compensations, the little pleasures, the little joys."[9] This ethic is the antipode of the logic of chance articulated in the previous chapter on *Open Water*. There, violence involves the contingency of a counting error, a cast of dice that sets the subsequent anxious film in motion and brings about every terrible formal and material end. But in the joyful ethic of the what-might-take-place of any situation, as formulated by

Deleuze, "*Nietzsche turns chance into an affirmation.*" This affirmation is not achieved by isolating the figure of the throwing of the die (which would affirm only chance itself), but by binding that figural toss to the "combination which they form on falling," which also affirms necessity.[10] Thus, the eternal return, as Deleuze writes of the risky pitch, "is the second moment, the result of the dice-throw, the affirmation of necessity, the number which brings together all the parts of chance."[11] Affirming the whole of chance entails affirming not only the probable possible but also the necessary and the certain. Nietzsche's figuring of the eternal return is thus both ethical, as in the imperative formulated as, "Whatever you will, will it in such a way that you also will its eternal return," and, Deleuze reminds us, ontological: "it is the universal being of becoming, but the universal being of becoming ought to belong to a single becoming."[12] Joy, then, after Nietzsche, does not recuse itself from the messy facticity of being a Being-in-time, nor bracket the actual or active, either suffering or becoming. Rather, it places the infinity of chance and possibility into an existence marked by finitude. It also, therefore, radically changes the relationship between the self and the past that has taken place. The law in *Zarathustra* that embodies this shift is that one must become a retrospective or retroactive force (*rückwirkende Kraft*), transforming the brute past, willing backward "to transform every 'It was' into an 'I wanted it thus.'"[13] Every contingency becomes a retroactive determination of will. And to imagine the great struggle for affirmation, the urgency but also profound difficulty of Nietzschean joy, one need only consider what it would have meant to transform every "It was" of *Open Water* into "I, we, wanted it thus."

The eternal return is the bringing forth not only of this transformation but also of the joyful willing of this new form of becoming. In the section of *Zarathustra* titled "Of Redemption," the key word is *Freudebringer*: "the will [has] become its own redeemer and bringer of joy."[14] The significance of this departure from the history of thought on joy prior to the nineteenth century cannot be overstated. Adam Potkay's genealogy of joy notes its long-standing link to recollection or anticipation, either taken place (now lost) or future promises of unity, fulfillment (or fullness), plenitude, and harmony, just as the news of the birth of Christ—"I bring you good news of a great joy" (Luke 2:10)—only defers or anticipates a later and greater joy in the death and resurrection; the apotheosis of Romanticism's joy in Schiller's *An die Freude* (1785), set iconically in a revised version by Beethoven, promises that "every sin shall be forgiven, / Hell forever cease to be."[15] By contrast, the insistently present and immanent joy of Nietzsche's eternal recurrence "does not offer a convenient way of dividing one's life into a before and an after," in Gary Shapiro's language, "for the moments (*Augenblicke*) of all my past are as eternal, as significant, as all of my future."[16] This is why the thought experiment also requires a willed forgetting, an affirmation of the dissolving of the taken-place so that an eternity of all possible taking-places might also occur. If anxiety is the form in which nothing will have taken place but the place—where not enough transforms on the level of form, where an insufficiency of being and of comprehension of its demise is staged—then the form of joy, we might say, is precisely where *something* (all prior and future possibles) in fact, indeed, actually, takes place.

When one takes from the philosopher of intensities, laughter, and dance this shape of joy, the form of the affect as the affirmation of recurrence, and reads it not for a life or a will in relation to eternity but in relation to a text, the theoretical translation is tricky. Without ascribing agency to form or clinging to an authorial subjectivity, it is not immediately clear how the willing of "*all* prior possibilities" might manifest in or as cinematic structure. However, as one possible way of introducing the aesthetic dimension, consider Shapiro's reading of the figure of the Ugliest Man, who is awoken through a mere and brief "one day, one festival with Zarathustra." This character study provides an instructive nuance on the relation between affirmation and repetition that suggests a broader formal possibility in the *ewige Wiederkehr*.[17] Shapiro writes, "The Ugliest Man's ability to base his affirmation on a brief episode suggests that one need not see one's entire life as an aesthetic totality in order to make the requisite affirmation. Rather, the thought of recurrence, when understood in circumstances that dramatize its sense, shows itself to be affirmable."[18] The import in Shapiro's carefully worded argument—that "one need not see one's entire life as an aesthetic totality"—is that the content of those "prior possibilities" need not be determined (nor as "*all* prior possibilities" could they be determined) but that *recurrence as such is abstractly affirmable.* The passive grammatical construction Shapiro uses is telling: the very thought of recurrence—or, let us say, the *form* of return or recurrence—shows itself to be affirmable without recourse to the specificity of the contents of "one's entire life" that would be repeated. A "Yes" may be issued without any particular utterer speaking. Divorced from any subject's particular affirmation, a subjectless recurrence is affirmable because its content or particulars cannot be determined in advance. In other words, recurrence is able to be affirmed precisely because it is fundamentally a form.

Q.: What's round, yellow, and equivalent to the axiom of choice?
A.: Zorn's lemon.

That the notion or idea or thought (and not the *thinking*) of recurrence is itself affirmable is the rigorous formal insistence of Hollis Frampton's structuralist film *Zorns Lemma* (1970). The sixty-minute film is divided into three sections, at least one of which constitutes a meta-section: (1) a five-minute vocal reading of alphabetically-ordered, albeit alinearly inflected, lines from the early American *Bay State Primer* over a black screen ("In *Adam's* Fall, we sinnèd all. Thy life to mend, God's *Book* attend"); (2) a forty-five minute parataxis of sorts, a soundless series of one-second shots of photographed signs that run through a twenty-four letter version of the alphabet (following colonial typography by combining, or treating as interchangeable, "I" and "J" and "U" with "V")—what one critic calls "a phantasmagoria of environmental language"—followed by a complex logic of substitutions of arbitrary images of mostly motor activities for each letter, in a pattern that will remain constant throughout the subsequent cycles of the alphabet (e.g., the washing of hands for "G"; painting a wall white for "K," and so on); and (3) a final shot in long take, about ten minutes in duration and seemingly without the division of a cut, of a man, woman, and dog walking across a snowy field, away from the fixed camera, toward a black horizon, while six female voices in hocket read from a text on the metaphysics of light by the medieval philosopher Robert Grosseteste, beginning, "The first bodily form I judge to be Light."[19]

Zorns Lemma takes its title from Max Zorn's 1935 principle of set theory, albeit losing in the process the apostrophic mark of possessive belonging or origin, pluralizing—which is to say, destroying—the singular identity of the proper name. Logically equivalent to the axiom of choice, Zorn's lemma states, "If X is a partially ordered set such that every chain in X has an upper bound, then X contains a maximal element."[20] Frampton's title, however, misspeaks—or, rather, miscategorizes or misrecognizes itself—because it is less Zorn's lemma than its logical equivalent, the "well-ordering principle," that actually structures Frampton's film. This corollary to Zorn's lemma suggests just what its name says: that any set can be endowed with an order, or arranged such that it is well ordered (which means that every non-empty subset of a set will have a least element). This principle is applied, in the middle section of the film, to an infinite number of sets, both the visible—ordinal numbers, Latin or Roman alphabets, substitution patterns, natural elements, found footage, images with superimposed text, images with bodies in them, bodiless images, and so forth—and those that do not appear, including the largest set of all images that are possible but do not appear, and ranging also to footage not shown in the film, but taken for it, to the images of words that do not appear because their substitution schema has locally begun, to all the images attributed to either "I" or "J" or "U" or "V" that fail to appear, and so forth. The principle of well-ordering is not a metaphor for the (or any) authorial act of choosing footage or merely another discipline's name for the plastic processes of montage. It is, instead, the structural possibility for a rabid ethic of cataloguing: the gesture of organizing, dividing, partitioning, and ordering an infinite number of possible sets in order to extend beyond those closed systems to open up the possibility of all other, prior, or future possible sets.

What Frampton takes from set theory is the founding structural principle that, in reference to a universal set, the complement of a set is also a set: for example, if A is the set of all even numbers, then the complement of A is the set of all odd numbers. In *Zorns Lemma,* therefore, from a universal set of every possible (one-second) image, every "A"-beginning word that does not appear in that first unit of the sequence is a set (of not-appearing "A" words), just as the appearing "A" words are themselves a set. Because set theory recognizes both as sets, the non-appearing elements appear as the complement of what appears, which means that presence entails absence not as its photographic negative but as its equivalent. Each is the other's mutual consequence. The value of set theory for thinking about structural repetition is precisely in its formal generality: one can define a set without having a reason for defining a set. Any group of elements is a set, by definition, so the language of set theory not only embraces but insists on the arbitrariness of membership, or the non-determination of membership. The advantage Frampton derives from set theory, and the one that bonds the form of *Zorns Lemma* to the explicitly Nietzschean conception of "joy in the actual and active of *every kind,*" is the inclusion in the order of unordered elements, the fact that arbitrariness actively creates a relation between unordered elements. Put another way, arbitrariness as a foundational principle in the film is what allows a relation to be defined among unordered elements. That set theory is indifferent to any given *what* of a set to focus on the relations between sets creates an open field in Frampton's film for every and all possibles to be negotiated in the middle section of alphabetic substitution. What is elsewhere non-arbitrary as necessary or meaningful is here only and ever structure as an overarching aesthetic principle. Because any word, any particular image, could have found its place in that structure pending the broad rules governing membership, any other word or image might have.

Following from the titular and structural appeal to set theory, we can say that form in Frampton's film affirms the idea of recurrence by recurring without regard for forming a meaningful narrative for *what* recurs, by formally willing the repetition of all and every possible visual content, and all content that has yet to be, or that might become, in its becoming, its taking shape as repeatable unit. The joyful possibility of "all prior possibilities" is the ground for this wild structural (and, yes, also a structuralist) joy. This is a language of repetition that is not motivated by the subject or a metaphoricity or a narrative of and for the iterated units for the film. The vitality of repetition as a speed, as the intensity of recurrence itself, is what is affirmed in the film through the affirming act alone of repeating, indifferent to what is or has been, or might be, repeated. In other words, the animating question, the inquisitive ethic, of Frampton's film—and of post-Nietzschean joy—is: how do you affirm the form of the certain (that which *has* taken place such that any prior or future possible might take place) without affirming its substance or content (*that* which has taken place)? Frampton's answer affirms the recurrence of the image as *thing,* which encompasses images of both words and actions, through the arbitrary choice from an infinite set of all visual possibilities. In the middle section of the film, these repeat without regard for what is repeated so that, and because, ultimately, anything could be repeated. The arbitrariness of the items within the larger total set, as much as the rigorous repeated form, is what affirms every and *all* prior possibilities as having been willed. That repetition is what is affirmed makes all possibilities possible but also confirms them as necessary (and actual, and active), insists on the certainty that has taken place by affirming that any other certainty could have, and will, take place in its stead. My argument in this concluding chapter is that the final form of the last (and only positive) affect in this book returns us to a pure notion of affective bliss through the presencing and affirming of reading for formalism as such—that the purest form of joy is formal repetition.

Readings of *Zorns Lemma* have ranged from the rabidly narrativizing (that it is autobiographical, a highly problematic claim co-dependently enabled by Frampton's appeal to authorial authority in his numerous film-theoretical writings and lectures) to the broadly metaphorical or allegorical (that it represents the stages of infant language acquisition or dawning religious consciousness) and to the cognitivist-inspired interest in arguing that the film creates an engaged spectator through ludic play organized around expectation, anticipation, and confirmation in relation to the alphabet substitution process.[21] (The last argument need not be refuted on a broad philosophical level. It fails a priori in its unwillingness and, frankly, inability to deal with the final ten-minute section, as though it were an annoying itch to be willed away from the tidy schematic of structuralist film as guessing game.[22])

Film theorists approaching *Zorns Lemma* from the perspective of its role in American avant-garde film have done somewhat better at isolating the formal language of repetition, arbitrary choice, and set selection—thus heeding the import of the film's title.[23] However, even when critics attend to the film's innovations for the cinematic avant-garde, they tend to retreat into the language of meaning and narrative—it is, not unlike metaphysics, almost impossible to do away with—as when James Peterson writes that the third part of the film "serves as a kind of retroactive explanatory articulation . . . [that] reprises some of the basic *themes* of the film."[24] Even in a reading that emphasizes the systematicity of structure in *Zorns Lemma* in the context of broader efforts in culture to enact "seriality, exemplification, listing, and cataloguing," Allen Weiss cannot avoid appeals to a transcendent, non-arbitrary logic for the terms of the film. At first, Weiss provides an extraordinary and productive list of Frampton's schemas, arguing that listing is either subversive, "destroying all taxonomic schemes," decentering events by pointing to "the aleatory conditions of existence," or, antithetically, wild listing serves as "formal imperatives, constituting structures and systems," in which case this hermeneutics centers systems by "constituting a determinate axiomatics."[25] The formal analogues of these opposing epistemologies are accumulation's disjunctive relations, in the former case, and enumeration's hierarchized relations, in the latter.[26] Weiss sees both structures at play in *Zorns Lemma;* ultimately, however, he reads the enumeration system as deriving from a grounding term he calls individual consciousness, which gives the rest of his reading a theological urgency that undermines the investment in structure with which the exegesis began. That codifications of accumulation and enumeration ultimately, for Weiss, "refer respectively to the world and to God," culminating in the notion that "God is the infinite film projector," obliterates the very essence of the film, which is nothing but the arbitrariness of structure.[27] This reading praxis betrays the set-theory aesthetic of the film precisely by refusing to stay on the side of the arbitrary, by refusing the ethical imperative to retroactively will the very arbitrariness that constitutes the film, and by interpreting repetition as ultimately providing the instrumental means by which a metaphysical promise (call it cinema; call it God) is realized and conveyed.

Not unlike the claim made so often for Peter Greenaway's taxonomies and grids—that they are radically (and necessarily) divorced from affect, warmth, or feeling—criticism on Frampton's film has been marked by a persistent tendency to rend its formal innovations from affective intensity. Take this typical suggestion for the zero-sum game between structure and sense: "most conventional narrative films . . . place their viewers within the complex web of their own feelings and responses. Structural films do just the opposite by refusing the viewer all such pleasures, thus producing rather a rude confrontation."[28] By the time Federico Windhausen published an article on Frampton in 2004, a form of this argument had ossified. Windhausen blithely asserts that Frampton was "rejecting the clichés of feeling and conventions of form associated with the psychology model"[29]—which, while historically accurate, also segregates feeling from form without so much as asking whether a non-psychological feeling is possible. Yet another critic writes of Frampton's "impulse to drain both the image and speech of their affective, prescriptive relationships to representation." In a stronger formulation, she writes that Frampton's turn to language helped him "figure film's relationship to legibility," while the photograph's historical concern with selection and classification "propelled Frampton's desire to empty film of its diegetic affect."[30] The result of this argument—and the consequence of this division between an investment in formal techniques such as saturation, duration, and repetition, on the one hand, and a twisting of form to narrative's emotive arc, on the other—is a split whereby affectivity is produced in the meaning of the latter arguments and omitted entirely from the former.

While widespread and persistent, this critical impulse is particularly at odds with *Zorns Lemma*, which could be said to perplex a tradition based on finding sense in language. The relation between meaning and the image is not only broken in the arbitrary and delinked presentation of a series of signifiers; it is also decimated in the form of its other site of meaning—the human body—in the final scene, about which I will write more later. My argument is that not only is the structuralist logic of the film *not* the site of an unsuturable rending from affect, but that the grounding for the formal joy iterated and reiterated in the film is precisely in this rigorous aesthetic ethic of repetition. Regard how *Zorns Lemma* conforms to the tidy definition of structuralism provided by Robert Scholes: "the perception of order or structure where only undifferentiated phenomena had seemed to exist before is the distinguishing characteristic of structuralist thought. In this mental operation we give up our general sense of all the observable data in exchange for a heightened sense of some specific items."[31] Scholes opens up, through this definition, a way for affectivity to be seen as deeply intertwined with the history of formalism and structuralism itself. For all that an attention to forms is accused of being affectless, Scholes writes that in this operation of perceiving the formal relations of parts, "what is lost in mass here is gained in energy."[32] Grasping structures, then, or reading for form, is the *passionate* act of giving up totality in exchange for the energetic possibility of the detail and the particular. For all that heartless structure is as durable a trope as the heartless structuralist (as in the famous May 1968 opposition, described and criticized by Lacan, between structures and "those who march in streets"; no less a voice than Deleuze once described structuralism as "a cold and concerted destruction of the subject"), both formulations are misleading and misled.[33] As with the readings in previous chapters, returning affect and form to each other suggests that highly formalist films are suffused with affect—that affects have structured forms and that form has an affective intensity that must be read for. Joy, no less than grief, disgust, or anxiety, cannot be known in advance—and is, like those other affects, in a fundamental sense *difficult*. Not only is it neither immediate nor obvious, but it also requires an investment in the duration of closely interpreting the forms of texts. (Let it be noted, then, that if the explicit goal of this chapter is to reclaim joy for structuralist film, it is also an effort at reclaiming joyfulness for structures more broadly.) For all that the pleasures and unpleasures of popular cinema, cinephiliac bliss in the avant-garde, or Deleuzian visceral shudders have been written about in film theory of the past thirty years, it is joy, and the form of joy loosed from spectatorial affect, that reminds us that in many ways film theorists have not yet asked: What might affectivity do to (or on or for) an *image*? What might a form of joy formally affirm?

(SHALL WE) LET X =

The middle segment of *Zorns Lemma* ventures an answer to this question. The forty-five minute section involves an effort to exhaust the infinity of the letter and of the image amid and against the shape of a finite duration, both the one-second duration of each shot of each letter or its substitution, which in the broader temporal shape of twenty-four letters per alphabetic cycle evokes the twenty-four frames per second of the ontology of cinema, and the arbitrary but fixed duration of the forty-five minute block. The images cut from one to the next without segue or transition; the visual asyndetism fights hierarchization, ordering, or dramatic linkage to emphasize instead the isolated units from which could be assembled an infinite number of possible sets—and the even pacing of the one-second rhythm, which the substitutions notably do not interrupt, itself repeats this nonhierarchical system of difference. Meaning here is not only subordinated to the word, the word is subordinated to the letter, the letter subordinated to rhythm. Each time, the image of any word in its appearance is singular and is all, is everything, but also each time it is temporary; each time it will disappear; each time it will disappear again until the structure is exhausted of possibles for this particular set of arbitrary constraints. Frampton, for his part, frames this structural conceit as an explicitly cinematic one in his anti-Eisensteinian claim, "There is nothing in the structural logic of the cinema filmstrip that precludes sequestering any single image. A still photograph is simply an isolated frame taken out of the infinite cinema."[34] But the effort to isolate and thereby exhaust an infinite possibility within a finite shape or duration is not necessarily or only authorized by a visual or technological possibility unique to cinema. There is a long history of its impulse from the *Encyclopédistes* of the Enlightenment to Joyce's exhaustive *Ulysses*. It is also the ethical possibility demanded by Nietzsche for joy, in which the ethical maxim of willing solely that which one wills for eternity requires affirming no particular past or possible act or event, but willing the totality of possibilities, the active, actual, and every kind—out of which any instant is merely an isolation from an infinity of possibilities.

The arbitrary visual choices that comprise the one-second units of the set called "alphabet" in Frampton's film produce formal and visual fecundity within the rigorous, but also arbitrary, boundary of the larger unit of film duration. What this structure also holds off is the notion that infinite possibility is itself derived from language or sign systems, as much as it resists the notion that it results from the essential nature of the cinematic animation of still images. The repetitions as they take place in the present of the projection of the film affirm every and all prior possibilities that might have been repeated in just this form. Why is repetition the purest form of affirmable form? Because it responds to the possible with the certain and specific; repetition holds open the possible, allows it to remain possible, by activating and displaying the necessary. The otherwise, and a specifically joyful otherwise, does not require the (still metaphysical) holding open of another scene—rather, Nietzsche's immanence demands that the otherwise itself be a part of the necessary and actual. Repetition's specific formal value is that it is an amplification of possibility that takes place through a narrowing, a constriction and constraint that nevertheless touches on the new. In other words, *repetition requires that a constructed form take place so that it might take place again.* This gesture by which repetition affirms and opens up new possibilities precisely because iteration has taken place evokes Derrida's account of the signature, which happens so that it can happen again; (it may well be that *Zorns Lemma* best answers Derrida's demand in "Signature Event Context" to construct a "typology of forms of iteration").[35] The new, then, results from form, shape, specificity, and constraint, over and instead of formless amorphousness. The new also results from the infinite prior possibilities affirmed in willed recurrence, an ethic that can also serve as a model for a critical praxis. Thus, it is not precisely that I am arguing against Barthes's claim that "bliss may come only with the *absolutely new.*" My contention, rather, is that bliss comes only with the absolutely repeated because only iteration produces the absolutely new.[36]

Of these infinite numbers of possible lines of flight set loose by *Zorns Lemma,* consider just one—and, in this thought experiment, judge the absurdity of fixing the arbitrariness of the all-possibles of the film for the privileging of one selected narrative.

I present to you the story of X.

It begins with the end, in the first section of the film, as the lesson "Xerxes the Great did die, And so must you and I." The *Bay State Primer* narration would, on the one hand, pose the very certainty of the certain: that finitude is inevitable and the ground for the concept of the "must" or the necessary. It also poses certainty, however, in relation to the homonym for the subject as a figure of non-appearance or a failure to fully appear, for the alphabet in the *Primer* omits "I" (skipping from "My Book and *Heart* Shall never part" to "*Job* feels the Rod, Yet blesses God"). I-the-initial-letter appears solely as the I-that-will-die in the entry of "X"—or, rather, the subject *as* "I" is deferred to appear as the missing sign at the moment its appearance is foretold as future disappearance of the grammatical placeholder for Self. In the second section of the film, the X words of the alphabetic cycle before substitutions take place are: (1) a violet photographic negative with a tiny box at its heart, almost imperceptibly containing the word "xenon"; (2) "X-ray"; (3) "Xylene"; and (4) "Xylophone"*. At the next cycle, X disappears into the first substituting image of the lapping peaks of a fire. The fourth visual appearance of an

X sign is particularly striking: a medium shot of a disembodied arm and hand writing out a cursive form of the word while the filmstrip runs backward. Thus "Xylophone" does not appear (hence, the qualifying star above)—instead, "Xylophon" then "Xylopho" do. The word appears in its failure to fully appear, in its becoming the image that it is taken to be but interrupted in that active gesture of completion. Indeed, because the image runs backward, the becoming-undone and disintegration of "Xylophone" is, in essence, an *ex-ing* out of that word—neither written nor posited, but erased. The bodily motion in producing the partial sign is unique among the footage of the middle section, and puts motion into the incompletion of the signifier, visually anticipating the wild movements of the substituting images, organized around forms of movement (wild lapping flames, bending reeds, a tracking camera or a walk around a block or the painting of some wall). That X marks the spot of the first sign of substitution, that site a site of the movements of the body in penning the image—so that its image is the image of the signifier coming into visual existence—seems a significant mark on the cinematic map, but the film refuses to confirm or reflect on a privilege for this position.

Let us follow this wandering X to some further consequences. Since Descartes's seventeenth-century *La géometrie,* x has named the unknown algebraic variable and is therefore the term for possibility in mathematics. (More precisely, Descartes deployed x, y, and z to represent unknown quantities and a, b, and c to signify known ones. The use of x, however, predominates: "in a paper on Cartesian ovals, prepared before 1629, x alone occurs as unknown, y being used as a parameter."[37]) At the same time, the widespread use of x in mathematics has been traced to typographical utility, or to its signifying value for equations due to its rare appearance in words in French. What x is is a nothing—it is an unknown, a variable, the very concept of the variable. And what is a variable but an algebraic name for possibility? In being a snapshot of becoming that which will change and become otherwise, writing over itself in the act, x is the name for the otherwise of mathematics, the possibility of alternatives—which is also to say, it is the locus of historicity in mathematical thought itself. The variable is also, however, constitutively finite. If, on the one hand, x is the totality of that which is unknown and yet possible—the everything implied in the notion of the "variable"—it is also continually expunged in its link to, overcoming by, necessity. Particularity erases, decimates the letter: let $x = \ldots$ This is every time a death.

But could X also be the sign of the gaud, marking the spot of a smudgy form of thingish joy? An early twentieth-century account in *Webster's* claimed that "X was used as an abbreviation for Arabic *shei,* a thing, something, which in the Middle Ages, was used to designate the unknown, and was then prevailingly transcribed as *xei.*"[38] While the OED suggests there is no evidence for the "thing" root of *xei* or *shei* for X, the persistence of the account for marking the unknown or the variable as also the site of a thing suggests a slip between the heavy weight of gaud and its lightness of being as the variable, mutable, changeable, or possible.[39] In the cold logic of the substitution cycle in *Zorns Lemma,* X must die—like you and I—and must go first, must go so early, before its time, because it is the letter that least frequently begins words in English (so vaguely goes the logic for the order of sign substitution). Hence, the extraordinary entry made for the crossed bars in Samuel Johnson's *A Dictionary of the English Language* (1755), which includes X only to elide it: "X is a letter, which, though found in Saxon words, begins no word in the English language."[40] So reads the entire entry. X is therefore the sign of the unknown, the variable and the totality of possible concrete values that it might come to take on, while simultaneously being impossibility, the unbecoming letter, that which begins nothing, the beginning of the nothing, and thus that of which nothing more can be said. Scrawled in a shaky pen in its fourth and final visual appearance before being yet another thing lost in the flames, it signs a form of an assenting name for those who cannot sign their own. It is also, of course, an abbreviation for Christ.

X needs a vowel, hungers for it to begin (a word); the compounds it names on its own in Frampton's film, on full display before being consumed by the substitutive flames—*xeno-, xero-,* or the wooden *xylo-*—are each Greek in origin. Bound to the prefix "ex-," it comes to imply absence, abstention, vanishing, deletion, depletion; it is the very sign and manifestation of the spectral, the un- or yet to be known, the possible and mysterious, the undefinable, even the unspeakable. X is the letter of wonderment as such. (It is also, therefore, something of an affective letter.) When X marks the spot, it opts in as gesture of presence; where it is variable and unknown, it abstains from presence, shows itself only through its absence. As "xenon," it is named in and as the violet light that it enables (in flash lamps and lasers); xenon short-arc lamps are standard in movie theater projection. In its form as "X-ray," it is the very possibility of translucence, the form of radiation that renders the body a shadow of its line and tissue. As "Xylene" it is the sweet, colorless solvent for printing ink. Notable for its highly flammable nature, does it give rise to the conflagration that erases that very word, and all other ex-words forever more in the subsequent cycles of the series? As the Roman numeral ten, it also returns in the metaphysics of light read in parts at the end of the film, in which $1 + 2 + 3 + 4$ are deemed to be "the full Number of the Universe" in Grosseteste's metaphysics. ("When the Number One of Form and the Number Two of Matter and the Number Three of Composition and the Number Four of Entirety are added together, they make up the Number Ten."[41]) That numerical form of perfection is repeated in the final scene in ten partitioned segments of white space, itself like an X-ray of soft and hard tissue, all white gaps and black dividers.

The vertical ticks of the fence in the final image of *Zorns Lemma* are like an X taken apart at its hinging cross to set side by side, short lines, deconstructed bars. In "Pentagram for Conjuring the Narrative," Frampton formulates literary history in relation to the labile, secretive X. "Joseph Conrad insisted that any man's biography could be reduced to a series of three terms: 'He was born. He suffered. He died.' It is the middle term that interests us here. Let us call it 'X.'"[42] The different expansions Frampton provides, what he calls "true accounts of the suffering of X," are given in narrative-mathematical forms, such as "Henry James: x = "; (another, compellingly, is "Gertrude Stein: $x = x$").[43] All this would seem to suggest that X is unique, is like no other, is privileged and holds—as its letter might suggest—the key to unlocking the secreted structure or metaphysical promise of Frampton's film. But this is not the case, for yes, yes, all this has been said, and more could be said, of X, but this reading, this very choice of X, is of course itself an arbitrary one (*my* arbitrary one). This reading offers no center, origin, or substance to the film. There is nothing on the other side of the promise to let X = something meaningful about Frampton's film.

And if suggested otherwise: throw these pages to the fire.

For the story of X is only one story that might be told of *Zorns Lemma*— no doubt, A has its own adventures (ask Derrida; and consider the world contained in its substituting images: the turning of the pages of a book). Or reflect on C, the last letter to disappear, holdout to the end, homonym for the optical activity of the spectator. It is also, of course, the constant for the speed of light—indeed, marked by its persistence over the duration of the film, it is also the trace of the constancy of light. Other readings might tell a story for the cinematically reflexive moments (signifiers Lens, X-ray, Film, Light, Art; tracking cameras and broad painting strokes); another for the adventures of the serif as it pulsatingly appears at the borders of textual worlds. The film's de-privileging of all and every site of hierarchy (its radical undoing of *any* letter's privilege) is what sets loose these possible tales, what promises but also maddens the fecundity of these stories. My critical reading, called here a set, produces as its complement—and explicitly this time—the set of every story left neglected, every thread unfollowed. At the same time that the film exhausts one form of its structure through the substitution logic of letter and image in the finite shape of the alphabet, it frees and sends forth an inexhaustible set of possibles for any reader of the film. Following *Zorns Lemma,* any other story might have been here told—and criticism, in a reading that could always itself be and have been and become otherwise, is itself organized around the arbitrary choices made not only in reading but in order to take place *as* reading. The affirmation of choice becomes a gesture for criticism necessitated by its structural centrality to the film. It is not only the infinite possibility put into the finite duration of the film that structures and strains what takes place—and that I am arguing is the form, following Nietzsche, of recurrence as formal joy. It is also that critical labor repeats this structure. The question for film and for theorist is whether one can own and affirm this gesture, can transform every "It was" into an "I willed it thus." If so, then the form of elation's affect also shapes every theoretical arc. Criticism is also capable of performing the act of becoming a "retroactive force," willing backward so that reading can function as energetic and passionate insistence. Reading for the forms of the affects in the previous chapters has enabled a sensitivity to the hidden structure of formal affectivity in critical theory, philosophy, psychoanalysis, and film, and has brought out the ways in which affect on the level of structure is as present in theoretical work as in representation. Thinking together form and affect—and textual and representational formal affectivity—opens up a space where joy may be regarded as a possible critical stance. Theoretical speculation can also, and specifically through reading for form, affirm the actual and the active of every kind.

But a bit more is yet to come.

PUTTING ONE'S FAITH IN FORM

The third and final section of *Zorns Lemma* takes the semiotically dense arena of human figure in landscape and reduces it to its barest graphic forms. In a spare and stark image, one-third of the way up the frame of the snowy field is a series of nine short vertical ticks, marking out ten units of horizontal space; two-thirds up, constituting the background and horizon, is a swath of black into which, eventually, the individuated forms of man, woman, and dog will disappear. If you held their images firm—snapshots at every instant in a kind of vertical perspective—as they appear from the theatrical space behind the camera, walk away from it into the image, toward the left of the screen and world, over the fence bifurcating the image, past it and toward the right of the undifferentiated dark mass, they would form a curve like an open parenthesis, enclosing the landscape through their motor gestures' traversing it. The dark shapes on the brightest white become only their outlines soon enough, but as they progress farther across the image and into the ten-minute depth, their bodies, sexual difference marked, species difference marked, begin to disappear into brute shapes and blocks. As they walk over the one-third mark, presumably lifting legs over the fence of the nine posts, their bodies become less dense, increasingly blur into the more fundamental graphic difference of upright vertical forms and the frenetic horizontal energies of what used to be a dog.

Deeper still, now into the expanse of the last field of white before the black edge of the world, outlines promising epistemological certainty fade altogether: sexual difference is now gone, even the integrity of the human is lost. The bodies over time come to resemble an equal sign rotated ninety degrees; while lost are the particulars of their shape and substance, the darkness of their upright forms foregrounds the speed of their shapes in the curving loop toward the back of the image. Recalling a Spinozan conception of the body, such that anything can be a body—dog, woman, fence, snow, whiteness, metronomic pulse, the alternating voices—each thing that affects other things is dispersed into mutually-affecting formal forces in space. By the time the shades of figure against ground reach the limits of visible possibility, the radical effect of the final scene is clear: in the depth of the deep field of the image, bodies made abstract mass now serve, like the nine fence posts, merely to define some unit of bright space between marks. Frampton's film, in other words, has turned bodies into lines. Eventually, the bodies do not even do the labor of lines, as those marks ultimately merge with black field at the far edge of the world's frame. Under the pressure of the duration of the final uncut image, the body is rendered abstract formal element against a world as visible field.

This is the final substitution in the schema of *Zorns Lemma*. It is not that bodies disappear into the duration and the inky swath of deep space (thus retaining their bodiliness), so much as the pressure of duration in this shot enables the line to come into being and appear. The film effects this appearance through an explicit swap; the end of the film involves a replacement of body with line. Make no mistake: the logic of substitution is not limited to the alphabetic one-to-one of the middle section, the replacements in time, the syntagmatic substitutions of the *Primer*. Serving as yet another repetition of the overarching structure, the end, in exchanging mark for corpus, thereby and irretrievably substitutes abstract form for meaning, gains structure at the expense of the traditional ground of sense. And the final section of the film does so not on the back of the letter or the word, but on the frame of flesh itself.

In this way, the second and third sections of *Zorns Lemma* resemble Deleuze's reading of Spinoza's *Ethics*—that it is "a book written twice simultaneously: once in the continuous stream of definitions, propositions, demonstrations, and corollaries, which develop the great speculative themes with all the rigors of the mind; another time in the broken chain of scholia, a discontinuous volcanic line, a second version underneath the first, expressing all the angers of the heart and setting forth the practical theses of denunciation and liberation."[44] Frampton's twice-written film makes present in the third section the site of the possibility of action, transformation, meaning—the *body*, the human, the family, the reproducible ,on the level of the social or the biological—solely as it is converted into the precision of the formal. Body made band, figural made formal, is both a decimation—of the corpus as what by definition means something—and a positing of the new openness of the graphic. *Zorns Lemma* ventures that there is more hope in the line than in the being. The film places its faith for the transformation of the possible in the formal: in saturation and light, in metronomic rhythm, in figure and ground, in gesture and space, and in this, this final repetition of the constraint of the structure of the film. *There is bliss in this replacement of body with line.* Affirming the repetition of the structure that came before it by launching the body, and all that it means, into formal value, it also brings to presence the open empty space of the ground of representation in the broad white canvas prepared for beginning once more—*Wohlan! Noch Ein Mal!* Very well, once more then, out of that bright white into the black image and simple schema of an ordering of letters with which the film began.

It is not enough to repeat, Nietzsche's ethic of joy insists. One must affirm that repetition. One must will it as a retroactive force; one must shout, Yes! This final section of *Zorns Lemma*, which takes the consequence of formal repetition to its most radical extreme, affirms repetition not merely by exhausting the local structure of the alphabet (the ethic of the middle part) but by persisting past that exhaustion and consumption to launch the possibility for the newness of form into the world itself, by launching the body into line. Instead of affiliating joy with ecstasy's dissolution of the self or a shattering of structure, which would position joy as a release from form or as an excess resistant to form or as a de-formation of forms, Frampton's film suggests how joy might be figured as a release *into* form or a re-formation of forms. The approach of a visual infinity through a dispersion of bodies in space as line is an affirmation of every possible formal transmutation that has taken place, and that might also, in the future as the possible, take place.

One of Spinoza's most extraordinary claims in his *Ethics,* excised and made to reappear across Deleuze's immanent philosophy, is that "*etenim quid corpus possit, nemo hucusque determinavit*" (indeed, no one has yet determined all the things the body can do [or is capable of]). Deleuze likes to render this formula as "*on ne sait pas ce que peut le corps.*"[45] But past this wonderment wander the figures of the final section of Frampton's film. What goes forth to begin again, to repeat or to create, to set in motion every active and actual, every prior and future possible is a de-subjectivized form, a line on ground, a white space between dark bars. If this affirmation of form holds out eternity and infinity not for bodies but for form, it also refuses to settle that form. The film releases the line from the body, sets forth the newness of this transition as the exuberant possibility of the very materiality of the cinema. This joyful form, and this form of joy, does not fix affectivity as an exhausted, prior something in a text, but looses every gaudium in each and every act of reading. If the figure of the body is here made a gaud, it is given this quality of being *something* for form, for abstraction, for the sake of the frame, the field, the line, the dark, the mark, the light. Ecstatic wonder is thus not despite structure, does not resist or fight back against it, but imagines how much more formality there ever might be. Taking forms and affects as mutually consequent, reading for their shaping of each other, instructs us in a lesson about the possibility for the new, the not-yet vitality of both form and affectivity. It is a lesson that reading for affect uniquely teaches, and that reading, indeed, makes possible and creates—because interpretation itself is also always infinite. This conclusion is therefore, certainly, another instance of joyful affirmation:

We do not yet know all it is that form can do.

FIG 9.1. *Zorns Lemma* (Hollis Frampton, 1970)

Acknowledgments

It is, of course, a kind of admitting or concession of a certain kind of truth, a recognizing (which is to say, a kindred mode of knowing), but also an understanding, a debt, even receipt (as of a letter), and I accede above all to this confession: it has always been my greatest pleasure, the claim of being a student of.

My gratitude is therefore first owed to the academic programs through which I have passed in the last decade, ones that indelibly shaped me in their curious, sometimes contradictory, and always wonderfully complicated interactions. I am the proud product of the Film Studies Program at Yale University, the Center for the Study of Psychoanalysis and Culture at the University at Buffalo, and the Department of Modern Culture and Media at Brown University, and my scholarly debt to the abstractions of the traditions represented therein is as real and felt as to any named body that breathes.

Moira Fradinger and John MacKay taught me how to form intellectual commitments—to the rigors of close reading, to the wild speculations of theory—while Brigitte Peucker bestowed kindnesses on me that I can never requite, including introducing me to many of the filmmakers about whom I write and modeling the promise and challenge of attending to the nuances of representation in even the most maligned texts. I was their formal charge for only a few years, but I have been their student for half my life.

Tim Dean, for me, is the mode of the unexpected. I am continually taken aback by the reach of his sincerity, goodness, and intellectual generosity. To be his student, to experience the technique of perpetual mentorship, involves bearing witness to an ethic of unfearful questioning, an observance that is also a challenge and is also a call.

As a student of Mary Ann Doane's, I appreciated immensely her admonitions for pushing arguments without losing precision in writing. She was a keen auditor of assumptions and an exceptionally valuable tutor. I was also very fortunate to work closely with Lynne Joyrich for many years, and the particularly exhilarating time spent in her seminar for the Pembroke Center shaped the formless open days of this project.

Ellen Rooney appears in these pages in the form of an argument that directly and powerfully made mine possible, but her signature is also here in hundreds of minor, essential ways. Ellen's exhaustive, patient, thoughtful questions to this book not only made it stronger but also, filtered through her reading, paradoxically made it mine. My work has been bettered in proportion to the degree I took her counsel. She will always typify, for me, the grand spirit of a generous reader.

Rey Chow rendered me a beginner at a late stage, forever altering the canon to which I turn for my work, renewing my love of RB and GD, but adding the now essential MF; I make no secret that, here, student means recruit. Her ability to read this book incisively for the argument that it should have been making enhanced and refined every page. The rigor, wit, and curiosity of her scholarship is a renewable excitement to me, and I am perhaps most grateful that to learn from Rey, as I still do, is to heed, among other things, an undiluted affection for difficult thought.

In the years in which I wrote and edited this book, numerous conferences and communities served as welcome inducements to keep grappling with all the important questions. An early version of chapter 5 was published in Tina Kendall, ed., "The Disgust Issue," *Film-Philosophy* 15, no. 2 (2011), and a slightly modified version of chapter 6 previously appeared in Ellen Rooney and Elizabeth Weed, eds., "Reading Remains," *Differences* 21, no. 3 (2010). My gratitude to the editors of both of those special issues for their curation of the different debates in which I situate my work. I will forever be thankful to Brian Price, John David Rhodes, and Meghan Sutherland for their creation of the vibrant intellectual assembly that is the conference and journal *World Picture*. I am also deeply indebted to interlocutors at the Society for Cinema and Media Studies, the Robert Penn Warren Center for the Humanities at Vanderbilt University, and the Susan and Donald Newhouse Center for the Humanities at Wellesley College, where I had the great fortune to spend a fellowship year editing this book in wonderful company.

One could not ask for warmer colleagues than mine in the Literature Section at the Massachusetts Institute of Technology. They are daily reminders that the most animated conversations happen across the humanities and not in disciplinary isolation. I am especially grateful to Noel Jackson for his careful, perceptive reading of the entire manuscript. My immense gratitude also to Rosalind Galt and an anonymous second reader for the press. Although it was their enthusiasm that was most privately meaningful, the superlative care each took with considering the book as a whole made for a revision process that was an unexpected pleasure and a chance to return with fresh eyes to the very familiar. At Duke, Christine Choi, Amy Ruth Buchanan, and Sara Leone offered generous help at critical junctures. Above all, I am so thankful to have Courtney Berger as my editor. She not only brought this book forth with conviction and calm and an astuteness at which I marvel, but her company is also a complete delight.

John and Leonie Brinkema, in addition to being my favorite people in the world, are models for lives joyfully tethered to meaningful vocation. They were supportive when need be, honest and challenging when need be, and always a vital part of this process. Having been raised in a house where wonder and curiosity were taken as preeminent values, where there was always a reason to buy one more book—one cannot thank one's parents for that so much as humbly say, Without you, there could not be this. (And, yes, I am your student, too.)

More than a decade ago, I soldered myself to my ideal reader and have spent every day since with the better embodiment of my intellectual passions. Evan Johnson saw the stakes of the idea first, and he read these many pages last. He is the long conversation that will always seem too brief. Were he a stranger and not my husband, his unreasonable beautiful work alone would indelibly shape mine. So I wonder, Evan, if you knew that I was writing this for you all along.

Notes

PREFACE

1. One of the best attempts to answer this question is in Ruth Leys, "The Turn to Affect: A Critique," *Critical Inquiry* 37 (Spring 2011): 434–72. A year later, in the Summer 2012 issue of *Critical Inquiry,* her provocations were still being debated in a series of responses by the likes of Adam Frank, Elizabeth Wilson, Charles Altieri, and Leys herself. See also Michael Hardt, "Foreword: What Affects Are Good For," in *The Affective Turn: Theorizing the Social,* ed. Patricia Ticineto Clough with Jean Halley (Durham, NC: Duke University Press, 2007), ix–xiii; Gregory J. Seigworth and Melissa Gregg, "An Inventory of Shimmers," in *The Affect Theory Reader,* ed. Melissa Gregg and Gregory J. Seigworth (Durham, NC: Duke University Press, 2010), 1–26.

2. Work on affect has exploded in the past decade. A mere two-year period (2004–2005) saw the publication of a canon-defining list that includes Teresa Brennan, *The Transmission of Affect* (Ithaca, NY: Cornell University Press, 2004); Sara Ahmed, *The Cultural Politics of Emotion* (New York: Routledge, 2004); Charles Altieri, *The Particulars of Rapture: An Aesthetics of the Affects* (Ithaca, NY: Cornell University Press, 2004); Denise Riley, *Impersonal Passion: Language as Affect* (Durham, NC: Duke University Press, 2005); and Sianne Ngai, *Ugly Feelings* (Cambridge, MA: Harvard University Press, 2005). For a compendium specific to media studies, see Catherine Grant, "On 'Affect' and 'Emotion' in Film Studies," Film Studies for Free (blog), http://filmstudies forfree.blogspot.com (accessed November 4, 2011).

3. The term was coined by the Dutch critics Timotheus Vermeulen and Robin van den Akker in "Notes on Metamodernism," *Journal of Aesthetics and Culture* 2 (2010), published November 15, 2010, http://aestheticsandculture.net/index.php/jac/article /view/5677/6304.

4. Lone Bertelsen and Andrew Murphie, "An Ethics of Everyday Infinities and Powers: Félix Guattari on Affect and the Refrain," in *The Affect Theory Reader,* ed. Melissa Gregg and Gregory J. Seigworth (Durham, NC: Duke University Press, 2010), 145.

5. Hermann Lotze, *Metaphysik* (Leipzig: Weidmann, 1841), "Einleitung" Section 9.

6. This fine formulation, from the film theorist Raymond Bellour, serves as an epigraph to this book. Raymond Bellour, "Cinema and . . . ," *Semiotica* 112, nos. 1–2 (1996): 207–29.

1. William Rothman, *Hitchcock—The Murderous Gaze* (Cambridge, MA: Harvard University Press, 1982), 309.

2. See, e.g., Donald Spoto, *The Art of Alfred Hitchcock: Fifty Years of His Motion Pictures* (New York: Anchor, 1992): chap. 33; Raymond Bellour, "Psychosis, Neurosis, Perversion (on *Psycho*)," trans. Nancy Huston, in *The Analysis of Film,* ed. Constance Penley (Bloomington: Indiana University Press, 2000), 238–61.

3. For a summary of other philosophical approaches to the question "Why do we cry?" see Adela Pinch, *Strange Fits of Passion: Epistemologies of Emotion, Hume to Austen* (Palo Alto, CA: Stanford University Press, 1999); the title essay in Jerome Neu, *A Tear Is an Intellectual Thing: The Meanings of Emotion* (Oxford: Oxford University Press, 2000); Stephen Leighton, ed., *Philosophy and the Emotions: A Reader* (Ontario: Broadview, 2003). An attempt to answer that question from the perspective of experimental psychology is in William Frey and William Langseth, *Crying: The Mystery of Tears* (New York: Harper and Row, 1985). A more recent addition to the literature, especially valuable for its wide historical and disciplinary scope, is Tom Lutz, *Crying: The Natural and Cultural History of Tears* (New York: W. W. Norton, 1999). Finally, see James Elkins, *Pictures and Tears: A History of People Who Have Cried in Front of Paintings* (New York: Routledge, 2004). While Elkins's subtitle suggests that it treats the question of why we cry from the perspective of art history, the analysis is more concerned with the underside of that question: the failure to tear up, particularly in the case of the art critic.

4. Plato, *Republic,* trans. Paul Shorey, in *The Collected Dialogues of Plato, Including the Letters,* ed. Edith Hamilton and Huntington Cairns (Princeton, NJ: Princeton University Press, 1989), III.395d–e.

5. Aristotle, *De Poetica* (Poetics), trans. Ingram Bywater, in *The Basic Works of Aristotle,* ed. Richard McKeon (New York: Random House, 1941), 1449b.

6. Aristotle, *Poetics,* 1467 (1453b).

7. Aristotle, *Rhetorica* (Rhetoric), trans. W. Rhys Roberts, in *The Basic Works of Aristotle,* ed. Richard McKeon (New York: Random House, 1941), 1386a.

8. Aristotle, *Rhetoric,* 164 (1386a).

9. Gorgias of Leontini, "The Encomium of Helen," in *The Greek Sophists,* trans. John Dillon and Tania Gergel (New York: Penguin, 2003), 80 [9].

10. Roland Barthes, *A Lover's Discourse: Fragments,* trans. Richard Howard (New York: Noonday Press, 1978), 180.

11. On the gratia lacrimarum, see Diane Apostolos-Cappadona, "'Pray with Tears and Your Request Will Find a Hearing': On the Iconology of the Magdalene's Tears," in *Holy Tears: Weeping in the Religious Imagination,* ed. Kimberley Christine Patton and John Stratton Hawley (Princeton, NJ: Princeton University Press, 2005), 201–28. For an account of the suffering of the female saints, which takes the form (and technique) of

floods of tears, see Emile M. Cioran, *Tears and Saints,* trans. Ilinca Zarifopol-Johnston (Chicago: University of Chicago Press, 1995).

12. David Hume, "Of Tragedy," in *Eight Great Tragedies,* ed. Sylvan Barnet, Morton Berman, William Burto (New York: Meridian, 1996), 433. The essay of 1757 was first published as the third dissertation in Hume's *Four Dissertations,* of which the fourth was his companion work on aesthetics, "Of the Standard of Taste."

13. Hume, "Of Tragedy," 435.

14. Hume, "Of Tragedy," 435.

15. Adam Smith, *The Theory of Moral Sentiments,* ed. Knud Haakonssen (Cambridge: Cambridge University Press, 2002), 11, 23. *The Theory of Moral Sentiments* was originally published in 1759. It was compiled from Smith's lectures on ethics, delivered in Edinburgh starting in 1748.

16. Smith, *The Theory of Moral Sentiments,* 15.

17. Smith, *The Theory of Moral Sentiments,* 15.

18. Smith, *The Theory of Moral Sentiments,* 15.

19. Smith, *The Theory of Moral Sentiments,* 16.

20. Smith, *The Theory of Moral Sentiments,* 16.

21. Smith, *The Theory of Moral Sentiments,* 12; emphasis added.

22. Smith, *The Theory of Moral Sentiments,* 20.

23. Smith, *The Theory of Moral Sentiments,* 18–19.

24. Augustine, *Confessions,* VIII.12.

25. William James, "What Is an Emotion?" in *Philosophy and the Emotions: A Reader,* ed. Stephen Leighton (Ontario: Broadview, 2003), 22. The essay was first published in *Mind* 9 (1884): 188–205 and was expanded for publication in *The Principles of Psychology* (1890).

26. James, "What is an Emotion?" 22.

27. Neu, *A Tear Is an Intellectual Thing,* 18.

28. Rejlander was one of several photographers involved in the project, itself a meta-archive of illustrations composed of photographs and wood engravings: see Phillip Prodger, *Darwin's Camera: Art and Photography in the Theory of Evolution* (Oxford: Oxford University Press, 2009).

29. Charles Darwin, *The Expression of Emotions in Man and Animals,* In *From so Simple a Beginning: The Four Great Books of Charles Darwin,* ed. Edward O. Wilson (New York: W. W. Norton, 2006), 1344–45.

30. Darwin, *The Expression of Emotions in Man and Animals,* 1345.

31. Samuel Beckett, *Murphy* (New York: Grove Press, 1957) 51, 115.

32. Darwin, *The Expression of Emotions in Man and Animals,* 1348.

33. Darwin, *The Expression of Emotions in Man and Animals,* 1348.

34. Darwin, *The Expression of Emotions in Man and Animals,* 1356.

35. Darwin, *The Expression of Emotions in Man and Animals,* 1359.

36. Darwin, *The Expression of Emotions in Man and Animals,* 1360.

37. Darwin, *The Expression of Emotions in Man and Animals*, 1353.

38. Sigmund Freud, "Hysterical Phantasies and Their Relation to Bisexuality," in *Freud on Women: A Reader*, ed. Elisabeth Young-Bruehl (New York: W. W. Norton, 1990), 147–48.

39. Jean-Paul Sartre, *The Emotions: Outline of a Theory*, trans. Bernard Frechtman (New York: Philosophical Library, 1948), 58–59.

40. Sartre, *The Emotions*, 59.

41. Sartre, *The Emotions*, 60.

42. Sartre, *The Emotions*, 61.

43. Sartre, *The Emotions*, 62–63.

44. Sartre, *The Emotions*, 64.

45. Sartre, *The Emotions*, 65.

46. Sartre, *The Emotions*, 70.

47. Sartre, *The Emotions*, 31.

48. Sartre, *The Emotions*, 31–32.

49. Sartre, *The Emotions*, 66.

50. See René Descartes, "Discours cinquième. Des images qui se forment sur le fond de l'oeil," in *La dioptrique*, Leiden 1637.

51. Barthes, *A Lover's Discourse*, 181.

52. George Toles, "'If Thine Eye Offend Thee . . .': *Psycho* and the Art of Infection," in *Alfred Hitchcock: Centenary Essays*, ed. Richard Allen and S. Ishii-Gonzales (London: BFI, 1999), 163.

53. Gilles Deleuze, *Foucault*, trans. Seán Hand (Minneapolis: University of Minnesota Press, 1988), 96.

54. Deleuze, *Foucault*, 97.

55. Deleuze, *Foucault*, 97.

56. Deleuze, *Foucault*, 100.

57. Deleuze, *Foucault*, 101.

58. Deleuze, *Foucault*, 118.

59. *Oxford English Dictionary*, 2d ed. (1989), s.v. "affect."

60. Gilles Deleuze, "Spinoza and the Three 'Ethics,'" trans. Daniel W. Smith and Michael A. Greco, in *Essays Critical and Clinical* (Minneapolis: University of Minnesota Press, 1997), 138.

61. Gilles Deleuze, *Francis Bacon: The Logic of Sensation*, trans. Daniel W. Smith (Minneapolis: University of Minnesota Press, 2002); Gilles Deleuze, *Cinema 1: The Movement-Image*, trans. Hugh Tomlinson and Barbara Habberjam (Minneapolis: University of Minnesota Press, 1986); Gilles Deleuze, *Cinema 2: The Time-Image*, trans. Hugh Tomlinson and Robert Galeta (Minneapolis: University of Minnesota Press, 1989).

62. Gilles Deleuze and Félix Guattari, *A Thousand Plateaus: Capitalism and Schizophrenia*, trans. Brian Massumi (Minneapolis: University of Minnesota Press, 1987), 270.

Brian Massumi continues this logic when he insists that, unlike affects, emotions necessarily have a subject attached to them: "An emotion is a subjective content, the sociolinguistic fixing of the quality of an experience which is from that point onward defined as personal. Emotion is qualified intensity . . . into narrativizable action-reaction circuits, into function and meaning. It is intensity owned and recognized. It is crucial to theorize the difference between affect and emotion. If some have the impression that affect has waned, it is because affect is unqualified. As such, it is not ownable or recognizable and is thus resistant to critique" (Brian Massumi, *Parables for the Virtual: Movement, Affect, Sensation* [Durham, NC: Duke University Press, 2002], 28).

Ruth Leys makes the important point that "the claim that affect is a formless, unstructured, nonsignifying force or 'intensity' that escapes the categories of the psychologists suggest that Tomkins's or Ekman's or Damasio's talk about the existence of six or seven or eight or nine structured, evolved categories of innate emotions is incompatible with the view of writers such as Massumi who espouse Spinozist-Deleuzian ideas about affect" (Ruth Leys, "The Turn to Affect: A Critique," *Critical Inquiry* 37 [Spring 2011]: 442).

TWO. FILM THEORY'S ABSENT CENTER

1. As late as March 2011, well into the turn to affect, participants in the workshop "Affect as Rhetorical Strategy" at the annual Society for Cinema and Media Studies Conference repeatedly insisted that affect needed to be attended to in the discipline of film studies; that, as per the title of the workshop, its rhetorical strategies had not yet been considered. The esteemed scholars on the panel could not have been ignorant of the extensive work on affect that had been published by that date. Rather, their renewed call for attention to affect just shows how seductive the term "affect" is as an empty heralding of the unsaid.

2. See also the work of Tarja Laine, Anna Powell, Elena del Rio, and Anne Rutherford. Intersecting with work on affect, though with its own sensual commitments, is the "turn to touch," or interest in hapticity, in film and media studies, most strongly associated with the work of Laura U. Marks and Jennifer Barker.

3. See Hugo Münsterberg, *The Film: A Psychological Study* (New York: Dover, 2004); Jean Epstein, "*Bonjour Cinema* and Other Writings," trans. Tom Milne, *Afterimage,* no. 10 (Autumn 1981): 8–38; Jean Epstein, "*Magnification* and Other Writings," trans. Stuart Liebman, *October* 3 (Spring 1977): 9–25; Siegfried Kracauer, "Cult of Distraction," in *The Mass Ornament: Weimar Essays,* trans. and ed. Thomas Levin (Cambridge, MA: Harvard University Press, 1995), 323–30; Sergei Eisenstein, *Film Form,* trans. Jay Leyda (San Diego, CA: Harcourt, 1977); Sergei Eisenstein, *The Film Sense,* trans. Jay Leyda (San Diego, CA: Harcourt, 1970).

4. Thomas Elsaesser and Mary Ann Doane have pointed to the wrenching of the body and centrality of affect to the narrative and cinematographic organization of

melodrama. Doane, for example, writes, "In maternal melodrama, the violence is displaced onto affect—producing *tearjerkers*. Its sentimentality is, in some respects, quite sadistic" for the way in which it violently wrings movement and emotion from the spectator: Mary Ann Doane, *The Desire to Desire: The Woman's Film of the 1940s* (Bloomington: Indiana University Press, 1987), 95. In work on pornography and horror, respectively, Linda Williams and Carol Clover have emphasized the crucial role of affect in defining the bodily aims of those genres. See also Williams's canonical "Film Bodies: Gender, Genre, Excess," in *Film and Theory: An Anthology*, ed. Robert Stam and Toby Miller (Malden, MA: Blackwell, 2000), 207–21.

5. Steven Shaviro, *The Cinematic Body* (Minneapolis: University of Minnesota Press, 1993), viii.

6. Steven Shaviro, *The Cinematic Body*, 16, 25.

7. For this rhetorical strategy, see, e.g., Anne Rutherford, "Cinema and Embodied Affect," *Senses of Cinema* 25, no. 3 (2003), available online at http://sensesofcinema .com/2003/feature-articles/embodied_affect; Tim Groves, "Cinema/Affect/Writing," *Senses of Cinema* 25, no. 3 (2003), available online at http://sensesofcinema.com/2003 /feature-articles/writing_cinema_affect. While Rutherford argues that film theory has "thwarted the articulation of an aesthetics of embodiment which recognises the full resonance of embodied affect in the experience of cinema spectatorship," Groves claims that psychoanalytic and semiotic film theory displayed "a certain anxiety about affect."

8. See, for example, the essays in the anthology *Passionate Views: Film, Cognition, and Emotion*, ed. Carl Plantinga and Greg M. Smith (Baltimore: Johns Hopkins University Press, 1999).

9. Noël Carroll, "Film, Emotion, and Genre," in *Passionate Views: Film, Cognition, and Emotion*, ed. Carl Plantinga and Greg M. Smith (Baltimore: Johns Hopkins University Press, 1999), 21. For other cognitivist accounts of emotion in/and film, see Greg Smith, *Structure and the Emotion System* (Cambridge: Cambridge University Press, 2003); Ed S. Tan, *Emotion and the Structure of Narrative Film: Film as an Emotion Machine*, trans. Barbara Fasting (Mahwah, NJ: Erlbaum, 1996); and, more recently, Torben Grodal, *Embodied Visions: Evolution, Emotion, Culture, and Film* (New York: Oxford University Press, 2009); Torben Grodal, *Moving Pictures: A New Theory of Film Genres, Feelings, and Cognition* (New York: Oxford University Press, 1999). A background to cognitivist film theory can be found in David Bordwell, "A Case for Cognitivism," *Iris* 9 (Spring 1989): 11–40; David Bordwell and Noël Carroll, eds., *Post-Theory: Reconstructing Film Studies* (Madison: University of Wisconsin Press, 1996).

10. Giuliana Bruno, *Atlas of Emotion: Journeys in Art, Architecture, and Film* (London: Verso, 2007), 16.

11. Lisa Cartwright, *Moral Spectatorship: Technologies of Voice and Affect in Postwar Representations of the Child* (Durham, NC: Duke University Press, 2008), 4.

12. "I am trying to suggest that semiotic and psychoanalytic film theory is largely a phobic construct. Images are kept at a distance, isolated like dangerous germs; some-

times, they are even made the object of the theorist's sadistic fantasies of revenge." Shaviro, *The Cinematic Body,* 16.

13. Rutherford, "Cinema and Embodied Affect."

14. Paul Willemen, *Looks and Frictions: Essays in Cultural Studies and Film Theory* (Bloomington: Indiana University Press, 1994), 231.

15. Jean-François Lyotard, "Gesture and Commentary," in *Between Ethics and Aesthetics,* ed. Dorota Glowacka and Stephen Boos (Buffalo: State University of New York Press, 2002), 80.

16. Abel, *Violent Affect,* 7.

17. Shaviro, *The Cinematic Body,* 10.

18. William K. Wimsatt, *The Verbal Icon: Studies in the Meaning of Poetry* (Lexington: University of Kentucky Press, 1954), 21. The first two essays in this collection, "The Intentional Fallacy" and "The Affective Fallacy," were co-written with Monroe Beardsley.

19. Wimsatt, *The Verbal Icon: Studies in the Meaning of Poetry,* 21.

20. Wimsatt, *The Verbal Icon: Studies in the Meaning of Poetry,* 32.

21. Ngai, *Ugly Feelings,* 6.

22. Ngai, *Ugly Feelings,* 28.

23. Ngai, *Ugly Feelings,* 28. See also her discussion at ibid., 42–44.

24. Jennifer Barker, *The Tactile Eye: Touch and the Cinematic Experience* (Berkeley: University of California Press, 2009), 92.

25. Abel, *Violent Affect,* 5, 7, 13.

26. Bordwell has most vocally framed neo-formalism as the righteous enemy of poststructuralism, which he pejoratively calls "SLAB Theory" (for Saussure, Lacan, Althusser, Barthes) or "Grand Theory." For example, he asserts, "Neoformalism has even less in common with what has been called 'Grand Theory,' that development in the humanities that has embraced ever more wide-ranging intellectual programs": David Bordwell, "Historical Poetics of Cinema," in *The Cinematic Text: Methods and Approaches,* ed. R. Barton Palmer (New York: AMS Press, 1989), 379.

27. Jean-François Lyotard, "Note on the Meaning of 'Post-,'" in *Postmodern Literary Theory: An Anthology,* ed. Niall Lucy (Oxford: Blackwell, 2000), 412.

28. The primal scene of this return was the issue of *Modern Language Quarterly* dated March 2000, titled "Reading for Form," which was republished as a book with additional essays in 2006. Susan Wolfson's introduction locates the "demonizing of aesthetic form" in literary studies at exactly the same moment at which one glimpses the turn to affect in film theory. Susan J. Wolfson, "Reading for Form," *Modern Language Quarterly* 61, no. 1 (March 2000): 15. See also Alison James, "Introduction: The Return of Form," *L'esprit Créateur* 48, no. 2 (2008): 2.

29. Ellen Rooney, "Form and Contentment," *Modern Language Quarterly* 61, no. 1 (March 2000): 29.

30. Ellen Rooney, "Form and Contentment," 18.

31. Rey Chow's account of the sentimental in contemporary Chinese cinema is a perfect example of how sensitivity to form need not involve insensitivity to theory. An analysis of this mode does not lead Chow away from postcolonial, feminist, and historical analyses: precisely the opposite, as the sentimental is the "affective orientation/ tendency" that puts under duress a political epistemology of visibility and instates an aesthetic praxis of difficult living that simultaneously resists and adapts to the pressures of filiality. Rey Chow, *Sentimental Fabulations, Contemporary Chinese Films: Attachment in the Age of Global Visibility* (New York: Columbia University Press, 2007), 14, 199.

32. V. I. Pudovkin, *Film Technique and Film Acting: The Cinema Writings of V. I. Pudovkin,* trans. Ivor Montagu (New York: Bonanza Books, 1949), 140.

33. Roland Barthes, "The Third Meaning," in *Image/Music/Text,* trans. Stephen Heath (New York: Hill and Wang, 1977), 53.

34. Roland Barthes, "The Third Meaning," 53.

35. Roland Barthes, "The Third Meaning," 61.

36. Stephen Heath, "Film and System: Terms of Analysis, Part 1," *Screen* 16, no. 1 (Spring 1975): 10. See also Heath, "Film, System, Narrative." A review of the literature on the concept is in Kristin Thompson, "The Concept of Cinematic Excess," in *Narrative, Apparatus, Ideology,* ed. Philip Rosen (New York: Columbia University Press, 1986), 130–142.

37. Thomas Elsaesser, "Tales of Sound and Fury: Observations on the Family Melodrama," in *Film Genre Reader III,* ed. Barry Keith Grant (Austin: University of Texas Press, 1986), 375.

38. Thomas Elsaesser, "Tales of Sound and Fury," 378.

39. Anne Rutherford, "Precarious Boundaries: Affect, *Mise en scene,* and the Senses," in *Art and the Performance of Memory: Sounds and Gestures of Recollection,* ed. Richard Smith (New York: Routledge, 2002), 75.

40. Anne Rutherford, "Precarious Boundaries."

41. Alexandre Astruc, "What Is *Mise-en-Scene?*" trans. Liz Heron, in *Cahiers du Cinema: The 1950s,* ed. Jim Hillier (Cambridge, MA: Harvard University Press, 1985), 267.

42. Alexandre Astruc, "What Is *Mise-en-Scene?*"

43. Astruc, quoted in Lutz Bacher, *The Mobile Mise-en-Scene: A Critical Analysis of the Theory and Practice of Long-Take Camera Movement in the Narrative Film* (New York: Arno Press, 1978), 231.

44. Astruc, quoted in Lutz Bacher, *The Mobile Mise-en-Scene,* 232.

45. Jacques Derrida, "Structure, Sign, and Play in the Discourse of the Human Sciences," in *Writing and Difference,* trans. Alan Bass (Chicago: University of Chicago Press, 1978), 292. This translation is found in Macksey and Donato, 264. This attention to forms of absence and to what fails to appear has literary resonances with Pierre Macherey, *A Theory of Literary Production,* trans. Geoffrey Wall (London: Routledge, 2006). See, e.g., "Implicit and Explicit" and "The Spoken and the Unspoken."

46. Sigmund Freud, "The 'Uncanny,'" in *Writings on Art and Literature,* ed. Werner Hamacher and David E. Wellbery (Stanford, CA: Stanford University Press, 1997), 222.

1. Jacques Derrida, "The Taste of Tears," trans. Pascale-Anne Brault and Michael Naas, in *The Work of Mourning*, ed. Pascale-Anne Brault and Michael Naas (Chicago: University of Chicago Press, 2001), 107.

2. Jacques Derrida, "By Force of Mourning," in *The Work of Mourning*, ed. Pascale-Anne Brault and Michael Naas (Chicago: University of Chicago Press, 2001), 159.

3. Derrida, "The Taste of Tears," 107.

4. Derrida, "The Taste of Tears," 107.

5. Derrida, "The Taste of Tears," 110.

THREE. THE ILLUMINATION OF LIGHT

1. Augustine, *Confessions*, trans. R. S. Pine-Coffin (New York: Penguin, 1961), IV.4.

2. Charlotte Mew's early twentieth-century war plaint "June, 1915" repeats this motif, with the emendation that now it is grief's horrible visage, instead of its affective intensity, that causes an exhaustion of light: "What's little June to a great broken world with eyes gone dim/from too much looking on the face of grief, the face of dread?" Charlotte Mew, "June, 1915," in *Complete Poems*, ed. John Newton (London: Penguin, 2000), 77–78.

3. *OED*, s.v. "blind."

4. Gerard Manley Hopkins, "No Worst, There Is None," in *Gerard Manley Hopkins: The Major Works*, ed. Catherine Phillips (Oxford: Oxford University Press, 2002), 167.

5. Sigmund Freud, "Mourning and Melancholia," trans. Joan Riviere, in *Freud: General Psychological Theory*, ed. Philip Rieff (New York: Touchstone, 1991), 164.

6. Freud, "Mourning and Melancholia," 166.

7. Freud, "Mourning and Melancholia," 166.

8. Freud, "Mourning and Melancholia," 165.

9. Laplanche, "Time and the Other," 241.

10. Laplanche, "Time and the Other," 241, 242.

11. Laplanche, "Time and the Other," 254.

12. Freud, "Mourning and Melancholia," 164, 165.

13. Freud, "Mourning and Melancholia," 174.

14. Freud, "Mourning and Melancholia," 167.

15. Freud, "Mourning and Melancholia," 161.

16. Emphasis added. Shaun Whiteside's modernized translation of Freud, in the series edited by Adam Phillips, figures the opening line as "dreams having served us as the normal model for narcissistic mental disorders, we shall now attempt to cast some light on the nature of melancholia by comparing it to the normal affect of mourning": Sigmund Freud, *On Murder, Mourning, and Melancholia* (London: Penguin, 2005).

17. Laplanche, "Time and the Other," 248.

18. Sigmund Freud, "On Transience," in *The Standard Edition of the Complete Psychological Works of Sigmund Freud*, ed. and trans. James Strachey (London: Hogarth, 1957), 14:305.

19. Freud, "On Transience," 14:306.

20. Freud, "On Transience," 14:306.

21. Sigmund Freud, *Inhibitions, Symptoms, and Anxiety*, trans. Alix Strachey, ed. James Strachey (New York: W. W. Norton, 1960), 105.

22. Freud, "On Transience," 14:306.

23. Freud, *Inhibitions, Symptoms, and Anxiety*, 59.

24. Freud, *Inhibitions, Symptoms and Anxiety*, 105. "Wann macht die Trennung vom Objekt Angst, wann Trauer und wann vielleicht nur Schmerz?": Sigmund Freud, *Hemmung, Symptom, und Angst, Gesammelte Werke, Werke aus den Jahren 1925–1931* (London: Imago, 1948), 202.

25. Ultimately, Freud concludes that pain is the actual reaction to a loss of an object while anxiety is "the reaction to the danger which that loss entails." Pain is then defined in *Inhibitions, Symptoms, and Anxiety*, extending work from *Beyond the Pleasure Principle* (1920), as a reaction to a stimulus breaking through the subject's protective shield: Freud, *Inhibitions, Symptoms, and Anxiety*, 107.

26. Freud, *Inhibitions, Symptoms and Anxiety*, 109.

27. Laplanche, "Time and the Other," 248.

28. Sigmund Freud, *The Ego and the Id*, trans. Joan Riviere, ed. James Strachey (New York: W. W. Norton, 1960), 23–24.

29. One critic who points to the fluid relationship between mourning and melancholia in Freud's work is Kathleen Woodward. She argues for "a grief that is lived in such a way that one is still *in* mourning but no longer *exclusively* devoted to mourning": see Kathleen Woodward, "Freud and Barthes: Theorizing Mourning, Sustaining Grief," *Discourse* 13, no. 1 (Fall–Winter 1990–91): 93–110; Kathleen Woodward, "Grief-Work in Contemporary American Cultural Criticism," *Discourse* 15, no. 2 (Winter 1992–93): 94–112.

30. Freud, "Mourning and Melancholia," 167–68.

31. Although an abiding interest in understanding melancholia is visible in Freud's own work, and the notion of objectal loss retains its centrality to the work of later psychoanalytic thinkers (cf. Julia Kristeva, *Black Sun: Depression and Melancholia*, trans. Leon S. Roudiez [New York: Columbia University Press, 1989]; Melanie Klein, "Mourning and Its Relation to Manic-Depressive States," in *The Selected Melanie Klein*, ed. Juliet Mitchell [New York: Free Press, 1987], 146–74), it is later in the twentieth century that a full-scale politics and ethics of melancholia starts to emerge. Fittingly, trauma studies arose in American academia around the same historical moment as the valorization of melancholia. For example, Alessia Ricciardi echoes a critique most often associated with Dominick LaCapra, arguing that a theory of loss as "an a priori, ontological condition" elides historical traumas (a position she associates with Lacan

and against Freud's vision of loss as contingent and historical): Alessia Ricciardi, *The Ends of Mourning: Psychoanalysis, Literature, Film* (Stanford, CA: Stanford University Press, 2003), 27.

32. David L. Eng and David Kazanjian, "Introduction: Mourning Remains," in *Loss: The Politics of Mourning*, ed. David L. Eng and David Kazanjian (Berkeley: University of California Press, 2003), 4.

33. Eng and Kazanjian, "Introduction," 2.

34. Eng and Kazanjian, "Introduction," 2.

35. Douglas Crimp's contribution to *Loss* positions mourning-cum-melancholia as an important ongoing queer stance that functions as a performative antidote to "the regimes of the normal" and to moralism and normativity: Douglas Crimp, "Melancholia and Moralism," in *Loss: The Politics of Mourning*, ed. David L. Eng and David Kazanjian (Berkeley: University of California Press, 2003), 201.

36. Eng and Kazanjian, "Introduction," 2.

37. Max Pensky finds in Benjamin "the theme of melancholy not just as a dialectic of lost meaning, or of illness and insight, or of self and its half-forgotten origin, but also . . . as a remarkable, difficult form of subjective temperament in which these traits are unified." Max Pensky, *Melancholy Dialectics: Walter Benjamin and the Play of Mourning* (Amherst: University of Massachusetts Press, 2001), 32. See esp. Walter Benjamin, *The Origin of German Tragic Drama,* trans. John Osborne (London: NLB, 1977); Walter Benjamin, "Theses on the Philosophy of History," trans. Harry Zohn, in *Illuminations,* ed. Hannah Arendt (New York: Schocken Books, 1969), 253–64.

38. Judith Butler, "Afterword: After Loss, What Then?" in *Loss: The Politics of Mourning*, ed. David L. Eng and David Kazanjian (Berkeley: University of California Press, 2003), 472.

39. Eng and Kazanjian, "Introduction," 4.

40. Giorgio Agamben, *Stanzas: Word and Phantasm in Western Culture* (Minneapolis: University of Minnesota Press, 1993), 20.

41. Eng and Kazanjian, "Introduction," 5.

42. Marc Nichanian, "Catastrophic Mourning," in *Loss: The Politics of Mourning*, ed. David L. Eng and David Kazanjian (Berkeley: University of California Press, 2003), 99.

43. Nichanian, "Catastrophic Mourning," 120.

44. Dennis King Keenan, *The Question of Sacrifice* (Bloomington: Indiana University Press, 2005), 49.

45. Derrida, "From Restricted to General Economy," 275.

46. It remains an open question whether the centrality of dialectics to theories of rehabilitated melancholia as a public engagement with collective loss derives from Hegel's reading of Antigone's crime in administering funeral rites as a figure for the conflict between community and singularity, as in "individuals in whom the universal appears as 'pathos.'" G. W. F. Hegel, *Phenomenology of Spirit,* trans. A. V. Miller (Oxford: Oxford University Press, 1977), 287.

47. Against the notion that "grief is privatizing," Butler imbues grief/mourning with the quality of "bringing to the fore the relational ties that have implications for theorizing fundamental dependency and ethical responsibility": Judith Butler, *Precarious Life: The Powers of Mourning and Violence* (London: Verso, 2004), 22.

48. Butler, *Precarious Life,* xi-xii.

49. Butler, *Precarious Life,* xix.

50. Tammy Clewell, "Mourning beyond Melancholia: Freud's Psychoanalysis of Loss," *Journal of the American Psychoanalytic Association* 52, no. 1 (2002): 44.

51. John Archer, *The Nature of Grief: The Evolution and Psychology of Reactions to Loss* (London: Routledge, 1999), 16. "Grieving" and "mourning" are used interchangeably throughout Archer's study. When distinctions are made elsewhere in the literature, they are often neither extensively theorized nor committed to. Laura Tanner insists on a difference between grief and mourning—and figures her work in *Lost Bodies* as grappling with the former—but does so in a footnote: see Laura Tanner, *Lost Bodies: Inhabiting the Borders of Life and Death* (Ithaca, NY: Cornell University Press, 2006), 243n1. She routinely slides between the two in the body of her text.

52. The only form of "mourn" that is substantive is the obsolete form of sorrow or a murmur: Malory, for instance, speaks of someone making a great mourne: OED, s.v. "mourn."

53. *Oxford English Dictionary,* 2nd ed., s.v. "grief."

54. Joan Didion, *The Year of Magical Thinking* (New York: Vintage, 2006), 26–27.

55. Didion, *The Year of Magical Thinking,* 26.

56. Didion, *The Year of Magical Thinking,* 27-28.

57. The (mis)quotation in Burton is from Tully (Cicero): "Omnis perturbatio miseria, et carnificina est dolor." Robert Burton, *The Anatomy of Melancholy,* ed. Holbrook Jackson (New York: New York Review Books, 2001), 259 (IV.—Sorrow a Cause of Melancholy).

58. Didion, *The Year of Magical Thinking,* 143.

59. Didion, *The Year of Magical Thinking,* 189.

60. Didion, *The Year of Magical Thinking,* 225–26.

FOUR. GRIEF AND THE UNDIALECTICAL IMAGE

1. Jacques Derrida, "The Deaths of Roland Barthes," in *The Work of Mourning,* ed. Pascale-Anne Brault and Michael Naas (Chicago: University of Chicago Press, 2001), 47.

2. Roland Barthes, *Camera Lucida: Reflections on Photography,* trans. Richard Howard (New York: Hill and Wang, 1981), 3, 63.

3. Roland Barthes, *La chambre claire. Note sur la photographie* (Paris: Gallimard, 1980), 13, 99.

4. For his critique of classical phenomenology, see Barthes, *Camera Lucida,* 19–20.

5. Gary Shapiro, " 'To Philosophize Is to Learn to Die,' " in *Signs in Culture: Roland*

Barthes Today, ed. Steven Ungar and Betty R. McGraw (Iowa City: University of Iowa Press, 1989), 6.

6. Shapiro, " 'To Philosophize Is to Learn to Die,' " 10.

7. Martin Heidegger, *Being and Time,* trans. John Macquarrie and Edward Robinson (New York: HarperCollins, 1962), 284.

8. Heidegger, *Being and Time,* 284.

9. Jacques Derrida, *The Gift of Death,* trans. David Wills (Chicago: University of Chicago Press, 1995), 43.

10. Emmanuel Levinas, "La mort et le temps," *L'Herne* 60 (1991): 42.

11. Barthes, *Camera Lucida,* 9, 14.

12. Barthes, *Camera Lucida,* 97.

13. Barthes, *Camera Lucida,* 96.

14. Barthes, *Camera Lucida,* 66.

15. Barthes, *Camera Lucida,* 67.

16. Barthes, *Camera Lucida,* 72.

17. Hegel's *Lectures* of 1803–1804, vol. 19, quoted in Alexandre Kojève, "The Idea of Death in the Philosophy of Hegel," in *Hegel and Contemporary Continental Philosophy,* ed. Dennis King Keenan (Albany: State University of New York Press, 2004), 55.

18. Barthes, *Camera Lucida,* 65.

19. Barthes, *Camera Lucida,* 90.

20. Barthes, *Camera Lucida,* 75.

21. Barthes, *Camera Lucida,* 90.

22. Barthes, *Camera Lucida,* 21.

23. Barthes, *Camera Lucida,* 113.

24. Barthes, *Camera Lucida,* 79.

25. Barthes, *Camera Lucida,* 80.

26. What the photograph makes certain is that "the photographed body touches me with its own rays and not with a superadded light." Barthes describes the Winter Garden Photograph as "the treasury of rays which emanated from my mother as a child, from her hair, her skin, her dress, her gaze, *on that day.*" Barthes, *Camera Lucida,* 81–82.

27. Barthes, *Camera Lucida,* 81.

28. Barthes, *Camera Lucida,* 88.

29. Barthes, *Camera Lucida,* 106.

30. See Jonathan Crary, "The Camera Obscura and Its Subject," in *Techniques of the Observer: On Vision and Modernity in the Nineteenth Century* (Cambridge, MA: MIT Press, 1990), 25–66.

31. Barthes, *Camera Lucida,* 81.

32. This quotation is on the back of the French edition of Barthes, *La chambre claire.*

33. Derrida, "The Deaths of Roland Barthes," 63.

34. Roland Barthes, *Mourning Diary: October 26, 1977–September 15, 1979,* trans. Richard Howard (New York: Hill and Wang, 2010), 56.

35. Mary Lydon, "Amplification: Barthes, Freud, and Paranoia," in *Signs in Culture: Roland Barthes Today,* ed. Steven Ungar and Betty R. McGraw (Iowa City: University of Iowa Press, 1989), 127–28.

36. Lydon's argument is compelling, although to it I would add that, in addition to the photographic history into which the camera lucida is placed, there is a philosophical room that has equally been deployed in shadow and darkness: Plato's allegorical subterranean cave in *Republic,* super-metaphor for the metaphysical suspicion of representation and illusions taken for the real. Against any denigration of representation, Barthes figures the image and its affective powers as already on the side of the evidential, of the self-presencing, of the force of a mobile, generative, affective light.

37. On this coy "or" that seems to equate mother and wife, see Carol Mavor, "Pulling Ribbons from Mouths: Roland Barthes's Umbilical Referent," in *Representing the Passions: Histories, Bodies, Visions,* ed. Richard Meyer (Los Angeles: Getty, 2003), 184–86.

38. Jean-Paul Sartre, *The Imaginary: A Phenomenological Psychology of the Imagination,* trans. Jonathan Webber (London: Routledge, 2004), 4.

39. Sartre, *The Imaginary,* 18.

40. Sartre, *The Imaginary,* 17.

41. Sartre, *The Imaginary,* 69.

42. Sartre, *The Imaginary,* 69.

43. Sartre, *The Imaginary,* 71.

44. Sartre, *The Imaginary,* 72.

45. Barthes, *Camera Lucida,* 81.

46. The photograph varies in tone depending on the book one is holding in one's hands. It is a remarkably bright, rich teal in my English-language edition and a pale, washed-out turquoise (almost a glaucous) in my French edition. (This is pleasantly odd, as the level of detail in the shaded areas remains fairly consistent. It is uniquely that blue-green that is not stable in the printing and reprinting.) Across the various editions of Barthes's book, then, the color photograph that opens the text remarkably also performs his argument that color is an artifice, a coating applied over the more essential (stable, certain) truth of the photograph.

47. Barthes, *Camera Lucida,* 66. In language that reinserts mediation into a text in which it explicitly has no place, Diana Knight reads Barthes's reference to this light as "the mediating light that will lead him at last to the essence of her face, a blue-green luminosity which is also that of the Boudinet Polaroid": Diana Knight, "Roland Barthes, or the Woman without a Shadow," in *Writing the Image after Roland Barthes,* ed. Jean-Michel Rabaté (Philadelphia: University of Pennsylvania Press, 1997), 138.

48. Jean-Michel Rabaté, *The Ghosts of Modernity* (Gainesville: University Press of Florida, 1996), 72.

49. Colin MacCabe writes that, due to the similarities in the ontologies of photography, "it becomes absolutely extraordinary that Barthes makes no mention of Bazin in his bibliography": Colin MacCabe, "Barthes and Bazin: The Ontology of the Im-

age," in *Writing the Image after Roland Barthes,* ed. Jean-Michel Rabaté (Philadelphia: University of Pennsylvania Press, 1997), 75. There is at least one further complicated matter in the distinction between photography and cinema that Barthes avows. In "Deliberation," originally published in *Tel Quel,* Barthes writes in fragmentary diary entries about going to see an exhibit of Boudinet's photographs on April 25, 1979, one of which will eventually silently stand before his last work. Not only is his account of "D. B.'s photographs (of windows and blue curtains, taken with a Polaroid camera)" suffused with the language of weak affectivity—he writes about disappointment at "the chilly atmosphere of the opening"—but he also then notes, "I took French leave and indulged in a futile spree, from bus to bus and movie house to movie house." While photography exhibit and cinema equally leave him cold, he notes a vivid pleasure in the recollection of those sensations, not from what he had written but from "the interstices of notation." Again, this is a Barthes whose affection is above all for affectivity itself: Roland Barthes, "Deliberation," in *The Rustle of Language,* trans. Richard Howard (Berkeley: University of California Press, 1986), 368.

50. Barthes, *Camera Lucida,* 55–57.

51. Barthes, *Camera Lucida,* 57.

52. Barthes, *Camera Lucida,* 78.

53. Barthes, *Camera Lucida,* 79.

54. Likewise, in *Roland Barthes by Roland Barthes,* he writes that unlike the photograph's certificate of presence, in the cinema "the image is the *irremediable* absence of the represented body": Roland Barthes, *Roland Barthes by Roland Barthes,* trans. Richard Howard (Berkeley: University of California Press, 1977), 84.

55. Barthes, *Camera Lucida,* 90.

56. See Roland Barthes, "The Photographic Message," "The Rhetoric of the Image," "The Third Meaning," and "Diderot, Brecht, Eisenstein," in *Image/Music/Text,* trans. Stephen Heath (New York: Hill and Wang, 1977), 15–31, 32–51, 52–68, 69–78.

57. Roland Barthes, "Leaving the Movie Theater," in *The Rustle of Language,* trans. Richard Howard (Berkeley: University of California Press, 1986), 346.

58. Barthes, *Camera Lucida,* 117.

59. That spectator is numb, awkward, chilly, sleepy. "His body has become something soporific, soft, peaceful": Barthes, "Leaving the Movie Theater," 345. The connection between this less well-known essay of Barthes's and acedia is from Victor Burgin, "Barthes's Discretion," in *Writing the Image after Roland Barthes,* ed. Jean-Michel Rabaté (Philadelphia: University of Pennsylvania Press, 1997), 27.

60. Siegfried Wenzel, *The Sin of Sloth: Acedia in Medieval Thought and Literature* (Chapel Hill: University of North Carolina Press, 1960), 13.

61. Victor Burgin's reading of Barthes emphasizes the role of desire in the hypnotic experience of the spectator. He concludes, "The cinema audience—a totally aleatory conglomeration of alterities—sleeps together in a space of finely judged proximities, a *touching* space": Burgin, "Barthes's Discretion," 29.

62. Barthes, *Camera Lucida,* 91.

63. Barthes, *Mourning Diary,* 14.

64. Raymond Bellour, "A Bit of History," trans. Mary Quaintance, in *The Analysis of Film,* ed. Constance Penley (Bloomington: Indiana University Press, 2000), 16.

65. Christian Metz, *The Imaginary Signifier: Psychoanalysis and the Cinema,* trans. Celia Britton, Annwyl Williams, Ben Brewster, and Alfred Guzzetti (Bloomington: Indiana University Press, 1982), 246.

66. Metz, *The Imaginary Signifier,* 15. He puts this theoretical philosophy into practice, writing later, "I have loved the cinema, I no longer love it. I still love it": Metz, *The Imaginary Signifier,* 79.

67. Christian Metz, *Le signifiant imaginaire. Psychanalyse et cinéma* (Paris: Christian Bourgois, 1984), 117. In the English, the film is "a beautiful closed object which must remain unaware of the pleasure it gives us (literally, over its dead body)": Metz, *The Imaginary Signifier,* 94.

68. Gilles Deleuze, "Preface," *Cinema 1.*

69. Leon Battista Alberti, *On Painting,* trans. John R. Spencer (New Haven, CT: Yale University Press, 1966), 63.

70. Much has been written on melodramas and their incitement of spectatorial leaks: see Mary Ann Doane, *The Desire to Desire: The Woman's Film of the 1940s* (Bloomington: Indiana University Press, 1987); Christine Gledhill, ed., *Home is Where the Heart Is: Studies in Melodrama and the Woman's Film* (London: BFI, 1987). Joan Copjec goes so far as to argue that "crying was an invention of the late eighteenth century" because at that moment "there emerged a brand new literary form—melodrama—which was specifically designed to give people something to cry about." Copjec, "The Invention of Crying and the Antitheatrics of the Act," 109. In a canonical essay on the genre, Thomas Elsaesser redescribes pathos as a formal problematic, though he retains spectatorial strivings as the telos of the melodramatic project. See Thomas Elsaesser, "Tales of Sound and Fury: Observations on the Family Melodrama," in *Film Genre Reader III,* ed. Barry Keith Grant (Austin: University of Texas Press, 1986), 366–95.

71. Sergei Eisenstein, "The Structure of the Film," in *Film Form,* ed. and trans. Jay Leyda (San Diego, CA: Harcourt, 1977), 150.

72. Grief is deployed by Eisenstein as a meta-example of the authorial-affective challenge. "*The problem of portraying an attitude toward the thing portrayed*": Eisenstein, "The Structure of the Film," 151.

73. Eisenstein, "The Structure of the Film," 166.

74. Eisenstein, "The Structure of the Film," 167. For more on Eisenstein's theory of ecstasy and departure, see James Goodwin, *Eisenstein, Cinema, and History* (Urbana: University of Illinois Press, 1993), 175–78.

75. Eisenstein, "The Structure of the Film," 171–72.

76. Barthes, *Camera Lucida,* 57.

77. See, e.g., Willy Riemer, "Beyond Mainstream Film: An Interview with Michael

Haneke," in *After Postmodernism: Austrian Literature and Film in Transition,* ed. Willy Riemer (Riverside, CA: Ariadne, 2000), 160–75.

78. While the images are often bereft of violence, the assaultive realism of sound "wages war against the inauthenticity of postmodernity"; thus, the coldness of pro-liferating mediation is countered by the warmth of the affective jolts experienced by the sensitive plane of the spectatorial body: Peucker, "Violence and Affect," in *The Material Image,* 131.

79. Haneke's *Le temps du loup* (Time of the Wolf; 2003) has some similar aural and visual structures. Bodies are cloaked in prohibitive darkness; faces are turned away from the screen; hands take the place of the face in the close-up. The film opens with an immediate loss and is another of Haneke's films of grief, although the formal techniques are not identical to those in *Funny Games.* As with choking sounds in the earlier film, in *Time of the Wolf* time is stilled and meaning is drained around the visceral wailing of a mother at the death of her child in the postapocalyptic chaos.

80. Only infrequently noted in criticism on the film, this shot is also rarely if ever discussed in terms of its presentation of a structure of illumination; instead, the pres-ence of light is converted into a symbol, as in Peter Brunette's claim that the first cut "takes us to an ironic shot of the outside of the apparently peaceful house." The con-verting of light to irony is a perfect example of putting grief to work for a recuperative dialectic: in this case, an anesthetized rhetorical device. See Peter Brunette, *Michael Haneke (Contemporary Film Directors)* (Champaign, IL: University of Illinois Press, 2010), 64.

81. Haneke's remake of *Funny Games* in English in 2007 (which is sometimes titled *Funny Games U.S.*) is purportedly a shot-by-shot remake, but actually takes some lib-erties with the original composition. It makes slight changes to this tableau: the lines of dripping blood are less even, the camera is inexplicably closer to the figures, and Naomi Watts continually wriggles movement into the stillness of the scene. Yet it preserves the three central aspects of this extraordinary structure: it lasts for ten minutes without a cut; a tipped-over lamp burns a white hole of light into the center of the image; and the moment the characters exit, the tableau is covered over with a cut to the outside of the house. These are the *essential* elements of this scene—what does not go missing (as so much does) in translation.

82. Brigitte Peucker, *The Material Image: Art and the Real in Film* (Stanford, CA: Stanford University Press, 2007), 30.

83. Coates, "Crying in the Dark," 60.

84. Coates, "Crying in the Dark," 60.

85. Lawrence Gowing, *Vermeer* (Berkeley: University of California Press, 1997), 137–38.

86. Arthur Danto's formulation of this law argues that the camera does not sim-ply document the pose. "The pose itself draws on the language of the still in such a way that even if it were never photographically recorded, the pose would be the photographic equivalent of a tableau vivant": Arthur Danto, "Photography and Per-

formance: Cindy Sherman's Stills," in Cindy Sherman, *Untitled Film Stills* (London: Jonathan Cape, 1990), 13.

87. Craig Owens, "Posing," in *Beyond Recognition: Representation, Power, and Culture,* ed. Scott Bryson, Barbara Kruger, Lynne Tillman, and Jane Weinstock (Berkeley: University of California Press, 1992), 210.

88. Kaja Silverman's reading of this adoption of materiality to the image is that, like anamorphosis, "the pose puts the subject who assumes it 'in the picture'": Kaja Silverman, *The Threshold of the Visible World* (New York: Routledge, 1996), 203.

89. Silverman, *The Threshold of the Visible World,* 203.

90. Silverman, *The Threshold of the Visible World,* 203.

91. And yet, this insistence on treating affect as a problem of expression, consumption, and interiority persists in critical treatments of this scene. Take, for an example, Tarja Laine's claim that during the extreme stillness of the long shot, "Instead of having to watch the pain reflected on Anna's and Georg's faces, we now have to listen to it in Georg's desperate and heart-wrenching wounded animal cries that enter into us without distance, and it is with the most inward part of ourselves that we establish their affective meaning." Tarja Laine, "Haneke's 'Funny' Games with the Audience (Revisited)," in *On Michael Haneke,* ed. Brian Price and John David Rhodes (Detroit, MI: Wayne State University Press, 2010) 55. This argument has the added problem of figuring affect as what lacks distance, or what is in collusion with the immediate imposition of the sonic—in either case, the claim that affective intensity penetrates the body without the act of interpretation establishes the affective payoff as an empathetic experience undergone by some "us" and "we." It therefore takes (and is only capable of taking) the durational and visual form of this scene as a means to that spectatorial end.

92. As Jean-Luc Nancy notes, "Light is not itself a luminous substance: it is the give and distance of the world, the absolute velocity of the appearing of bodies, the sculpture of their mass, the curvature and brilliance of their edges." This light that gives the world is *lux,* the "radiant source" of primary light, and is thus distinguished from *lumen,* "the secondary or incidental light in the translucency of surfaces or bits of matter, their reflections and refractions. At the very edge of bodies, *lux* is folded, modulated, and diffused in *lumen*": Jean-Luc Nancy, "Lux Lumen Splendor," in *Multiple Arts: The Muses II,* ed. Simon Sparks (Stanford, CA: Stanford University Press, 2006), 171.

93. Jean-Luc Nancy, "Image and Violence," in *The Ground of the Image,* trans. Jeff Fort (New York: Fordham University Press, 2005), 26.

94. Nancy, "Image and Violence," 26.

FIVE. AESTHETIC EXCLUSIONS

1. Gilles Deleuze, *Francis Bacon: The Logic of Sensation,* trans. Daniel W. Smith (Minneapolis: University of Minnesota Press, 2002), xxix.

2. Deleuze, *Francis Bacon,* 122.

3. Deleuze, *Francis Bacon,* 122.

4. Deleuze, *Francis Bacon,* 123.

5. "When Pausanias had paused—you see the kind of tricks we catch from our philologists, with their punning derivations—the next speaker, so Aristodemus went on to tell me, should have been Aristophanes; only as it happened, whether he'd been overeating I don't know, but he had got the hiccups so badly that he really wasn't fit to make a speech": Plato, *Symposium,* trans. Paul Shorey, in *The Collected Dialogues of Plato, Including the Letters,* ed. Edith Hamilton and Huntington Cairns (Princeton, NJ: Princeton University Press, 1989), 185c.

6. Daniel E. Anderson, *The Masks of Dionysos: A Commentary on Plato's "Symposium"* (Albany: State University of New York Press, 1993), 12.

7. Seth Benardete, "On Plato's *Symposium,*" in *Plato's "Symposium,"* trans. Seth Benardete (Chicago: University of Chicago Press, 2001), 184–85.

8. Plato, *Symposium,* 192c. These hiccups have also been deployed for a meta-reading of the history of philosophy as such: see, e.g., Rolf Hughes, "The Drowning Method," in *Critical Architecture,* ed. Jane Rendell, Jonathan Hill, Murray Fraser, and Mark Dorrian (New York: Routledge, 2007), 93.

9. Quoted in Mladen Dolar, *A Voice and Nothing More* (Cambridge, MA: MIT Press, 2006), 25. Originally in Jacques Lacan, *Le transfert* (*Le séminaire, Livre VIII*), ed. Jacques-Alain Miller (Paris: Seuil, 1960–61).

10. Dolar, *A Voice and Nothing More,* 25.

11. Plato, *Symposium,* 189a. The ignoring of this disrupting aural dimension is especially problematic given that "hiccup" derives from the Greek *singult* (cough or choke) and refers to the sound made by the body in its lived production.

12. The Greek for "hiccup," *lugx* (*luzo* [to have the hiccup]), can also mean "belching": Drew Hyland, *Plato and the Question of Beauty* (Bloomington: Indiana University Press, 2008), 34. See also H. G. Liddell and R. Scott, eds., *A Greek–English Lexicon,* 9th ed. (Oxford: Clarendon, 1996). Thucydides's use of *lugx,* as in *lugx kene,* is likewise usually translated in this expanded sense to suggest hiccupping but also unproductive heaving or even the spasms of "empty retching."

13. Hyland, *Plato and the Question of Beauty,* 34.

14. Plato, *Phaedo,* trans. Paul Shorey. In *The Collected Dialogues of Plato, Including the Letters,* ed. Edith Hamilton and Huntington Cairns (Princeton, NJ: Princeton University Press, 1989), 40-98. These abstentions are outlined in Plato, *Symposium,* 176. *Phaedo* 64d repeats the admonition about the indifference the philosopher should feel toward the pleasures of food and drink.

15. Plato, *Timaeus,* trans. Paul Shorey. In *The Collected Dialogues of Plato, Including the Letters,* ed. Edith Hamilton and Huntington Cairns (Princeton, NJ: Princeton University Press, 1989), 69d–71a. This map of the body is highly condensed in the quotation. For the full plan, see *Timaeus* 69–82.

16. "Man is an animal organism with (like others) an unmistakably bisexual dis-

position. The individual corresponds to a fusion of two symmetrical halves, of which, according to some investigators, one is purely male and the other female. It is equally possible that each half was originally hermaphrodite." Aristophanes appears to enter Freud's text under the sign of "It is equally possible"—one way in which philosophical history runs a speculative furrow through psychoanalytic discourse: Sigmund Freud, *Civilization and Its Discontents,* trans. and ed. James Strachey (New York: W. W. Norton, 1961), 61fn.

17. Freud, *Civilization and Its Discontents,* 54. Freud's genealogy of this shift simultaneously emplaces another affect into sexuality: shame. "The diminution of the olfactory stimuli," he writes, "seems itself to be a consequence of man's raising himself from the ground, of his assumption of an upright gait; this made his genitals, which were previously concealed, visible and in need of protection, and so provoked feelings of shame in him." In an insightful reading that has the supplementary advantage of demonstrating how textual bodies are given their own zones of propriety, Leo Bersani reads "the upper body of the text" in relation to the lower, repressed footnotes, which "play the role of the psychoanalytic unconscious in this work," pushing back and resisting Freud's authorized version: Leo Bersani, *The Freudian Body: Psychoanalysis and Art* (New York: Columbia University Press, 1986), 18.

18. Aristotle: "All men by nature desire to know. An indication of this is the delight we take in our senses; for even apart from their usefulness they are loved for themselves; and above all others the sense of sight. [. . .] The reason is that this, most of all of the senses, makes us know and brings to light many differences between things.": Aristotle, *Metaphysica* (Metaphysics), trans. W. D. Ross, in *The Basic Works of Aristotle,* ed. Richard McKeon (New York: Random House, 1941), 689 (980a).

Descartes concurred with Plato and Aristotle that "sight is the noblest and most comprehensive of the senses"; Hegel's "theoretical senses" are sight and hearing, as opposed to smell, taste, and touch, which "have to do with matter as such and its immediately sensible qualities.": René Descartes, "Optics," trans. John Cottingham, in *The Philosophical Writings of Descartes,* 3 vols. (Cambridge: Cambridge University Press, 1985), 1:152; G. W. F. Hegel, *Aesthetics: Lectures on Fine Arts,* 2 vols., trans. T. M. Knox (Oxford: Clarendon, 1975), 1:38–39.

This tradition does not extend to all of European philosophy without qualification. The German tradition has at times emphasized hearing as a privileged sense (see, for example, the role of music in Romanticism). Likewise, touch is crucial for much twentieth-century French feminist philosophy and in the contemporary work of Jean-Luc Nancy.

19. See an excellent discussion of this in Carolyn Korsmeyer, *Making Sense of Taste: Food and Philosophy* (Ithaca, NY: Cornell University Press, 1999), 11–37; Abbé Etienne Bonnot de Condillac, *Treatise on the Sensations,* trans. Geraldine Carr (Los Angeles: University of Southern California Press, 1930), xxxi.

20. This is as opposed to writing, which "has no *smell:* produced (having accom-

plished its process of production), it *falls,* not like a collapsing soufflé but like a meteorite disappearing; it will *travel* far from my body and yet it is not a detached, narcissistically retained fragment, like speech; its disappearing is not disappointing; it passes, it traverses—no more": Roland Barthes, "Writers, Intellectuals, Teachers," in *The Rustle of Language,* trans. Richard Howard (Berkeley: University of California Press, 1986), 321–22.

21. Derrida notes this sensual structure of permissible philosophical metaphor, writing, "Thus one does actually speak of visual, auditory, and tactile metaphors, (where the problem of knowledge is in its element), and even, more rarely, which is not insignificant, olfactory or gustatory ones": Jacques Derrida, "White Mythology: Metaphor in the Text of Philosophy," in *Margins of Philosophy,* trans. Alan Bass (Chicago: University of Chicago Press, 1982), 227.

22. Moses Mendelssohn, quoted in Winfried Menninghaus, *Disgust: Theory and History of a Strong Sensation,* trans. Howard Eiland and Joel Golb (Albany: State University of New York Press, 2003), 38.

23. Korsmeyer, *Making Sense of Taste,* 25. Most generously, she argues, "In virtually all analyses of the senses in Western philosophy the distance between object and perceiver has been seen as a cognitive, moral, and aesthetic advantage": Korsmeyer, *Making Sense of Taste,* 12. Korsmeyer proposes to remedy the problem of the splitting of embodied senses from knowledge (which for her is both a feminist and a philosophical problem) by insisting on the knowledge of the world that is made available through (literal) taste. Although her detailed exploration of the losses attending the hierarchy of the senses is valuable, her proposed recuperation of taste hinges on the refusal to delink valuation from knowledge acquisition and thus makes even this critique of the sensual hierarchy in thrall to its ladder of terms. In his version of this argument, though with a very different critical aim, Jean-Luc Nancy hedges, "In a sense, one is tempted to say that if there has never been any body in philosophy—other than the signifier and the signified—in literature, on the contrary, there is nothing but bodies." Unlike Korsmeyer, though, Nancy accepts this division, writing that "the body does not have any way of knowing, and there is no lack here, because the body does not belong to the domain in which 'knowledge' or 'non-knowledge' is at stake, any more than knowledge itself belongs to the domain of bodies": Jean-Luc Nancy, *The Birth to Presence,* trans. Brian Holmes et al. (Stanford, CA: Stanford University Press, 1993), 193, 200–1.

24. Friedrich Nietzsche, *The Will to Power,* trans. Walter Kaufmann and R. J. Hollingdale, ed. Walter Kaufmann (New York: Vintage, 1967), 349. Deleuze likewise argues that "the body is a multiple phenomenon, its unity is that of a multiple phenomenon": Gilles Deleuze, *Nietzsche and Philosophy,* trans. Hugh Tomlinson (New York: Columbia University Press, 2006), 40.

25. See Luce Irigaray, *This Sex Which Is not One,* trans. Catherine Porter (Ithaca, NY: Cornell University Press, 1985); Elizabeth Grosz, *Space, Time and Perversion* (New York: Routledge, 1996); Kelly Oliver, *Womanizing Nietzsche: Philosophy's Relation to*

the *"Feminine"* (New York: Routledge, 1995); Kelly Oliver and Marilyn Pearsall, eds., *Feminist Interpretations of Friedrich Nietzsche* (University Park: Penn State Press, 1998).

26. Menninghaus, *Disgust*, 9. Jacques Derrida, *The Ear of the Other: Otobiography, Transference, Translation,* trans. Peggy Kamuf, ed. Christie McDonald (Lincoln: University of Nebraska Press, 1988), 23. Jean-Paul Sartre, *Nausea,* trans. Lloyd Alexander (New York: New Directions, 1964), 136.

27. Georges Bataille, "Attraction and Repulsion II: Social Structure," in *The College of Sociology 1937–39,* ed. Denis Hollier (Minneapolis: University of Minnesota Press, 1988), 114. Note, though, that Sartre writes of nausea while Bataille writes of disgust. The two notions are not identical, and nausea appears to resist aesthetic recuperation in the philosophical literature in a way that disgust does not.

28. This translation is from Menninghaus. In Stoekl's translation, "Thus *formless* is not only an adjective having a given meaning, but a term that serves to bring things down in the world, generally requiring that each thing have its form. What it designates has no rights in any sense and gets itself squashed everywhere, like a spider or an earthworm": Georges Bataille, "Formless," in *Visions of Excess: Selected Writings, 1927–1939,* ed. and trans. Allan Stoekl (Minneapolis: University of Minnesota, Press, 1985), 31.

29. The theorization of disgust as a figure of exclusion, an Ur-rejection, is a robust theme in disciplinary contexts far from philosophy. Darwin figures revulsion as the "not" or "no" in any system by grouping his discussion of disgust with other "signs of affirmation and negation." Disgust is a binary toggle that accepts or rejects food as a defensive and protective gesture for a vulnerable biology. Hence, the reason his name is lent to the notion of "Darwinian gastronomy," the theory that gastronomic developments in climates friendly to food-borne fungi and bacteria favored the use of spices that are antimicrobial. Try your hand at harissa, the fiery North African condiment: pestle ten red chili peppers soaked in water and drained, three smashed garlic cloves, a pinch of salt, a few tablespoons of olive oil, and caraway, coriander, and cumin seeds to taste. See Paul Sherman and Jennifer Billing, "Darwinian Gastronomy: Why We Use Spices," *Bioscience* 49, no. 6 (1999): 453–63.

Despite his definition's suggestion of the innate defensive function of disgust and revulsion, Darwin's emphasis on the habitual nature of emotional expressions allows him to make no distinction between a kind of moral or social disgust and a literal repulsion, noting that the slight upturning of the nose is the same "when we perceive an offensive odour, and wish to exclude or expel it" as when we express disdain. Despite his theory's suggestion that disgust is an innate protective mechanism, the most unpacked example in Darwin's text suggests colonial revulsion. "In Tierra del Fuego a native touched with his finger some cold preserved meat which I was eating at our bivouac, and plainly showed utter disgust at its softness; whilst I felt utter disgust at my food being touched by a naked savage, though his hands did not appear dirty." The *idea* alone of consuming bad (spoiled, rotten) food can prompt disgust. Surmising that "our progenitors must formerly have had the power . . . of voluntarily rejecting food which disagreed with them, or which they thought would disagree with them," Darwin writes, "now, though this power has been lost, as far as the will is concerned, it is called into involuntary action, through the force of a formerly well-established habit." The highly speculative proposals about the prehistory of man, found in both Freud and Darwin, position disgust as a primary or original affect, a link to the bestial and the forgotten truth of the body. Of particular note in Darwin's argument is that vomiting is willful for this earlier man. The myth of a habit-made ejection involves a controllable gag reflex, responsive to the judgment at a remove that what one has eaten *may* be disagreeable. In other words, what is reinstated theoretically against the threat of disgust's immediacy and distinctness is the notion that at an earlier time now lost, it was under the control of will: Charles Darwin, *The Expression of Emotions in Man and Animals,* in *From so Simple a Beginning: The Four Great Books of Charles Darwin,* ed. Edward O. Wilson (New York: W. W. Norton, 2006), 1409–14.

30. Menninghaus, *Disgust,* 2.

31. Even in contemporary readings of disgust, these terms are still in play. For a treatment of disgust and shame, see Sara Ahmed, *The Cultural Politics of Emotion* (New York: Routledge, 2004); Martha Nussbaum, *Hiding from Humanity: Disgust, Shame, and the Law* (Princeton, NJ: Princeton University Press, 2004). For work on contempt and disgust, see William Ian Miller, *The Anatomy of Disgust* (Cambridge, MA: Harvard University Press, 1997); William Ian Miller, *Humiliation: And Other Essays on Honor, Social Discomfort, and Violence* (Ithaca, NY: Cornell University Press, 1993).

32. Menninghaus, *Disgust,* 3.

33. Greenblatt, "Filthy Rites," 60.

34. Menninghaus, *Disgust,* 7. See also Simon Richter, *Laocoon's Body and the Aesthetics of Pain: Winckelmann, Lessing, Herder, Moritz, Goethe* (Detroit: Wayne State University Press, 1992).

35. Menninghaus, *Disgust,* 26. He continues, "This prominent feature of the new aesthetics inaugurated by Baumgarten [the idea of infinite reflection] furnishes an urgently needed *antivomitive:* an apotropaic response to the disgust of satiation that results from the unmixed and uncontaminated beautiful": Menninghaus, *Disgust,* 33.

36. Menninghaus, *Disgust,* 29.

37. Menninghaus, *Disgust,* 30.

38. Quoted in Menninghaus, *Disgust,* 35.

39. Immanuel Kant, *Critique of the Power of Judgment,* 2d ed., ed. Paul Guyer, trans. Paul Guyer and Eric Matthews (Cambridge: Cambridge University Press, 2000), 190.

40. Jacques Derrida, "Economimesis," trans. R. Klein, *Diacritics* 11 (1981): 16.

41. Derrida, "Economimesis," 16.

42. Derrida, "Economimesis," 16.

43. Derrida, "Economimesis," 20.

44. Derrida, "Economimesis," 21.

45. Derrida, "Economimesis," 21.

46. Jacques Derrida, *The Truth in Painting,* trans. Geoff Bennington and Ian Mc-Leod (Chicago: University of Chicago Press, 1987), 56.

47. "The ugly, the evil, the horrible, the negative in general," Derrida continues, "are therefore not unassimilable to the system." This may recall what is done to mediate the negativity of mourning in the previous chapters: Derrida, "Economimesis," 22.

48. Derrida, "Economimesis," 22.

49. Derrida, "Economimesis," 22.

50. Derrida, "Economimesis," 22.

51. Derrida, "Economimesis," 23.

52. Derrida, "Economimesis," 23.

53. Immanuel Kant, *Anthropology, History, and Education,* trans. Robert Louden, Mary Gregor, and Paul Guyer (Cambridge: Cambridge University Press, 2007), 269.

54. Derrida, "Economimesis," 23.

55. Derrida, "Economimesis," 25.

56. Menninghaus, *Disgust,* 1.

57. There is a vigorous debate in the literature centered on the figure of vomit or vomiting: is it *the* privileged form of disgust or just one instance among many? Complicating matters is the etymological intimacy between taste (*goût*) and distaste (*degoût*), which exists in the English and French but not in the German (*Ekel*). The development of parallel theoretical and philosophical traditions on the affect reflects these differences.

58. Mary Douglas, *Purity and Danger: An Analysis of the Concept of Pollution and Taboo* (London: Routledge, 2007), 2.

59. Entire subgenres of pornography, such as the productions of Extreme Associates, are organized around the imperative to produce ever more instances of disgust with the claim that the image is the thing: here, this, then this, then further still—this. Equally, a film like Lucas Moodysson's *A Hole in My Heart* (2004) follows the logic whereby after all that can be done to bodies and all that can be done to disgust—the worms, the fucking, the violence, the gorging, the pissing—pro-filmically real vomit appears as the sign of having reached the limit, that transgression can go no further, that the film can end no other way than having a man stick his finger down his throat, lean over inches from a woman's face and vomit into her mouth for her to take it in, to swallow, to consume. Such a film purports to cross the threshold, to transcend, to take the spectator to a limit case, to the realm of the excluded. This kind of relation to disgust consumes the non-place designated by the worse than the worst—in other words, such a film purports to eat and become the "something more disgusting than the disgusting," instead of designating as uninhabitable the properly impossible position of the absolute excluded. (It is therefore an ultimately conservative move, despite any controversies such a film may generate.)

60. Menninghaus, *Disgust,* 48. "As the aesthetic's entirely other, it remains basically

unrepresentable, invisible, unidentifiable for the field that it limits: an empty cipher for that which the world of beautiful forms cannot appropriate or integrate."

61. Sigmund Freud, "The 'Uncanny,'" in *Writings on Art and Literature,* ed. Werner Hamacher and David E. Wellbery (Stanford, CA: Stanford University Press, 1997), 194.

62. As one of many possible examples of this tendency, take Murray Pomerance, ed., *Bad: Infamy, Darkness, Evil, and Slime on Screen* (Albany: State University of New York Press, 2004), which brings forth a series of tropes and spectacles of the negative (genocide, Chinese villainy, Nazis) whose meaning is affirmatively recuperable by ideological analysis. Tom Gunning's contribution, an analysis of a longstanding suspicion that cinema as a medium is dangerous and evil, is a lone exception to the "images-of" criticism.

63. See Mikita Brottman, *Offensive Films: Toward an Anthropology of Cinéma Vomitif* (Westport, CT: Greenwood, 1997); Cynthia Freeland, *The Naked and the Undead: Evil and the Appeal of Horror* (Boulder, CO: Westview, 2000).

64. See Barbara Creed, *The Monstrous-Feminine: Film, Feminism, Psychoanalysis* (London: Routledge, 1993); Mary Russo, *The Female Grotesque: Risk, Excess, and Modernity* (London: Routledge, 1995).

65. Noël Carroll, *The Philosophy of Horror, or, Paradoxes of the Heart* (New York: Routledge, 1990), 14.

66. Carroll, *The Philosophy of Horror,* 17.

67. Carroll, *The Philosophy of Horror,* 17. For a summary of the cognitivist view of film spectatorship, see Carroll, *The Philosophy of Horror,* 24-27.

68. Carroll, *The Philosophy of Horror,* 34.

69. Carroll, *The Philosophy of Horror,* 18.

70. Carroll, *The Philosophy of Horror,* 38–39.

71. Carroll, *The Philosophy of Horror,* 158.

72. Carroll, *The Philosophy of Horror,* 159. See also Edmund Burke, *A Philosophical Enquiry into the Origin of our Ideas of the Sublime and Beautiful* (Notre Dame, IN: University of Notre Dame Press, 1968); David Hume, "Of Tragedy," in *Eight Great Tragedies,* ed. Sylvan Barnet, Morton Berman, William Burto (New York: Meridian, 1996), 433–39.

73. Carroll, *The Philosophy of Horror,* 190–91.

74. Julia Kristeva, *Powers of Horror: An Essay on Abjection,* trans. Leon S. Roudiez (New York: Columbia University Press, 1982), 4.

75. Kristeva, *Powers of Horror,* 2.

76. Kristeva, *Powers of Horror,* 3.

77. Kristeva, *Powers of Horror,* 2.

78. Creed, *The Monstrous-Feminine,* 10.

79. Katarzyna Marciniak, "Transnational Anatomies of Exile and Abjection in Milcho Manchevski's *Before the Rain* (1994)," *Cinema Journal* 43, no. 1 (Fall 2003): 78.

80. Kristeva, *Powers of Horror,* 1.

81. Kristeva, *Powers of Horror,* 1.

82. Kristeva, *Powers of Horror,* 3.

83. Daryl Buckley, "ELISION: Philosophy Defining a Performance Practice." http ://www.elision.org.au/ELISION_Ensemble/ELISION_Articles__Philosophy.html. Accessed July 2009. On experiencing the piece, "Visitors were led like Jews to the gas chambers around the darkened foundry. Inside a dilapidated warehouse they encountered a shattered landscape of rusting machinery, ambiguous film symbology, a disturbing loud electronic soundscape, and most confronting of all, the putrid stench of decaying fish heads which potently conveyed the bloodletting of Nazi-designed genocide. I nearly vomited": Stewart Dawes, "Opening of the Mouth: Perth, Australia," *X-Press Magazine,* vol. 525, March 6, 1997.

84. Mary Ann Doane, "The Close-Up: Scale and Detail in the Cinema," *Differences* 14, no. 3 (Fall 2003): 90–91.

85. Doane, "The Close-Up," 107.

86. "As Eisenstein and others have pointed out, the concept is inflected differently through its varying nomenclature in different languages. In Russian and in French, the term for close-up denotes largeness or large scale (e.g., *gros plan* in French); while in English, it is nearness or proximity that is at stake. The close-up thus invokes two different binary oppositions—proximity vs. distance and the large vs. the small. In the American context, it is conceptualized in terms of point of view, perspective, the relation between spectator and image, the spectator's place in the scene, and an assumed identification between viewer and camera. In the Soviet and French context, it is thought as a quality of the image, as extensiveness, scale, an imposing stature, the awe of the gigantic as opposed to the charm of the miniature": Doane, "The Close-Up," 92.

87. Menninghaus, *Disgust,* 1. Jonathan Swift, *Gulliver's Travels,* ed. Martin Price (Indianapolis: Bobbs-Merrill, 1963), chap. 5.

88. This translation of Lessing is Menninghaus's, quoted in Menninghaus, *Disgust,* 61. Mikhail Bakhtin, *Rabelais and His World,* trans. Hélène Iswolsky (Bloomington: Indiana University Press, 1984), 317.

89. Critical derision such as this, from David Denby: "given complete freedom, [Lynch] gives way to his obsessions. It becomes a procession of freaks which is now getting grotesque" (quoted in David Hughes, *The Complete Lynch* [London: Virgin, 2001], 153).

90. Derrida, "Economimesis," 21. Nochimson's reading of the other scene of vomit, in which Lula's mother hysterically vomits all over herself, spectacularly succumbs to the error of subjectifying vomit that Derrida decries: "the involuntary process of vomiting creates a tension between the direct sensory presence of the bodies of Lula and Marietta and their contrived styles of glamour." Nochimson's conflation of vomit with vomiting emphasizes the issue of control (loss of, retention of, display of), epitomized in either the abandonment to involuntarism in vomiting or the abandonment to love figured in the film's saccharine ending: Martha P. Nochimson, *The Passion of David Lynch: Wild at Heart in Hollywood* (Austin: University of Texas Press, 1997), 39.

91. Denis Diderot, *Élements de physiologie. Oeuvres completes,* ed. Herbert Dieck-mann, Jacques Proust, and Jean Varloot (Paris: Hermann, 1975), 1:1308.

92. Žižek's most extensive analysis of the Bobby Peru exhorting scene occurs in *The Plague of Fantasies,* but as with many of his favorite bits from films, he vomits this example up in subsequent texts. In *The Plague of Fantasies,* Žižek elaborates his basic thesis that "there is, however, something which is even worse than being swallowed by the pre-ontological Real of the sexual act not sustained by the phantasmatic screen: its exact opposite, the confrontation with the phantasmatic screen deprived of the act." Žižek reads this scene as a forced exteriorization of a fantasy that is then thrown back at the utterer: Slavoj Žižek, *The Plague of Fantasies* (London: Verso, 1997), 185–90.

93. Attempts have been made to reincorporate that excluded element in cinematic exhibitions (John Waters's Odorama cards preeminent among them) and in recent film theory by Laura U. Marks. Marks studies how cinema "can appeal to senses that it cannot technically represent" and argues that the inexpressible trio (smell, taste, touch) can be expressed through the bridging labors of memory: Laura U. Marks, *The Skin of the Film: Intercultural Cinema, Embodiment, and the Senses* (Durham, NC: Duke University Press, 2000), 129. Sense perceptions, she writes, require a mediating memory that is cerebral and emotional; therefore, cinema's posited relation between spectator and text is that of an embodied spectator and a perception system that pulls on retained evocations. However, Marks's theory of film's grasping by "the complex perception of the body as a whole" defines perception "not as something that must be analyzed and deciphered in order to deliver forth its meaning but as something that means in itself": Marks, *The Skin of the Film,* 145. This anti-semiotic (and anti-psychoanalytic) argument posits embodied visuality at the cost of figuring both embodiment and visuality as asignifying, immediate, and transparent. Redefining spectatorial understanding and perception as taking place through embodied experiences of smell, taste, and touch memories reasserts the hegemony of meaning and knowledge, merely reinscribing which senses top the new hierarchy of terms previously erected by Western philosophy.

94. Deleuze, *Francis Bacon,* xxix.

95. There is an extraordinary amount of confusion about the title of this piece, as though its mixed ontology of sculpted screen compelled a permanent uncertainty as to what it actually is. Hughes, for example, writes "*Six Figures Getting Sick* is often referred to, erroneously, as *Six Men Getting Sick,* or simply *Six Figures.* 'It's *Six Figures Getting Sick,*' Lynch confirms. In fact, the piece was originally untitled; Lynch gave it a name in order to make it easier to reference": Hughes, *The Complete Lynch,* 5. However, on the DVD compilation *The Short Films of David Lynch,* the piece is titled *Six Men Getting Sick,* and other critics (e.g., Kenneth Kaleta) persist in referring to it as *Six Men Getting Sick.* The matter of the differing titles is ultimately more interesting as a symptomatic confusion than as a riddle to be solved with certainty. It may be the case that the piece exists in the gap or difference between Figures and men.

96. Deleuze, *Francis Bacon,* 124.

97. Kenneth Kaleta, *David Lynch* (New York: Twayne, 1993), 7. Hughes, *The Complete Lynch,* 6.

98. Nochimson, *The Passion of David Lynch,* 149–50.

99. Nochimson, *The Passion of David Lynch,* 150.

100. Eric Wilson, *The Strange World of David Lynch: Transcendental Irony from "Eraserhead" to "Mulholland Dr."* (New York: Continuum, 2007), 1.

101. Lynch's own creation myth about this work emphasizes the dimension of movement, insisting that he grew tired of the stillness of painting and therefore decided to animate this early piece.

102. Michel Foucault, *Madness and Civilization,* trans. Richard Howard (New York: Vintage, 1965), 11. For a reading of this structure, see Gilles Deleuze, *Foucault,* trans. Seán Hand (Minneapolis: University of Minnesota Press, 1988), 94–123.

103. Freud, quoted in Ilse Grubrich-Simitis, "'No Greater, Richer, More Mysterious Subject . . . than the Life of the Mind': An Early Exchange of Letters between Freud and Einstein," *International Journal of Psychoanalysis* 76 (1995): 117.

104. Jean-Luc Nancy, "Corpus," in *Corpus,* trans. Richard Rand (New York: Fordham University Press, 2008), 55. Lynch's film also confirms one of Nancy's "Fifty-eight Indices"—that "the head consists only of holes, its empty center representing the spirit, the point, an infinite concentration in itself": Jean-Luc Nancy, "Fifty-eight Indices on the Body," in *Corpus,* trans. Richard Rand (New York: Fordham University Press, 2008), 153.

105. Michael Gershon, *The Second Brain* (New York: Harper Perennial, 1998), 84.

SIX. DISGUST AND THE CINEMA OF HAUT GOÛT

Julia Child's quote under the subheading "Gastronomy According to Peter Greenaway," is from Julia Child, Louisette Bertholle, and Simone Beck, *Mastering the Art of French Cooking,* vol. 1 (New York: Knopf, 2002), 79. While Harold McGee writes elsewhere about the pleasures of ingenuity in sauce making, Julia Child describes *Sauce Hollandaise* as marked by the negative affect of dread.

1. Jacques Derrida, "Différance," in *Margins of Philosophy,* trans. Alan Bass (Chicago: University of Chicago Press, 1982), 3.

2. Auguste Escoffier, *The Escoffier Cookbook* (New York: Crown, 1969).

3. On the difference, see Jean-François Revel, "Retrieving Tastes: Two Sources of Cuisine," in *The Taste Culture Reader: Experiencing Food and Drink,* ed. Carolyn Korsmeyer (Oxford: Berg, 2005).

4. Pierre Bourdieu, *Distinction: A Social Critique of the Judgment of Taste,* trans. Richard Nice (Cambridge, MA: Harvard University Press, 1984), 177.

5. The former claim comes from Ruth D. Johnston, "The Staging of the Bourgeois Imaginary in *The Cook, the Thief, His Wife, and Her Lover* (1990)," *Cinema Journal* 41, no. 2 (Winter 2002): 19–40, while the latter is in Michael Walsh, "Allegories of

Thatcherism: The Films of Peter Greenaway," in *Fires Were Started: British Cinema and Thatcherism,* ed. Lester Friedman (Minneapolis: University of Minnesota Press, 1993), 255–77. Amy Lawrence reads the film as a revival of the gangster genre, while Nita Rollins explores the punk Gaultier costumes as ambivalent deconstructive sites, which "equivocate between enhancement and indictment just as the spectator vacillates between (Dutch) description and (Renaissance) condemnation": Amy Lawrence, *The Films of Peter Greenaway* (Cambridge: Cambridge University Press, 1997); Nita Rollins, "Greenaway-Gaultier: Old Masters, Fashion Slaves," *Cinema Journal* 35, no. 1 (Autumn 1995): 76.

6. One telling example of putting gastronomy to work as metaphor or theme instead of as form is Lawrence's take on the film's ending. "Spica's last bite brings the film's investigation of food-as-metaphor full circle. As a last meal, Richard's pièce de résistance is presented not to prolong life (to nourish) but to condemn": Lawrence, *The Films of Peter Greenaway,* 187.

7. Weiss, "Tractatus Logico-Gastronomicus," in *Feast and Folly,* 89.

8. See, e.g., the Sauce Robert in La Varenne's 1651 *Le Cuisinier François.* What La Varenne calls "fragrant sauce" is an identifiable precursor to *hollandaise;* Harold McGee posits that "it may be the first recorded recipe for an egg-based emulsified sauce." Harold McGee, *On Food and Cooking* (New York: Fireside, 1984), 330.

Carême's "Preliminary Discourse" to *Le Maître d'Hôtel français* notes that the "splendor of the old cuisine" was due to lavish private expenses and depended on extensive private resources. One of the unintended consequences of the social upheavals of the French Revolution—the displacement of the private chefs of the aristocratic great houses—was the rise of restaurants in France. With the Revolution, cooks "were thus obliged, for want of help, to simplify the work in order to be able to serve dinner, and then to do a great deal with very little." The Revolution plays a crucial role in the film as the subject of the tome shoved down Michael's strangling throat, but it also signifies the historical conditions that made the restaurant as an institution possible, that made "the Cook" possible as a public category, and that therefore made the events— gastronomic, erotic, violent—of Le Hollandais possible: Carême, quoted in McGee, *On Food and Cooking,* 330. See also Marie-Antoine Carême, *Le Maître d'Hôtel français,* 2 vols. (Paris: Firmin Didot, 1822).

9. McGee, *On Food and Cooking,* 332. It goes without saying that both senses of "taste"—flavor and texture, discernment and refinement—were imagined to be improved in this historical shift.

10. McGee, *On Food and Cooking,* 332. See Marie-Antoine Carême, *L'art de la cuisine française au dix-neuvième siècle,* 2 vols. (Paris: chez l'auteur, 1833), pt. 4. See also Philip Hyman, "Culina Mutata: Carême and *l'ancienne cuisine,*" in *French Food: On the Table, on the Page, and in French Culture,* ed. Lawrence Schehr and Allen Weiss (New York: Routledge, 2001), 71–82; Priscilla Parkhurst Ferguson, *Accounting for Taste: The Triumph of French Cuisine* (Chicago: University of Chicago Press, 2004), chap. 2.

11. Carême, quoted in McGee, *On Food and Cooking,* 332.

12. "Hollandaise is so called because it was developed by Huguenots exiled in Holland, and 'mayonnaise' is thought to derive from a Minorcan port": McGee, *On Food and Cooking,* 330. The importance of Dutch painting in this and other of Greenaway's films is another importation, and another point of contact between gastronomic and representational concerns in his works. Lawrence notes that "Le Hollandais re-creates a familiar triumvirate. French and Dutch and British . . . , Le Hollandais joins in a word food, country, and home": Lawrence, *The Films of Peter Greenaway,* 213n16.

William Van Wert likewise argues that "what is English in this film is both Jacobean revenge tragedies and Margaret Thatcher's England; what is Dutch in the film is both the preponderance of gifted portrait painters and table painters as well as the name of the restaurant. . . . What is French in this film is both the refinement of cuisine, aspired to but never reached, as well as the barbarism of the French Revolution": William Van Wert, "*The Cook, the Thief, His Wife, and Her Lover,*" *Film Quarterly* 44, no. 2 (Winter 1990–91): 48.

13. McGee, *On Food and Cooking,* 349.

14. McGee, *On Food and Cooking,* 350.

15. Dayana Stetco, "The Crisis of Commentary: Tilting at Windmills in Peter Greenaway's *The Cook, the Thief, His Wife, and Her Lover,*" in *Peter Greenaway's Postmodern/ Poststructuralist Cinema,* ed. Paula Willoquet-Maricondi and Mary Alemany-Galway (Lanham, MD: Scarecrow, 2001), 208.

16. Van Wert, "*The Cook, the Thief, His Wife, and Her Lover,*" 43.

17. Lawrence, *The Films of Peter Greenaway,* 175.

18. Aurel Kolnai, *On Disgust,* ed. Barry Smith and Carolyn Korsmeyer (Chicago: Open Court, 2004), 29–30. The book collects "Disgust" (Der Ekel), written in 1927 and published in 1929, and "The Standard Modes of Aversion: Fear, Hate, and Disgust," published in *Mind.*

19. Kolnai, *On Disgust,* 30. The language of disgust—Kolnai calls it "primordial," "immediate and more sensual than abhorrence"—is linked to a primitive organicism. William Ian Miller likewise figures disgust as subtended by the horror of "life soup": see William Ian Miller, *The Anatomy of Disgust* (Cambridge, MA: Harvard University Press, 1997), 40–41.

20. Kolnai, *On Disgust,* 33.

21. Kolnai, *On Disgust,* 34.

22. Kolnai, *On Disgust,* 38.

23. Kolnai, *On Disgust,* 39.

24. Kolnai, *On Disgust,* 44.

25. Kolnai, *On Disgust,* 40.

26. Kolnai, *On Disgust,* 40. The history of disgust could well be mapped by the senses linked most strongly to it: touch for Benjamin, Sartre, and Miller; smell for Kant; taste for Darwin and Paul Rozin; and so forth. Vision has its proponents, but in

a claim that deserves more scrutiny, the strong consensus in the literature is that there can be no disgust of the sense of hearing.

27. Kolnai, *On Disgust,* 41.

28. Kolnai, *On Disgust,* 39.

29. Kolnai, *On Disgust,* 47.

30. Kolnai, *On Disgust,* 47.

31. "What is missing is a specially dedicated qualitative diction of odor that matches the richness of distinctions we make with the tactile as with squishy, oozy, gooey, . . . dank, and damp. Odor qualifiers, if not the names of things emitting the odor, are usually simple adjectives and nouns expressing either the pleasantness or unpleasantness of the smell": Miller, *The Anatomy of Disgust,* 67.

32. Roland Barthes, "The Grain of the Voice," in *Image/Music/Text,* trans. Stephen Heath (New York: Hill and Wang, 1977), 180.

33. See Naomi Schor's theory of the detail, which, in the words of Ellen Rooney's introduction, offers "a brilliant instantiation of the detail as a mode of reading, rather than a catalogue or hoard of details": Ellen Rooney, "Foreword: An Aesthetic of Bad Objects," in Naomi Schor, *Reading in Detail: Aesthetics and the Feminine* (New York: Routledge, 2007), xxvi. See esp. "Sublimation: Hegel's *Aesthetics*" and "Desublimation: Roland Barthes's Aesthetics," in Naomi Schor, *Reading in Detail: Aesthetics and the Feminine* (New York: Routledge, 2007).

34. Schor, *Reading in Detail,* 3. It bears further consideration how Schor's argument that the detail "as negativity" is gendered feminine, and its recuperable importance for feminism and aesthetics, might relate to the long history in the philosophical literature on women and disgust, as in Kant and Nietzsche, or the disgusting as "feminine," as in Sartre's work on *visqueux* (the slimy).

35. Weiss, "Tractatus Logico-Gastronomicus," 85.

36. Naomi Schor, *Reading in Detail: Aesthetics and the Feminine* (New York: Routledge, 2007). The Sosein of disgust is itself a telling detail in the expanding network of connections between Kolnai and Freud, for it is the particular and contingent revelations of the minor that are the most "telling" in the sense of speaking and being readable in psychoanalytic praxis. On Freud's use of the detail in opposition to the figure of the fragment.

37. See Kolnai, *On Disgust,* 53–62. Korsmeyer and Smith's introduction to *On Disgust* describes Kolnai's taxonomy of the disgusting as sharing "the impression of life gone bad, of flesh turning towards death, and of a primordial and profuse regeneration of life from the mulch of decaying organic matter": Carolyn Korsmeyer and Barry Smith, "Visceral Values: Aurel Kolnai on Disgust," in Kolnai, *On Disgust,* 16.

38. Kolnai, *On Disgust,* 74.

39. Kolnai, *On Disgust,* 42.

40. Kolnai, *On Disgust,* 43.

41. Kolnai, *On Disgust,* 66.

42. "There exists," Kolnai notes, "the perverse type of preference for slightly putrescent tastes, namely the *haut-goût* of roast game. The Chinese were said to prefer completely rotten eggs, something I would credit less to the 'differences of taste' which are so much overestimated by foolish relativists, then [*sic*] to a passion for esoteric refinement on the part of an extraordinarily overcultivated civilization." He continues, though, "Whether the disgustingness of rotten eggs is intentionally apparent to the Chinese as the disgustingness of rotten meat is to the lovers of *faisandé,* I do not know: the states of consciousness may well be here somehow different": Kolnai, *On Disgust,* 60.

43. Kolnai, *On Disgust,* 60. For an overview of what she calls "terrible eating," see Carolyn Korsmeyer, "Delightful, Delicious, Disgusting," *Journal of Aesthetics and Art Criticism* 60, no. 3 (Summer 2002): 217–25; Carolyn Korsmeyer, *Savoring Disgust: The Foul and Fair in Aesthetics* (Oxford: Oxford University Press, 2011).

44. Kolnai, *On Disgust,* 53.

45. Kolnai, *On Disgust,* 71–72.

46. Brillat-Savarin, *The Physiology of Taste,* 378–79 (Varieties XII: Pheasant). See also his earlier remarks on timing and game ("Gastronomical Meditations": VI. Specialties).

47. Brillat-Savarin, *The Physiology of Taste,* 379.

48. Brillat-Savarin, *The Physiology of Taste,* 379.

49. Of the role of duration in lustful or excessive libertinage, Kolnai writes that just as one may begin to eat a dish that is no longer fresh, "here the tonality of this 'no longer' is just as important," for moral haut goût involves a subject "as if by destiny putrefied in a permanent motion towards what is evil": Kolnai, *On Disgust,* 85.

50. Roland Barthes, "Reading Brillat-Savarin," in *The Rustle of Language,* trans. Richard Howard (Berkeley: University of California Press, 1986), 250. The original was a preface to Jean Anthelme Brillat-Savarin, *Physiologie du goût* (Paris: C. Hermann, 1975).

51. Brillat-Savarin, *The Physiology of Taste,* 51.

52. Brillat-Savarin, *The Physiology of Taste,* 52–53.

53. Barthes, "Reading Brillat-Savarin," 250.

54. One inclined to explore the relationship between gastronomy and representation in Greenaway might well note Barthes's description of the "gourmand's body" as "a glowing painting, illuminated from *within*": Barthes, "Reading Brillat-Savarin," 253.

55. Brillat-Savarin, *The Physiology of Taste,* 138 (VII. Theory of Frying). Barthes, "Reading Brillat-Savarin," 262.

56. Barthes, "Reading Brillat-Savarin," 250–51. The appetitive is further linked to a specifically hallucinatory time. "When I have an appetite for food, do I not imagine myself eating it? And, in this predictive imagination, is there not the entire memory of previous pleasures? I am the constituted subject of a scene to come, in which I am the only actor": Barthes, "Reading Brillat-Savarin," 264.

57. Brillat-Savarin, *The Physiology of Taste,* 54.

58. Bourdieu, *Distinction,* 196.

59. In another philosophical treatment of disgust that links it to temporality, Sartre's meditation on the *visqueux* in *Being and Nothingness,* the problem of the sticky/slimy itself slides along a chain of philosophical problems, a quality of the thought of which it is also the subject. The indeterminate state is an ontological obscenity: "Slime is the agony of water," Sartre memorably argues. In its imitation of liquidity, "it manifests to us a being which is everywhere fleeing and yet everywhere similar to itself, which on all sides escapes yet on which one can float." The "horrible image" the slimy offers is that of consciousness "transformed by the thick stickiness of its ideas," unable to take flight into the new. Like Darwin's colonial revulsion at his food being touched by a native, Sartre's nervous references to "a moist and feminine sucking" theorize a mediated body under the guise of disgust's immediacy: Jean-Paul Sartre, *Being and Nothingness,* trans. Hazel Barnes (New York: Washington Square Press, 1956), 774–78.

60. Kolnai, *On Disgust,* 53. In a provocative argument that flows rot to the aesthetic through a different canal altogether, Kolnai also suggests that one may experience disgust toward certain types of sentimental (particularly Russian) literature. The genre itself is seen as aligned with "the soft gushing type of life which resists all solid formations, all discrimination, selection": Kolnai, *On Disgust,* 71.

61. Jacques Lacan, *The Seminar of Jacques Lacan VII: The Ethics of Psychoanalysis 1959–1960,* trans. Dennis Porter, ed. Jacques-Alain Miller (New York: W. W. Norton, 1992), 216.

62. Spica does not merely imagine he possesses an excellent taste palate; he also purports to be the better palette artist in the logic of the film. Of the murder, he insists, "They're going to admire the style" by which Michael is stuffed with his favorite tome. As though following a classical law of aesthetics, Spica insists that the act of horrific violence contain "no unnecessaries."

63. Or the changing colors of Georgina's frock are noted only to be provided with symbolic meaning in a metaphorical displacement of likenesses. She is gray in the kitchen; red in the restaurant—like the night; like a knife; like the curtains. This approach attempts to return color to the objects of the world, to act as though they never changed, to re-suture them to dress; to subsume color to costumes puts the color to work for fabric. I disagree, then, with Brigitte Peucker's claim that Georgina's "body is trapped within the mise-en-scene, subsumed within the palette much in the manner in which the bodies of Gustav Klimt's female figures are trapped behind the excessively decorative quality of their clothing." Quite the contrary: in place of being trapped within the mise-en-scène, Georgina constitutes it through her bearing of the force of autonomous color through the spaces of the film: Brigitte Peucker, *Incorporating Images: Film and the Rival Arts* (Princeton, NJ: Princeton University Press, 1995), 163. See also "Dutch Realism: Vermeer, Greenaway, Wenders," in Brigitte Peucker, *The Material Image: Art and the Real in Film* (Stanford, CA: Stanford University Press, 2007), 30-48.

64. Greenaway allows, "Telling a story is something completely arbitrary and to

escape this arbitrariness, I invent systems, universal structures that organize this contingency": Andreas Kilb, "I Am the Cook: A Conversation with Peter Greenaway," in *Peter Greenaway: Interviews,* ed. Vernon Gras and Marguerite Gras (Jackson: University Press of Mississippi, 2000), 62.

65. Joel Siegel, "Greenaway by the Numbers," in *Peter Greenaway: Interviews,* ed. Vernon Gras and Marguerite Gras (Jackson: University Press of Mississippi, 2000), 76.

66. Roland Barthes, "Cy Twombly: Works on Paper," in *The Responsibility of Forms,* trans. Richard Howard (Berkeley: University of California Press, 1985), 166.

67. Barthes, "Cy Twombly," 166.

68. Gilles Deleuze, *Francis Bacon: The Logic of Sensation,* trans. Daniel W. Smith (Minneapolis: University of Minnesota Press, 2002), 121.

69. Charles Riley, *Color Codes: Modern Theories of Color in Philosophy, Painting and Architecture, Literature, Music, and Psychology* (Hanover, NH: University Press of New England, 1995), 8–9.

70. Riley, *Color Codes,* 8–9. "Color as fact is an event—almost an accident—characterized by imprecision and a malformed spontaneity. It sounds just like what happens when a painter tries something out on a palette before applying it to the canvas. Color retains in this manner a freshness and unforeseeable variety": ibid., 60. Greenaway's films in general are obsessed with the painterly. In this film, he explicitly invokes the genre of "table painting" and the problem for the painter who "has to find a viewpoint where you can satisfactorily position everybody without masking anyone": Siegel, "Greenaway by the Numbers," 79–80.

71. Roland Barthes, "The Wisdom of Art," in *The Responsibility of Forms,* trans. Richard Howard (Berkeley: University of California Press, 1985), 180.

INTERVAL

1. Walsh, "Allegories of Thatcherism," 294. Joel Siegel makes a similarly problematic point, writing, "The extreme formalism of Greenaway's movies tends to distract audiences from perceiving his sometimes oblique but nevertheless demonstrable populist sympathies": Siegel, "Greenaway by the Numbers," 80.

SEVEN. INTERMITTENCY, EMBARRASSMENT, DISMAY

1. Søren Kierkegaard, *The Concept of Anxiety: A Simple Psychologically Orienting Deliberation on the Dogmatic Issue of Hereditary Sin,* ed. and trans. Reidar Thomte (Princeton, NJ: Princeton University Press, 1980), 43, 77.

2. Martin Heidegger, "What Is Metaphysics?" in *Martin Heidegger: Basic Writings,* ed. David Farrell Krell, 89–110 (San Francisco: HarperCollins, 1993), 96–97, 101.

3. Jean-Paul Sartre, *Being and Nothingness,* trans. Hazel Barnes (New York: Washington Square Press, 1956), 69.

4. Kierkegaard, *The Concept of Anxiety*, 61.

5. "*That in the face of which one has anxiety is Being-in-the-world as such.* What is the difference phenomenally between that in the face of which anxiety is anxious and that in the face of which fear is afraid? That in the face of which one has anxiety is not an entity within-the-world. . . . That in the face of which one is anxious is completely indefinite": Martin Heidegger, *Being and Time*, trans. John Macquarrie and Edward Robinson (New York: HarperCollins, 1962), 186.

6. Kierkegaard, *The Concept of Anxiety*, 41. Likewise, because of the nothingness of ignorance, the demonic is ultimately figured as "anxiety about the good": Kierkegaard, *The Concept of Anxiety*, 123.

7. Kierkegaard, *The Concept of Anxiety*, 42, 44, 61, 91.

8. Kierkegaard, *The Concept of Anxiety*, 113.

9. Kierkegaard, *The Concept of Anxiety*, 155.

10. Jacob Grimm and Wilhelm Grimm, "The Tale of the Boy Who Set Out To Learn Fear," in *Grimm: Selected Tales*, trans. Joyce Crick (Oxford: Oxford University Press, 2005), 20.

11. Grimm, "The Tale of the Boy Who Set Out To Learn Fear," 127.

12. Gilles Deleuze, *Foucault*, trans. Seán Hand (Minneapolis: University of Minnesota Press, 1988), 101.

13. Kierkegaard, *The Concept of Anxiety*, 159.

14. Reidar Thomte note in Kierkegaard, *The Concept of Anxiety*, 254n8.

15. Unless, of course, one accepts Marx and Engels's famous critique of the Kaleidoscope as what feigns the new but only reflects itself: see Karl Marx and Friedrich Engels, *The German Ideology*, ed. R. Pascal (New York: International Publishers, 1963), 109–11.

16. This reference is from the section in *Either/Or* titled "Equilibrium between the Aesthetic and the Ethical in the Development of Personality": see Søren Kierkegaard, *Either/Or*, 2 vols., trans. Howard V. Hong and Edna H. Hong (Princeton, NJ: Princeton University Press, 1987), Part 2:549.

17. As though inverting Mary Ann Doane's claim that the appearance in modernity of the cinema "appears to extract a magical continuity from what is acknowledged to be discontinuous," it is more the case that the *Heksebrev* extracts a magical discontinuity from what is acknowledged and perceived to be continuous: Mary Ann Doane, *The Emergence of Cinematic Time* (Cambridge, MA: Harvard University Press, 2002), 176.

18. Jonathan Crary, *Techniques of the Observer: On Vision and Modernity in the Nineteenth Century*, (Cambridge, MA: MIT Press, 1990), 125.

It may be objected, fairly, that the magic picture cannot be regarded as any kind of proto-cinematic object, given that the location of sorcery, which here is synonymous with the capacity for transformation and movement, is on the side of the physical object—the letter or picture is dubbed magic or bewitched in its shape-shifting dimension—in place of a deceived or conjured vision. Specifically, in Crary's genealogy of perception, the common bond in the optical toys at the time of Kierkegaard's writing—such as the thaumatrope or the phenakistoscope—"was the notion that perception was not instantaneous, and the notion of a disjunction between eye and object." In the witch's letter, deception and duration are addressed not principally to the eye but to the malleability and mobility of the physical image as such and as subjected to an individual's tactile labors. Indeed, a stronger form of the objection would note that, departing from Crary's argument that "like the study of afterimages, new experiences of speed and machine movement disclosed an increasing divergence between appearances and their external causes," the *Heksebrev* precisely provides an external cause in individual agency for each and every instance of manipulated transformation. In this sense, the witch's letter does not transform an observer, ushering him into modernity, but confirms the tight coincidence between cause and appearance. The strongest form of this objection might claim that in place of the subjective vision Crary describes, the witch's letter confirms classical vision at the expense of a transfixed image: ibid., 104, 112.

19. Crary, *Techniques of the Observer*, 126. "Like the phenakistoscope and other nonprojective optical devices, the stereoscope also required the corporeal adjacency and immobility of the observer": Crary, *Techniques of the Observer*, 129. The *Heksebrev* requires not only this corporeal adjacency but a haptic interaction with the book.

20. This new form of space is technically "Riemannian patches of space." In their treatment of Riemannian space, they quote Albert Lautman's description of the linkages this shift makes possible from *Les schemas de structure* (Paris: Hermann, 1938), 34–35, quoted in Gilles Deleuze and Félix Guattari, *A Thousand Plateaus: Capitalism and Schizophrenia*, trans. Brian Massumi (Minneapolis: University of Minnesota Press, 1987), 485.

21. Deleuze and Guattari, *A Thousand Plateaus*, 485.

22. Deleuze and Guattari, *A Thousand Plateaus*, 488.

23. Kierkegaard, *The Concept of Anxiety*, 12, note at IV285.

24. Kierkegaard, *The Concept of Anxiety*, 12, note at IV285.

25. Kierkegaard likens them to Lulu's appearance on stage without cause, when she "comes running without anyone's being able to observe the mechanism of movement": Kierkegaard, *The Concept of Anxiety*, 12, note at IV285.

26. Emmanuel Levinas, "Kierkegaard: Existence and Ethics," *Proper Names*, trans. Michael B. Smith (Stanford: Stanford University Press, 1996), 72. Levinas figures this leap as an abandoning gesture. "Kierkegaardian violence begins when existence is forced to abandon the ethical stage in order to embark on the religious stage, the domain of belief. But belief no longer sought external justification. Even internally, it combined communication and isolation, and hence violence and passion. That is the origin of the relegation of ethical phenomena to secondary status and the contempt of the ethical foundation of being which has led, through Nietzsche, to the amoralism of recent philosophies."

27. See Kierkegaard, *The Concept of Anxiety*, sec. III, for theories of time and movement in relation to transition and the leap.

28. Kierkegaard, *Either/Or*, 1:129, 2:186.

29. Kierkegaard, *Either/Or I*, 152–53.

30. Kierkegaard, *Either/Or I*, 153.

31. Samuel Weber, *Return to Freud: Jacques Lacan's Dislocation of Psychoanalysis*, trans. Michael Levine (Cambridge: Cambridge University Press, 1991), 167.

32. One other, and significant, reference in the literature to this figure is in Lyndsey Stonebridge, "Anxiety in Klein: The Missing Witch's Letter," in *Reading Melanie Klein*, ed. Lyndsey Stonebridge and John Phillips (London: Routledge, 1998), 190–202. Stonebridge quotes Weber quoting Kierkegaard on the figure of flux and change that the *Heksebrev* stands for, and argues that unlike Freud, for whom it remains lacking, Klein appears to be able to provide the missing witch's letter. Stonebridge's conclusion is that "Klein refuses to put anxiety in its proper place but insists on leaving the ego shattered and dislocated" by its vicissitudes, linked to guilt but also to freedom and to possibility. In addition to Stonebridge, see Melanie Klein, *Love, Guilt and Reparation and Other Works, 1921–1945* (London: Virago, 1988), and *Envy and Gratitude and Other Works, 1946–1963* (London: Virago, 1988). For its articulation of a relationship between anxiety and aesthetics, specifically painting and the figure of "blank space," see Klein's essay on Ruth Kjär, "Infantile Anxiety Situations Reflected in a Work of Art and in the Creative Impulse," in *The Selected Melanie Klein*, ed. Juliet Mitchell (New York: Free Press, 1987), 84–94.

33. Kierkegaard, *The Concept of Anxiety*, 43.

34. Accordingly, Joan Copjec dubs anxiety "something like the 'stem cell' of affects." The rabid mobility of the affect, however, suggests something like a horror film's view of stem cell division, multiplying wildly as though trapped in the perpetual loop of a Cronenberg film: Joan Copjec, "The Object-Gaze: Shame, *Hejab*, Cinema." *Filozofski vestnik* 27, no. 2 (2006): 22.

35. Jacques Lacan, *Le Séminaire X: L'angoisse (Anxiety) 1962–63*, trans. Cormac Gallagher, 14.11.62. The unedited transcripts of Lacan's Seminar X are dated in the European style, beginning Wednesday, November 14, 1962 (14.11.62), and ending Wednesday, July 3, 1963 (3.7.63). It is by those dates of the weekly meetings, and not pages from the unedited transcript, that I identify passages.

36. Sigmund Freud, "Lecture XXV: Anxiety," in *Introductory Lectures on Psychoanalysis*, trans. and ed. James Strachey (New York: W. W. Norton, 1966), 393.

37. This is Weber's translation of this passage in Lacan, which begins "*Vous le verrez, je pense, l'angoisse est très précisément le point de rendez-vous*": see Weber, *Return to Freud*, 153 and Lacan, *Le Séminaire X*, 14.11.62.

38. Weber, *Return to Freud*, 156.

39. Sigmund Freud, "Lecture XXXII: Anxiety and Instinctual Life," in *New Introductory Lectures on Psychoanalysis*, trans. and ed. James Strachey (New York: W. W. Norton, 1965).

40. Freud, *New Introductory Lectures on Psychoanalysis*, 85.

41. Freud, *Inhibitions, Symptoms, and Anxiety,* 33.

42. Freud, *Inhibitions, Symptoms and Anxiety,* 100.

43. Freud, *Inhibitions, Symptoms and Anxiety,* 45.

44. Freud, *Inhibitions, Symptoms and Anxiety,* 45–46.

45. Freud, *Inhibitions, Symptoms and Anxiety,* 46.

46. Freud, *Inhibitions, Symptoms and Anxiety,* 46. That things repeat because they never took place is also the lesson of Freud's essay on the uncanny, the concept that best anticipates anxiety as a formal problematic of awkward, difficult, repetitious movements—and on the level of textual form, no less.

47. Freud, *Inhibitions, Symptoms and Anxiety,* 47.

48. Freud, *Inhibitions, Symptoms and Anxiety,* 47.

49. These varying models of anxiety's movements hinge on perhaps the oldest philosophical debate about the structure of time. Freud's account of the privileged role of coitus interruptus in the formation of anxiety recalls Zeno's model of movement as interruptions in his image of the arrow's non-continuous trajectory. Freud's accounts of anxiety pose a broader disciplinary problem about time and motion, then: Does one, following Zeno, regard movement as a compendium of immobilities or archive of divisible fixed halts (which would suggest that *coitus completus* is in fact impossible)? Or, following Bergson's critique of Zeno in *Creative Evolution,* is movement an indivisible continuity that takes place in the interval between two states, "slips through the interval" in his formulation—which might suggest that coitus cannot be truly interrupted, for any imagined breach in mobility would be potential or virtual, not actual?

50. Crary, *Techniques of the Observer,* 124. Weber, *Return to Freud,* 163.

51. Freud, *Inhibitions, Symptoms, and Anxiety,* 60.

52. Freud, *Introductory Lectures on Psychoanalysis,* 401.

53. Weber, *Return to Freud,* 157. "Freud's discussion of anxiety thus turns upon a question that it will never entirely resolve: Is anxiety a constitutive process by which the psyche maintains its coherence and identity, or does it ultimately entail their dissolution?": Weber, *Return to Freud,* 154.

54. Jacques Derrida, *The Post Card,* trans. Alan Bass (Chicago: University of Chicago Press, 1987), 405.

55. Freud, *Inhibitions, Symptoms, and Anxiety,* 35.

56. Freud, *Inhibitions, Symptoms and Anxiety,* 17, 51, 60.

57. Freud, *Inhibitions, Symptoms and Anxiety,* 60.

58. Freud, *Inhibitions, Symptoms and Anxiety,* 34.

59. Freud, *Inhibitions, Symptoms and Anxiety,* 59.

60. Freud, *Inhibitions, Symptoms and Anxiety,* 81.

61. As though anticipating the future impotence of the psychoanalytic thinker, one of Freud's early examples of inhibition in the essay symptomatically focuses on the act of writing. "As soon as writing, which entails making a liquid flow out of a tube on to a piece of white paper, assumes the significance of copulation," he posits, writing will

be stopped because it represents "the performance of a forbidden sexual act": Freud, *Inhibitions, Symptoms and Anxiety,* 6–7.

62. Curiously, anxiety's etymology emphasizes this spatial constriction-restriction, while it is "panic" that has the dimension of time and rhythm in its link to Pan and the *sudden* appearance of a gripping fear.

63. Freud, *Inhibitions, Symptoms, and Anxiety,* 88.

64. Freud is reported to have said this in 1909 at the Vienna Psychoanalytical Society: quoted in Freud, *Inhibitions, Symptoms and Anxiety,* xxxiv.

65. For the critique of Rank's theory of birth trauma, see Freud, *Inhibitions, Symptoms and Anxiety,* chaps. 8–10.

66. Sigmund Freud, *The Ego and the Id,* trans. Joan Riviere, ed. James Strachey (New York: W. W. Norton, 1960), 61.

67. "The act of birth, as the individual's first experience of anxiety, has given the affect of anxiety certain characteristic forms of expression": Freud, *Inhibitions, Symptoms, and Anxiety,* 12–13.

68. Freud, *Inhibitions, Symptoms and Anxiety,* 52.

69. Freud, *Inhibitions, Symptoms and Anxiety,* 100.

70. Joan Copjec, "May '68, the Emotional Month," in *Lacan: The Silent Partners,* ed. Slavoj Žižek (London: Verso, 2006), 98. See Lacan, *Le Séminaire X,* 30.1.63, 6.3.63.

71. Copjec, "May '68, the Emotional Month," 99.

72. Lacan, *Le Séminaire X,* 30.1.63.

73. Lacan, *Le Séminaire X,* 30.1.63.

74. Lacan, *Le Séminaire X,* 30.1.63.

75. Lacan, *Le Séminaire X,* 22.5.63.

76. If it is the case, as Lacan writes, that "this emergence of the *heimlich* in the frame . . . constitutes the phenomenon of anxiety," then anxiety functions as the punctum of the *heimlich–unheimlich* in the trajectory of Lacanian psychoanalysis Lacan, *Le Séminaire X,* 19.12.62. Jacques-Alain Miller's elegant phrase for this shift in Lacan's version of psychoanalysis is "the replacement of mythology by topology": Jacques-Alain Miller, "On Jacques Lacan's *Anxiety,*" *Lacanian Ink* 26 (Autumn 2005): 51.

77. Miller, "On Jacques Lacan's *Anxiety,*" 14.

78. Lacan, *Le Séminaire X,* 19.12.62.

79. Lacan, *Le Séminaire X,* 19.12.62.

80. Lacan, *Le Séminaire X,* 19.12.62.

81. Lacan, *Le Séminaire X,* 19.12.62.

82. See Lacan, *Le Séminaire X,* 19.12.62 and 6.3.63 for the most succinct presentation of these articulations of anxiety. For the famous formula for anxiety, that it is the "lack of lack"—"if all of a sudden all norms are lacking, namely what constitutes the lack–because the norm is correlative to the idea of lack–if all of a sudden it is not lacking . . . it is at that moment that anxiety begins"—see Lacan 28.11.62. By this phrase as the formulation for anxiety, Lacan means that "*le point d'angoisse*" (an echo of the quilting

point from Seminar III on the psychoses) manifests at "the total filling of a certain void which should be preserved which has nothing to do with either the positive or negative content of the demand." He repeats a version of this in 6.12.62: anxiety-provoking for the child is "when there is no possibility of lack." For the claim that the real "does not lack anything," see Lacan, *Le Séminaire X*, 20.3.63.

83. Lacan, *Le Séminaire X*, 14.11.62.

84. Lacan, *Le Séminaire X*, 14.11.62.

85. In defense of rereading Freud's text on anxiety as being about locomotion, Lacan says that "movement exists in every function, even if it is not locomotory. It exists at least metaphorically, and in inhibition, it is the stopping of movement that is involved": Lacan, *Le Séminaire X*, 14.11.62.

86. Lacan, *Le Séminaire X*, 14.11.62.

87. Lacan, *Le Séminaire X*, 14.11.62. Emphasis added.

88. Lacan, *Le Séminaire X*, 14.11.62.

89. Lacan, *Le Séminaire X*, 14.11.62.

90. Anticipating a version of the radical split of emotion from affect that one sees in Deleuze and Massumi, Lacan will later formally pronounce that anxiety is an affect, not an emotion.

91. Miller, "On Jacques Lacan's *Anxiety*," 20.

92. Lacan, *Le Séminaire X*, 14.11.62.

93. Lacan, *Le Séminaire X*, 19.12.62.

94. Lacan, *Le Séminaire X*, 23.1.63. This, in addition to the reading of shame in Seminar XVII, should put to rest any claim that psychoanalysis has no theory of affect. Lacan's seminars are suffused with theories of affect (and, not unlike Deleuze's treatment of the term, its absolute difference from emotion). On affect as displacement— "Affect is always displaced, or: always out of place" and, more broadly, "Affect is the discharge, the movement of thought. If readers of Freud, blinded by the word 'discharge,' failed to see that it was the term by which he attempted to theorize affect as the movement of thought, readers of Lacan, blinded by the word 'signifier,' were misled into believing that he had neglected affect altogether"—see Copjec, "May '68, the Emotional Month," 93, 95.

95. Lacan, *Le Séminaire X*, 23.1.63. Dora's famous slap is just such a "switching point in a particular destiny."

96. Lacan, *Le Séminaire X*, 26.6.63.

97. Lacan, *Le Séminaire X*, 3.7.63.

98. Alain Badiou, "Anxiety," *Lacanian Ink* 26 (Autumn 2005): 71.

99. Miller, "On Jacques Lacan's *Anxiety*," 14. Lacan eventually creates a new version of the table that repeats like an uncanny structure the earlier one, in which dismay is replaced with the object *o* [*a*], embarrassment with cause, impediment with "not to be able," emotion with the specific one of not knowing how to respond, and so forth. The most radical rewriting of the table appears at the end of *Seminar X*. There, the

most curious substitution involves Lacan writing Kierkegaard's title in the upper-right corner where "embarrassment" was. One of Lacan's justifications for this switch is Freud's humiliation at failing to adequately distinguish in his appendices to *Inhibitions, Symptoms, and Anxiety* the various forms of pain in relation to loss (e.g., anxiety from mourning), such that it is the psychoanalytic formulation of the *concept* of anxiety that textually bears out a formal embarrassment where Freud's inadequate, failed thought is not all and not enough.

100. Weber, *Return to Freud,* 153.

101. Weber, *Return to Freud,* 166.

102. Copjec, "May '68, the Emotional Month," 96. See Copjec, "May '68," 100–3, for her discussion of the feeling of "being riveted, of the inescapability of being" in relation to shame. It is worth noting, however, that shame is not embarrassment—and while more needs to be said about this difference, this is not, it should be noted, the place for that cleaving.

EIGHT. OPEN WATER ANXIETY

1. Søren Kierkegaard, *Journals and Papers,* ed. and trans. Howard Hong and Edna Hong (Bloomington: Indiana University Press, 1970), entry 1405.

2. In this sense, *Open Water*'s structure is the inverse of that of *Psycho,* from which one learns nothing from the end. In *Open Water,* the sociological cliché of the beginning is inadequate as a meta-narrative for what is to come; in *Psycho,* psychiatric scientific discourse is inadequate to account for the power of what has happened or came before. In this and other ways, this chapter and this film answer some of the issues presented in the opening of this book.

3. There is a great deal of extra-textual discourse about *Open Water* and realism, given the film's production history and use of real sharks baited by a wrangler in the water containing filmmaker and actors. Those who are interested can refer to Marcia Garcia, "Bait Noir: Kentis and Lau's *Open Water* Hooks Audiences with Shark Scare," *Film Journal International* 107, no. 7 (July 2004): 12–14.

4. Dennis Lim, "Reality Bites," *Village Voice,* August 2, 2004.

5. Lim. He contrasts this negatively to the praised "structural stunt" of *The Blair Witch Project.*

6. Randy Shulman, "Not So Chummy: *Open Water* Is a Stunt That Quickly Grows Tiresome," *Metro Weekly* (Washington, DC), August 12, 2004.

7. Walter Metz, "Shark Porn: Film Genre, Reception Studies, and Chris Kentis' *Open Water,*" *Film Criticism* 31, no. 3 (Spring 2007): 44. Graham Benton likewise suggests that *Open Water* "participates in the category of naturalism" and reads the film in relation to a "deliberate aesthetic and philosophical approach that presents human beings as passive victims of natural forces and their environment": Graham Benton, "Shark Films: Cinematic Realism and the Production of Terror," in *This Watery World:*

Humans and the Sea, ed. Vartan P. Messier and Nandita Batra (Newcastle: Cambridge Scholars, 2007), 129. The film review that comes the closest to this chapter's claim that the sharks are a structural force is by Stephanie Zacharek, who writes of *Open Water* that the sharks are fundamentally "unreadable." She elsewhere calls them a "novelty" and says that the film is marked with "obviousness," both of which are provocative terms. (Glenn Whip, the reviewer for the *Milwaukee Journal Sentinel,* likewise says that the film "is often too simple for its own good.") These remarks are compelling productions of a sense that the film exists on the surface. The reviewers fail to see, however, that that surface takes a specific visual form, that that obviousness on the level of visuality is also linked to a finitude of form. In the end, unfortunately, Zacharek also gives in to the need to find meaning in the film under the master signifier of them all, writing that it is "ultimately a serious film about the unknowability and uncontrollability of nature": see Stephanie Zacharek, "Open Water," Salon.com, August 6, 2004; Glenn Whip, "Diving into Danger: Two Swim with Sharks in *Open Water,*" *Milwaukee Journal Sentinel,* August 16, 2004.

8. Metz, "Shark Porn," 46.

9. Metz, "Shark Porn," 48.

10. Metz, "Shark Porn," 51. A different form of this allegorical claim is in Jameson's well-known essay on *Jaws,* "Reification and Utopia in Mass Culture." Writing about how critics "have tended to emphasize the problem of the shark itself, what it 'represents,'" he argues that while those readings of the shark as the Other, as the unconscious, and so on, are not wrong, "their very multiplicity suggests that the vocation of the symbol—the killer shark—lies less in any single message or meaning than in its very capacity to absorb and organize all of these quite distinct anxieties together." The shark "as a symbolic vehicle," he concludes, is "essentially polysemous," and it is ideological precisely because "it allows essentially social and historical anxieties to be folded back into *apparently* 'natural' ones": Jameson, "Reification and Utopia in Mass Culture," 26.

11. Metz, "Shark Porn," 51.

12. Immanuel Kant, *Critique of Pure Reason,* trans. Norman Kemp Smith. New York: St. Martin's Press, 1965, 77.

13. Roland Barthes, *Mythologies,* trans. Annette Lavers (New York: Hill and Wang, 1972), 112.

14. Spoto describes *Lifeboat* as confined to "what may be the narrowest acting space ever filmed": Donald Spoto, *The Art of Alfred Hitchcock: Fifty Years of His Motion Pictures* (New York: Anchor, 1992), 129.

15. Spoto, *The Art of Alfred Hitchcock,* 133–34.

16. Slavoj Žižek, "Kierkegaard with Lacan," *Lacanian Ink* 26 (Autumn 2005): 112.

17. Stephen Jay Gould, "Seeing Eye to Eye, through a Glass Clearly," in *Leonardo's Mountain of Clams and the Diet of Worms* (New York: Harmony Books, 1998), 59.

18. The terrarium or Wardian case as a domestic adornment displaying ferns, in fact,

is a more salient precursor to the aquarium than innovations stemming from marine biology. Gould links this to a series of events that included the repeal on a tax on glass and the Victorian penchant for exploring—imperialists away at sea could be sure that their plants survived at home: Gould, "Seeing Eye to Eye," 63.

19. J. G. Wood, quoted in Gould, "Seeing Eye to Eye," 63.

20. Gould, "Seeing Eye to Eye," 65.

21. Gould, "Seeing Eye to Eye," 67.

22. Noël Burch, *To the Distant Observer: Form and Meaning in Japanese Cinema* (Berkeley: University of California Press, 1979), 200.

23. Burch, *To the Distant Observer,* 200.

24. Certainly, many disaster films trace characters who break down under the pressure of suspenseful waiting (as does *Open Water*), but the majority of those films do so without formally breaking down. Indeed, a constancy of form provides an antidote to the anxieties of the terrified.

25. This break is also therefore reminiscent of the shot from outside the house in *Funny Games,* which covers over the exit from the space of the tableau, and the black cut over the darkness of the wall that severs color from dress in Greenaway's film.

26. Emmanuel Levinas, *On Escape,* trans. Bettina Bergo (Stanford: Stanford University Press, 2003), 67. This is why Sianne Ngai's reading of anxiety is so problematic. She considers the affect, following Heidegger, as projection or thrownness, but her reading of, say, Scottie flying through space in *Vertigo* is akin to saying that Kierkegaard's leap can be thought through images of figures bounding across a screen. In other words, she takes bodies and characters for form as a way of re-privileging bodies above all. Anxiety, then, is never more than a thematic acted out in the mise-en-scène as presence, and vertigo and finitude are limited to the experiences of being(s): see Ngai, *Ugly Feelings,* chap. 5.

Another example of thematizing anxiety is Vincent Rocchio, *Cinema of Anxiety: A Psychoanalysis of Italian Neorealism* (Austin: University of Texas Press, 1999).

27. Johann Wolfgang von Goethe, *Theory of Colours,* trans. Charles Lock Eastlake (Cambridge, MA: MIT Press, 1970), 787. The most famous claim in this work is that color is "subdued light" (*gedämpfte Licht*) or a "degree of darkness," often mistranslated as "troubled light," following Mondrian's reference of 1917: See Goethe, *Theory of Colours,* 231 (574), 31 (69).

28. Goethe, *Theory of Colours,* 313 (790).

29. Metz, "Shark Porn," 52–54. He reads this scene as Susan "killing herself" in such a way that she "retains discursive control over her own death."

30. Maurice Blanchot, *The Space of Literature,* trans. Ann Smock (Lincoln: University of Nebraska Press, 1982), 97.

31. One wonders whether this "death of a distinction" is an entry point for a form of sexual difference in the film. Susan recalls Julia Kristeva's description of Virginia Woolf, "who sank wordlessly into the river, her pockets weighed down with stones."

For Kristeva, the suicide of a woman can carry on "as though it were simply a matter of making an inevitable, irresistible and self-evident transition." To Dostoevsky's Kirilov, who commits suicide "to prove that his will is stronger than God's," she counterpoises Tsvetaeva's suicide as the desire to want merely "not to be": Julia Kristeva, "About Chinese Women," in *The Kristeva Reader,* ed. Toril Moi (New York: Columbia University Press, 1986), 157–58.

32. Alain Badiou, *Being and Event,* trans. Oliver Feltham (London: Continuum, 2005), 193.

33. Badiou, *Being and Event,* 193. Likewise, "Hesitation in Mallarmé enacts the intermittence of meaning and non-meaning. Trapped in the uncertainty of the moment all the poet can do is explore the meaning of non-meaning; that is, to make the non-event an event": Elizabeth McCombie, *Mallarmé and Debussy: Unheard Music, Unseen Text* (Oxford: Oxford University Press, 2003), 62.

34. This is a "cancellation of the event by its total invisibility, the only representable figure of the concept of the event is the staging of its undecidability": Badiou, *Being and Event,* 194.

35. Badiou, *Being and Event,* 196.

36. Mallarmé follows the proviso RIEN / N'AURA EU LIEU / QUE LE LIEU, however, with "EXCEPT . . . PERHAPS . . . A CONSTELLATION," which Badiou reads as placing in the outside place, as exception, number in the equivalence of casting and not casting the dice. This pure form of exception suggests the violence of the crew's written numbers as the original and external cause of violence. "That 'nothing,'" Badiou writes, "has taken place therefore means solely that nothing *decidable within the situation* could figure the event as such." The counting error on the boat is not decidable—or comprehensible—within the scenario of the event that it nevertheless casts out. In *Open Water,* finitude is a formal abstraction put in play externally to the event by the purest form of abstraction, number, made present in the purest form of visual abstraction, the frustrations of form to take place: Badiou, *Being and Event,* 197.

37. Martin Heidegger, *Being and Time,* trans. John Macquarrie and Edward Robinson (New York: HarperCollins, 1962), 241.

NINE. TO BEGIN AGAIN

Epigraph: "Fling to the cave of War / A gaud, a ribbon, a dead flower, something / That once has touched thee, and I'll bring it back / Though all the hosts of Christendom were there, / Inviolate again! ay, more than this, / Set me to scale the pallid white-faced cliffs / Of mighty England, and from that arrogant shield / Will I raze out the lilies of your France / Which England, that sea-lion of the sea, / Hath taken from her!": Oscar Wilde, "The Duchess of Padua," *The Works of Oscar Wilde: Volume 10: The Duchess of Padua: A Play,* repr. ed. (London: Methuen and Co., 1908), 58.

1. Robert Creeley, *The Collected Poems of Robert Creeley, 1945–75* (Berkeley: Univer-

sity of California Press, 1982), 350. See also Charles Altieri, *The Particulars of Rapture: An Aesthetics of the Affects* (Ithaca, NY: Cornell University Press, 2004), 133–41. Altieri links his study of emotion to formal issues of rhythm and speaker and thus may be productive to consider in dialogue with this book's thesis. However, while I appreciate Altieri's interest in "the aesthetic aspect of our affects," his theory of identification retains a link between affective dynamics and bodies and subjects: Altieri, *The Particulars of Rapture*, 25, 27.

2. The translation is R. J. Hollingdale's (Harmondsworth: Penguin, 1969). Kaufmann's translation of this passage is, "'Was *that* life?' I want to say to death. 'Well then! Once more!'": Friedrich Nietzsche, *Thus Spoke Zarathustra*, in *The Portable Nietzsche*, trans. Walter Kaufmann (New York: Viking, 1954), 430.

3. Nietzsche, *Thus Spoke Zarathustra*, 435. Section 11 of "The Drunken Song."

4. *Oxford English Dictionary,* 2d ed. (1989), s.v. "joy." Another etymological history of the word "joy" can be found in Adam Potkay, *The Story of Joy: From the Bible to Late Romanticism* (Cambridge: Cambridge University Press, 2007).

5. An interesting exploration of the notion that "happiness is what happens to us" is in Darrin McMahon, *The Pursuit of Happiness: A History from the Greeks to the Present* (London: Penguin, 2006). See also the very different Barbara Ehrenreich, *Dancing in the Streets: A History of Collective Joy* (New York: Holt, 2006); Scott Wilson, *The Order of Joy: Beyond the Cultural Politics of Enjoyment* (New York: State University of New York Press, 2008). Finally, a philosopher who takes joy seriously, and does not assimilate it to the negativity of *jouissance,* is Jean-Luc Nancy: see, e.g., his account of how "joy is possible, it has meaning and existence, only through community and as its communication," in *The Inoperative Community,* ed. and trans. Peter Connor (Minneapolis: University of Minnesota Press, 1991), 34.

6. Friedrich Nietzsche, *Human, All Too Human,* trans. R. J. Hollingdale (Cambridge: Cambridge University Press, 1996), 266.

7. Nietzsche, *Thus Spoke Zarathustra*, 434.

8. Alex McIntyre, *The Sovereignty of Joy: Nietzsche's Vision of Grand Politics* (Toronto: University of Toronto Press, 1997), 5. McIntyre takes the crucial phrase from Nietzsche, "joy in the actual and active of *every kind,*" and puts it to work for a reading of sovereignty, morality, and politics.

9. Gilles Deleuze, *Nietzsche and Philosophy,* trans. Hugh Tomlinson. New York: Columbia University Press, 2006, 68.

10. Deleuze, *Nietzsche and Philosophy,* 26.

11. Deleuze, *Nietzsche and Philosophy,* 27–28.

12. Deleuze, *Nietzsche and Philosophy,* 68, 72.

13. The notion of "retroactive force" is from Friedrich Nietzsche, *The Gay Science,* trans. Josefine Nauckhoff, ed. Bernard Williams (Cambridge: Cambridge University Press, 2003), 53. For the transformation of "It was" into "I willed it thus," see Nietzsche, *Thus Spoke Zarathustra,* 251. In Klossowski's summation of this temporal paradox as

ethical imperative, "the Eternal Return is a necessity that must be willed: only he who I am now can will the necessity of my return and all the events that have led to what I am. . . . Now this subject is no longer able to will itself as it has been up to now, but wills *all* prior possibilities": Pierre Klossowski, *Nietzsche and the Vicious Circle,* trans. Daniel W. Smith (Chicago: University of Chicago Press, 1997), 57.

14. Nietzsche, *Thus Spoke Zarathustra,* 251.

15. See the discussion in Potkay, *The Story of Joy,* 162–67. Potkay's summation of Nietzsche's departure from this tradition is that "Nietzsche transformed the basic story of joy, which concerns recollected or anticipated unities and their momentary recuperation or foretaste, into a story in which the fullness of joy occurs now or never, in an unfolding present that will eternally come back to delight or disappoint": Potkay, *The Story of Joy,* 210.

16. Gary Shapiro, *Nietzschean Narratives* (Bloomington: Indiana University Press, 1989), 103.

17. Nietzsche, *Thus Spoke Zarathustra,* 429.

18. Shapiro, *Nietzschean Narratives,* 121.

19. Robert Grosseteste, *On Light,* trans. Clare C. Riedl (Milwaukee: Marquette University Press, 2000), 10. For the narration from the *Bay State Primer,* a list of letters and their substitution images, and Frampton's translation of Grosseteste's passage, see Hollis Frampton, *On the Camera Arts and Consecutive Matters: The Writings of Hollis Frampton,* ed. Bruce Jenkins (Cambridge, MA: MIT Press, 2009), 192–202.

20. Paul R. Halmos, *Naive Set Theory* (New York: Springer, 1974) 62.

21. P. Adams Sitney's influential early version of the participatory argument posits, "The substitution process sets in action a guessing game and a timing device. Since the letters seem to disappear roughly in inverse proportion to their distribution as initial letters of words in English, the viewer can with occasional accuracy guess which letter will drop out next. He also suspects that when the alphabet has been completely replaced, the film or the section will end": P. Adams Sitney, *Visionary Film: The American Avant-Garde, 1943–1978* (New York: Oxford University Press, 1979), 394.

The fervent desire to produce a narrative in the midst of the rigorously formalist film produces comically general assertions about what that narrative might be, as in the broad claim, "The most fruitful approach to the progression . . . is to see it as a narrative mapping of human intellectual development. . . . Essentially, the three sections of *Zorns Lemma* correspond to three phases of life—childhood, youth or young adulthood, and maturity—phases that are often characterized by different forms of intellectual process": Scott MacDonald, *Avant-Garde Film/Motion Studies* (Cambridge: Cambridge University Press, 1993), 71.

22. This claim is made in a soft form by Sitney and a strong one by Peterson. See Sitney, *Visionary Film,* 369–97. Peterson's argument is exemplified in the query, "Frampton's ambitions for progressively complex *a priori* schemes raise an important question: at what point does graded complication exceed the perceptual and cognitive capacities

of viewers?": James Peterson, *Dreams of Chaos, Visions of Order* (Detroit: Wayne State University Press, 1994), 116.

23. See, e.g., a canonical early essay by Wanda Bershen and a series of articles published in *October* in 1985 and in 2004. Bershen productively places the film in dialogue with other structuralist avant-garde works, especially those by Stan Brakhage, and focuses on the way in which the final snowy image "fades to a rectangle of white light, the minimum definition of cinema." However, she sets in place a problematic trend by making this argument in deference to Frampton's notes on his film to support much of her reading. There is insufficient space to explore fully the degree to which Frampton is not a post-Barthesian dead author in critical work on his films. Indeed, Bershen repeats almost verbatim a line from Frampton's "A Lecture" in her analysis of the film: see Wanda Bershen, "*Zorn's Lemma*," *Artforum* 9, no. 1 (September 1971): 41–45; Annette Michelson, "Frampton's Sieve," *October* 32 (Spring 1985): 151–66; Federico Windhausen, "Words into Film: Toward a Genealogical Understanding of Hollis Frampton's Theory and Practice," *October* 109 (Summer 2004), 76–95.

24. Peterson, *Dreams of Chaos*, 114; emphasis added.

25. Allen Weiss, "Frampton's Lemma, Zorn's Dilemma," *October* 32 (Spring 1985): 118.

26. "Accumulation," Weiss writes, "is a mode of listing independent of any necessary formal or material connection between the constituent terms. Enumeration is a listing of attributes, a mode of predication, defining a central term by means of ancillary terms": Weiss, "Frampton's Lemma," 121.

27. Weiss, "Frampton's Lemma," 128.

28. "What *is* this thing that calls itself a movie? That is the underlying question posed by structural cinema": Bershen, "*Zorn's Lemma*," 42. For all of this attention to film form, she does not get rid of the spectator. "The film proposes a possible construct, a model in mathematical or scientific parlance, for the component parts and dynamic of the specific perceptual experience of film-viewing": Bershen, "*Zorn's Lemma*," 42.

29. Federico Windhausen, "Words into Film: Toward a Genealogical Understanding of Hollis Frampton's Theory and Practice," *October* 109 (Summer 2004), 92.

30. Melissa Ragona, "Hidden Noise: Strategies of Sound Montage in the Films of Hollis Frampton." *October* 109 (Summer 2004): 108, 112. This move is made with many of Frampton's works in some form. In her study of Frampton's *(nostalgia)*, Rachel Moore argues for the division of cinematic form and structure from the affect named in that film's title. Moore writes of *(nostalgia)* that her interest in the film "is not animated by a structural investigation of film's formal properties, but by nostalgia itself." I would claim, of course, that this is a false opposition: Rachel Moore, *Hollis Frampton: (nostalgia)* (London: Afterall, 2006), 4.

31. Robert Scholes, *An Introduction to Structuralism in Literature* (New Haven, CT: Yale University Press, 1974), 41.

32. Scholes, *An Introduction to Structuralism*, 41.

33. Gilles Deleuze, quoted in Richard Macksey and Eugenio Donato, eds. *The Structuralist Controversy* (Baltimore: Johns Hopkins University Press, 2007), xvi.

34. Frampton, "For a Metahistory of Film," 134.

35. Jacques Derrida, "Signature Event Context," in *Margins of Philosophy*, trans. Alan Bass (Chicago: University of Chicago Press, 1982), 326.

36. Roland Barthes, *The Pleasure of the Text*, trans. Richard Miller (New York: Hill and Wang, 1975), 40. The argument I am putting forward is mentioned, albeit only to be disavowed, by Barthes. "Yet one can make a claim for precisely the opposite (though I am not the one who would make such a claim): repetition itself creates bliss. There are many ethnographic examples: obsessive rhythms, incantatory music, litanies, rites, and Buddhist nembutsu, etc.: to repeat excessively is to enter into loss, into the zero of the signified. But: in order for repetition to be erotic, it must be formal, literal, and in our culture this flaunted (excessive) repetition reverts to eccentricity, thrust toward various marginal regions of music": Barthes, *The Pleasure of the Text*, 41.

37. Florian Cajori, *A History of Mathematical Notations, Volume 1: Notations in Elementary Mathematics* (1928), repr. ed. (Alcester, UK: Read Books, 2007), 381.

38. Quoted in Cajori, *A History of Mathematical Notations*, 383. For another history of this account, see William Kottmeyer, *Except after C: The Story of English Spelling* (New York: McGraw-Hill, 1988), 52.

39. "X" is also the twenty-fourth letter in the full iteration of the Roman alphabet, twenty-four being the mark of the temporality of the cinema and the upper bound of the reduced alphabet in Frampton's cycle.

40. Quoted in Henry Hitchings, *Defining the World: the Extraordinary Story of Dr. Johnson's Dictionary* (New York: Farrar, Straus and Giroux, 2005), 251. This is the version of the entry found in volume 2 of Johnson's sixth edition (1785).

41. Grosseteste, *On Light*, 17. The version quoted earlier is Frampton's translation: see Frampton, *On the Camera Arts and Consecutive Matters*, 195.

42. Frampton, "A Pentagram for Conjuring the Narrative," 146.

43. Frampton, "A Pentagram for Conjuring the Narrative," 146.

44. Gilles Deleuze, *Spinoza: Practical Philosophy*, trans. Robert Hurley (San Francisco: City Lights, 1988), 28–29.

45. Benedict de Spinoza, *Ethics*, ed. James Gutmann (New York: Hafner, 1949), 131. Deleuze repeats this phrase (ever lovingly) in numerous places. See, at minimum, Deleuze, *Spinoza*, and Deleuze, *Nietzsche and Philosophy*, as well as Gilles Deleuze, *Cinema 1: The Movement-Image*, trans. Hugh Tomlinson and Barbara Habberjam (Minneapolis: University of Minnesota Press, 1986), and *Cinema 2: The Time-Image*, trans. Hugh Tomlinson and Robert Galeta (Minneapolis: University of Minnesota Press, 1989).

Bibliography

Abel, Marco. *Violent Affect: Literature, Cinema, and Critique after Representation.* Lincoln: University of Nebraska Press, 2007.

Agamben, Giorgio. *Stanzas: Word and Phantasm in Western Culture.* Minneapolis: University of Minnesota Press, 1993.

Ahmed, Sara. *The Cultural Politics of Emotion.* New York: Routledge, 2004.

Alberti, Leon Battista. *On Painting,* trans. John R. Spencer. New Haven, CT: Yale University Press, 1966.

Altieri, Charles. *The Particulars of Rapture: An Aesthetics of the Affects.* Ithaca, NY: Cornell University Press, 2004.

Anderson, Daniel E. *The Masks of Dionysos: A Commentary on Plato's "Symposium."* Albany: State University of New York Press, 1993.

Apostolos-Cappadona, Diane. "'Pray with Tears and Your Request Will Find a Hearing': On the Iconology of the Magdalene's Tears." In *Holy Tears: Weeping in the Religious Imagination,* ed. Kimberley Christine Patton and John Stratton Hawley, 201–28. Princeton, NJ: Princeton University Press, 2005.

Archer, John. *The Nature of Grief: The Evolution and Psychology of Reactions to Loss.* London: Routledge, 1999.

Aristotle. *De Poetica* (Poetics), trans. Ingram Bywater. In *The Basic Works of Aristotle,* ed. Richard McKeon, 1455-1487. New York: Random House, 1941.

———. *Metaphysica* (Metaphysics), trans. W. D. Ross. In *The Basic Works of Aristotle,* ed. Richard McKeon, 689-926. New York: Random House, 1941.

———. *Rhetorica* (Rhetoric), trans. W. Rhys Roberts. In *The Basic Works of Aristotle,* ed. Richard McKeon, 1325-1451. New York: Random House, 1941.

Astruc, Alexandre. "What Is *Mise-en-Scene?*" trans. Liz Heron. In *Cahiers du Cinema: The 1950s,* ed. Jim Hillier, 266–68. Cambridge, MA: Harvard University Press, 1985.

Augustine. *Confessions,* trans. R. S. Pine-Coffin. New York: Penguin, 1961.

Bacher, Lutz. *The Mobile Mise-en-Scene: A Critical Analysis of the Theory and Practice of Long-Take Camera Movement in the Narrative Film.* New York: Arno Press, 1978.

Badiou, Alain. "Anxiety." *Lacanian Ink* 26 (Autumn 2005): 70–71.

———. *Being and Event,* trans. Oliver Feltham. London: Continuum, 2005.

Bakhtin, Mikhail. *Rabelais and His World,* trans. Hélène Iswolsky. Bloomington: Indiana University Press, 1984.

Barker, Jennifer. *The Tactile Eye: Touch and the Cinematic Experience.* Berkeley: University of California Press, 2009.

Barthes, Roland. *A Lover's Discourse: Fragments,* trans. Richard Howard. New York: Noonday Press, 1978.

———. *Camera Lucida: Reflections on Photography,* trans. Richard Howard. New York: Hill and Wang, 1981.

———. *La chambre claire. Note sur la photographie.* Paris: Gallimard, 1980.

———. "Cy Twombly: Works on Paper." In *The Responsibility of Forms,* trans. Richard Howard, 157–76. Berkeley: University of California Press, 1985.

———. "Deliberation." In *The Rustle of Language,* trans. Richard Howard, 359–73. Berkeley: University of California Press, 1986.

———. "Diderot, Brecht, Eisenstein." In *Image/Music/Text,* trans. Stephen Heath, 69–78. New York: Hill and Wang, 1977.

———. "The Grain of the Voice." In *Image/Music/Text,* trans. Stephen Heath, 179–89. New York: Hill and Wang, 1977.

———. "Leaving the Movie Theater." In *The Rustle of Language,* trans. Richard Howard, 345–49. Berkeley: University of California Press, 1986. (Originally published as "En sortant du cinéma," *Communications* 23 [1975]: 104–7.)

———. *Mourning Diary: October 26, 1977–September 15, 1979,* trans. Richard Howard. New York: Hill and Wang, 2010.

———. *Mythologies,* trans. Annette Lavers. New York: Hill and Wang, 1972.

———. "The Photographic Message." In *Image/Music/Text,* trans. Stephen Heath, 15–31. New York: Hill and Wang, 1977.

———. *The Pleasure of the Text,* trans. Richard Miller. New York: Hill and Wang, 1975.

———. "Reading Brillat-Savarin." In *The Rustle of Language,* trans. Richard Howard, 250–70. Berkeley: University of California Press, 1986.

———. "Rhetoric of the Image." In *Image/Music/Text,* trans. Stephen Heath, 32–51. New York: Hill and Wang, 1977.

———. *Roland Barthes by Roland Barthes,* trans. Richard Howard. Berkeley: University of California Press, 1977.

———. "The Third Meaning." In *Image/Music/Text,* trans. Stephen Heath, 32–51. New York: Hill and Wang, 1977.

———. "The Wisdom of Art." In *The Responsibility of Forms,* trans. Richard Howard, 177–94. Berkeley: University of California Press, 1985.

———. "Writers, Intellectuals, Teachers." In *The Rustle of Language,* trans. Richard Howard, 309–31. Berkeley: University of California Press, 1986.

Bataille, Georges. "Attraction and Repulsion II: Social Structure." In *The College of Sociology 1937–39,* ed. Denis Hollier, 113–24. Minneapolis: University of Minnesota Press, 1988.

———. "Formless." In *Visions of Excess: Selected Writings, 1927–1939,* ed. and trans. Allan Stoekl, 31. Minneapolis: University of Minnesota Press, 1985.

Bazin, André. *What Is Cinema?* vol. 2, trans. Hugh Gray. Berkeley: University of California Press, 1971.

Bellour, Raymond. "A Bit of History," trans. Mary Quaintance. In *The Analysis of Film,* ed. Constance Penley, 1–20. Bloomington: Indiana University Press, 2000.

———. "Cinema and . . ." *Semiotica* 112, nos. 1–2 (1996): 207–29.

———. "Psychosis, Neurosis, Perversion (on *Psycho*)," trans. Nancy Huston. In *The Analysis of Film,* ed. Constance Penley, 238–61. Bloomington: Indiana University Press, 2000.

Benardete, Seth. "On Plato's *Symposium.*" In *Plato's "Symposium,"* trans. Seth Benardete, 179–99. Chicago: University of Chicago Press, 2001.

Benjamin, Walter. *The Origin of German Tragic Drama,* trans. John Osborne. London: NLB, 1977.

———. "Theses on the Philosophy of History," trans. Harry Zohn. In *Illuminations,* ed. Hannah Arendt, 253–64. New York: Schocken Books, 1969.

Benton, Graham. "Shark Films: Cinematic Realism and the Production of Terror." In *This Watery World: Humans and the Sea,* ed. Vartan P. Messier and Nandita Batra, 123–34. Newcastle: Cambridge Scholars, 2007.

Bersani, Leo. *The Freudian Body: Psychoanalysis and Art.* New York: Columbia University Press, 1986.

Bershen, Wanda. "*Zorn's Lemma.*" *Artforum* 9, no. 1 (September 1971): 41–45.

Bertelsen, Lone, and Andrew Murphie. "An Ethics of Everyday Infinities and Powers: Félix Guattari on Affect and the Refrain." In *The Affect Theory Reader,* ed. Melissa Gregg and Gregory J. Seigworth, 138–60. Durham, NC: Duke University Press, 2010.

Blanchot, Maurice. *The Space of Literature,* trans. Ann Smock. Lincoln: University of Nebraska Press, 1982.

Bordwell, David. "A Case for Cognitivism." *Iris* 9 (Spring 1989): 11–40.

———. "Historical Poetics of Cinema." In *The Cinematic Text: Methods and Approaches,* ed. R. Barton Palmer, 369–98. New York: AMS Press, 1989.

Bordwell, David, and Noël Carroll, eds. *Post-Theory: Reconstructing Film Studies.* Madison: University of Wisconsin Press, 1996.

Bourdieu, Pierre. *Distinction: A Social Critique of the Judgment of Taste,* trans. Richard Nice. Cambridge, MA: Harvard University Press, 1984.

Brennan, Teresa. *The Transmission of Affect.* Ithaca, NY: Cornell University Press, 2004.

Brillat-Savarin, Jean Anthelme. *Physiologie du goût,* Paris: C. Hermann, 1975.

———. *The Physiology of Taste, or, Meditations on Transcendental Gastronomy,* trans. M. F. K. Fisher. New York: Vintage, 2009.

Brottman, Mikita. *Offensive Films: Toward an Anthropology of Cinéma Vomitif.* Westport, CT: Greenwood, 1997.

Brunette, Peter. *Michael Haneke (Contemporary Film Directors).* Champaign, IL: University of Illinois Press, 2010.

Bruno, Giuliana. *Atlas of Emotion: Journeys in Art, Architecture, and Film.* London: Verso, 2007.

Buckley, Daryl. "ELISION: Philosophy Defining a Performance Practice," ELISION Ensemble website, n. d. Accessed July 2009. http://www.elision.org.au/ELISION _Ensemble/ELISION_Articles__Opening_of_the_Mouth.html.

Burch, Noël. *To the Distant Observer: Form and Meaning in Japanese Cinema.* Berkeley: University of California Press, 1979.

Burgin, Victor. "Barthes's Discretion." In *Writing the Image after Roland Barthes,* ed. Jean-Michel Rabaté, 19–31. Philadelphia: University of Pennsylvania Press, 1997.

Burke, Edmund. *A Philosophical Enquiry into the Origin of our Ideas of the Sublime and Beautiful.* Notre Dame, IN: University of Notre Dame Press, 1968.

Burton, Robert. *The Anatomy of Melancholy,* ed. Holbrook Jackson. New York: New York Review Books, 2001.

Butler, Judith. "Afterword: After Loss, What Then?" In *Loss: The Politics of Mourning,* ed. David L. Eng and David Kazanjian, 467–73. Berkeley: University of California Press, 2003.

———. *Precarious Life: The Powers of Mourning and Violence.* London: Verso, 2004.

Cajori, Florian. *A History of Mathematical Notations, Volume 1: Notations in Elementary Mathematics* (1928), repr. ed. Alcester, UK: Read Books, 2007.

Carême, Marie-Antoine. *L'art de la cuisine française au dix-neuvième siècle,* 2 vols. Paris: chez l'auteur, 1833.

———. *Le Maître d'Hôtel français,* 2 vols. Paris: Firmin Didot, 1822.

Carroll, Noël. "Film, Emotion, and Genre." In *Passionate Views: Film, Cognition, and Emotion,* ed. Carl Plantinga and Greg M. Smith, 21–47. Baltimore: Johns Hopkins University Press, 1999.

———. *The Philosophy of Horror, or, Paradoxes of the Heart.* New York: Routledge, 1990.

Cartwright, Lisa. *Moral Spectatorship: Technologies of Voice and Affect in Postwar Representations of the Child.* Durham, NC: Duke University Press, 2008.

Child, Julia, Louisette Bertholle, and Simone Beck. *Mastering the Art of French Cooking,* vol. 1. New York: Alfred A. Knopf, 2002.

Chow, Rey. *Sentimental Fabulations, Contemporary Chinese Films: Attachment in the Age of Global Visibility.* New York: Columbia University Press, 2007.

Cioran, E. M. *Tears and Saints,* trans. Ilinca Zarifopol-Johnston. Chicago: University of Chicago Press, 1995.

Clewell, Tammy. "Mourning beyond Melancholia: Freud's Psychoanalysis of Loss." *Journal of the American Psychoanalytic Association* 52, no. 1 (2002): 43–67.

Clover, Carol. *Men, Women, and Chain Saws: Gender in the Modern Horror Film.* Princeton, NJ: Princeton University Press, 1992.

Coates, Paul. *Film at the Intersection of High and Mass Culture.* Cambridge: Cambridge University Press, 1994.

Condillac, Abbé Etienne Bonnot de. *Treatise on the Sensations,* trans. Geraldine Carr. Los Angeles: University of Southern California Press, 1930.

Copjec, Joan. *Imagine There's No Woman: Ethics and Sublimation.* Cambridge, MA: MIT Press, 2002.

———. "May '68, the Emotional Month." In *Lacan: The Silent Partners,* ed. Slavoj Žižek, 90–114. London: Verso, 2006.

———. "The Object-Gaze: Shame, *Hejab,* Cinema." *Filozofski vestnik* 27, no. 2 (2006): 11–29.

Crary, Jonathan. *Techniques of the Observer: On Vision and Modernity in the Nineteenth Century.* Cambridge, MA: MIT Press, 1990.

Creed, Barbara. *The Monstrous-Feminine: Film, Feminism, Psychoanalysis.* London: Routledge, 1993.

Creeley, Robert. *The Collected Poems of Robert Creeley, 1945–75.* Berkeley: University of California Press, 1982.

Crimp, Douglas. "Melancholia and Moralism." In *Loss: The Politics of Mourning,* ed. David L. Eng and David Kazanjian, 188–202. Berkeley: University of California Press, 2003.

Danto, Arthur. "Photography and Performance: Cindy Sherman's Stills." In *Cindy Sherman, Untitled Film Stills,* 5–14. London: Jonathan Cape, 1990.

Darwin, Charles. *The Expression of Emotions in Man and Animals.* In *From so Simple a Beginning: The Four Great Books of Charles Darwin,* ed. Edward O. Wilson, 1255–1477. New York: W. W. Norton, 2006.

Dawes, Stewart. "Opening of the Mouth: Perth, Australia." *X-Press Magazine,* vol. 525, March 6, 1997.

del Río, Elena. *Deleuze and the Cinemas of Performance: Powers of Affection.* Edinburgh: Edinburgh University Press, 2008.

Deleuze, Gilles. *Cinema 1: The Movement-Image,* trans. Hugh Tomlinson and Barbara Habberjam. Minneapolis: University of Minnesota Press, 1986.

———. *Cinema 2: The Time-Image,* trans. Hugh Tomlinson and Robert Galeta. Minneapolis: University of Minnesota Press, 1989.

———. *Foucault,* trans. Seán Hand. Minneapolis: University of Minnesota Press, 1988.

———. *Francis Bacon: The Logic of Sensation,* trans. Daniel W. Smith. Minneapolis: University of Minnesota Press, 2002.

———. *Nietzsche and Philosophy,* trans. Hugh Tomlinson. New York: Columbia University Press, 2006.

———. "Spinoza and the Three 'Ethics,'" trans. Daniel W. Smith and Michael A. Greco. In *Essays Critical and Clinical,* 138–51. Minneapolis: University of Minnesota Press, 1997.

———. *Spinoza: Practical Philosophy,* trans. Robert Hurley. San Francisco: City Lights, 1988.

Deleuze, Gilles, and Félix Guattari. *A Thousand Plateaus: Capitalism and Schizophrenia,* trans. Brian Massumi. Minneapolis: University of Minnesota Press, 1987.

Derrida, Jacques. "By Force of Mourning." In *The Work of Mourning,* ed. Pascale-Anne Brault and Michael Naas, 139–64. Chicago: University of Chicago Press, 2001.

———. "The Deaths of Roland Barthes." In *The Work of Mourning,* ed. Pascale-Anne Brault and Michael Naas, 31–68. Chicago: University of Chicago Press, 2001.

———. "Différance." In *Margins of Philosophy,* trans. Alan Bass, 1–28. Chicago: University of Chicago Press, 1982.

———. *The Ear of the Other: Otobiography, Transference, Translation,* trans. Peggy Kamuf, ed. Christie McDonald. Lincoln: University of Nebraska Press, 1988.

———. "Economimesis," trans. R. Klein. *Diacritics* 11 (1981): 3–25.

———. "From Restricted to General Economy: A Hegelianism without Reserve." In *Writing and Difference,* trans. Alan Bass, 251–77. Chicago: University of Chicago Press, 1978.

———. *The Gift of Death,* trans. David Wills. Chicago: University of Chicago Press, 1995.

———. *The Post Card,* trans. Alan Bass. Chicago: University of Chicago Press, 1987.

———. "Signature Event Context." In *Margins of Philosophy,* trans. Alan Bass, 307–30. Chicago: University of Chicago Press, 1982.

———. "Structure, Sign, and Play in the Discourse of the Human Sciences." In *Writing and Difference,* trans. Alan Bass, 278–93. Chicago: University of Chicago Press, 1978.

———. "The Taste of Tears," trans. Pascale-Anne Brault and Michael Naas. In *The Work of Mourning,* ed. Pascale-Anne Brault and Michael Naas, 105–10. Chicago: University of Chicago Press, 2001.

———. *The Truth in Painting,* trans. Geoff Bennington and Ian McLeod. Chicago: University of Chicago Press, 1987.

———. "White Mythology: Metaphor in the Text of Philosophy." In *Margins of Philosophy,* trans. Alan Bass, 207–71. Chicago: University of Chicago Press, 1982.

Descartes, René. *La dioptrique,* in *Oeuvres de Descartes,* vol. 6, *Discours de la méthode et essais,* ed. Charles Adam and Paul Tannery, 114–129. Paris: Librairie Philosophique J. Vrin, 1996.

———. "Optics," trans. John Cottingham, Robert Stoothoff and Dugald Murdoch. In *The Philosophical Writings of Descartes,* 3 vols. 152–176. Cambridge: Cambridge University Press, 1985.

Diderot, Denis. *Élements de physiologie. Oeuvres completes,* ed. Herbert Dieckmann, Jacques Proust, and Jean Varloot. Paris: Hermann, 1975.

Didion, Joan. *The Year of Magical Thinking.* New York: Vintage, 2006.

Doane, Mary Ann. "The Close-Up: Scale and Detail in the Cinema." *Differences* 14, no. 3 (Fall 2003): 89–111.

———. *The Desire to Desire: The Woman's Film of the 1940s.* Bloomington: Indiana University Press, 1987.

———. *The Emergence of Cinematic Time*. Cambridge, MA: Harvard University Press, 2002.

Dolar, Mladen. *A Voice and Nothing More*. Cambridge, MA: MIT Press, 2006.

Douglas, Mary. *Purity and Danger: An Analysis of the Concept of Pollution and Taboo*. London: Routledge, 2007.

Ehrenreich, Barbara. *Dancing in the Streets: A History of Collective Joy*. New York: Henry Holt, 2006.

Eisenstein, Sergei. *Film Form*, trans. Jay Leyda. San Diego, CA: Harcourt, 1977.

———. *The Film Sense*, trans. Jay Leyda. San Diego, CA: Harcourt, 1970.

———. "The Structure of the Film." In *Film Form*, ed. and trans. Jay Leyda, 150–78. San Diego, CA: Harcourt, 1977.

Elkins, James. *Pictures and Tears: A History of People Who Have Cried in Front of Paintings*. New York: Routledge, 2004.

Elsaesser, Thomas. "Tales of Sound and Fury: Observations on the Family Melodrama." In *Film Genre Reader III*, ed. Barry Keith Grant, 366–95. Austin: University of Texas Press, 1986.

Eng, David L., and David Kazanjian. "Introduction: Mourning Remains." In *Loss: The Politics of Mourning*, ed. David L. Eng and David Kazanjian, 1–25. Berkeley: University of California Press, 2003.

Epstein, Jean. "*Bonjour Cinema* and Other Writings," trans. Tom Milne. *Afterimage*, no. 10 (Autumn 1981): 8–38.

———. "*Magnification* and Other Writings," trans. Stuart Liebman. *October* 3 (Spring 1977): 9–25.

Escoffier, Auguste. *The Escoffier Cookbook*. New York: Crown, 1969.

Ferguson, Priscilla Parkhurst. *Accounting for Taste: The Triumph of French Cuisine*. Chicago: University of Chicago Press, 2004.

Foucault, Michel. *Madness and Civilization*, trans. Richard Howard. New York: Vintage, 1965.

Frampton, Hollis. *On the Camera Arts and Consecutive Matters: The Writings of Hollis Frampton*, ed. Bruce Jenkins. Cambridge, MA: MIT Press, 2009.

Freeland, Cynthia. *The Naked and the Undead: Evil and the Appeal of Horror*. Boulder, CO: Westview, 2000.

Freud, Sigmund. *Beyond the Pleasure Principle*, trans. and ed. James Strachey. New York: W. W. Norton, 1961.

———. *Civilization and Its Discontents*, trans. and ed. James Strachey. New York: W. W. Norton, 1961.

———. *The Ego and the Id*, trans. Joan Riviere, ed. James Strachey. New York: W. W. Norton, 1960.

———. *Hemmung, Symptom und Angst. Gesammelte Werke, Werke aus den Jahren 1925–1931*. London: Imago, 1948.

———. "Hysterical Phantasies and Their Relation to Bisexuality." In *Freud on Women: A Reader*, ed. Elisabeth Young-Bruehl, 146–52. New York: W. W. Norton, 1990.

———. *Inhibitions, Symptoms, and Anxiety,* trans. Alix Strachey, ed. James Strachey. New York: W. W. Norton, 1960.

———. *Introductory Lectures on Psychoanalysis,* trans. and ed. James Strachey. New York: W. W. Norton, 1966.

———. "Mourning and Melancholia," trans. Joan Riviere. In *Freud: General Psychological Theory,* ed. Philip Rieff, 164–79. New York: Touchstone, 1991.

———. *On Murder, Mourning, and Melancholia.* London: Penguin, 2005.

———. *New Introductory Lectures on Psychoanalysis,* trans. and ed. James Strachey. New York: W. W. Norton, 1965.

———. "On Transience." In *The Standard Edition of the Complete Psychological Works of Sigmund Freud,* ed. and trans. James Strachey, 14:303–8. London: Hogarth, 1957.

———. "Trauer und Melancholie." In *Studienausgabe Band III, Psychologie des Unbewußten.* Frankfurt am Main: Fischer Taschenbuch, 1982.

———. "The 'Uncanny.'" In *Writings on Art and Literature,* ed. Werner Hamacher and David E. Wellbery, 193–233. Stanford, CA: Stanford University Press, 1997.

Frey, William, and William Langseth. *Crying: The Mystery of Tears.* New York: Harper and Row, 1985.

Garcia, Marcia. "Bait Noir: Kentis and Lau's *Open Water* Hooks Audiences with Shark Scare." *Film Journal International* 107, no. 7 (July 2004): 12.

Gershon, Michael. *The Second Brain.* New York: Harper Perennial, 1998.

Gledhill, Christine, ed. *Home Is Where the Heart Is: Studies in Melodrama and the Woman's Film.* London: BFI, 1987.

Goethe, Johann Wolfgang von. *Theory of Colours,* trans. Charles Lock Eastlake. Cambridge, MA: MIT Press, 1970.

Goodwin, James. *Eisenstein, Cinema, and History.* Urbana: University of Illinois Press, 1993.

Gorgias of Leontini. "The Encomium of Helen." In *The Greek Sophists,* trans. John Dillon and Tania Gergel, 76–84. New York: Penguin, 2003.

Gould, Stephen Jay. "Seeing Eye to Eye, through a Glass Clearly." In *Leonardo's Mountain of Clams and the Diet of Worms,* 57–76. New York: Harmony Books, 1998.

Gowing, Lawrence. *Vermeer.* Berkeley: University of California Press, 1997.

Grant, Catherine. "On 'Affect' and 'Emotion' in Film Studies." Film Studies for Free (blog). Available at http://filmstudiesforfree.blogspot.com. Accessed November 4, 2011.

Greenblatt, Stephen. "Filthy Rites" in *Learning to Curse: Essays in Early Modern Culture.* London: Routledge, 1990.

Grimm, Jacob, and Wilhelm Grimm. "The Tale of the Boy Who Set Out to Learn Fear." In *Grimm: Selected Tales,* trans. Joyce Crick, 20–26. Oxford: Oxford University Press, 2005.

Grodal, Torben. *Embodied Visions: Evolution, Emotion, Culture, and Film.* New York: Oxford University Press, 2009.

———. *Moving Pictures: A New Theory of Film Genres, Feelings, and Cognition.* New York: Oxford University Press, 1999.

Grosseteste, Robert. *On Light,* trans. Clare C. Riedl. Milwaukee: Marquette University Press, 2000.

Grosz, Elizabeth. *Space, Time, and Perversion.* New York: Routledge, 1996.

Groves, Tim. "Cinema/Affect/Writing." *Senses of Cinema* 25, no. 3 (2003). Available online at http://sensesofcinema.com/2003/feature-articles/writing_cinema_affect.

Grubrich-Simitis, Ilse. "'No Greater, Richer, More Mysterious Subject . . . than the Life of the Mind': An Early Exchange of Letters between Freud and Einstein," *International Journal of Psychoanalysis* 76 (1995): 115–22.

Halmos, Paul R. *Naive Set Theory.* New York: Springer, 1974.

Hardt, Michael. "Foreword: What Affects Are Good For." In *The Affective Turn: Theorizing the Social,* ed. Patricia Ticineto Clough with Jean Halley, ix–xiii. Durham, NC: Duke University Press, 2007.

Heath, Stephen. "Film and System: Terms of Analysis, Part 1," *Screen* 16, no. 1 (Spring 1975): 7–77.

———. *Questions of Cinema.* Bloomington: Indiana University Press, 1981.

Hegel, G. W. F. *Aesthetics: Lectures on Fine Arts,* 2 vols., trans. T. M. Knox. Oxford: Clarendon, 1975.

———. *Phenomenology of Spirit,* trans. A. V. Miller. Oxford: Oxford University Press, 1977.

Heidegger, Martin. *Being and Time,* trans. John Macquarrie and Edward Robinson. New York: HarperCollins, 1962.

———. "What Is Metaphysics?" In *Martin Heidegger: Basic Writings,* ed. David Farrell Krell, 89–110. San Francisco: HarperCollins, 1993.

Hitchings, Henry. *Defining the World: the Extraordinary Story of Dr. Johnson's Dictionary.* New York: Farrar, Straus and Giroux, 2005.

Hopkins, Gerard Manley, "No Worst, There Is None." In *Gerard Manley Hopkins: The Major Works,* ed. Catherine Phillips, 167. Oxford: Oxford University Press, 2002.

Hughes, David. *The Complete Lynch.* London: Virgin, 2001.

Hughes, Rolf. "The Drowning Method." In *Critical Architecture,* ed. Jane Rendell, Jonathan Hill, Murray Fraser, and Mark Dorrian, 92–102. New York: Routledge, 2007.

Hume, David. "Of Tragedy." In *Eight Great Tragedies,* ed. Sylvan Barnet, Morton Berman, William Burto, 433–39. New York: Meridian, 1996.

Hyland, Drew. *Plato and the Question of Beauty.* Bloomington: Indiana University Press, 2008.

Hyman, Philip. "Culina Mutata: Carême and *l'ancienne cuisine.*" In *French Food: On the Table, on the Page, and in French Culture,* ed. Lawrence Schehr and Allen Weiss, 71–82. New York: Routledge, 2001.

Irigaray, Luce. *This Sex Which Is not One,* trans. Catherine Porter. Ithaca, NY: Cornell University Press, 1985.

James, Alison. "Introduction: The Return of Form." *L'esprit Créateur* 48, no. 2 (2008): 1–4.

James, William. "What Is an Emotion?" In *Philosophy and the Emotions: A Reader,* ed. Stephen Leighton, 21–37. Ontario: Broadview, 2003.

Jameson, Fredric. "Reification and Utopia in Mass Culture." In *Signatures of the Visible.* New York: Routledge, 1992.

Johnston, Ruth D. "The Staging of the Bourgeois Imaginary in *The Cook, the Thief, His Wife, and Her Lover* (1990)." *Cinema Journal* 41, no. 2 (Winter 2002): 19–40.

Kaleta, Kenneth. *David Lynch.* New York: Twayne, 1993.

Kant, Immanuel. *Anthropology, History, and Education,* trans. Robert Louden, Mary Gregor, and Paul Guyer. Cambridge: Cambridge University Press, 2007.

———. *Critique of the Power of Judgment,* 2d ed., ed. Paul Guyer, trans. Paul Guyer and Eric Matthews. Cambridge: Cambridge University Press, 2000.

———. *Critique of Pure Reason,* trans. Norman Kemp Smith. New York: St. Martin's Press, 1965.

Keenan, Dennis King. *The Question of Sacrifice.* Bloomington: Indiana University Press, 2005.

Kierkegaard, Søren. *The Concept of Anxiety: A Simple Psychologically Orienting Deliberation on the Dogmatic Issue of Hereditary Sin,* ed. and trans. Reidar Thomte. Princeton, NJ: Princeton University Press, 1980.

———. *Either/Or: A Fragment of Life,* trans. Alastair Hannay. London: Penguin Books, 1992.

———. *Either/Or,* 2 vols., trans. Howard V. Hong and Edna H. Hong. Princeton, NJ: Princeton University Press, 1987.

———. *Journals and Papers,* ed. and trans. Howard V. Hong and Edna H. Hong. Bloomington: Indiana University Press, 1970.

Kilb, Andreas. "I Am the Cook: A Conversation with Peter Greenaway." In *Peter Greenaway: Interviews,* ed. Vernon Gras and Marguerite Gras, 60–65. Jackson: University Press of Mississippi, 2000.

Klein, Melanie. *Envy and Gratitude and Other Works, 1946–1963.* London: Virago, 1988.

———. "Infantile Anxiety Situations Reflected in a Work of Art and in the Creative Impulse." In *The Selected Melanie Klein,* ed. Juliet Mitchell, 84–94. New York: Free Press, 1987.

———. *Love, Guilt and Reparation and Other Works, 1921–1945.* London: Virago, 1988.

———. "Mourning and Its Relation to Manic-Depressive States." In *The Selected Melanie Klein,* ed. Juliet Mitchell, 146–74. New York: Free Press, 1987.

Klossowski, Pierre. *Nietzsche and the Vicious Circle,* trans. Daniel W. Smith. Chicago: University of Chicago Press, 1997.

Knight, Diana. "Roland Barthes, or the Woman without a Shadow." In *Writing the Image after Roland Barthes,* ed. Jean-Michel Rabaté, 132–43. Philadelphia: University of Pennsylvania Press, 1997.

Kojève, Alexandre. "The Idea of Death in the Philosophy of Hegel." In *Hegel and Contemporary Continental Philosophy,* ed. Dennis King Keenan, 27–74. Albany: State University of New York Press, 2004.

Kolnai, Aurel. *On Disgust,* ed. Barry Smith and Carolyn Korsmeyer. Chicago: Open Court, 2004.

Korsmeyer, Carolyn. "Delightful, Delicious, Disgusting." *Journal of Aesthetics and Art Criticism* 60, no. 3 (Summer 2002): 217–25.

——. *Making Sense of Taste: Food and Philosophy.* Ithaca, NY: Cornell University Press, 1999.

——. *Savoring Disgust: The Foul and Fair in Aesthetics.* Oxford: Oxford University Press, 2011.

Korsmeyer, Carolyn, and Barry Smith. "Visceral Values: Aurel Kolnai on Disgust." In *On Disgust,* ed. Carolyn Korsmeyer and Barry Smith, 1-28. Chicago: Open Court, 2004.

Kottmeyer, William. *Except after C: The Story of English Spelling.* New York: McGraw-Hill, 1988.

Kracauer, Siegfried. "Cult of Distraction." In *The Mass Ornament: Weimar Essays,* trans. and ed. Thomas Levin, 323–30. Cambridge, MA: Harvard University Press, 1995.

Kristeva, Julia. "About Chinese Women." In *The Kristeva Reader,* ed. Toril Moi, 138–59. New York: Columbia University Press, 1986.

——. *Black Sun: Depression and Melancholia,* trans. Leon S. Roudiez. New York: Columbia University Press, 1989.

——. *Powers of Horror: An Essay on Abjection,* trans. Leon S. Roudiez. New York: Columbia University Press, 1982.

Lacan, Jacques. *Le Séminaire X: L'angoisse (Anxiety) 1962–63,* trans. Cormac Gallagher from unedited French typescripts. Unpublished seminar transcript.

——. *The Seminar of Jacques Lacan VII: The Ethics of Psychoanalysis 1959–1960,* trans. Dennis Porter, ed. Jacques-Alain Miller. New York: W. W. Norton, 1992.

——. *Le transfert (Le séminaire, Livre VIII),* ed. Jacques-Alain Miller. Paris: Seuil, 1960–61.

Laine, Tarja. *Feeling Cinema: Emotional Dynamics in Film Studies.* New York: Continuum, 2011.

——. "Haneke's 'Funny' Games with the Audience (Revisited)," In *On Michael Haneke,* ed. Brian Price and John David Rhodes, 51–60. Detroit, MI: Wayne State University Press, 2010.

Laplanche, Jean. *Essays on Otherness,* trans. Luke Thurston, ed. John Fletcher. New York: Routledge, 1999.

Lautman, Albert. *Les schemas de structure.* Paris: Hermann, 1938.

Lawrence, Amy. *The Films of Peter Greenaway.* Cambridge: Cambridge University Press, 1997.

Leighton, Stephen, ed. *Philosophy and the Emotions: A Reader.* Ontario: Broadview, 2003.

Levinas, Emmanuel. "Kierkegaard: Existence and Ethics," *Proper Names,* trans. Michael B. Smith. Stanford: Stanford University Press, 1996.

———. "La mort et le temps." *Cahier de l'Herne* 60 (1991): 21-75.

———. *On Escape,* trans. Bettina Bergo. Stanford: Stanford University Press, 2003.

Leys, Ruth. "The Turn to Affect: A Critique." *Critical Inquiry* 37 (Spring 2011): 434-72.

Liddell, H. G., and R. Scott, eds. *A Greek-English Lexicon,* 9th ed. Oxford: Clarendon, 1996.

Lotze, Hermann. *Metaphysik.* Leipzig: Weidmann, 1841.

Lutz, Tom. *Crying: The Natural and Cultural History of Tears.* New York: W. W. Norton, 1999.

Lydon, Mary. "Amplification: Barthes, Freud, and Paranoia." In *Signs in Culture: Roland Barthes Today,* ed. Steven Ungar and Betty R. McGraw, 119-38. Iowa City: University of Iowa Press, 1989.

Lyotard, Jean-François. "Gesture and Commentary." In *Between Ethics and Aesthetics,* ed. Dorota Glowacka and Stephen Boos, 73-82. Buffalo: State University of New York Press, 2002.

———. "Note on the Meaning of 'Post-.'" In *Postmodern Literary Theory: An Anthology,* ed. Niall Lucy, 409-12. Oxford: Blackwell, 2000.

MacCabe, Colin. "Barthes and Bazin: The Ontology of the Image." In *Writing the Image after Roland Barthes,* ed. Jean-Michel Rabaté, 71-76. Philadelphia: University of Pennsylvania Press, 1997.

MacDonald, Scott. *Avant-Garde Film/Motion Studies.* Cambridge: Cambridge University Press, 1993.

Macherey, Pierre. *A Theory of Literary Production,* trans. Geoffrey Wall. London: Routledge, 2006.

Macksey, Richard, and Eugenio Donato, eds. *The Structuralist Controversy.* Baltimore: Johns Hopkins University Press, 2007.

Marciniak, Katarzyna. "Transnational Anatomies of Exile and Abjection in Milcho Manchevski's *Before the Rain* (1994)." *Cinema Journal* 43, no. 1 (Fall 2003): 63-84.

Marks, Laura U. *The Skin of the Film: Intercultural Cinema, Embodiment, and the Senses.* Durham, NC: Duke University Press, 2000.

Marx, Karl, and Friedrich Engels. *The German Ideology,* ed. R. Pascal. New York: International Publishers, 1963.

Massumi, Brian. *Parables for the Virtual: Movement, Affect, Sensation.* Durham, NC: Duke University Press, 2002.

Mavor, Carol. "Pulling Ribbons from Mouths: Roland Barthes's Umbilical Referent." In *Representing the Passions: Histories, Bodies, Visions,* ed. Richard Meyer, 175-206. Los Angeles: Getty, 2003.

McCombie, Elizabeth. *Mallarmé and Debussy: Unheard Music, Unseen Text.* Oxford: Oxford University Press, 2003.

McGee, Harold. *On Food and Cooking*. New York: Fireside, 1984.

McIntyre, Alex. *The Sovereignty of Joy: Nietzsche's Vision of Grand Politics*. Toronto: University of Toronto Press, 1997.

McMahon, Darrin. *The Pursuit of Happiness: A History from the Greeks to the Present*. London: Penguin, 2006.

Menninghaus, Winfried. *Disgust: Theory and History of a Strong Sensation*, trans. Howard Eiland and Joel Golb. Albany: State University of New York Press, 2003.

Metz, Christian. *Le signifiant imaginaire. Psychanalyse et Cinéma*. Paris: Christian Bourgois, 1984.

———. *The Imaginary Signifier: Psychoanalysis and the Cinema*, trans. Celia Britton, Annwyl Williams, Ben Brewster, and Alfred Guzzetti. Bloomington: Indiana University Press, 1982.

Metz, Walter. "Shark Porn: Film Genre, Reception Studies, and Chris Kentis' *Open Water*." *Film Criticism* 31, no. 3 (Spring 2007): 36–58.

Mew, Charlotte. "June, 1915." In *Complete Poems*, ed. John Newton, 77–78. London: Penguin, 2000.

Michelson, Annette. "Frampton's Sieve." *October* 32 (Spring 1985): 151–66.

Miller, Jacques-Alain. "On Jacques Lacan's *Anxiety*." *Lacanian Ink* 26 (Autumn 2005): 8–69.

Miller, William Ian. *The Anatomy of Disgust*. Cambridge, MA: Harvard University Press, 1997.

———. *Humiliation: And Other Essays on Honor, Social Discomfort, and Violence*. Ithaca, NY: Cornell University Press, 1993.

Moore, Rachel. *Hollis Frampton: (nostalgia)*. London: Afterall, 2006.

Münsterberg, Hugo. *The Film: A Psychological Study*. New York: Dover, 2004.

Nancy, Jean-Luc. *The Birth to Presence*, trans. Brian Holmes et al. Stanford, CA: Stanford University Press, 1993.

———. "Corpus." In *Corpus*, trans. Richard Rand, 2–121. New York: Fordham University Press, 2008.

———. "Fifty-eight Indices on the Body." In *Corpus*, trans. Richard Rand, 150–60. New York: Fordham University Press, 2008.

———. "Image and Violence." In *The Ground of the Image*, trans. Jeff Fort, 15–26. New York: Fordham University Press, 2005. (Originally published as "Image et violence," *Le portique* 6 [2000]).

———. *The Inoperative Community*, ed. and trans. Peter Connor. Minneapolis: University of Minnesota Press, 1991.

———. "Lux Lumen Splendor." In *Multiple Arts: The Muses II*, ed. Simon Sparks, 171–74. Stanford, CA: Stanford University Press, 2006.

Neu, Jerome. *A Tear Is an Intellectual Thing: The Meanings of Emotion*. Oxford: Oxford University Press, 2000.

Ngai, Sianne. *Ugly Feelings*. Cambridge, MA: Harvard University Press, 2005.

Nichanian, Marc. "Catastrophic Mourning." In *Loss: The Politics of Mourning*, ed. David L. Eng and David Kazanjian, 99–124. Berkeley: University of California Press, 2003.

Nietzsche, Friedrich. *The Gay Science*, trans. Josefine Nauckhoff, ed. Bernard Williams. Cambridge: Cambridge University Press, 2003.

———. *Human, All Too Human*, trans. R. J. Hollingdale. Cambridge: Cambridge University Press, 1996.

———. *Thus Spoke Zarathustra*. In *The Portable Nietzsche*, trans. Walter Kaufmann, 103-439. New York: Viking, 1954.

———. *The Will to Power*, trans. Walter Kaufmann and R. J. Hollingdale, ed. Walter Kaufmann. New York: Vintage, 1967.

Nochimson, Martha P. *The Passion of David Lynch: Wild at Heart in Hollywood*. Austin: University of Texas Press, 1997.

Nussbaum, Martha. *Hiding from Humanity: Disgust, Shame, and the Law*. Princeton, NJ: Princeton University Press, 2004.

Oliver, Kelly. *Womanizing Nietzsche: Philosophy's Relation to the "Feminine."* New York: Routledge, 1995.

Oliver, Kelly, and Marilyn Pearsall, eds. *Feminist Interpretations of Friedrich Nietzsche*. University Park: Penn State Press, 1998.

Owens, Craig. "Posing." In *Beyond Recognition: Representation, Power, and Culture*, ed. Scott Bryson, Barbara Kruger, Lynne Tillman, and Jane Weinstock, 201–17. Berkeley: University of California Press, 1992.

Pensky, Max. *Melancholy Dialectics: Walter Benjamin and the Play of Mourning*. Amherst: University of Massachusetts Press, 2001.

Peterson, James. *Dreams of Chaos, Visions of Order*. Detroit: Wayne State University Press, 1994.

Peucker, Brigitte. *Incorporating Images: Film and the Rival Arts*. Princeton, NJ: Princeton University Press, 1995.

———. *The Material Image: Art and the Real in Film*. Stanford, CA: Stanford University Press, 2007.

Pinch, Adela. *Strange Fits of Passion: Epistemologies of Emotion, Hume to Austen*. Palo Alto, CA: Stanford University Press, 1999.

Plato. *Phaedo*, trans. Paul Shorey. In *The Collected Dialogues of Plato, Including the Letters*, ed. Edith Hamilton and Huntington Cairns, 40-98. Princeton, NJ: Princeton University Press, 1989.

———. *Republic*, trans. Paul Shorey. In *The Collected Dialogues of Plato, Including the Letters*, ed. Edith Hamilton and Huntington Cairns, 575-844. Princeton, NJ: Princeton University Press, 1989.

———. *Symposium*, trans. Paul Shorey. In *The Collected Dialogues of Plato, Including the Letters*, ed. Edith Hamilton and Huntington Cairns, 526-574. Princeton, NJ: Princeton University Press, 1989.

———. *Timaeus*, trans. Paul Shorey. In *The Collected Dialogues of Plato, Including the Letters,* ed. Edith Hamilton and Huntington Cairns, 1151-1211. Princeton, NJ: Princeton University Press, 1989.

Pomerance, Murray, ed. *Bad: Infamy, Darkness, Evil, and Slime on Screen.* Albany: State University of New York Press, 2004.

Potkay, Adam. *The Story of Joy: From the Bible to Late Romanticism.* Cambridge: Cambridge University Press, 2007.

Powell, Anna. *Deleuze, Altered States, and Film.* Edinburgh: Edinburgh University Press, 2007.

———. *Deleuze and Horror Film.* Edinburgh: Edinburgh University Press, 2005.

Prodger, Phillip. *Darwin's Camera: Art and Photography in the Theory of Evolution.* Oxford: Oxford University Press, 2009.

Pudovkin, V. I. *Film Technique and Film Acting: The Cinema Writings of V. I. Pudovkin,* trans. Ivor Montagu. New York: Bonanza Books, 1949.

Rabaté, Jean-Michel. *The Ghosts of Modernity.* Gainesville: University Press of Florida, 1996.

Ragona, Melissa. "Hidden Noise: Strategies of Sound Montage in the Films of Hollis Frampton." *October* 109 (Summer 2004): 96–118.

Revel, Jean-François. "Retrieving Tastes: Two Sources of Cuisine." In *The Taste Culture Reader: Experiencing Food and Drink,* ed. Carolyn Korsmeyer, 51–56. Oxford: Berg, 2005.

Ricciardi, Alessia. *The Ends of Mourning: Psychoanalysis, Literature, Film.* Stanford, CA: Stanford University Press, 2003.

Richter, Simon. *Laocoon's Body and the Aesthetics of Pain: Winckelmann, Lessing, Herder, Moritz, Goethe.* Detroit: Wayne State University Press, 1992.

Riemer, Willy. "Beyond Mainstream Film: An Interview with Michael Haneke." In *After Postmodernism: Austrian Literature and Film in Transition,* ed. Willy Riemer, 160–75. Riverside, CA: Ariadne, 2000.

Riley, Charles. *Color Codes: Modern Theories of Color in Philosophy, Painting and Architecture, Literature, Music, and Psychology.* Hanover, NH: University Press of New England, 1995.

Riley, Denise. *Impersonal Passion: Language as Affect.* Durham, NC: Duke University Press, 2005.

Rocchio, Vincent. *Cinema of Anxiety: A Psychoanalysis of Italian Neorealism.* Austin: University of Texas Press, 1999.

Rollins, Nita. "Greenaway-Gaultier: Old Masters, Fashion Slaves." *Cinema Journal* 35, no. 1 (Autumn 1995): 65–80.

Rooney, Ellen. "Foreword: An Aesthetic of Bad Objects." In Naomi Schor, *Reading in Detail: Aesthetics and the Feminine,* xiii–xxxv. New York: Routledge, 2007.

———. "Form and Contentment." *Modern Language Quarterly* 61, no. 1 (March 2000): 17–40.

Rothman, William. *Hitchcock—The Murderous Gaze.* Cambridge, MA: Harvard University Press, 1982.

Russo, Mary. *The Female Grotesque: Risk, Excess, and Modernity.* London: Routledge, 1995.

Rutherford, Anne. "Cinema and Embodied Affect," *Senses of Cinema* 25, no. 3 (2003). Available online at http://sensesofcinema.com/2003/feature-articles/embodied _affect.

———. "Precarious Boundaries: Affect, *Mise en scene,* and the Senses." In *Art and the Performance of Memory: Sounds and Gestures of Recollection,* ed. Richard Smith, 63–84. New York: Routledge, 2002.

———. *What Makes a Film Tick? Cinematic Affect, Materiality, and Mimetic Innervation.* Bern: Peter Lang, 2011.

Sartre, Jean-Paul. *Being and Nothingness,* trans. Hazel Barnes. New York: Washington Square Press, 1956.

———. *The Emotions: Outline of a Theory,* trans. Bernard Frechtman. New York: Philosophical Library, 1948.

———. *The Imaginary: A Phenomenological Psychology of the Imagination,* trans. Jonathan Webber. London: Routledge, 2004.

———. *Nausea,* trans. Lloyd Alexander. New York: New Directions, 1964.

Scholes, Robert. *An Introduction to Structuralism in Literature.* New Haven, CT: Yale University Press, 1974.

Schor, Naomi. *Reading in Detail: Aesthetics and the Feminine.* New York: Routledge, 2007.

Seigworth, Gregory J., and Melissa Gregg. "An Inventory of Shimmers." In *The Affect Theory Reader,* ed. Melissa Gregg and Gregory J. Seigworth, 1–26. Durham, NC: Duke University Press, 2010.

Shapiro, Gary. *Nietzschean Narratives.* Bloomington: Indiana University Press, 1989.

———. "To Philosophize Is to Learn to Die." In *Signs in Culture: Roland Barthes Today,* ed. Steven Ungar and Betty R. McGraw, 3–31. Iowa City: University of Iowa Press, 1989.

Shaviro, Steven. *The Cinematic Body.* Minneapolis: University of Minnesota Press, 1993.

———. *Post-Cinematic Affect.* Winchester: Zero, 2010.

Sherman, Paul, and Jennifer Billing. "Darwinian Gastronomy: Why We Use Spices." *Bioscience* 49, no. 6 (1999): 453–63.

Siegel, Joel. "Greenaway by the Numbers." In *Peter Greenaway: Interviews,* ed. Vernon Gras and Marguerite Gras, 66–90. Jackson: University Press of Mississippi, 2000.

Silverman, Kaja. *The Threshold of the Visible World.* New York: Routledge, 1996.

Sitney, P. Adams. *Visionary Film: The American Avant-Garde, 1943–1978.* New York: Oxford University Press, 1979.

Smith, Adam. *The Theory of Moral Sentiments,* ed. Knud Haakonssen. Cambridge: Cambridge University Press, 2002.

Smith, Greg M. *Structure and the Emotion System.* Cambridge: Cambridge University Press, 2003.

Spinoza, Benedict de. *Ethics,* ed. James Gutmann. New York: Hafner, 1949.

Spoto, Donald. *The Art of Alfred Hitchcock: Fifty Years of His Motion Pictures.* New York: Anchor, 1992.

Stetco, Dayana. "The Crisis of Commentary: Tilting at Windmills in Peter Greenaway's *The Cook, the Thief, His Wife, and Her Lover.*" In *Peter Greenaway's Postmodern/ Poststructuralist Cinema,* ed. Paula Willoquet-Maricondi and Mary Alemany-Galway, 203–22. Lanham, MD: Scarecrow, 2001.

Stonebridge, Lyndsey. "Anxiety in Klein: The Missing Witch's Letter." In *Reading Melanie Klein,* ed. Lyndsey Stonebridge and John Phillips, 190–202. London: Routledge, 1998.

Swift, Jonathan. *Gulliver's Travels,* ed. Martin Price. Indianapolis: Bobbs-Merrill, 1963.

Tan, Ed S. *Emotion and the Structure of Narrative Film: Film as an Emotion Machine,* trans. Barbara Fasting. Mahwah, NJ: Erlbaum, 1996.

Tanner, Laura. *Lost Bodies: Inhabiting the Borders of Life and Death.* Ithaca, NY: Cornell University Press, 2006.

Thompson, Kristin. "The Concept of Cinematic Excess." In *Narrative, Apparatus, Ideology,* ed. Philip Rosen, 130–42. New York: Columbia University Press, 1986.

Tillich, Paul. *Systematic Theology,* 3 vols. Chicago: University of Chicago Press, 1954–64.

Toles, George. "'If Thine Eye Offend Thee . . . ': *Psycho* and the Art of Infection." In *Alfred Hitchcock: Centenary Essays,* ed. Richard Allen and S. Ishii-Gonzales, 159–74. London: BFI, 1999.

Van Wert, William. "*The Cook, the Thief, His Wife, and Her Lover.*" *Film Quarterly* 44, no. 2 (Winter 1990–91): 42–50.

Vermeulen, Timotheus, and Robin van den Akker. "Notes on Metamodernism." *Journal of Aesthetics and Culture* 2 (2010). doi:10.3402/jac.v1i0.5677.

Walsh, Michael. "Allegories of Thatcherism: The Films of Peter Greenaway." In *Fires Were Started: British Cinema and Thatcherism,* ed. Lester Friedman, 282–300. Minneapolis: University of Minnesota Press, 1993.

Weber, Samuel. *Return to Freud: Jacques Lacan's Dislocation of Psychoanalysis,* trans. Michael Levine. Cambridge: Cambridge University Press, 1991.

Weiss, Allen. *Feast and Folly: Cuisine, Intoxication, and the Poetics of the Sublime.* Albany: State University of New York Press, 2002.

———. "Frampton's Lemma, Zorn's Dilemma." *October* 32 (Spring 1985): 118–28.

Wenzel, Siegfried. *The Sin of Sloth: Acedia in Medieval Thought and Literature.* Chapel Hill: University of North Carolina Press, 1960.

Willemen, Paul. *Looks and Frictions: Essays in Cultural Studies and Film Theory.* Bloomington: Indiana University Press, 1994.

Williams, Linda. "Film Bodies: Gender, Genre, Excess." In *Film and Theory: An Anthology,* ed. Robert Stam and Toby Miller, 207–21. Malden, MA: Blackwell, 2000.

———. *Hard Core: Power, Pleasure, and the "Frenzy of the Visible."* Berkeley: University of California Press, 1989.

Wilson, Eric. *The Strange World of David Lynch: Transcendental Irony from "Eraser-head" to "Mulholland Dr."* New York: Continuum, 2007.

Wilson, Scott. *The Order of Joy: Beyond the Cultural Politics of Enjoyment.* New York: State University of New York Press, 2008.

Wimsatt, William K. *The Verbal Icon: Studies in the Meaning of Poetry.* Lexington: University of Kentucky Press, 1954.

Windhausen, Federico. "Words into Film: Toward a Genealogical Understanding of Hollis Frampton's Theory and Practice," *October* 109 (Summer 2004), 76–95.

Wolfson, Susan J. "Reading for Form." *Modern Language Quarterly* 61, no. 1 (March 2000): 1–16.

Woodward, Kathleen. "Freud and Barthes: Theorizing Mourning, Sustaining Grief." *Discourse* 13, no. 1 (Fall–Winter 1990–91): 93–110.

———. "Grief-Work in Contemporary American Cultural Criticism." *Discourse* 15, no. 2 (Winter 1992–93): 94–112.

Žižek, Slavoj. "Kierkegaard with Lacan." *Lacanian Ink* 26 (Autumn 2005): 102–17.

———. *The Plague of Fantasies.* London: Verso, 1997.

Index

Burgin, Victor, 281n61
Burke, Edmund, 136
Burton, Robert, 74
Butler, Judith, 67, 71, 278n47

Camera Lucida (Barthes), 42, 76–93; on cinema, 90–93, 281n54; on death and grief, 79–84; dedication of, 86–87; narrative of ontological quest of, 78–79, 83; paratextual supplements to, 84–89, 280nn46–47, 280–81n49; on partial truth of images, 80–84; on the punctum, 80; on the undialectical photograph, 82–84, 89–93; Winter Garden Photograph of, 80–87, 279n26, 280n36
camera lucida, the, 84
Cannibal Holocaust (Deodato), 133
Carême, Marie-Antoine, 156–57, 295n8
Carroll, Noël, 29, 38, 133, 134–37, 160
Cartwright, Lisa, 27, 28, 29–30
catharsis, 4–5, 6, 29
chambre claire, La (Barthes). See Camera Lucida
chien andalou, Un (Buñuel), 140
Child, Julia, 155
Chow, Rey, 274n31
Cinema 1 and 2 (Deleuze), 24, 44, 94
Cinematic Body, The (Shaviro), 28–29, 272n12
cinéma vomitif, 133
cinephilia, 27, 31, 133, 252
Civilization and Its Discontents (Freud), 120–21, 199
Clewell, Tammy, 72
close-up, the, 139–41, 292n86
Clover, Carol, 271n4
Coates, Paul, 106–7
cognitivist film theory, 29, 38; taxonomy of visual strategies of, 36–37; on Zorns Lemma, 249–50

color: the artist's palette and, 174–77, 299n62, 300n70; death and, 164; Francis Bacon's use of, 115–16; in Greenaway's The Cook, the Thief . . . , 170–77, 179, 299n63, 300n70, 309n25; in Kentis's Open Water, 227–28, 231–35, 309n27; in Lynch's Six Figures Getting Sick, 146–48; in photography, 87–89, 280n46
Concept of Anxiety, The (Kierkegaard), 183–91, 202; Grimm Brothers' fairy tale in, 185–88; on Hegelian dialectics, 189–90; on the magic picture (Heksebrev), 187–91, 212, 301n15, 301nn17–18
Condillac, Étienne Bonnot de, 121
Confessions (Augustine), 9, 18, 53–56
Conrad, Joseph, 257
contingency, xii, 30; in Camera Lucida, 77–78; form and, 173; in Kentis's Open Water, 212, 220–21, 235–40, 310n36; in Nietzsche's formulation of joy, 244–46
Cook, the Thief, His Wife, and Her Lover, The (Greenaway), 151–77, PLATES 1–2; aesthetics of disgust in, 159–70; aspic and Spica in, 152–57, 169–70, 175; black food and death in, 164, 169–77; characters of, 152, 153; formal language of gastronomy in, 154–59; Hals's table painting in, 156, 159, 168–69, 175, 296n12, 300n70; modes of relation in, 158; repetition without depth in, 158–59; spaces of, 157; structure of color in, 172–80, 299nn63–64, 300n70
Copjec, Joan, 202, 208, 303n34, 307n102
corporeality. See spectators
corpse, the, 7, 94–96; disgust and, 129–30, 138–39; in Greenaway's The Cook, the Thief . . . , 169–70; in Haneke's Funny Games, 107; in Kentis's Open Water, 232–33; in photography, 83, 87–88

in Lynch's *Wild at Heart*, 141–45, 292n90; psychoanalytic investigation of, 133; smell and, 120–23, 128–30, 143–45, 161, 164, 286–87nn20–21, 293n93; spatial-temporal models of, 131–32; structures of good taste in, 151, 166–67, 179; visible character of, 161, 175–77; vomit as exteriority of, 127–30, 143–51, 165, 290n57, 290n59, 292n90

Doane, Mary Ann, 26, 140, 271n4, 301nn17–18

Dolar, Mladen, 118

Don't Look Now (Roeg), 95

Dostoevsky, Fyodor, 309n31

Douglas, Mary, 130, 131, 134

Dreyer, Carl Theodor, 7

Drowning by Numbers (Greenaway), 178

"Drunken Song" (Nietzsche), 243

"Economimesis" (Derrida), 125–32, 292n90

Ego and the Id, The (Freud), 61, 64, 193, 200

Ehrenreich, Barbara, 311n5

Eisenstein, Sergei, 27, 41, 97–98; on close-ups, 140, 292n86; on spectatorship and grief, 97–98, 282n72

Either/Or (Kierkegaard), 188, 190–91

Der Ekel (Kolnai), 159–64

Élements de physiologie (Diderot), 143

ELISION Ensemble, 140, 292n83

Elsaesser, Thomas, 43, 44, 271n4

embarrassment, 187, 202–9, 219, 230–31, 238–39

emotion, 23–24, 27–31, 43–44, 270–71n62

Emotions: Outline of a Theory, The (Sartre), 15–16

Eng, David L., 65

"En sortant du cinéma" (Barthes), 91–92

Epstein, Jean, 27

Escoffier, Auguste, 157

Essays Critical and Clinical (Deleuze), 24

Ethics (Spinoza), 24, 259–61

excess, 41–42

Expression of the Emotions in Man and Animals, The (Darwin), 11–13

exteriority of affect, 186; in death and putrefaction, 170–77, 297n37; in decay, 151, 155, 164–77, 297n37, 298n42, 298n49; as fear and the creeps, 185–88; in joy, 241–61; loss of the body in, 24–25; movement of space and time as, 187–201, 203–12, 216–31, 233–35, 303n32, 309n26; in the ontology of the photograph, 92–93; as self-folding, 24–25, 36–41, 45–46, 48–49, 76–77, 93; structure of color in, 172–80, 231–33, 299nn63–64, 300n70, 309n27; tears as, 22–25; in undialectical images of grief, 71, 76–112; in vomit, 127–30, 143–51, 165, 290n57, 290n59, 292n90

Extreme Associates, 290n59

Fairy Tale about a Boy Who Left Home to Learn about Fear, A (Grimm Brothers), 185–88

faisandage, 166–77, 297n37, 298n42, 298n49. *See also* decay; gastronomy

fear, 160–61, 185–87

feminist theory, 122–23

Figures (Bacon), 115–16, 120, 146

film theory, 21–22, 26–46; apparatus/*Screen* theory in, 28–29, 30, 42; of Barthes's *Camera Lucida*, 92–93; on body genres, 28; Carroll's theory of monstrosity in, 134–37; cognitivist theory in, 29, 36–37, 38, 249–50; on digital cinema, 26–27; on disgust, 133–41, 161, 291n62; historical turn in, 26; intentional affect model in, 31–36;

76, 81, 92–93, 95, 98–99; in Haneke's
  Funny Games, 103–5, 109, 284n91; in
  Kentis's *Open Water*, 232; tears and,
  4–6, 11–12
painting, 268n3; absence and, 94,
  303n32; color in, 115–16, 173–75,
  300n70; disgust and, 125; in Greenaway's *The Cook, the Thief . . .* ,
  295n12, 298n54, 299n63; in Haneke's
  Funny Games, 106–8, 283nn80–81;
  in Lynch's *Six Figures Getting Sick*,
  146–47, 149, 151, 294n101; of table
  scenes, 168–69, 296n12, 300n70
palate, 174–77. *See also* gastronomy; taste
palette, 174–77. *See also* color
panic, 305n62
Paris, Texas (Wenders), 171
Passion of David Lynch, The (Nochimson), 148
Pensky, Max, 277n37
"Pentagram for Conjuring the Narrative" (Frampton), 257
Peterson, James, 250, 312–13n22
Peucker, Brigitte, 99, 106, 283n79,
  299n63
pheasant, 166–67, 179
phenomenology: in Barthes's *Camera
  Lucida*, 78–80, 82–83, 86, 90–92,
  278n4; in film theory, 26–29, 32–33;
  in Kolnai's formulation of disgust,
  159–63
*Philosophy of Horror, or, Paradoxes of the
  Heart, The* (Carroll), 134
photography: affective mobility in, 83–84;
  Barthes on cinema and, 90–93,
  281n54; Barthes on grief and, 76–93,
  108, 279n26, 280nn46–47; Barthes
  on partial truth of, 80–84; etymology
  of, 59–60; affect as guarantee of being in, 82–84, 89–93, 98; materiality
  of grief in, 75, 90; materialization of

light, 59–60, 75, 84; material return
  of the dead in, 79–81, 83–84; the pose
  in, 108–9, 283n86; proto-tools of,
  188–89; Sartre on, 86–87
Physiologie du goût (Brillat-Savarin),
  166–69
Plague of Fantasies, The (Žižek), 293n92
Plato: allegorical cave of, 280n36; on
  Aristophanes's hiccups, 117–18,
  285n5, 285n8, 285n11; creation myth
  of, 120; on tears, 4–5, 21
Poetics (Aristotle), 2, 4–5
"Polaroid, 1979" (Boudinet), 84, 87–89,
  280nn46–47, 280–81n49
Pomerance, Murray, 291n62
pornography, 28, 271n4, 290n59
pose, the, 108–9, 283n86
Post Card, The (Derrida), 197–98
Post-Cinematic Affect (Shaviro), 28
poststructuralist theory, 41–42, 252, 273n26
Potemkin (Eisenstein), 140
Potkay, Adam, 245, 312n15
Powell, Anna, 28
Powers of Horror: An Essay on Abjection
  (Kristeva), 134, 137–39
Pratique de la voie tibétaine, 85
Precarious Life (Butler), 71
Psycho (Hitchcock): Carroll's theory of
  horror and, 135–36; Marion's tear
  in, 1–2, *3f*, 18–25, 36, 45–46, 48–49;
  structure of, 307n2
psychoanalytic theory, 29–30; on mel-
  ancholia, 57–59, 61, 63–71, 276n31; on
  mourning, 56–64, 68–69
Pudovkin, V. I., 41
punctum, the, 42, 78, 80, 90, 110, 163
putrescence. *See* decay

Rabaté, Jean-Michel, 88–89
radical formalism. *See* formal dimensions of affect

Ragona, Melissa, 313n30
Rancière, Jacques, 39
Rank, Otto, 199–200
Ray, Man, 19
reading for affect, xv–xvi, 20–21, 36–41, 237–38; affect as self-folding exteriority in, 24–25, 36–41, 45–46, 48–49, 76–77, 92–93; disciplinary precedents for, 41–46; the mise-n'en-scène in, 46, 237–39, 241; radical formalism of, 37–41, 273n28, 274n31. *See also* formal dimensions of affect
reading for form, xiv–xvi, 31–37, 39–40, 163. *See also* formal dimensions of affect
"Reading for Form" (Wolfson), 273n28
reflexivity, 18–19, 105–9, 145–49, 154, 257
Reign over Me, 95
Rejlander, Oscar, 11, 269n28
rejoicing, 243
Rembrandt van Rijn, 107
Remember Me, 95
repetition: anxiety and, 195–96, 200, 209; bliss and, 254, 314n36; in Frampton's *Zorns Lemma*, 247–54, 260; in Greenaway's *The Cook, the Thief . . .*, 156, 158–59, 171, 178–79; in Nietzsche's formulation of joy, 243–46
Republic, The (Plato), 4–5, 21, 280n36
return to form. *See* formal dimensions of affect
Return to Freud (Weber), 191
Rhetoric (Aristotle), 4–5
Ricciardi, Alessia, 276n31
Richard (character, *The Cook, The Thief . . .*), 153, 158, 164, 172–74, 176–77
Riley, Charles, 174–75
Riley, Denise, 267n2
Rocchio, Vincent, 309n26
Roeg, Nicolas, 95
Rollins, Nita, 294–95n5

Rooney, Ellen, 39, 286n33
rot. *See* decay
Rothman, William, 2, 20
Rozin, Paul, 296n26
Russo, Mary, 133
Rutherford, Anne, 30, 43–44, 273n7

Sartre, Jean-Paul: on Antivalue, 131; on anxiety, 160, 183; on disgust, 296n26, 296n34, 299n59; on nausea, 123, 288n27; on the photographic image, 86–87; on the tear, 3, 13–18
Schiller, Friedrich, 245
Schlegel, A. W., 124, 125
Scholes, Robert, 252
Schor, Naomi, 163, 286nn33–34
Screen theory, 28, 30, 42
Le Séminaire X (Lacan), 191, 202–8
senses, the, 287n23; adjectival lexicon of, 162–63, 286n31; aesthetic inquiry into, 120–23, 128–30, 143–45, 286–87nn20–21, 287n23, 296n26; of taste, 115–18, 126, 144; of touch (hapticity), 116, 147, 161, 271n2, 296n26. *See also* disgust; smell
sentiments, the, 41; Hume's formulation of, 5–6; Smith's formulation of, 6–9
September 11, 2001 attacks, 95
sequence, 167–70, 175, 178, 197, 221, 248
set theory, 248–50
shame, 201–2, 306n94
Shapiro, Gary, 78, 246
sharks, 210, 215–31, 236, 308n10
Shaviro, Steven, 27; on affectivity, 28–29, 30, 42, 272n12; on writing theory, 33
Shelley, Mary, 8
Siegel, Joel, 300n1 (Interval)
Silverman, Kaja, 108, 284n88
Sitney, P. Adams, 312nn21–22
Six Figures Getting Sick (Lynch), 145–51, 293n95, 294n101, 294n104, PLATE 3

smell: adjectival lexicon of, 162, 286n31; aesthetic inquiry into, 120–23, 128–30, 143–45, 286–87nn20–21, 293n93; decay and, 164–70; intimacy of, 161. *See also* disgust

Smith, Adam, 6–9, 18

Smith, Barry, 296n37

Sosein, 160–63, 170, 174, 297n36

Sous le Sable (Ozon), 96–97

spectators: affective work of, 19–20, 31–36, 43–44, 94–95, 133–35, 252, 282n70; Barthes on the drowsiness of, 91–92, 281n59, 281n61; "body genres" and, 28, 43, 44, 271n4; disgust and, 133–41; in Eisenstein's model of grief, 97–98, 282n72; Haneke's indifference to, 99; in structuralist and poststructuralist theory, 41–42, 252; theoretical rejection of, 36, 40–41. *See also* affectivity/the affective turn

Spinoza, Baruch, 24, 122, 259–61, 270–71n62

Spoto, Donald, 223

Stanzas (Agamben), 68

stereoscopes, 188–89, 197, 301–2nn18–19

Stonebridge, Lyndsey, 303n32

structuralist theory, 41–42, 252

"The Structure of the Film" (Eisenstein), 97–98

studium, the, 78, 89

sympathy, 6–8, 18

Symposium (Plato), 117–18, 121, 285n5, 285n8, 285n11

tableaux vivants, 101–12, 283nn80–81

table paintings, 168–69, 296n12, 300n70

Tactile Eye, The (Barker), 35–36

"Tales of Sound and Fury: Observations on the Family Melodrama" (Elsaesser), 43

Tanner, Laura, 278n51

taste, 115–18, 144; Barthes on temporal possibilities of, 167–70; in high cuisine, 116, 154–59, 168–70; palate in, 174–75; smell and, 120–23, 128–30, 143–45, 161, 286–87nn20–21, 293n93; two forms of, 126, 176. *See also* disgust

"The Taste of Tears" (Derrida), 47

tears, 1–22, 47–49; as catharsis, 4–5, 6; evolutionary function of, 11–13; as exteriority of interior states, 2–4, 9, 22–25; film theory of, 21–22; as gendered behavior, 4; as grief, 8–9; indifference of, 18, 20, 36; interpretive imperative of, 20–21; as paradoxical pleasure, 5–6, 9; as performative, 13–18; as physiological state, 9–11; in *Psycho*, 1–2, 3*f*, 18–25, 36, 45–46, 48–49; as sympathy, 6–8, 18; as weakness, 5

Le Temps du loup (Haneke), 283n79

Theory of Moral Sentiments, The (Smith), 6–9

"The Third Meaning" (Barthes), 41–42, 91

Thompson, Kristin, 36–37

Thus Spoke Zarathustra (Nietzsche), 243–46

Timaeus (Plato), 120

time, 252–53, 259–61; of clocks, 219–22; as duration, 57–58, 67, 102–9, 112, 162–63, 176–77, 210, 225, 284n91, 298n49; sharks as operators of (in *Open Water*), 216–22

Toles, George, 20

Tompkins, Silvan, 29

"Tractatus Logico-Gastronomicus" (Weiss), 163–64

"Trauer und Melancholie" (Freud), 57–71, 96–97

Truth in Painting, The (Derrida), 127

turn to affect. *See* affect; affectivity/the affective turn

turn to form. *See* formal dimensions of affect; formalism

Twombly, Cy, 173–74

Ugly Feelings (Ngai), 34–36, 267n2, 309n26

Ulysses' Gaze (Angelopoulos), 43–44

uncanny, the. *See unheimlich*

undialectical images of grief, 71, 76–112; in Barthes's *Camera Lucida*, 76–93; in cinematic portrayals of absence, 93–98, 282n56; as duration of suspended form, 112; in Haneke's *Funny Games*, 98–112, 178–80; resistance to opposition or permutation in, 98

unheimlich: Freud's formulation of, 45–46, 133, 137, 304n46; Lacan's formulation of, 203, 305n76

"Das Unheimliche" (Freud), 133

Vampyr (Dreyer), 7

van den Akker, Robin, 267n3

Van Wert, William, 158, 296n12

Vermeer, Johannes, 107

Vermeulen, Timotheus, 267n3

Vertigo (Hitchcock), 309n26

violence: Benjamin's formulation of, 69; eating and, 168–69; in Haneke's *Funny Games*, 99–100, 283n78; in Kentis's *Open Water*, 214–17, 226–28; Kierkegaardian forms of, 190, 302n26; melodramatic portrayals of, 271–72n4; Nancy's formulation of, 110–12; numbers and, 220–21, 310n36; of sensation, 28, 115–16, 146; smell and, 143–45, 151

Violent Affect (Abel), 31–32

visqueux, the, 297n34, 299n59. *See also* Sartre, Jean-Paul

vomit, 127–30; Derrida's theory of, 123, 142; as exteriority of disgust, 127–30, 143–51, 165, 290n57, 290n59, 292n90; in Kristeva's theory of abjection, 138–39; in Lynch's *Six Figures Getting Sick*, 145–51, 293n95, 294n101, 294n104; in Lynch's *Wild at Heart*, 141–45, 292n90; mobilization by smell of, 144–45, 293n93. *See also* disgust

Walsh, Michael, 178–79, 294n5

Waters, John, 293n93

Weber, Samuel, 191, 192, 197, 201, 208

Weiss, Allen, 163–64, 250, 313n26

Wenders, Wim, 171

"What Is an Emotion?" (James), 10

Whitman, Walt, 89

Wild at Heart, 141–45, 292n90

Wilde, Oscar, 154

Willemen, Paul, 31

Williams, Linda, 271n4

Wilson, Scott, 311n5

Wimsatt, W. K., 34

Windhausen, Federico, 251

Winter Garden Photograph, 80–87, 279n26, 280n36

Wolfson, Susan, 273n28

Wollaston, William, 84

women who cry, 4

Woodward, Kathleen, 276n29

Woolf, Virginia, 309n31

Work of Mourning, The (Derrida), 47–48

WTC View, 95

X (in *Zorns Lemma*), 254–58, 314n39

x (the algebraic unknown), 255